How do we translate New Testament σῶμα (body), ψυχή (soul), πνεῦμα (spirit), and καρδία (heart)?  tend to interpret these concepts in ... ... they right? Dr Sunny Chen takes his readers on a fascinating exegetical fieldtrip during which he ably discusses the meanings of anthropological terms in the Pauline corpus. Following sound methodological principles provided and informed by discourse analysis, the author makes a plausible and laudable case for interpreting these concepts as primarily social concepts. Highly recommended for every student of Paul's letters, especially those who tend to underestimate the sociocentric aspects of Paul's theology!

Dr Dick Kroneman, *SIL International Translation Coordinator*

Dr Chen's book examines four key anthropological terms in the letters of Paul: σῶμα (body), ψυχή (soul), πνεῦμα (spirit), and καρδία (heart). It helpfully establishes that in most cases these four terms focus on the place of the human person within the ecclesial community, rather than the ontological nature of the human person. This book deserves special attention by all those seeking to come to terms with Pauline anthropology.

Dr Colin G Kruse, *Emeritus Scholar, Melbourne School of Theology*

Discourse analysis can easily be seen as an exegetical tool devoted to literary or grammatical issues, with little direct point of contact with the way that scriptural texts function theologically or ethically in the church. In this detailed study, Dr Sunny Chen shows how the use of technical theories of semantic meaning bears fruit. His analysis of the key anthropological terms in Paul takes us to the heart of Paul's theology, and provides resources for ongoing reflection on a Christian understanding of the nature of the human person. A highly recommended study.

Rev. Dr Sean Winter, *Head of College, Pilgrim Theological College, University of Divinity, Melbourne*

Paul's Anthropological Terms in the Light of Discourse Analysis

SIL International®
Publications in Translation and Textlinguistics
9

Publications in Translation and Textlinguistics is a peer-reviewed series published by SIL International®. The series is a venue for works concerned with all aspects of translation and textlinguistics, including translation theory, exegesis, pragmatics, and discourse analysis. While most volumes are authored by members of SIL, suitable works by others also form part of the series.

Series Editor
Susan McQuay

Editorial Staff
George Huttar, Copy Editor
Gene Burnham, Proofreader

Production Staff
Lois Gourley, Production Director
Judy Benjamin, Compositor
Barbara Alber, Graphic Designer

Cover Image
Illustration by Barbara Alber. Image is a derivative of: https://pixabay.com/en/boy-human-male-man-people-person-2025115/#comments. CC0.

Paul's Anthropological Terms in the Light of Discourse Analysis

Sunny Chen

SIL International®
Dallas, Texas

Copies of this and other publications of SIL International® may be obtained through distributors such as Amazon, Barnes & Noble, other worldwide distributors and, for select volumes, publications.sil.org:

SIL International® Publications
7500 W Camp Wisdom Road
Dallas, TX 75236-5629 USA

General inquiry: publications_intl@sil.org
Pending order inquiry: sales@sil.org

Contents

Figures

Tables

Abstract

The study of theological anthropology significantly depends on the resource of the biblical tradition, including relevant material in the Pauline epistles. A solid understanding of Paul's anthropology inevitably requires an analysis of the key anthropological terms used in the Pauline epistles.

However, the task of understanding Paul, with a view to using his thought as the basis for reflection on theological anthropology, is difficult. Although James Barr's *The Semantics of Biblical Language* (1961) has provided ground-breaking insights by highlighting the importance of applying linguistic principles in conducting biblical semantic study and various scholars have been attentive to Barr's comments for the last forty years in studying Paul's anthropological terms, many of these works fail to follow Barr's comments adequately. In particular, they fail to pay sufficient attention to the textual context of the specific terms. Thus, in this book I adopt the method of discourse analysis to overcome some of the deficiencies in previous scholarship.

Following a survey of scholarship and consideration of an appropriate methodology, I study four key terms: σῶμα (body), ψυχή (soul), πνεῦμα (spirit), and καρδία (heart), as these occur in different Pauline letters. I argue that there are social and corporate dimensions, the focus of community or communal unity in particular, connoted by some occurrences of Paul's anthropological terms. Although not every single occurrence carries a corporate and relational reference, many occurrences, which together form a coherent thematic meaning, point in that direction. My study indicates that Paul's anthropology shows less concern for the ontological nature of a human person. Instead, the apostle uses anthropological terms to focus on the place of the human person within the ecclesial community, a theme which is, ultimately, inseparable from his Christology.

I therefore propose that reflection on the nature and identity of the human person should take the notions of communal relationship and social identity into serious consideration.

Acknowledgements

It is with immense gratitude that I acknowledge the support and help of a number of people whom the Lord has placed around me. Without their assistance and inspiration, this book would not have been possible.

I owe my sincerest gratitude to several teachers during my time studying at Dallas Theological Seminary and SIL: Prof. Daniel B. Wallace and Prof. R. Elliott Greene, who inspired me to master New Testament Greek; and Assoc. Prof. Shin Ja Hwang, who showed me fascinating elements in linguistics.

I am deeply indebted to my PhD supervisor, Assoc. Prof. Sean Winter, who offered me his relentless guidance, advice, and encouragement throughout this journey. I would also like to express my heartfelt thanks to Bruce Symons and Irene Haywood at SIL Australia, who offered me their valuable advice and assistance throughout my research endeavour.

I am grateful for the generous support of Prof. David Runia by providing me a wonderful opportunity to be part of an academic residential community at Queen's College, The University of Melbourne, during my doctoral studies in 2009–2013.

Last but not the least, I would like to give my heartfelt thanks to my family and friends: Chee Ho, who reignited my desire to pursue doctoral research; my mother Jenny, sister Pauline, and brother-in-law Raymond, who provided me much needed emotional and prayer support; my nephews, Bon and Jon, who offered their help and presence; Claire Pickering, who conducted proofreading; Kelvin Chang, Ian and Angeline Lo, Nick Teo, and Ann Chan and her family, who lent me their unreserved support during this roller-coaster experience.

Abbreviations

BAGD	A Greek-English Lexicon of the New Testament and Other Early Christian Literature (Bauer, Walter. 1979. *A Greek-English lexicon of the New Testament and other early Christian literature*. William F. Arndt and F. Wilbur Gingrich, trans. Chicago, IL: University of Chicago Press.)
BHS	Biblica Hebraica Stuggartensia (Elliger, K., and W. Rudolph, eds. 1990. *Biblica Hebraica Stuggartensia*. Stuttgart: Deutsche Bibelgesellschaft.)
LXX	Septuagint (Rahlfs, Alfred, and R. Hanhart, eds. 2006. *Septuaginta*. Second edition. Stuttgart: Deutche Bibelgesellschaft.)
NA28	Nestle-Aland 28th edition of Novum Testamentum Graece (*Novum Testamentum Graece*. 2012. Nestle-Aland 28th edition. Stuttgart: Deutche Bibelgesellschaft.)
NT	New Testament
OT	Old Testament
SIL	SIL International®

TDNT   Theological Dictionary of the New Testament (Kittel, Gerhard, and Gerhard Friedrich, eds. *Theological dictionary of the New Testament.* 1964–1976. 10 vols. Geoffrey W. Bromiley, trans. Grand Rapids, MI: Eerdmans.)

TLG   Thesaurus Linguae Graecae® Digital Library. Maria C. Pantelia, ed. Irvine, CA: University of California. Accessed 26 March 2019. http://www.tlg.uci.edu.

1

Introduction

1.1 Why this book?

Christian accounts of the nature of the human person—theological anthropology—significantly depend on the resources of the biblical tradition. Central to that tradition is the relevant material found in the Pauline epistles. A solid understanding of Paul's anthropology inevitably requires an analysis of the apostle's key anthropological terms, including σῶμα (body), πνεῦμα (spirit), ψυχή (soul), καρδία (heart), σάρξ (flesh), and συνείδησις (conscience). Throughout church history, various New Testament (NT) scholars have sought to better understand the semantic value, and theological and anthropological connotations of these terms, from John Chrysostom in the fourth century, who provided an early analysis of the anthropological use of πνεῦμα (spirit) (Chrysostom 1889:47–48), to two recent studies of σῶμα (body) and σάρξ (flesh) by Emma Wasserman and Lorenzo Scornaienchi (Wasserman 2007, Scornaienchi 2008). However, the task of understanding Paul, and using his thought as the basis for reflection on theological anthropology, is difficult. Werner Georg Kümmel argues that it is "a priori impossible" to provide accurate definitions for different anthropological terms, due to their arbitrary use in the description of a human being.[1] Nevertheless, through careful study of several

---

[1] Although Laato (1995:174–175) provides detailed textual analysis of Gal 6:4, 13–14, his analysis is too brief in explaining how the text relates to the whole letter (Laato 1995:177–178). Similarly, in discussing the notion of flesh as the "home" of a person's selfish desires, Laato (2004:354–359) provides a comprehensive exegetical

1

key anthropological terms, I intend to identify and describe one aspect of Paul's anthropology.

Several NT interpreters maintain that some anthropological terms are occasionally used in a metaphorical sense by Paul, with a corporate and social connotation. For instance, ψυχή (soul) in Phil 1:27 highlights community sharing or sharing among friends (Hansen 2009:8), καρδία (heart) in 2 Cor 1:22 points to the "messianic community" (O'Brien 1991:152) and πνεῦμα (spirit) in Gal 6:18 denotes the spiritual fellowship of the faith community (Burton 1921:362). Although this communal understanding is not particularly popular amongst NT scholars, the corporate and social connotations of Paul's anthropological terms must not be overlooked. I seek to revisit and investigate Paul's anthropological terms with particular focus on their corporate, relational, and thus ecclesiological connotations. By "corporate" I mean the unity of a community (corporate unity), or a community acting as a single entity sharing the same identity (corporate entity); "social" denotes the relationship amongst different members in a community (communal relation), or the relationship between Paul and a community.

1.2 The problems of previous studies

James Barr, in *The Semantics of Biblical Language* published in 1961, changed the landscape of biblical semantic study by exposing problematic approaches in previous scholarship (Barr 1961). According to Barr, earlier work suffered from a gross negligence of linguistic principles in conducting biblical semantic study.[2] Barr's insights were in part a response to the Biblical Theological Movement (BTM), which sought to uncover the theological connotations of key biblical terms. The BTM approached biblical language as a special "divine language" (Childs 1970:47), and criticised previous scholarship for undermining this uniqueness (ibid. 1970:33–35). Many NT words were perceived as closely related to their so-called Hebrew roots (ibid. 1970:44–47). Paul was perceived as thinking "more consciously along OT lines," rather than employing a Hellenistic understanding of anthropological terms.[3] Therefore, scholarship in the BTM largely investigated the

---

analysis of Gal 3:10, but only briefly mentions the connection between Gal 3:22–23, Gal 5:17, and Rom 7:7–25. Kümmel (1963:43) states that the terms do not simply denote "psychologically different functions" and instead are used "promiscuously." Likewise, Joel Green (2008:54–60) argues that biblical writers do not develop "a specialized or technical, denotative vocabulary for theoretical discussion of the human person," since biblical anthropological terms are polysemous.

[2] According to Barr (1961:2), the term 'linguistics' denotes "the science of linguistics and the material it handles: phonology, grammar and lexicography of various languages and the semantic value of the various forms observed and classified in these processes."

[3] This quote by Schweizer, a BTM scholar, concerns the meaning of σῶμα (body) in Paul's work (Schweizer 1971a:1060).

meanings of the Hebrew equivalents of key biblical words. According to Barr, such previous scholarship tended to adopt two flawed approaches to the NT data. First, theological presuppositions were superimposed onto a word whilst ignoring its textual context.[4] Second, these semantic studies were overly diachronic.

Semantics became a distinct field of enquiry in 1883 when Michel Bréal demarcated the term 'sémantique' as the study of "the laws which govern the transformation of sense, the choice of new expressions, and the birth and death of locutions" (Norrick 2003:76). Within this field, Ferdinand de Saussure defined two different dimensions of semantic study, the diachronic and the synchronic.[5] The diachronic is the study of the historical development of a word, and the synchronic is the study of a word's meaning in light of its contemporary literary context. The diachronic and the synchronic loosely represent the temporal and the spatial dimensions of semantic meaning respectively. Thus, Saussure argues that every word "is at the crossroads between the diachronic and the synchronic viewpoint."[6] These two terms were thereafter used to describe the two different foci of semantic study.[7]

In commenting the problematic method adopted in previous scholarship, Barr mentions several essentials in conducting biblical semantic study. Barr first contends that biblical semantic study must take into account the modern science of linguistics and apply the general linguistic rules that are applied in studying other languages. Based on this, Barr then emphasises the importance of adopting a synchronic approach by seriously attending to the context of a word. Barr identifies two different notions of context: the textual context and the wider context. The textual context refers to the place of a word in the whole discourse, and the wider context refers to how a word is employed in contemporary usage. An examination of the wider context should be a much higher priority than an examination of its historical development.

Over the last forty years, scholars investigating Paul's anthropological terms have been attentive to Barr's criticism and have adopted a more synchronic approach, attending to the textual context and the wider context in their work. Nonetheless, much of this scholarship arguably fails to follow Barr's comments adequately. Some scholars examining the textual context are either overly speculative about or rely heavily on presuppositions about the likely situation behind the text. Others scholars focus on the place of a

---

[4] The term 'textual context' is equivalent to Barr's term 'literary context.'

[5] Saussure, known as "the founder of modern linguistics," presupposes that language "is an object for an empirical science" (Ricoeur 1974:81).

[6] At the beginning of his work, Saussure sets forth that duality is the 'first and last' principle in terms of linguistic points of view. The duality of 'time and space' is also prominent in his analysis (Saussure 2006:3–4, 6–7, 80, 112–113).

[7] Burton, a NT grammarian in the same era as Saussure, similarly identified two dimensions in the study of syntax. However, he names them differently, as 'historical grammar' and 'exegetical grammar' (Burton 1898:2–3).

word in a sentence or paragraph, and undertake little analysis at the discourse level. On the other hand, scholars examining the wider context for Paul's anthropological terms either do not sufficiently attend to the textual context or fail to include any textual analysis.[8]

1.3 Approaching a text through discourse analysis

One way to address Barr's criticism is to employ discourse analysis, which originates from the field of linguistics and focuses on textual context. This method explicates the semantic value of key words in light of their usage in the whole discourse. Linguists use this method to examine written and oral forms, namely discourse. The term discourse refers to "the entirety of the author's communication to his or her audience…[it] represents the largest linguistic level of communication" (Reed 1997:45). A written discourse usually comprises a combination of various levels, including grapheme, word, clause, sentence, and paragraph (ibid. 1997:43–45). A narrative containing many paragraphs and segments is a single discourse, as is a letter comprising many segments.

The application of discourse analysis in NT scholarship is relatively new. Some well-known NT scholars who apply this method include Stanley Porter, Moisés Silva, Jeffrey Reed, and J. P. Louw. Discourse analysis can provide a new perspective regarding the function and significance of Pauline anthropological terms. By adopting this method, in my opinion, we can overcome some of the deficiencies in previous scholarship as identified by Barr. Discourse analysis does not rely on investigating the historical development of words, nor does it speculate about the situation behind a text. Instead, it focuses on the textual context, enabling exegetical and semantic analysis at both the discourse level and paragraphic-sentential-clausal level. The highest priority of this method is examining how a term is used within the discourse, instead of focusing on the diachronic aspects of semantic meaning. I am confident that discourse analysis offers a more secure approach to these terms than has been provided thus far in the scholarship.

1.4 Aims, hypotheses, and overview

In the following chapters, I investigate Paul's anthropological terms with particular focus on their corporate, relational, and thus ecclesiological connotations. Primarily, I seek to ascertain whether some of Paul's anthropological terms connote social and corporate dimensions in some instances, using the method of discourse analysis. I do not presuppose that all of Paul's

---

[8] See chapter 2 for a detailed explanation of Barr's criticism and his proposals for conducting biblical semantic study, and for a critical analysis of subsequent scholarship.

anthropological terms always denote a social and corporate dimension. Instead, I undertake the more modest task of ascertaining whether some of the terms, on some occasions, are used by the apostle to highlight or denote for the audience the corporate and relational dimensions of human identity. I argue that the corporate and relational dimensions of Paul's terms are increasingly perceptible, when applying the tools of discourse analysis.

My study shows that the corporate and relational dimensions of Pauline anthropology are deeply connected to his ecclesiology. Paul's audiences are united, and are a single communal entity due to the work and faithfulness of Christ. This united entity operates under the new dispensation of grace, in which Christ is at the centre. Amidst various tribulations and distresses, they are waiting for the eschatological realisation that brings forth the perfection of their community through the redemption of Christ. Hence, Christian practice should not be understood as an individualistic endeavour. Rather, it must be accomplished in and through community.

Accordingly, I explore the following questions. First, what are the social and corporate dimensions of the key anthropological terms, and what are the implications of this for understanding Paul's anthropology? Second, how are the key anthropological terms understood given Paul's wider thought about the person of Christ and the identity of the church? Third, how might a better understanding of the key anthropological terms assist Christian reflection on the nature of the human person?

I address these questions in the following chapters. In chapter 2, my literature review identifies and details key methodological flaws in previous scholarship. Subsequently, I establish a method for semantic study based on discourse analysis, leading to an investigation of the key anthropological terms in four stages.

In Stage I, which is chapter 3, I analyse a single anthropological term within a single discourse: σῶμα (body) in 1 Corinthians. Given that τὸ σῶμα τοῦ Χριστοῦ (the body of Christ) in 1 Corinthians is widely accepted by scholars as denoting the church, the corporate and relational dimensions of σῶμα (body) are already well-established. The purpose of this stage is two-fold: to prove the value of discourse analysis for the investigation of such terms, and to provide further insights regarding σῶμα (body) in 1 Corinthians.

In Stage II (chapter 4) I analyse multiple anthropological terms within a single discourse: πνεῦμα (spirit), ψυχή (soul), καρδία (heart), and σῶμα (body) in Philippians.

In Stage III (chapter 5) I will analyse a single anthropological term within multiple discourses: καρδία (heart) in all of the Pauline epistles, particularly focusing on Romans and 2 Corinthians.

In Stage IV (chapter 6) I analyse multiple anthropological terms within multiple discourses: πνεῦμα (spirit), σῶμα (body), and ψυχή (soul) in the benediction in 1 Thessalonians, and πνεῦμα (spirit) in the benedictions in Galatians, Philippians, and Philemon.

Lastly, I summarise the findings and suggest broader implications in chapter 7.

1.5 Scope and limitations

I do not attempt here to analyse all of Paul's anthropological terms as they occur in all of the Pauline epistles, both authentic and disputed. The definition of the Pauline corpus is broadly contested, with mainstream scholars widely upholding the authenticity of some letters, and disputing the authenticity of other letters. Seven letters are widely considered as written by Paul, namely Romans, 1 Corinthians, 2 Corinthians, Galatians, Philippians, 1 Thessalonians, and Philemon (Dunn 2006:13). For Ephesians, Colossians, 2 Thessalonians, 1 Timothy, 2 Timothy, and Titus, the authenticity of Paul's authorship is challenged in various degrees (Guthrie 1990:497, 572–577, 607–621). To limit the scope of my study, I focus only on the seven epistles listed above as commonly considered to be authentic.[9]

Furthermore, due to the immense scope that it would entail, I do not focus on some of the important elements in conducting biblical semantic study, for example, a detailed analysis of Paul's cultural context (primarily Stoicism).

Paul's key anthropological terms are: σῶμα (body), ψυχή (soul), πνεῦμα (spirit), καρδία (heart), σάρξ (flesh), νοῦς (mind), συνείδησις (conscience), and ἔσω ἄνθρωπος (inner human). I particularly concentrate on examining σῶμα (body), ψυχή (soul), πνεῦμα (spirit), and καρδία (heart). And even for these terms, I do not examine every single occurrence, since my purpose is to use discourse analysis as a complementary tool to provide a more adequate understanding of the possible connotations of Paul's anthropological terms.

In NT scholarship, applying linguistic methods to study the Scripture is not a common practice. Some consider it a complex task, as many NT scholars are not familiar with the discipline of linguistics. Consequently, resorting to traditional methods to conduct exegetical work is more appealing. On the other hand, a number of linguists have substantial experience in conducting biblical exegetical work and translating the Bible. Through this book, besides providing a study on Paul's anthropological terms, I attempt to bridge the wide gap by showing mainstream NT scholars and students the benefits of applying linguistic methods in studying the NT. Although this book would not be considered by linguists as a work that purely

---

[9] From this point onwards, these seven epistles that are widely accepted in NT scholarship to be Paul's authentic work are called Pauline epistles; and the letters that are suspected by some NT scholars to be pseudepigrapha are called Pauline disputed letters.

adopts linguistic approaches and employs sophisticated linguistic models, it introduces some basic and important elements of linguistics and demonstrates how to apply them, in addition to traditional exegetical methods, in conducting NT studies. Finally, I also attempt to make this book readily accessible to laypeople unfamiliar with NT Greek, and for this reason have frequently included English translations of Greek expressions.

2

James Barr and Discourse Analysis

In this chapter, I aim to establish a research method that can be used to investigate and accurately ascertain the semantic values and the theological implications of Paul's anthropological terms. First, I explain James Barr's revolutionary contribution to the field of biblical semantic study, more importantly, his significant suggestions on how to conduct semantic study. Second, I review the studies of Paul's anthropological terms in modern scholarship, examining both their strengths and limitations. Third, I explain the linguistic method called discourse analysis, and how this overcomes the limitations and problems in previous scholarship. In particular, my explanation introduces some key linguistic concepts for readers who are not familiar with linguistics. Fourth, I formulate a research method which is attentive to Barr's suggestions by applying the principles of discourse analysis. Finally, I provide an overview of the usage of the key anthropological terms in some first century Koine Greek literature.

2.1 Semantic study according to Barr

The publication of *The Semantics of Biblical Language* in 1961 by James Barr was arguably a watershed moment in the field of biblical semantic study. This monograph included valuable insights and exposed the problematic methodologies in previous scholarship.

2.1.1 Barr's critique of previous scholarship

Barr's fundamental criticism is the gross negligence of linguistic principles in conducting biblical semantic study. This criticism contains two main points, which are explained further below. First, some semantic research ignores the textual context and wrongfully superimposes particular theological presuppositions onto a word. Second, some semantic research is overly diachronic.

Concerning the first point, Barr heavily criticises the method in which presuppositions, usually theological, are superimposed onto a word to determine its meaning without considering its textual context. There are three fundamental issues: "the inability to keep to linguistic method strictly and the tendency to replace it by theological and philosophical argument; the blindness to any idea of the socially conditioned nature of language as an arbitrary system of semantic markers; [and] the inability to see and present linguistic evidence except where it appears to follow the lines of a thought-structure of metaphysical-theological type" (Barr 1961:204–205).[1] A prominent example of this flawed method is Gerhard Kittel's Wörterbuch, translated into English as *Theological Dictionary of the New Testament* (TDNT).[2] Although Barr acknowledges that Kittel's work is enormously influential in the study of the NT (ibid. 206), he expresses grave concerns, including the "failure to get to grips with the semantic value of words in their contexts" and the problematic approach in which "the value of context comes to be seen as something contributed by the word, and then it is read into the word as its contribution where the context is in fact different" (ibid. 231, 233). In summary, Barr contends that linguistic principles, especially textual context, should be afforded priority in biblical semantic study. Instead, in previous scholarship, particular theological presuppositions have been superimposed onto a word to determine its meaning.

Concerning his second point, Barr heavily criticises the adoption of an overly diachronic approach that focuses on a word's history. A belief underlying this approach concerns the "unity of the Bible" (ibid. 274–275) and the Hebrew language as "the language that fits the ultimate theological realities" (ibid. 44). The "extraordinary peculiarity of the Hebrew language" is highlighted and presupposed, which leads to an overemphasis on the Hebraic linguistic heritage of the NT,[3] whereby a NT word is always traced back to its Hebrew equivalent. The fundamental flaw is "starting from the theoretical end, from the assurance of understanding the Hebrew mind, and

---

[1] These three inabilities comprise Barr's criticism of Hebert and Torrance, who examine the two Pauline terms, faith and truth. This statement pinpoints the fundamental problems of this method.

[2] Barr devotes one chapter to discussing the problem of the TDNT (Barr 1961:206–262).

[3] Barr directs this criticism at Boman's method of contrasting Greek and Hebrew thought (Barr 1961:47–48).

working from there to its linguistic form" (ibid. 23). This facilitates two problematic practices in biblical semantic study. The first practice concerns that some semantic research overly emphasizes the historicity of a word, wrongly assuming that the meaning of a NT Greek word always stems from a Hebrew theological concept. As a result, the research fails to investigate how the Greek word functions in the Greek non-biblical system.[4] The second practice is that some semantic research commits the "root fallacy" (ibid. 100). A word is etymologised, "giving excessive weight to the origin of a word as against its actual semantic value" (ibid. 101).[5] To illustrate these two flawed practices, Barr cites Schlier's analysis of ἀνακεφαλαιόομαι (to sum up) in the TDNT and John Robinson's analysis of σάρξ (flesh) and σῶμα (body) as examples. In Schlier's case, Barr stipulates that the word is interpreted with a "particular theological importance" by incorrectly relating the word to its assumed root κεφαλή (head) (ibid. 237–238), and consequently, failing to investigate how the word functions given its context (ibid. 228). In Robinson's case, Barr contends that Robinson contrasts these two Greek terms with their supposed Hebrew equivalent בָּשָׂר (flesh), but fails to address "synchronic semantics" and investigate how these Greek terms function in "the Greek non-biblical system" (ibid. 37).[6] Nonetheless, Barr is most critical of TDNT, exposing the lexicon's overindulgence of "the realm of concept history." This leads to an excessively diachronic analysis of NT words, by correlating the NT Greek words with their so-called related theological concepts in the OT Hebrew and the LXX (ibid. 207). In other words, there is a clear emphasis on how a theological concept is transmitted from a particular OT Hebrew word to a NT Greek word.[7] According to Barr, a sole emphasis on concept history and a failure to understand a word in its textual

---

[4] Barr discusses the problematic approach of Robinson's study of σάρξ (flesh) and σῶμα (body) (Barr 1961:34–37).

[5] Despite his criticism, Barr does not undermine etymology. He recognises the value in tracing the "Hebraic root" of a NT word. However, he pinpoints a particular flaw, stating that "the etymology of a word is not a statement about its meaning but about its history...and it is quite wrong to suppose that the etymology of a word is necessarily a guide either to its 'proper' meaning in a later period or to its actual meaning in that period" (Barr 1961:109).

[6] The following statement of Robinson illustrates this flawed mentality: "τοῦ νοὸς τῆς σαρκός (the mind of the flesh)—another impossible combination for the Greek mind. Though the actual word νοῦς may be taken from Hellenistic terminology, we have here a good example of how, like every other term, it is drawn by Paul into his typical Hebrew usage" (Robinson 1952:25).

[7] This diachronic approach underpins various entries for anthropological terms in the TDNT. Schweizer makes a significant contribution to the lexical entries of different anthropological terms, including πνεῦμα (spirit) (Schweizer 1968:389–455), σάρξ (flesh) (Schweizer 1971a:98–105), σῶμα (body) (Schweizer 1971b:1024–1094), and ψυχή (soul) (Schweizer 1974:637–656), and constantly refers to the OT in his analysis of πνεῦμα (spirit) and ψυχή (soul).

context leads to "illegitimate totality transfer" (ibid. 218). This occurs when a word is isolated from its context and "the 'meaning' of a word (understood as the total series of relations in which it is used in the literature) is read into a particular case as its sense and implication."[8] Barr's criticisms are poignant. However, it is important to note that Barr does not negate the value of a diachronic approach; his criticism refers to those semantic studies that take an overly diachronic approach by ignoring a word's place in its textual context.

Various modern scholars support Barr's criticisms. For example, Meeks criticises the flawed method adopted in many entries of the TDNT: many NT words are treated as though they are "absorbed by the exclusiveness of their new content," and carry certain theological meanings not shared by other Koine Greek literature (Meeks 2004:513–544). He also repudiates the claim that NT Greek words "often take on a Hebrew content" because there is "a fundamental difference in mentality between Semitic and Greek consciousness" (ibid. 2004:41–42). Gene Green warns against an overreliance on lexicons, given the danger of "illegitimate transfer." Although lexicons can be helpful, he argues that "a simple survey of the semantic range" using lexicons does not guarantee successful identification of the specific conceptual schema represented by a word in its specific context (Green 2007:799–812). He also stipulates that the meaning of a word cannot be determined by etymology, because when biblical authors composed their work new concepts represented by a word were "being modified and constructed" (Green 2007:809). Louw (1982:41–42) and Silva (1983:25) also repudiate this problematic "illegitimate transfer." Likewise, Carson contends that the "root fallacy" is common in biblical semantic study, because some people are drawn to etymology and the search for a "hidden meaning bound up with etymologies" (Carson 1998:28, 30). For Osborne, even though a past meaning might consciously be in an author's mind at the time of writing, etymology must not be abused and has only limited value (Osborne 2006:112). He echoes Barr's concern, and contends that, in determining the semantic range of a word, a much higher priority should be given to its usage in contemporary literature, rather than focusing on its historical usage. Osborne also expresses caution towards Kittel's approach, and states that the TDNT is certainly a tool, but is not exhaustive in identifying semantic range because of its emphasis on 'theological usage' (Osborne 2006:102).

In my opinion, Barr's views are not completely exempted from theological and hermeneutical assumptions. Although his approach may be considered as dated given the postmodern developments, Barr's warning is still relevant and important. For instance, Berding indicates that flawed methods are still commonly practiced by those who do not realise that any meaning of a word can only be "defined more narrowly if the context suggests

---

[8] To illustrate "illegitimate totality transfer," Barr cites Schmidt's lexical entry of ἐκκλησία (assembly/church) in the TDNT (Barr 1961:218).

it" (Berding: 2000:51). Balentine indicates that scholars and students often wrongly bring "certain general theological convictions" to the exegetical task, and use a word to "describe" a certain theological concept that they have already embraced (Balentine and Barton 1994:13).

2.1.2 Barr's comments on semantic studies

Alongside heavy criticism of previous scholarship, Barr provides insightful comments on conducting biblical semantic study. The key comment is that any biblical semantic study must follow the modern science of linguistics. Barr succinctly sums up his comment: "It is probable that a greater awareness of general semantics, of general linguistic method in all its aspects, and an application of such awareness in biblical interpretation, would have valuable and important results for theology" (Barr 1961:296).[9] In other words, the semantic study of biblical Hebrew or Greek words cannot be excluded from the general linguistic rules that are applied in studying all other languages. Modern scholars also concur with Barr's view. For example, Porter echoes this key proposal, and acknowledges Barr's "ground-clearing" work and notes that various scholars in the Greek field are "explicitly utilizing the principles of modern linguistics" (Porter 1995:14–35). Louw states that semantic study involves "several dimensions: linguistic, logical, psychological, anthropological" whilst linguistics "must be the dominating dimension with others supporting it, since language is a linguistic entity in the first place" (Louw 1982:16).

In addition, Barr emphasises the importance of a synchronic approach, instead of a diachronic approach, and makes two clear suggestions. First, the textual context of a word must be prioritised in semantic study. Second, the wider context, including the particular writer and contemporary Greek thought, must be consulted. These two proposals are examined in greater detail below.

According to Barr, textual context is crucial in biblical semantic study. He argues that the theological connotation "of the type found in the NT has its characteristic linguistic expression not in the word individually but in the word-combination or sentence" (Barr 1961:233). Barr markedly contends that "the sentence (and of course the still larger literary complex such as the complete speech or poem)" is the "linguistic bearer of the usual theological statement, and not the word (the lexical unit)" (ibid. 263). Therefore, "the real communication of religious and theological patterns is by the larger word-combinations and not by the lexical units or words" (ibid. 264). Notably, as well as analysing a word in its sentence, Barr clearly

---

[9] At the beginning of his work, Barr similarly argues that "by studying language linguistically one is making a genuine and valid contribution to the understanding of it" (Barr 1961:2). As previously mentioned, according to Barr, the problem of previous scholarship rests on the failure to "relate what is said about either Hebrew or Greek to a general semantic method related to general linguistics" (Barr 1961:24).

asserts that any investigation must also consider "the still larger literary complex," pointing to a complete written or oral form.[10] This "larger literary complex" is equivalent to discourse, as discussed in 1.3 above. In other words, a thorough investigation of a word involves analysing its sentential context and its discourse context. Modern scholars affirm the importance of textual context. For example, modern linguists who deal primarily with non-biblical texts express the importance of referring to the sentence where a word is found (Collin and Guldmann 2005:41). Carson, in discussing various fallacies in word study, provides a headline "The Heart of the Matter: Coping with Context." He elaborates that "the heart of the issue is that semantics, meaning, is more than the meaning of words" (Carson 1998:64). Osborne maintains that the textual context of a word must be carefully considered, in order to avoid reading preconceived theological concepts into the word (Osborne 2006:110–111). Porter discusses the relevance of considering discourse in biblical studies (Porter 1995:21–35).

In addition to textual context, according to Barr, it is also important to investigate the wider context. According to Barr, the semantic value of a word should be understood through a systematic examination of the language: how a word is employed in literature that is contemporary to the biblical text. In criticizing the abuse of etymology, Barr points out a malpractice in which there is a general disregard of "the social nature of language as a means of communication" by ignoring a word's "current usage and current understanding" (Barr 1961:113). In other words, to ascertain the current usage and understanding of a biblical word one must examine how the same word is used in literature contemporary with it. On the other hand, solely relying on the assumption that a NT word is directly associated with a particular Greek thought is unreliable. For example, Barr argues that many contemporary scholars wrongly perceive the Pythagorean-Platonic tradition, which sees an immortal soul imprisoned in a mortal body, as the typical Greek tradition (ibid. 12). As such, rather than blindly assuming that a theological concept governs the meaning of a NT word, Barr emphasises the value of investigating the wider context by examining how the word is used in other contemporary Greek literature.

2.2 Recent work on Paul's anthropological terms

After the publication of Barr's work, there was a major shift within the field of biblical semantic study, with Barr's criticisms and comments drawing much attention.[11] In the post-Barr era, dozens of significant studies addressing

---

[10] Barr defines "literary" as both oral tradition and written literature (Barr 1961:269).

[11] For example, in his semantic study of NT soteriological terms published in 1967, Hill cautions against the danger of "illegitimate totality transfer" and provides a thorough investigation of the historical context of the chosen terms. Although

Paul's anthropological terms basically follow Barr's recommendations. They adopt a synchronic approach, with some focusing on the textual context and others attending to the wider context.

2.2.1 Textual context

Robert Jewett, James Dunn, Gordon Zerbe, Lorenzo Scornaienchi, Robert Gundry, E. Earle Ellis, and Sang-Won (Aaron) Son analyse Paul's anthropological terms by examining different aspects of the textual context. Jewett, Dunn, and Zerbe investigate multiple anthropological terms, and Scornaienchi investigates two anthropological terms. Gundry, Ellis, and Son investigate a single anthropological term, focusing only on σῶμα (body). The most comprehensive studies are by Jewett, Dunn, Zerbe, and Gundry, as they consider all of the Pauline epistles. By comparison, most studies concentrate on a single term within a particular Pauline epistle. However, despite their efforts, much of this work fails to adopt the synchronic approach in full.

Robert Jewett's work is undoubtedly the most comprehensive study post Barr. He analyses all of the authentic Pauline epistles, and examines all the key anthropological terms.[12] Importantly, Jewett was the first to explicitly address Barr's criticisms and insights (Jewett 1971:3). In describing his methodology, Jewett writes: "First of all, the approach will be to take account of the literary context of the sentence, the paragraph and the letter as a whole. We shall attempt to start with J. Barr's dictum that the basic semantic unit is not the word but the sentence, taking account of the grammatical structure in which a term is used" (ibid. 7).

Jewett employs a synchronic approach throughout his work. He focuses on the immediate context of a passage (sentence and paragraph) where a term occurs, and examines in detail the larger context by referring to the historical setting of the epistle. Jewett argues that historical reconstruction is important, despite its risk, in order to ascertain the usage of the key terms (ibid. 7). For example, before conducting a semantic analysis of σάρξ (flesh) and πνεῦμα (spirit) in Galatians, Jewett initially examines the circumstances of the audience, the Galatians (ibid. 17–20), and establishes a chronological framework of Paul's ministry and epistles to properly situate the anthropological terms (ibid. 11–14). This examination of the context is even extended to an investigation of the linguistic horizon of the first

Hill focuses on their usage in the LXX and their Hebrew equivalents in the OT, he is wholly aware of the value of attending to the immediate textual context (Hill 1967:18–19).

[12] For the discussion of Paul's authentic and disputed letters, see § 1.5. Jewett analyses the following epistles: 1 and 2 Thessalonians, Galatians, Philippians, 1 and 2 Corinthians, Philemon, and Romans; and examines the following terms: καρδία (heart), ψυχή (soul), νοῦς (mind), πνεῦμα (spirit), σάρξ (flesh), σῶμα (body), συνείδησις (conscience), and ἔσω ἄνθρωπος (inner human) (Jewett 1971:vii).

century (ibid. 8). As such, Jewett's semantic analysis employs a three-fold approach, examining the immediate context of a term, the historical set- ting of an epistle, and the linguistic usage in other contemporary Greek literature. Nonetheless, Jewett largely focuses on investigating how a term is used in light of its historical context, in particular, the polemical usage of an anthropological term.[13]

Jewett's approach can be demonstrated by his examination of σῶμα (body). Jewett initially considers the purpose of each Pauline epistle. He then argues that Paul faces different "opponents" throughout his ministry, and that the "extra personal, corporate dimensions" of σῶμα (body) are absent in the earlier epistles. For example, when Paul wrote 1 Thessalonians, Galatians and Philippians, he was tackling the "Libertinists" (who believed they were not bounded by the Law) and the "Enthusiasts" (who held the superiority of spirit over body and soul) (ibid. 250). However, despite his thorough his- torical construction and examination of the textual context, overall, Jewett's methodology exhibits two major problems. First, Jewett's approach is overly speculative. Second, his attention to the textual context is limited. Jewett reconstructs the chronological framework by producing a date for each Pauline epistle, then identifies Paul's opponents by interpreting the situation faced by the church, and then explains the polemical use of the anthropo- logical terms (ibid. 12–48). For example, in his examination of σάρξ (flesh) Jewett first establishes the date of Galatians as A.D. 52–53 by adopting the North Galatia theory (ibid. 18–19). He then identifies the "Judaizers" and the "Libertinists" as Paul's opponents by examining the apostle's response. Then, he uses the identified opponents to understand the meaning of σάρξ (flesh) in Galatians (ibid. 95–114). The adoption of the North Galatia theory, to establish the date of Galatians, is initially problematic.[14] Hence, Jewett's chronological reconstruction is not without risk. Furthermore, an examination of Paul's response to extrapolate his opponents and their thoughts is called mirror-reading. Despite its value, this method requires prudent treatment. As stipulated by Barclay, mirror-reading can lead to a biased selection of texts and wrong assumptions (Barclay 1987:73–93). Barclay refers to Jewett's work as an illustration of this method, and repudiates Jewett's identification of the opponents in Galatians as a shaky assumption.[15] In summary, Jewett's methodology is problematic given that the reconstructed timeline and his

---

[13] Jewett attempts to ascertain how the anthropological terms are used by the "conversational partners" (largely Paul's opponents), and how Paul redefines the terms to "fit to the needs of particular controversies" (Jewett 1971:10).

[14] For a detailed analysis of this theory, see Fung 1988:1–9 and Guthrie 1981:17–27.

[15] In Gal 5:3, Paul explicitly tells the Galatians that those who get circumcised would be obliged to keep the whole law. Barclay criticises Jewett's assumption that the opponents "had craftily refrained from passing on this information," and argues that the opponents "may have made very clear" the obligation, but Paul "may nevertheless feel it is necessary to hammer home their full unpalatable implication" (Barclay 1987:74–75). As well as the Judaizers and the Libertinists,

conjecture of Paul's opponents are questionable. Thus, his deduced polemical use of the anthropological terms is a product of speculation. Given that
Jewett focuses on the polemical use of the anthropological terms in Paul's
epistles by examining the historical situation, the attention to textual context
is limited. For example, in his study of σῶμα (body) in Philippians, Jewett's
textual analysis is mainly confined to sentential level by analysing σῶμα
(body) in 3:21 given its immediate context in 3:19. His analysis is also fixated
on how the term is used in relation to the Libertinists. As a result, Jewett fails
to examine the linguistic evidence in the whole epistle, and ascertain how this
evidence informs the use of σῶμα (body). His approach fails to attend to the
"larger literary complex" as suggested by Barr.

James Dunn discusses Paul's anthropological terms in his work, *The
Theology of Paul the Apostle*. In responding to the enduring debate about the
Hebrew over against Greek influence on Paul's work, Dunn contends that
there is a better approach than one that merely seeks "particular parallels
in Greek or Hebrew thought which could fully explain Paul's anthropology"
(Dunn 2008:55). He suggests that it is more fruitful to "look for the coherence
of Paul's thought in itself and only to draw attention to the points of possible influence where they are relevant to our better understanding of Paul"
(ibid. 55). For instance, in discussing σάρξ (flesh), Dunn agrees with Jewett's
criticism of pure semantic study without reference to context (ibid. 64). He
argues that σάρξ (flesh) has a spectrum of meaning, which is coherent with
Paul's theology. For example, the immediate context of κατὰ σάρκα (according to flesh) in Phil 3:3–4 suggests that the people placed their confidence in
the national identity of being Israelites, which was marked by circumcision.
Dunn argues that the phrase alone is neutral (for example, 1 Cor 10:18;
Rom 4:1), and is even something to be treasured (for example, Rom 9:3–5).
However, due to this physical kinship the people misplaced their confidence
and refused to have faith in Christ, a negative connotation (for example, Gal
4). In other words, Dunn contends that Paul's thought is coherent, and this
spectrum of meaning reflects such a coherency. According to Dunn, Paul is
not fixated on adopting Hebraic or Greek thoughts, and instead sometimes
creates a new usage that modifies the original Hebraic mind-set or Greek
philosophy. In contrasting σῶμα (body) and σάρξ (flesh), Dunn concludes
that Paul synthesises elements of Hebrew and Greek anthropology, concurrently affirming a holistic Hebrew concept of human embodiment and a
"negative Greek attitude to existence in the flesh" (ibid. 72). For Dunn, this
synthesis is largely due to Paul's apologetic and missionary strategy, and
the need to persuade audiences with both Jewish and Greek backgrounds
(ibid. 72). However, Paul's usage is coherent with his anthropology. Dunn
astutely surmises that Paul's concept of the human person comprises several dimensions, wherein each reflects one or more anthropological terms,

---

Jewett identifies other opponents, including the Gnostics, the Enthusiasts, and the
Divine-Man-Missionaries (Jewett 1971:119–130, 250–251).

and each anthropological term imbues a spectrum of meaning. Nonetheless, Paul's anthropology is coherent. A human person can be understood as a living being (ψυχή) existing in a social and relational dimension (σῶμα) with weakness and frailty (σάρξ), yet capable of deep emotions (καρδία) and being "touched by the profoundest reality within and behind the universe" (πνεῦμα) (ibid. 78). However, Dunn's analysis of Paul's anthropology and argument of coherency is problematic. Given that Paul developed his theology over a period of time as he composed the epistles, whether Paul always had a coherent and "neat" anthropology is questionable. Of most importance, Dunn gives less attention to the textual context, as he does not focus adequately on analysis at the discourse level and examining the linguistic evidence of a discourse to ascertain the usage of a term. Therefore, the rhetorical and contextual circumstances surrounding the composition of an epistle are flattened out in favour of Pauline coherence. As specified by Barr, the preconceived theological concept (in this case Paul's coherence) is imposed on an anthropological term in semantic study.

Gordon Zerbe's analysis focuses on three key terms, σῶμα (body), ψυχή (soul), and πνεῦμα (spirit), and contends that these terms do not have narrow semantic precision because some of them can be used interchangeably with an overlap in meaning (Zerbe 2008:168–184). Sometimes these terms are used colloquially by Paul, and other times they are used in a technical sense to elucidate a key theological argument. Zerbe argues that σῶμα (body) in the Corinthian epistles denotes the sacramental-spiritual-social being of the church, πνεῦμα (spirit) indicates the capacity of a person to relate directly to God, and ψυχή (soul) means the vitality of a living being, which relates to the "Hebrew notion of nephesh." Of interest, Zerbe contends that both the "essentialist anthropological dualism" and purely "monist understanding" cannot be established as the apostle's view, given that Paul is not interested in an ontological exposition of the human person. Paul's teaching is not "monist" in nature: "Paul is certainly...an apocalyptic dualist....For Paul the human being is faced with imperatives (modalities of living) that are God-ward (theological-spiritual), ethical (behavioral), and socio-political (having to do with allegiance, dominions, and identity). Paul's dualism has multiple dimensions" (ibid. 168). Zerbe concludes that Paul does not portray a "dualist anthropology with a distinct and separable soul." Paul is an apocalyptic dualist who emphasises social-ethical-political-spiritual "human living," rather than the ontology of "human being." Therefore, the resurrected body can be elucidated and understood as transformation into newness.

Zerbe's work primarily focuses on the textual context of the anthropological terms. In discussing σῶμα (body) in 1 Corinthians, Zerbe investigates how this term is used throughout the epistle. His attempt to address the textual context at the discourse level is commendable. However, his analysis does not demonstrate an attention to detailed contextual evidence. For example, Zerbe simply cites a biblical source without giving any detailed exegetical analysis.[16] Nonetheless, his most important finding is the social-ethical connotations of Paul's anthropological terms, rather than ontological. This study, drawing on a better formulated methodology, will endorse this finding.

Lorenzo Scornaienchi investigates the terms σῶμα (body) and σάρξ (flesh), and describes his methodology as a "neue Systematik." Scornaienchi demonstrates how Paul uses these terms to denote "Konstruktivität" and "Destruktivität" communities respectively, and primarily argues that this meaning stems from Paul's environment (Scornaienchi 2008:13). For Scornaienchi, σάρξ (flesh) denotes a destructive community (ibid. 67).[17] This community is characterised by hierarchical domination, and is full of differences (ibid. 62). By contrast, σῶμα (body) denotes togetherness and a constructive community. This community is characterised by constructive action that amalgamates a community and eliminates hierarchy, wherein believers come together despite their differences (gender, social group, and nationality) (ibid. 62, 67). Scornaienchi bases this argument on an analysis of various Pauline passages (Rom 7:7–25; 12:3–8; 1 Cor 6:12–20; 11:17–34; 12:1–31; 2 Cor 5:1–10; Gal 5:13–23). Scornaienchi concludes that while a person lives ἐν σαρκί (in flesh), the power of σάρξ (flesh) cannot be fully eliminated. Consequently, the person experiences a struggle between the consuming power of this destructiveness and the constructive life realised in Christ (ibid. 353). However, despite Scornaienchi's insights, his argument is limited to select Pauline passages and does not sufficiently investigate how the anthropological terms within chosen passages relate to the whole discourse. For example, in an analysis of σάρξ (flesh) in Rom 7, Scornaienchi discusses various understandings of the human person held by ancient Greek philosophers, including Plato, Aristotle, Stoics, and Epicurus (ibid. 308–316). However, a consideration of the wider discourse is limited.[18] Therefore, the semantics of these key terms are not examined through the "lenses" of the whole discourse, as suggested by Barr.

Three scholars—Robert Gundry, Earle Ellis, and Sang-Won (Aaron) Son—each investigate a single anthropological term, σῶμα (body).

Gundry first examines the usage of σῶμα (body) in contemporaneous extra-biblical literature, and concludes that the term always denotes a

---

[16] For example, "Paul can use the term [σῶμα (body)]...to denote the very sacramental-spiritual-social being of the church ("you are the body of Christ and individually members of it," 1 Cor. 12:27; "the body is one," 1 Cor. 12:12, 13; cf. 10:16–17; 1 Cor. 11:24–29)." Zerbe does not provide a further analysis of these cited passages (Zerbe 2008:168).

[17] Scornaienchi argues that σάρξ (flesh) does not merely indicate a material substance. This term points to the living flesh and those people who actively pursue their own desires contributing to this destructiveness.

[18] Scornaienchi only devotes a small portion of his analysis to discussing the wider discourse context of Romans in relation to Rom 7 (Scornaienchi 2008:299–300).

physical essence. Hence, the holistic definition of σῶμα (body) proposed by
Bultmann and Robinson is not supported by extra-biblical literature (Gundry
1976:15). Gundry then examines the usage of σῶμα (body) in the LXX by
reviewing its Hebrew equivalent, בָּשָׂר (flesh). He shares Barr's concern
about "illegitimate identity transfer," and concludes that "the LXX offers
no convincing support" for interpreting σῶμα as the whole human person.
Gundry maintains that "whatever the underlying Hebrew, בשׂר (flesh) or
another word – sōma refers to the physical body alone" (ibid. 25). Gundry
also examines the usage of σῶμα (body) in the Pauline epistles, especially
focusing on 1 Cor 6:12–20. Gundry concludes that σῶμα (body) usually
"denotes the physical body, roughly synonymous with 'flesh' in the neutral
sense" (ibid. 50). Hence, similarly, the holistic definition of σῶμα (body)
is not supported by biblical literature, including the LXX, the NT, and the
Pauline epistles (ibid. 79). Second, Gundry discusses various understandings of anthropological duality, including human identity in Greek thought.
He examines σῶμα (body) as the body of Christ, and heavily criticises
Bultmann who, according to Gundry, minimises the communal connotation
of the term to suit his theological framework (ibid. 223). Gundry adopts a
synchronic approach and focuses on the context of σῶμα (body). He analyses the wider context by reviewing contemporary philosophical thought,
such as the concept of anthropological duality, but prioritises the textual
analysis of various biblical and extra-biblical literature, particularly focusing on Pauline passages. While Gundry examines the historical development
of the term, for example in the LXX, such examination does not dominate
his investigation. His exegetical work provides a solid criticism of prior
scholarship, specifically Bultmann and Robinson who attempt to place the
term within their theological frameworks. However, apart from his specific
examination of 1 Cor 6 and 12, his exegetical analysis is arguably trun-
cated. For example, various Pauline passages are quoted to support an idea
without a detailed textual analysis.[19] In addition, the examination of 1 Cor
6 and 12 is limited to sentential and paragraphic levels. Hence, his exegetical analysis fails to review the place of the term within the whole epistle.
Therefore, Gundry's synchronic approach is limited as it does not attend to
the "larger literary complex," the whole discourse, as suggested by Barr.

Ellis specifically focuses on the term σῶμα (body) in 1 Corinthians.
First, he compares σῶμα (body) with other Pauline anthropological terms.
He repudiates the Platonic dualistic notion of the human person, and argues
that various anthropological terms, including spirit, heart, conscience, and

---

[19] For example, in explaining the phrase "absent in body" in 1 Cor 5:3, Gundry
argues that σῶμα (body) is "a reference to the external absence of the whole
man," and refers to Col 2:5 and 1 Thess 2:17. However, he does not provide any
contextual analysis of these passages (Gundry 1976:48). Gundry's conclusion may
be correct, but citing various Pauline passages without proper analysis can lead to
the malpractice of taking a passage out of context.

flesh, depict either the "outward self" or "inward self" (Ellis 1990:135), which resembles the OT "distinction between the person outwardly and the person inwardly" (ibid. 134–135). Ellis then focuses on and examines the "corporate body" in 1 Corinthians, particularly the contrast between the body of Christ and "the body of Adam" (ibid. 138–140). Ellis cites various Pauline passages in his analysis, but does not provide any detailed textual analysis. In most cases, he simply refers to the passage in a statement.

In two studies, Son examines σῶμα (body) in 1 Corinthians. In one study, Son demonstrates how various Pauline expressions, involving σῶμα (body), convey the corporate dimension of human existence. For example, ἐν Χριστῷ (in Christ) and its synonyms, the Adam-Christ typology, and σῶμα—in particular, ἓν σῶμα (one body) and σῶμα Χριστοῦ (body of Christ) in 1 Corinthians—are used by Paul to convey corporate personality (Son 2001a:183). In the other study, Son focuses on ἓν σῶμα (one body) in 1 Corinthians, demarcating the comparison between sexual union (between a man and a woman) and spiritual union (between Christ and his church) (Son 2001b:107–122). In both studies, he argues that a corporate solidarity is denoted by the usage of σῶμα (body). Paul employs this anthropological term and related expressions to highlight "the significance of the individual existence of believers in the light of their corporate reality in Christ" (Son 2001a:183). Son draws on particular passages from 1 Corinthians, Romans, Colossians, and Ephesians[20] to illustrate how σῶμα (body) refers to the church as the body of Christ and denotes "primarily the unity of believers with Christ" (ibid. 102). Although Son examines some contemporary philosophy, including the Stoic metaphor, the Gnostic myth, and the rabbinic tradition (ibid. 112–116), he predominantly focuses on exegetical analysis. However, this analysis is limited to σῶμα (body), and the explanation of ἓν σῶμα (one body) only considers 1 Cor 6 and 12 (Son 2001b:107–122). Thus, this study is far from exhaustive. In addition, the textual analysis is mostly limited to sentential and paragraphic levels, and accordingly Son's study fails to attend to "the complete speech," as suggested by Barr.

In my opinion, many modern commentaries critically elucidate the Pauline anthropological terms through exegetical analyses.[21] However, many of these are limited to sentential and paragraphic levels, and do not examine the terms in light of the textual context at the discourse level.

---

[20] These include 1 Cor 6:13–20; 10:14–22; 11:17–34; 12:12–27; Rom 12:3–8; Eph 1:22b–23; 2:14–16; 3:6; 4:4; 11–16; 5:23, 30; Col 1:18, 24; 2:16–19; 3:15 (Son 2001a:84–102).

[21] For example, Hawthorne studies πνεῦμα (spirit) and ψυχή (soul) in Phil 1:27 (Hawthorne 1983:57), Thiselton examines σῶμα (body) in 1 Cor 6 (Thiselton 2000:316, 474), and Furnish analyses καρδία (heart) in 2 Cor 6–7 (Furnish 1984:360). This research explores and understands these terms in light of their immediate sentential context.

2.2.2 Wider context

In addition to the textual context, various studies focus on the wider context, or the cultural and the philosophical context of Paul's anthropological terms. Some examine how the human person is understood in contemporaneous philosophical thought, and others examine how a particular term is employed in contemporary Greek literature. Although an investigation of the wider context is valuable, as suggested by Barr, and informs the meaning of key terms, many of these studies fail to apply the synchronic approach and attend to the textual context. The key findings of various studies are discussed below. Emma Wasserman, Adriana Destro and Mauro Pesce, and Brian Edgar investigate multiple anthropological terms, with most focusing on two terms. Troy Martin, Troels Engberg-Pedersen, David Brakke, and Timo Laato investigate only a single anthropological term.

Wasserman's discussion of the terms σῶμα (body) and σάρξ (flesh) in Rom 7 rejects the notion that a dualistic anthropology is being conveyed. Despite the probability that a Platonic logic is adopted in Rom 7, Wasserman contends that Paul does not need to agree with "Platonic metaphysics and epistemology to conceptualize the body or flesh as an ally of passion" (Wasserman 2007:793–816). Wasserman's focus on Platonic logic delimits an analysis of the textual context (Wasserman 2007:810–816). Thus, the level of synchronic analysis in this study is considerably limited.

Destro and Pesce briefly analyse the usage of ἔσω ἄνθρωπος (outer human) and σῶμα (body) in the Pauline epistles, and surmise that "the redefinition of spatial categories allows the conceptual elimination of the pre-existing boundaries between social group" (Destro and Pesce 1998:184–197). Their approach is largely based on investigating the contemporary philosophical background. However, an exegetical analysis and attention to the textual context is nearly nonexistent.[22]

Edgar, similarly to Wasserman, also repudiates the dualistic view in his investigation of how Paul's anthropological terms are employed in his soteriology. For example, Edgar argues that "Paul is more concerned with anthropological themes which develop and validate his central soteriological concerns than with the formulation of an all-encompassing anthropological ontology" (Edgar 2000:151–164). Edgar cites some Pauline passages, but does not provide any exegetical analysis of these.

Martin examines the usage of πνεῦμα (spirit) by comparing ancient medical texts and the Pauline epistles (Martin 2006:105–126). He concludes that the pneumatological statements found in the Pauline epistles are in accordance with those found in the medical texts (ibid. 106). In these medical texts, πνεῦμα is portrayed as entering a person through oro-nasal

---

[22] For example, passages are only cited in the discussion of the relation between "inner man" and "outer man," and there is little textual analysis (Destro and Pesce 1998:188).

channels, causing movement and providing health. Martin observes that this understanding is also found in the Corinthian correspondence, in which the Spirit enters the body and imparts life (ibid. 125–126). However, Martin's examination includes little exegetical analysis.[23]

Troels Engberg-Pedersen studies the usage of πνεῦμα (spirit) in the Pauline epistles by examining contemporary Greco-Roman philosophy. Engberg-Pedersen identifies and explains how Stoic philosophy influences the meaning of πνεῦμα (spirit) in 1 Cor 15 regarding the resurrected body. He maintains that Paul's account of "the pneumatic resurrection body presupposes Stoic cosmology...[Paul's] idea of a substantive change belongs within an Aristotelian tradition of physics" (Engberg-Pedersen 2009:179–197). As such, Engberg-Pedersen (2009:186) argues that πνεῦμα (spirit) does not reveal an immaterial understanding, and rather is employed to emphasise materiality in an apocalyptic framework, with a Stoic view of a bodily πνεῦμα (spirit). Although Engberg-Pedersen incorporates various Pauline passages in his argument, there is minimal textual analysis.[24]

Brakke (2000:119–134) investigates the notion of σῶμα (body) in the ancient world. Whilst acknowledging the complexity of Paul's usage of σῶμα (body), Brakke illustrates the relationship between Platonic teaching and Paul's anthropology. According to Brakke, certain elements of Platonic teaching are adopted by Paul to portray σῶμα (body) as a "tent," but other elements describing God's glory as manifested in human σῶμα (body) are rejected (ibid. 120). However, Brakke does not undertake any textual and exegetical analysis of the term.[25]

Timo Laato (1995:169–181) examines the usage of σάρξ (flesh) by contrasting Pauline and Jewish philosophical frameworks. Laato focuses on and discusses the connection between Galatians and the Jewish pattern of religion. However, his analysis predominantly relies on a reconstruction of events that occurred in Galatia, rather than attending to the textual context.[26]

As established above, many studies investigating the wider context fail to attend to the textual context.

---

[23] For example, Martin (2006:121) briefly describes the notion of spirit in 1 Cor 2:8–16, without providing any in-depth textual analysis.

[24] For example, Engberg-Pedersen (2009:185) provides a brief textual analysis of 1 Cor 15:35–50 in one paragraph, without addressing detailed textual evidence both within and beyond the pasage.

[25] For example, Brakke (2000:120) cites 2 Cor 5:2 to illustrate the "tent" language without analysing the context at sentential or paragraphic levels.

[26] Although Laato (1995:174–175) provides detailed textual analysis of Gal 6:4, 13–14, his analysis is too brief in explaining how the text relates to the whole letter (Laato 1995:177–178). Similarly, in discussing the notion of flesh as the "home" of a person's selfish desires, Laato (2004:354–359) provides a comprehensive exegetical analysis of Gal 3:10, but only briefly mentions the connection between Gal 3:22–23, Gal 5:17, and Rom 7:7–25.

2.2.3 Textual context and wider context

Some scholars investigate both the textual context and the wider context, including Hans Dieter Betz, Michelle Lee, and Dale Martin. However, all of these studies are limited in their scope by focusing only on a single anthropological term.

Betz examines the usage of ἔσω ἄνθρωπος (inner human). He considers some philosophical thought and provides a comparatively detailed analysis of the context. Betz argues that Paul rejects the Middle-Platonic dualism of an immortal soul imprisoned in a material body (Betz 2000a:315–341). He suggests that ἔσω ἄνθρωπος (inner human) is employed by Paul to denote "eschatological redemption through the Christ-ἄνθρωπος (human)" (ibid. 340). In another work, Betz also articulates Paul's struggle to teach the Christian faith to the Corinthians, among whom there is a "perceived conflict between Paul's preaching and conventional anthropological assumptions held by people educated in Greek culture," especially "with regard to the dualism of body and soul" (Betz 2000b:569). In both studies, Betz considers the immediate textual context and the wider context of the term, within the whole letter.[27]

Lee's analysis of σῶμα (body) suggests that Stoic philosophy influences Paul's usage of this term, and specifically informs the concept of bodily unity in the apostle's work (Lee 2006:6). She claims that comprehending "how the Stoics saw the universe and society as a 'body' may help us comprehend what lies behind Paul's statements that the believers are not 'like' a body, but also 'are' the body of Christ" (ibid. 6). The Stoics consider the universe a living being, which resembles the human body as an organism, and believed that people are unified bodies under the presence of a "persuasive πνεῦμα (spirit)" (ibid. 50). The concept of bodily unity, between humanity and the gods, is at the heart of Stoic philosophy, and forms the foundation of their ethical system and moral expectations (ibid. 46–101). Lee contends that Paul adopts a similar concept to convey his ideas to the Corinthians, and also uses "a similar method to train the Corinthians" to respond to the moral expectations within the church (ibid. 101). Detailed exegetical analysis is provided throughout Lee's study;[28] however, the analysis is limited to a single anthropological term within one Pauline epistle.

Martin considers the term σῶμα (body), and broadly examines contemporary philosophical thought and Greek literature. He argues that Greco-Roman philosophy is commonly assumed by modern biblical scholars "to share our modern notions of the body," and is portrayed as "more unified

---

[27] For example, the immediate textual context of ἔσω ἄνθρωπος (inner human) in 2 Cor 4:16 is analysed while the wider issues are addressed (Betz 2000a:329–335; Betz 2000b:565–8).

[28] For example, an analysis of 1 Cor 12 attends to both the paragraph and sentential levels while discussing the relevance of Stoic thought to the interpretation (Lee 2006:105–152).

and more homogeneous than it actually was" (Martin 1995:6). As a result, a form of Platonism that holds the radical separation of a mortal body and an immortal soul is considered "the Greek view" (ibid. 7). In particular, Martin argues that the philosophy of René Descartes adversely influenced modern scholarship. Unlike the ancient dualism of the body and the soul, Descartes created an ontological dualism in which "on one side were body, matter, nature, and the physical; on the other were soul or mind, nonmatter, the supernatural, and the spiritual or psychological" (ibid. 6). Martin contends that this dualism "still influences many modern minds, this was a system of which the ancients knew nothing" (ibid. 6).

Following a brief analysis of various Greek philosophical schools of thought, Martin asserts that first-century Platonism is more complex than perceived by many modern scholars and students. He argues that the influence of popular philosophy on the early Christian communities, within which Paul ministered, was "more related to Stoic than Platonic concepts" (ibid. 14). Martin examines the concept of "microcosmic body," which states that human bodies are part of the universe, the boundary between inner body and outer body is blurred, and the whole body is constantly influenced by and interacting with the universe (ibid. 17–21). This concept was widely embraced during Paul's era. Martin provides a succinct explanation, stating that "[a] few philosophers, Platonists perhaps, may have emphasized a dualism between the body and the soul. But such theorists represented a small minority. In the absence of such an ontological dualism, for most people of Greco-Roman culture the human body was of a piece with its environment...[and this concept was greatly different from] the individualism of modern conceptions" (ibid. 25).

Employing these findings, Martin provides a detailed exegetical analysis of σῶμα (body) in 1 Corinthians, examining the immediate textual context and the structure of the whole epistle. He argues that Paul assumes the microcosm of the body, whereby the human body is an analogy for human society and "unity can exist in diversity within the macrocosm of society" (ibid. 92). In addition, Martin considers the "opponents" who confronted Paul, namely a group of people who believed they were "stronger" in faith than the rest. By adopting a rhetorical strategy, Paul identifies himself "with the position of the Strong and [is] then calling on them to give up their own interests for the sake of the Weak" (ibid. 103). However, despite these insightful findings, Martin's study is limited to a single anthropological term, σῶμα (body), in one epistle, 1 Corinthians.

2.2.4 The limitations of recent work

As demonstrated in this discussion, many recent studies of Paul's anthropological terms attend to Barr's comments and adopt a synchronic approach, focusing on the textual context and/or the wider context. However, many of these studies fail to fully apply Barr's recommendations. Those that focus on the textual context either are overly speculative (Jewett), rely heavily on presuppositions (Dunn), or undertake limited textual analysis at the sentential level (Zerbe, Ellis) and the discourse level (Gundry, Son). Those that focus on the wider context either insufficiently address the textual context (Wasserman, Engberg-Pedersen, Laato) or do not include any textual analysis (Destro and Pesce, Edgar, Troy Martin, Brakke). Conversely, Betz, Lee, and Dale Martin provide detailed textual analysis while investigating the wider context. Yet, their work is limited to a single anthropological term within either multiple Pauline epistles (Betz) or a single epistle (Lee, Dale Martin).

Given these limitations, I have sought to formulate a research approach that principally attends to the modern science of linguistics. In other words, this must be a linguistic method that can be applied in the semantic study of different languages, both modern and ancient. In addition, this research approach must attend to Barr's comments and adopt the synchronic approach in full, providing textual analysis at clausal, sentential, and paragraphic levels, and in particular, a wider analysis of the larger literary context, the whole discourse. Furthermore, this research approach should be broader in scope and applicable for multiple anthropological terms within multiple Pauline epistles.

2.3 Research approach:
The basic principles of discourse analysis

To sum up, then, recent studies addressing Paul's anthropological terms have largely failed to fully attend to James Barr's comments and criticism about the best method for determining semantic meaning. Given their limitations, there is a need to formulate a sound research approach that carefully attends to the following key propositions. The first key proposition is that biblical semantic study must follow the modern science of linguistics, applying sound linguistic principles in conducting semantic study. The second key proposition is the importance of adopting the synchronic approach, and examining the textual context and the wider context. Barr emphasises the importance of treating the sentence as the linguistic bearer of a word's semantic meaning, and the importance of attending to the "larger literary complex," the whole discourse. The approach I take in this study, therefore, applies some basic principles of discourse analysis. Discourse analysis is a method in the field of linguistics that investigates what Barr calls the "larger literary complex."

2.3.1 Discourse analysis: A summary

In what follows I initially define the concepts of discourse and discourse analysis, then elucidate the connection between discourse analysis and NT studies, and finally identify the key features of discourse analysis relevant to this semantic study. After this overview, I formulate a research approach for examining Paul's anthropological terms, based on the principles of discourse analysis.

2.3.1.1 Discourse

A discourse is "the entirety of the author's communication to his or her audience" (Reed 1997:45). In the field of linguistics, a discourse can be broadly defined as anything "beyond the sentence" (Schiffrin, Tanner, and Hamilton 2003:1) from a structural unit[29] to an entire written or oral text, to "any aspect of language use" (Blakemore 2003:100).

In particular, written discourse comprises various grammatical elements, including grapheme, word, clause, sentence, and paragraph (Reed 1997:43–45).[30] For example, a narrative containing many paragraphs is a single discourse, as is a letter comprising various elements. Hence, a discourse is a combination of paragraphs or a complete speech, or as Barr expresses it, the "larger literary complex." In this study, a discourse is considered an entire written or oral text that comprises various structural units, which is communicated by an author to his or her audience.[31]

2.3.1.2 Discourse analysis

Discourse analysis originated as a method in the field of general linguistics,[32] and is employed by linguists to investigate a written or oral text.[33] Discourse analysis is the thorough examination of the structure and the pragmatics of a text, extending from the sentence to the entire discourse. There are four major schools of thought regarding discourse analysis: the North American model, the English and Australian model, the Continental European model,

---

[29] In this study, a structural unit is called a semantic unit. A unit is the grouping of sentences by an author to express a theme or a topic. A more detailed explanation of a semantic unit is provided later.

[30] Based on the definition of discourse in this study, a paragraph can be a single semantic unit or part of a semantic unit (which contains more than one paragraph).

[31] While this study adopts Reed's definition, examples by other linguists do not necessarily follow this definition. For example, Terry suggests that 1 Corinthians contains ten "discourses": (A) Church division 1:10–4:17; (B) Fornication 4:18–6:20; (C) Marriage 7; (D) Idol food 8:1–11:1; (E) Head coverings 11:2–16; (F) The Lord's Supper 11:17–34; (G) Spiritual gifts 12–14; (H) The Resurrection 15; (I) Contribution 16:1–11; and (J) Apollos 16:12. Terry treats each structural unit as one discourse. However, this study would identify 1 Corinthians as one entire discourse, and the ten "discourses" as ten "semantic units" (Terry 1995:38–43).

[32] Discourse analysis is often regarded as equivalent to text linguistics (Porter 1995:17). For a detailed account of the rise of discourse analysis, see Bodine 1995:1–5.

[33] Some scholars, such as Porter, focus on a written text (Porter 1995:17). Others focus on an oral text. For example, for Beaugrande and Dressler (1983:19) discourse analysis is the study of conversation.

and the South African model.[34] Stanley Porter suggests that the differentiation of these schools is not clear-cut since "there is more commonality in methods than has been realized" (Porter 1995:24). In addition, some scholars apply more than one school of thought in their work (Porter 1995:24).

Although there are various definitions of discourse analysis, there are three aspects commonly identified. Discourse analysis focuses on examining "(1) anything beyond the sentence, (2) language use, and (3) a broader range of social practice that includes nonlinguistic and nonspecific instances of language" (Schiffrin, Tanner, and Hamilton 2003:1). Jeffrey Reed defines discourse analysis as "a sub-discipline of modern linguistics that seeks to understand the relationships between language, discourse, and situational context in human communication" (Reed 2002:189).[35] Porter offers a succinct description, stating that discourse analysis can "provide as comprehensive a description as possible of the various components of a given discourse, including its meaning and structure, and the means by which these are created and conveyed" (Porter 1995:19). He argues that discourse analysis is a method that attempts to coherently integrate three areas of linguistic analysis: "semantics, concerned with the conveyance of meaning through the forms of the language; syntax, concerned with the organization of these forms into meaningful units; and pragmatics, concerned with the meanings of these forms in specific linguistic contest ('what speakers mean

---

[34] Porter (1995:24–35) provides a detailed discussion of these four schools, as well as the key linguists in each school and their publications. The North American model is represented by the Summer Institute of Linguistics (SIL International). This model is influenced by the works of some famous linguists, including Robert Longacre, Kenneth Pike, and Sydney Lamb. This model focuses on "the principle of levels and layers of language, proceeding from…the smallest parts of the language (whether phonetically or morphologically) to increasingly larger structures (Porter 1995:25). The English and Australian model is represented by M. Halliday and R. Hasan. This model is influenced by J. R. Firth, a leading British linguist in the 1940s, and professor of General Linguistics at the University of London. Firth regards language as "a social semiotic consisting of networks of systems." A discourse consists of "four categories of structure: experiential, interpersonal, logical and textual," and each category has "a number of networks of choices that are realized in the phenomena of the language" (Porter 1995:28). The Continental European model draws on the works of several linguists, including Robert Beaugrande, Wolfgang Dressler, Elizabeth Gülich, Wolfgang Raible, Teun A. van Dijk, R. Jacobson, and C. Perelman. This model addresses "the macro-structure" of text, leading to an examination of "syntax, semantics and pragmatics" (Porter 1995:30). The South African model is represented by J. P. Louw and A. B. du Toit. This emphasises the method of "colon analysis." As described, a colon is "a unit that is formed around a nominative and predicative structure. These cola are first isolated and then their interconnections are re-established in diagrammatic form, illustrating the semantic relations among them as increasingly larger semantic units are formed" (Porter 1995:32–33).

[35] Reed also (2002:189) states that discourse analysis is also known as Textlinguistics or Text Grammar.

when they use the form')" (ibid. 18). Thus, this study will gather these three areas into its structural and pragmatic analyses.

2.3.1.3 Discourse analysis and NT studies

The connection between discourse analysis and NT studies stems from the work of North American linguists in the area of NT translation, in the 1950s and 1960s (Bodine 1995:3–4). They recognised the importance of going beyond the sentential level of a text, in order to thoroughly understand the context (ibid. 3). Kenneth Pike, a prominent SIL linguist, emphasised the application of discourse analysis in the linguistic field work of Bible translation.[36] Hence, SIL has been using discourse analysis in their training and projects for many years. However, their work is not well known in wider NT scholarship, perhaps due to the tendency to publish work within their own organisation. For example, SIL has published a series on the discourse analysis of different NT books.[37]

Although discourse analysis is a relatively new method in NT studies, there are a number of NT scholars who discuss or apply it in their work. These scholars include, but are not limited to, Birger Olsson, Jean Calloud, Wolfgang Schenk, J. P. Louw, Bruce Johanson, George Guthrie, Jeffrey Reed, Moisés Silva, David Black, Stanley Porter, Cynthia Westfall, Mark Boda, Joel Green, Jae Hyun Lee, and Steven Runge.[38] Nonetheless, many NT scholars are reluctant to apply discourse analysis in their work partly due to the perception that "discourse analysis is something difficult to get a handle on and therefore difficult to use" (Porter 2012).

2.3.2 Key features of discourse analysis

The above explanation of discourse analysis identifies different schools of thought, and complex concepts and definitions. In this study, three key features of discourse analysis inform the examination of Paul's anthropological terms. These features do not thoroughly represent the conceptual principles of discourse analysis, and instead are the synthesis of some basic principles. These three features are: scope, structure, and pragmatics.

---

[36] Pike's (1967:9) tagmemic principles, an early theoretical concept of discourse analysis, are used in the field work of SIL.

[37] Some of the work in this series includes the following: Bank (1987, 1996, 1999); Callow (2000, 2002); Deibler (1998); Hart & Hart (2001); Johnson (1988, 2008); Rogers (1989); Sherman & Tuggy (1994); Sterner (1998);

[38] Some of the publications of these scholars are as follows: Black (1995); Bruce (1987); Calloud (1976); Green (2010); Guthrie (1994); Lee (2010); Louw (1987); Olsson (1974); Porter & Boda (2009); Reed (1995, 1997); Schenk (1977); Silva (1995); Steven (2010); Westfall (2005). Porter, Reed, and Guthrie apply the English and Australian model. Olsson and Schenk apply the Continental European model. Louw applies the South African model (Porter 1995:28, 30, 32–3).

2.3.2.1 Scope

First, the wider context is taken into account when conducting linguistic analysis of a text. Fundamentally, the analysis of a text must go beyond the sentential level, from merely studying the morpheme, word, phrase, clause, or sentence to examining the paragraph and whole discourse. M. Halliday highlights that "the sentences are...the realization of text" (Halliday 2002:45). Hence, sentential analysis fails to grasp the meaning intended by the author for his or her audience because human communication transcends words, phrases, and sentences (Green 2010:223–224).

As previously discussed, Barr perceives the sentence as the bearer of semantic meaning, and in the post-Barr era, many scholars undertaking semantic study focused on sentential exegetical analysis. Barr also articulates the importance of the "larger literary complex" in semantic study. Therefore, an emphasis on examining the wider textual context, rather than only considering the immediate textual context, addresses Barr's comments. Accordingly, a thorough semantic study must be conducted "beyond the sentence," whereby the whole discourse, defined as "the entirety of the author's communication to his or her audience," is the intended scope. Therefore, in this study, the discourse scope refers to conducting linguistic and semantic analysis at the level of the whole discourse.

2.3.2.2 Structure

Although the whole discourse is the primary concern of discourse analysis, this can also be divided into smaller units. In this study, the discourse structure refers to the identification, function, and correlation of these smaller units. Discourse structure denotes the segmentation of a discourse,[39] or "the pattern an author uses to organize [the entire] text" (Westfall 2005:28). This structure can be conceptualised as follows. A discourse is a coherent text formed by linguistic cohesion. A discourse is composed of different, yet cohesive, semantic units. Each semantic unit is formed by thematic grouping, and is usually marked by one or more discourse markers. Together these units form a coherent flow, through which the macrostructure can be identified. These concepts are discussed further below.

Cohesion, coherence, and prominence

A discourse does not consist of randomly inserted sentences. Instead, a discourse comprises sentences that are unified and connected through various grammatical and lexical devices employed by the author. This connectedness

---

[39] Kibrik argues that discourse structure can be further categorised into global structure and local structure. Global structure is "the segmentation of discourse into its immediate constituents or large chunks, such as paragraphs in an article." Local structure is "the structure consisting of minimal units" (Kibrik 2011:14).

is called cohesion (Schiffrin, Tanner, and Hamilton 2003:718).[40] This cohesion enables an audience to interpret different elements of a text and form "a single overall mental representation" (Dooley and Levinsohn 2001:23). This outcome is called coherence. In summary, cohesion (the connectedness of sentences through linguistic devices employed by the author) leads to coherence (an overall mental representation formed by the reader).

Within a discourse, a sentence does not stand alone and is closely related to neighbouring and distant sentences. All sentences in a discourse, except the first one, are "forcibly constrained by" the preceding text (Brown and Yule 1983:46).[41] In other words, there is a cohesion that is crucial to the correct interpretation of a discourse. The grammatical and lexical devices employed to achieve cohesion include synonyms, parallels, inclusion, and chiasm. These contribute to the coherence of a discourse,[42] which is arguably "of central importance to discourse analysis" (Schiffrin 1987:21).

One of the most important devices to achieve cohesion, and thus coherence, is prominence. Due to human limitations in processing information, it is easier for an audience to perceive something that stands out from its background. Prominence is the usage of linguistic devices to highlight and emphasise a point. One basic form of prominence is thematic repetition (thematic prominence), whereby the same theme is repeated (Pickering 1980:40).[43] A related form of prominence is lexical cohesion (lexical prominence), whereby the same word or words conveying the same theme are repeated (Halliday 2002:8).[44] The study of repetition at the textual level is well established in semantic study.

---

[40] Both Renkema (1993:35) and Beaugrande and Dressler (1983:48, 194) also use the term "cohesion." However, other linguists use other terms. For example, Reed (1997:89) uses the term "cohesiveness."

[41] Brown and Yule (1983:46) call these related sentences co-texts.

[42] There are at least three levels of coherence within a discourse: referential, situational, and structural. Referential coherence refers to the "sameness" of a particular textual element. Situational coherence refers to a consistent emotive tone in a semantic unit, characterised by the choice of words. For example, an author cannot be concurrently angry and happy, even though the successive units can display a change of tone. Structural coherence refers to the compatibility and correlation of different parts in a semantic unit, so that the reader can make sense of the text (Beekman, Callow, and Kopesec 1981:21).

[43] A similar concept is redundancy, which is the use of multiple means to convey a point in a text. Pickering (1980:29–30) cites Halliday and argues that all forms of grammatical agreement lead to redundancy, which contributes to the linear cohesion of a text. Human limitation is believed to be the reason behind repetition. Humans can only process a limited amount of information in a linear sequence and repetition helps humans grasp the meaning of a lengthy text.

[44] Halliday (2002:29) argues that when similar lexical items, with two or more occurrences, appear in close proximity in a discourse, these items possibly belong to the same lexical set. Halliday's argument is a direct attack on the diachronic approach in semantic study, as he clearly points out that any lexical item is defined

In summary, the usage of cohesive linguistic devices by an author (cohesion) leads to a coherent message, and one of the key devices to achieve this is prominence (thematic or lexical repetition).

To illustrate these concepts, let us look at John 15:5: ἐγώ εἰμι ἡ ἄμπελος, ὑμεῖς τὰ κλήματα (I am the vine, you are the branches). This passage is closely connected to preceding text. First, the expression ἐγώ εἰμι (I am)[45] occurs 20 times before 15:5,[46] which illustrates prominence: the author highlights ἐγώ εἰμι (I am) through lexical repetition (lexical cohesion). Second, the personal pronouns in the sentence function as a referential device, referring to the participants in a dialogue. These participants can be only identified by examining the previous context: ἐγώ (I) refers to Jesus; and ὑμεῖς (you) refers to his disciples.[47] Third, ἄμπελος (vine) and κλήματα (branches) are compatible since they belong to the semantic domain of viticulture. These three linguistic devices enable cohesion, which allows the audience to form a mental representation and perceive a coherent meaning.

Imagine this passage had been written as follows: εἰμι ἡ ἄμπελος, αὐτοί οἱ δέσμοι (I am the vine, they are the prisoners). The loss of cohesion would lead to the loss of coherence. First, the audience would fail to see the clear connection between εἰμι (I am) and previous occurrences of ἐγώ εἰμι (I am). Second, the audience would not identify who the personal pronoun αὐτοί (they) refers to, as this pronoun does not refer to any participants mentioned in the dialogue. Third, the audience would struggle to recognise the connection between ἄμπελος (vine) and δέσμοι (prisoners) because these two words do not belong to the same semantic domain. As a result, the audience would be unable to make sense of the text.[48]

Thematic groupings, semantic units, and macrostructure

In addition to employing linguistic devices (cohesion), the author also usually groups sentences into units according to different themes (known as thematic groupings).[49] These grouped units are called semantic units in this

---

by its environment. Therefore, analysing a de-contextualized word by purely consulting a dictionary or grammar book will fail to rightly grasp its intended meaning.

[45] The pronoun ἐγώ means "I," and the verb εἰμι means "I am." In the Greek language, simply using εἰμι is sufficient in expressing "I am." However, combining ἐγώ and εἰμι together creates emphasis.

[46] See John 4:26; 6:20, 35, 41, 48, 51; 8:12, 18, 24, 28; 9:9; 10:7, 9, 11, 14; 11:25; 13:19; 14:6; 15:1.

[47] The relationship between Jesus and his disciples is repeatedly depicted throughout John 1–14. The immediate context of John 15:5 concerns Jesus parting from his disciples during the Last Supper.

[48] This hypothetical text is an example of the absence of structural coherence.

[49] For example, in the English language, paragraphs can be used to achieve this thematic grouping (Dooley and Levinsohn 2001:35–36).

book.[50] A semantic unit refers to constituents of a discourse that are not necessarily immediate constituents of the discourse. The term is not used to specify a particular level in a discourse, since it can potentially refer to many levels.[51] In short, a discourse can be divided into smaller-themed segments, known as semantic units, and these semantic units are cohesively connected to form the whole discourse.

A discourse usually contains a core message intended and communicated by the author for his or her audience (known as macrostructure).[52] A macrostructure is the short summary that can be given by an audience member after engaging with a particular discourse. This term is also used by linguists for the summary of a theme portrayed in a semantic unit. For example, as previously mentioned, Terry's discourse analysis of 1 Corinthians identifies ten discourse or semantic units in the epistle,[53] and he then articulates a macrostructure for each unit. The macrostructure of the seventh unit is as follows: "Seek spiritual gifts, especially prophecy, which builds up the church, but above all, show love" (Terry 1995:54).

Discourse markers

A discourse, with a central macrostructure, contains various cohesive semantic units, and the boundaries of these units are marked by different linguistic devices. These devices are called discourse markers.[54] These markers provide clues about the boundary of a semantic unit within a discourse and the specific relationship between different sentences. Notably, a discourse

---

[50] As previously mentioned, these units are called structural units.

[51] I use this term in a fairly general way. For example, in the following chapters a higher level of constituent is called a major semantic unit, which comprises several lower level of constituents that are called minor semantic units. Porter and Boda use "discourse sub-unit" to describe the "units that join together a number of paragraphs, to mark off sub-sections within a discourse" (Porter and Boda 2009:120).

[52] The concept of macrostructure is a key part in the Continental European model, and is also known as global meaning, and according to Renkema, the concept was introduced by van Dijk who adopts the approach of the Continental Europeans School and has influenced Longacre (Renkema 1993:57).

[53] For some linguists, such as Terry, "discourse" denotes a major semantic unit. However, in this study, discourse denotes the entire text and smaller units are called semantic units.

[54] Different models emphasise different discourse markers. Some use connective particles to mark a semantic unit, such as conjunctions, while others use conceptual elements. Blakemore (2002:185) suggests that no single category of discourse markers can be identified as absolute, and that it is futile to unify these because scholars are divided in their classification. Therefore, Blakemore discredits research on discourse markers as a class or category, but upholds research on different expressions that have been called discourse markers.

marker can indicate either the beginning or the end of a semantic unit due to their "anaphoric and cataphoric character" (Schiffrin 1987:36–37).[55]

Some discourse markers include spatiotemporal changes, summary statements, rhetorical questions, vocatives, changes of cast, and changes of verb tense/mood/aspect (Levinsohn 2000:40–41). One of the most commonly used discourse markers are conjunctions.[56]

Steven Runge illustrates how different conjunctions function as discourse markers.[57] For example, Runge (2010:31–33) states δέ in Matt 2:1–10 is used to mark the boundaries of this short narrative and the sub-units, including the introduction to the incident (2:1–2), Herod's response (2:3–4), Herod's inquiry (2:5–6), Herod's instruction (2:7–8), and the response of the wise men (2:9–10).

Discourse flow

As previously discussed, different semantic units cohesively connect together to form a coherent discourse. Robert Longacre argues that a narrative discourse usually comprises a "plot," whereby the discourse displays "progress" and shows "some sort of climactic development" (Longacre 1983:33).[58] This plot development is also known as the flow of the discourse.[59] This plot can be perceived by dividing a discourse into different stages of progression: aperture, stage, pre-peak episodes, peak, post-peak, closure, and finis (ibid. 36).[60]

Longacre defines the peak as "a zone of turbulence" that occurs at the climax of the narrative (ibid. 38). The peak "is signified by a shift in

---

[55] Schiffrin also argues that a semantic unit, or in her words a "bracket," refers "simultaneously forward and backward." Therefore, discourse markers, which set the boundaries, can either mark the beginning or the end of a semantic unit (Schiffrin 1987:36–37).

[56] Conjunctions can be considered a discourse marker because they imbue cohesion within the linear perspective of a discourse (Pickering 1980:9, 34).

[57] Runge explains that in a narrative conjunctions mark "the semantic distinction of continuity versus discontinuity" (Runge2010:28–29).

[58] Longacre (1983:33) calls this climactic development the peak.

[59] This study adopts Longacre's concept (1983:38), calling this plot progress the flow of the discourse (or discourse flow).

[60] The following summarises Longacre's explanation of these terms (1983:34–38): Aperture is a formulaic phrase or sentence, serving as an introduction. Stage is usually an expository paragraph or discourse which lays out the issue. The key theme of a discourse is developed through various episodes. Peak episode contains the climax of the discourse, which can sometimes be subdivided into "climax," signifying the very climax itself (usually with a conflict element in it), and "dénouement," appearing after a resolution is offered right after the climax. Post-peak is the episode that follows peak. Closure is usually an expository paragraph, marking the end of the discourse. Finis is similar to aperture, a formulaic phrase or sentence.

the proportion of use of a particular grammatical device."[61] Importantly, Longacre argues that the peak occurs not only in narrative discourses, but also in expository and hortatory discourses (ibid. 48), and uses 1 John 4:7–21 to illustrate the "hortatory peak" (ibid. 49).

Similarly, Terry argues that this flow also occurs in non-narrative texts, such as epistles. By using statistical models to analyse 1 Corinthians, Terry determines that the peak or "Expository Climax" occurs in 1 Cor 12–15.[62] Lee (2010:442) also demonstrates this discourse flow in his discourse analysis of Romans.[63]

2.3.2.3 Pragmatics

Pragmatics is a complex subfield of the modern science of linguistics, and is primarily concerned with the bearing of context on meaning.[64] In particular, this considers how the audience (a reader or a listener) retrieves information from the "uttered sequence of words" of an author (Kempson 1997:562).[65] There are several elements of pragmatics that are relevant to this study, including relevance theory, thematic meaning, and sociolinguistics.

---

[61] This quote is Terry's succinct summary of Longacre's explanation of the peak. Longacre argues that there is usually a grammatical shift in the peak, which distinguishes it from the rest of the discourse. This shift may involve a change of tense, a change of pace, a change in the concentration of participants, or the introduction of new particles (Terry 2016; Longacre 1983:40–48).

[62] According to Terry (1995:120–121), the "expository climax" or "zone of grammatical turbulence" is indicated by the large number of verbless clauses starting in 1 Cor 12 and the change of tone in 1 Cor 15 (from hortatory to persuasive, indicated by a sudden lack of imperatives). Terry also cites Longinus, who discusses the use of various shifts in ancient Greek literature to create climax, which resembles the shifts in a peak episode. According to Terry, Longinus indicates that present tense is used to depict a past event, and the use of a single individual to represent the whole audience heightens the vividness. Terry's interpretation is persuasive. Longinus states that "the changes of case, tense, person, number, or gender" are used to achieve "κλίμακες," and then provides various examples to illustrate these shifts (Longinus 1995:23.1–29.2).

[63] As well as Terry and Lee, Clendenen also employs Longacre's concept of flow in his analysis of Malachi (Clendenen 1987:3–17).

[64] According to Levinson (1989:9, 20–21), pragmatics is the study of those relations between language and context that are grammaticalized, or encoded in the structure of a language. As such, semantic study must consider the sentences and the contexts where a word occurs. For van Dijk (1977:205), the pragmatics of discourse is the systematic relations between structures of text and context.

[65] Mey (1993:5, 42) contends that pragmatics is concerned with a user's context and is the study of language in relation to its user.

Relevance theory

According to proponents Sperber and Wilson (1995:1–3), relevance theory attempts to explain how the audience searches for meaning in a communicative situation. Within this theory, there is a crucial difference between sentences and utterances (ibid. 9). A sentence contains various grammatical elements. An utterance is the intended meaning of an author, and comprises both linguistic and non-linguistic elements (ibid.). Therefore, while informed by grammatical elements, the audience relies on implicated linguistic and non-linguistic elements in the context to retrieve the intended meaning (ibid. 9–10).[66] The author actively helps the audience attain and understand the intended meaning by producing an utterance that is relevant (Schiffrin, Tanner, and Hamilton 2003:105). For example, in the following English conversation, the intended meaning of the second speaker cannot be expressed without an understanding of the linguistic and non-linguistic context.

John (husband): Have you talked to my Mum lately?
Mary (wife): I haven't spoken to that woman for ages.

The meaning of "woman" in Mary's statement cannot be ascertained by isolating the sentence and addressing the grammatical elements: "I haven't spoken to that woman for ages." For Mary, "woman" does not simply denote a female human being. This meaning can only be ascertained by consider- ing the context. First, the textual context indicates that "woman" refers to Mary's mother-in-law, which is marked by a point of relevance uttered by her husband (John), "my Mum." Second, the socio-relational context (a hus- band and wife dialogue) reveals a negative connotation in Mary's statement by addressing her mother-in-law as "that woman." This implies a negative relationship between her and her mother-in-law. This meaning cannot be ascertained by solely analysing the grammatical elements, since there is no grammatical element in this sentence suggesting a negative connotation: "I haven't spoken to that woman for ages."[67]

Furthermore, the grammatical elements in the following sentence are insufficient to ascertain the meaning of ἄγωμεν καὶ ἡμεῖς (let us go too): So Thomas, called Didymus, said to his fellow disciples, "Let us go too (ἄγωμεν καὶ ἡμεῖς), so that we may die with him (ἵνα ἀποθάνωμεν μετ᾽ αὐτοῦ)." (John 11:16). The first person plural subjunctive of ἄγω (to go) and ἀποθνῄσκω (to die) seem to express Thomas' determination to follow Christ

---

[66] Horn elucidates that an audience needs to "compute implicated meaning...to fill our underspecified propositions where the semantic meaning contributed by the linguistic expression itself is insufficient to yield a proper accounting of...content" (Horn 1997:315).

[67] Sperber and Wilson (1995:9–15) provide many similar examples to illustrate relevance theory.

and to die with him.[68] However, when considering the point of relevance in the immediate context (the disciples question Jesus' decision to go to Judea because of the imminent danger, in John 11:8), and in the entire discourse (Thomas' character, in John 14:5; 20:24–28), the meaning of the sentence may be very different. Thomas' pronouncement may reflect his "unbelief and despair" (Michaels 2010:625), a meaning intended by the author.[69]

Thematic meaning

A word comprises three kinds of meaning, lexical meaning, sentence meaning, and thematic meaning.[70] The pragmatics subfield is primarily concerned with thematic meaning. Lexical meaning denotes "the meaning-potential of a word...in a system network of lexicogrammatical semantic options" (Lemke 1995:89). Sentence meaning refers to the "fully contextualized meaning" associated with the word as part of a sentence (ibid, 89).[71] Thematic meaning refers to the meaning of a word which is realised in "a recurrent discourse pattern that is familiar in many texts." The thematic meaning of a word is implicated in the utterance of the whole discourse, and may or may not match the conventional meaning.[72] In other words, the audience can only ascertain the meaning by examining the linguistic and non-linguistic elements in the context, rather than merely analysing the grammatical elements in the sentence. Hence, examining discourse structure is extremely important since it provides a framework to understand the context, through which the thematic meaning of a word can be identified.[73]

For example, the lexical meaning of οἶκος is 'house' or 'household' (Bauer 1979:560). The word occurs 25 times in Acts. In Acts 16:15, οἶκος occurs two times: but after her ὁ οἶκος was baptized, she urged us, "If you consider me to be a believer in the Lord, come and stay in my τὸν οἶκόν." Judging from the context, the first οἶκος denotes household (since a house cannot be baptised), and the second οἶκος denotes house (illustrated by "come and stay

---

[68] Beasley-Murray (1987:189) understands this expression as reflecting Thomas' blind devotion.

[69] This study neither defends nor repudiates this view, and instead uses this to illustrate the insufficiency of the analysis of grammatical elements in a sentence.

[70] Linguists use different sets of terms. For example, Lemke's "lexical meaning, use meaning, thematic meaning" (Lemke 1995:89) are similar to Grice's "word meaning, sentence meaning, utterer's meaning" (Grice 1991:65–76). This study uses lexical meaning, sentence meaning, thematic meaning.

[71] Lemke's "use meaning" is more general, referring to a text, rather than a particular sentence.

[72] This resembles Grice's utterer's meaning, which is the intended meaning of an author, and is implicated in the utterance of the author (Grice 1991:65).

[73] Louw (1973:104) argues that the structure of a discourse is a vital point in determining its intention. It is the hinge on which the communication turns; it is part and parcel of the semantics of a discourse.

in"). Hence, in 16:15, the sentence meaning of οἶκος is 'household' in the phrase "her ὁ οἶκος was baptized," and 'house' in the phrase "come and stay in my τὸν οἶκόν." Scholars observe that the occurrence of οἶκος throughout the discourse of Acts displays an intriguing pattern, in which "there is a regular shift of scene between house and temple" (Holmås 2005:400–401). On some occasions οἶκος is employed to denote the temple, and on other occasions it is used to denote a house in which religious activities take place, alluding to the concept of a church (ibid. 401) and the kinship shared by people who belong to the family of God (Elliott 1991:229). In other words, the thematic meaning of οἶκος may point to church or to God's family.[74] This meaning of οἶκος is neither a lexical meaning nor a sentence meaning. Instead, this connotation is deduced by investigating the discourse context and observing its pattern in the whole discourse.

Sociolinguistics

As discussed above, in relevance theory the audience relies on implicated linguistic and non-linguistic clues in the context to ascertain the intended meaning of an author. Sociolinguistics is an important non-linguistic clue in an utterance.[75]

Since language is culturally embedded, analysing a text without considering the situational and cultural settings of a text is "open to more misinterpretation than interpretation" (Kinneavy 1971:24). As indicated, the consideration of historical or cultural perspectives is well established in NT semantic study. However, in pragmatics there is a heavy emphasis on the social dimensions of a word (Mey 1993:185–188). The linguistic features of a word vary according to the social classes in a society.[76] In other words, the meaning of a word for people in a certain social class may be very different for those in a different social class.[77] Hence, to understand the

---

[74] This study neither defends nor repudiates this conclusion, and instead uses this illustration to differentiate the thematic meaning from the lexical meaning and the sentence meaning.

[75] Sperber and Wilson (1995:279) emphasise the importance of sociolinguistics, although admit that their study of sociolinguistics is limited and hope that relevance theory can contribute more.

[76] Although a regular relationship between social and linguistic factors can be demonstrated in many modern languages, Romaine (1994:1, 69–75) points out the prevailing trends in linguistics to marginalise the study of the social role of language.

[77] For example, Brown and Gilman, reflecting on ancient languages, argue that a "historical study of the pronouns of address reveals a set of semantic and social psychological correspondence. The nonreciprocal power semantic is associated with a relatively static society in which power is distributed by birthright and is not subject to much redistribution. The power semantic was closely tied with the feudal and manorial systems" (Brown and Gilman 2003:156–176).

meaning of a word in a discourse, it is necessary to investigate and understand the place and roles of the author and audience,[78] including the underlying institutional power and social hierarchy.

For example, Paul calls himself δοῦλος Χριστοῦ (slave/servant of Christ) in the epistles.[79] In this self-designation, the connotation of δοῦλος (slave/servant) can greatly differ from the meaning ascribed to a contemporary slave who has low social status. There are various interpretations of this self-designation. First, Paul employs this self-designation to indicate that his role being a δοῦλος (slave/servant) of Christ resembles the role of an OT prophet (Patte 2010:223–224).[80] Second, this is a metaphorical "designation of leadership" (Martin 1990:68), whereby Paul is a "slave agent" with the God-given authority to manage other slaves of Christ, believers, (ibid. 75–76). Third, δοῦλος (a slave/servant) of Christ denotes a slave of a Roman Emperor, "a position of honor" (Wuest 1947:12)[81] Nonetheless, whether this self-designation connotes Paul as an OT prophet, a slave manager, or an imperial slave, the noble status is implicated, which is vastly different from the experience of a low status δοῦλος (slave/servant).[82]

In summary, this analysis of Paul's self-designation as a δοῦλος Χριστοῦ (slave/servant of Christ) illustrates the importance of understanding the social dimensions implicated by the non-linguistic context, which is a key concern in sociolinguistics.

2.3.2.4 Summary

In this study, as shown in figure 2.1, I highlight three key features in my discourse analysis of Paul's anthropological terms: scope, structure, and pragmatics. Scope refers to the analysis of a text beyond the sentential level including at the level of the whole discourse. Structure refers to the

---

[78] Halliday (1986:49) names this relationship tenor.

[79] Rom 1:1; Gal 1:10; Phil 1:1.

[80] The phrase δοῦλος θεοῦ (slave/servant of God) occurs three times in the LXX (denoting Moses, the leaders who attempt to rebuild the Holy Temple, and possibly the nation Israel). Combes (1998:77–79) also repudiates Patte's interpretation. He notes that δοῦλος θεοῦ (slave/servant of God) is a rare expression in the LXX, and argues that δοῦλος Χριστοῦ (slave/servant of Christ) is not equivalent to δοῦλος θεοῦ (slave/servant of God), and should not be considered a depiction of a prophet.

[81] According to Wuest (1947:12), Christ is the King of kings and resembles the Roman emperor. Christ does not merely resemble an ordinary slave master in the Greco-Roman world. Wuest's suggestion is persuasive because he considers the role of Christ in an ecclesial community.

[82] However, Lyall (1984:37–38) argues that this self-designation indicates Paul's powerlessness and his surrender to Christ. Whilst Lyall considers the status of a slave, he fails to see the importance of Χριστοῦ (Christ's) in this self-designation. As mentioned above, the kingship of Christ should be considered in the interpretation of δοῦλος Χριστοῦ Ἰησοῦ (slave/servant of Christ Jesus).

organisation of semantic units within a text through linguistic devices, in order to enable cohesion (unified and connected sentences) and coherence (mental representation, meaning, and macrostructure). Pragmatics refers to the impact of linguistic and non-linguistic context on understanding the intended meaning of an author. Arguably, discourse analysis is a research method that attends to Barr's comments on biblical semantic study.

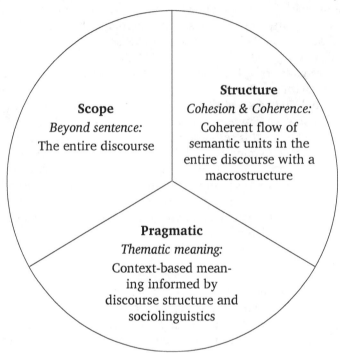

Figure 2.1. Key features of discourse analysis.

2.3.3 Research approach

As previously discussed, discourse analysis addresses Barr's key comments on biblical semantic study, by following the modern science of linguistics and attending to the context of the larger literary complex. Overall, I apply basic principles of discourse analysis to key anthropological terms in the Pauline epistles to ascertain their meaning.

In examining Paul's anthropological terms, I adopt a synthetic approach that employs three basic features of discourse analysis commonly used by linguists. These features are scope, structure, and pragmatics. However, it is crucial to recognise that there are many discourses within the corpus of the Pauline epistles (figure 2.2), and that within each discourse there may be various anthropological terms (figure 2.3). Therefore, a comprehensive analysis of Paul's anthropological terms can only be achieved by an approach that covers all of these dimensions (figure 2.4). This multifaceted approach and the specific analytical steps are detailed further below.

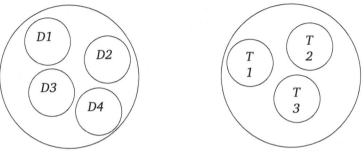

Figure 2.2. The Pauline epistles.[a]   Figure 2.3. Individual Pauline discourse.

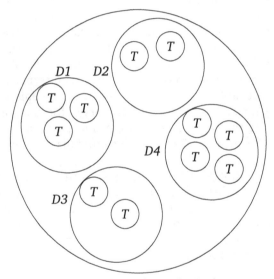

Figure 2.4. Paul's anthropological terms.

[a] Discourse is abbreviated as D, and term is abbreviated as T. The number of discourses and the number of terms in figures 2.2, 2.3, and 2.4 are merely illustrative, and do not represent the real numbers in the Pauline epistles.

My semantic study of key anthropological terms in the Pauline epistles occurs in four stages. Each stage integrates the three features of discourse analysis, as the analytical steps. The two attributes mentioned above, number of discourses and number of terms, are used to form the four research stages (table 2.1).

Table 2.1. Four research stages

	Single Discourse	Multiple Discourses
Single Term	I	III
Multiple Terms	II	IV

The three features of discourse analysis can be most adequately applied in Stage I and Stage II. Although all of the Pauline epistles can be loosely regarded as one corpus, the core principles of discourse analysis are best applied to one single discourse. Following this examination of first a single term, and then multiple terms, in one discourse, I turn to Stage III and Stage IV, which apply the core principles of discourse analysis to multiple discourses. My analysis may provide insights into how Paul establishes and employs anthropological terms across epistles. As mentioned in chapter 1, given that some Pauline epistles are considered pseudepigrapha, to minimise controversy I focus on analysing only the seven epistles that are commonly considered authentic: Romans, 1 Corinthians, 2 Corinthians, Galatians, Philippians, 1 Thessalonians, and Philemon.

Overall, the findings of these four stages can be used to verify the meaning of Paul's anthropological terms, and whether some of these on some occasions connote corporate and relational dimensions. I do not negate other connotations of Paul's anthropological terms; by no means is the social dimension the only thematic meaning. Rather, I simply seek to identify the corporate and relational connotations of some terms in certain contexts.

Below are the steps that I take in analysing the Pauline epistles and anthropological terms to ascertain their meanings, including their thematic meanings.

Scope: Consider an entire discourse, a specific Pauline epistle.

Structure: Examine the discourse structure of the Pauline epistle by:

  observing discourse markers to identify the semantic units of a discourse;

  examining the key cohesive linguistic devices displayed in and across all the semantic units, to ascertain the coherent theme of the discourse; and

  identifying the macrostructure of the entire discourse.

Pragmatics: Ascertain the thematic meaning of a term by:

  examining the term in relation to:

    the discourse structure, taking into account the linguistic context of each semantic unit and the entire discourse; and

    the sociolinguistic aspect, taking into account the non-linguistic context of the entire discourse.

  analysing the term according to the discourse flow.

My study is admittedly far from exhaustive. However, by choosing to investigate some Pauline epistles and some anthropological terms the scope is more manageable. Also, by adopting a multifaceted approach, my study is more synchronic and coherent. In addition, in terms of pragmatics, more emphasis is placed on the linguistic context than the non-linguistic context. As such, the sociolinguistic aspect only serves as a reference, and I focus on the thematic meaning informed by a detailed analysis of discourse structure. Below is a detailed description of the four stages.

Stage I—a single anthropological term within a single discourse: the corporate dimension of σῶμα in 1 Corinthians. The social and corporate dimensions of σῶμα (body) in 1 Corinthians have been thoroughly researched and well documented. Therefore, I use σῶμα (body) in 1 Corinthians as a test case with a two-fold purpose. I examine σῶμα (body) in 1 Corinthians to demonstrate the value of discourse analysis for the investigation of such key terms, and to provide further insights about this particular anthropological term.

Stage II—multiple anthropological terms within a single discourse: the key anthropological terms in Philippians. I analyse the terms ψυχή (soul), καρδία (heart), and πνεῦμα (spirit) in Philippians. These will initially be examined individually, and then collectively to see how they are related.

Stage III—a single anthropological term within multiple discourses: καρδία (heart) in Romans, 2 Corinthians, Philippians, and 1 Thessalonians. Καρδία (heart) occurs 37 times in the Pauline epistles, including 15 times in Romans and 11 times in 2 Corinthians. Accordingly, the meaning of καρδία (heart) in these two epistles is a primary focus. Similarly to Stage II, I initially examine the epistles individually, and then make a comparison of the usage of καρδία (heart) between the Pauline epistles.

Stage IV—multiple anthropological terms within multiple discourses: a focus on Pauline benedictions. The combination of a singular anthropological noun and a plural personal possessive pronoun is a peculiar grammatical construct that can be found in some benedictory phrases, including Phil 4:20, 1 Thess 5:23, Gal 6:18, and Phlm 1:25. In all four benedictory phrases, the singular noun, πνεῦμα (spirit), is present. In 1 Thessalonians, σῶμα (body) and ψυχή (soul) are also present. Traditionally, scholars have either treated benedictions as separate entities, independent from the epistle, or have simply ignored them. However, in light of the concept of coherence in discourse analysis, I aim to investigate these benedictory phrases at the discourse level. Again, I initially examine each benedictory phrase and anthropological term/s, and then make a comparison to ascertain any significant analogous meaning.

By comparing the overall findings, I then verify whether the key anthropological terms within different Pauline epistles have corporate, relational, and thus ecclesiological connotations.

2.3.3.4 *Limitations of research approach*

Although I adopt discourse analysis as a linguistically based research approach, my analysis does not aim to provide a detailed and holistic discourse analysis for each of the Pauline epistles. The works on discourse analysis of biblical literature mentioned in this chapter, both monographs and articles, each focus on only one biblical book, one single discourse. It is not my purpose in this book to conduct substantial discourse analyses for all of the seven Pauline epistles. Rather, I aim only to utilize some of the key principles in the field of discourse analysis for analysing the Pauline epistles.

For those who are experts in the field of linguistics, my book may seem to be tautological and overtly descriptive, which is largely due to the absence of a fully comprehensive statistical analysis of all the linguistic elements in any given epistle. However, the benefits of adopting this research approach, although far from ideal, in my opinion, outweigh its deficiencies. I employ the principles gleaned from the field of discourse analysis on top of exegetical analysis and literary analysis (for instance, inclusio and chiasm), enabling me to adopt a more linguistically based approach to overcome some of the deficiencies raised by Barr.

2.4 Key anthropological terms in first century Koine

In response to Barr's comments on biblical semantic studies, I intend to examine both the textual context and the wider context of the key Pauline anthropological terms. In the following chapters, I examine the key terms by attending to their textual context, their usage in various Pauline epistles.

However, it is important to first investigate how the key terms are employed in contemporary Greek literature—an attempt to attend to the wider context by identifying the semantic range of the key terms.

Although there are numerous works written in Koine Greek in the first century, I mainly focus on the work by Philo, Epictetus, and Plutarch. Philo was a Hellenistic Jew who "lived from about 20 B.C. to about A.D. 50" (Scholer 1993:xi). The corpus of his work was composed in the first half of the first century (B. Winter 1997:5). Studying his work reveals his understanding of the Bible, as he frequently "paraphrase[d] the biblical texts of Moses" (Scholer 1993:xii), and contributes to our "understanding [of] the early church and the writings of the New Testament, especially those of Paul" (ibid. xiii). Philo and Paul are considered as contemporaries. Both of them were skilled in Greek rhetoric (B. Winter 1997:233, 237–241), and both of their opponents were sophists in that era (ibid. 234–236).

Epictetus "was born probably in the years AD 50–60 at Hierapolis, a major Graeco-Roman city" (Long 2004:10). "Between 80 and 100 CE, Emperor Domitian banished him from Rome...[and he] died between 120 and 140 CE" (Huttunen 2009:4). As a teacher of philosophy, Epictetus was a Stoic philosopher who "aligned [himself] with the philosophy that elite citizens... found most in keeping with the traditional Roman virtues of rectitude in public and domestic life, material simplicity, and self-discipline" (Long 2004:15). His work occasionally "alludes without further comment to Christians" as he "could have encountered [Christian texts] while still a child" (ibid. 17). As previously mentioned, some modern scholars assert that there is a connection between Paul's theology and Stoicism (for example, refer to Lee's argument in *Paul, the Stoics, and the Body of Christ*) (Lee 2006). Huttunen's work, *Paul and Epictetus on Law*, demonstrates how studying Epictetus' work benefits our understanding of Paul's theology (Huttunen 2009:154–157).

Plutarch was a Platonic philosopher who was born in the forties in the first century; he lived a life of a wealthy person, and died approximately before A.D. 125 (Russell 1972:1–17). His philosophy is anti-Stoic, including his understanding of God (Reale 1990:215). Although Plutarch's corpus is "40 to 50 years later than [Paul's letters, his] works present quite well the opinions of educated people in his period" (Wojciechowski 2006:101). Studying Plutarch's work is believed to provide some insight into Paul's theology (ibid. 100–101). To sum up, I select the work of Philo, Epictetus, and Plutarch for the following reasons. First, they were contemporary authors of Paul, which is a key consideration in conducting synchronic semantic studies. Second, like Paul, they were thinkers (as theologian or philosopher) in the first century. Third, they also represented different philosophical or theological backgrounds: Philo as a representative of Hellenistic Judaism, Epictetus and Plutarch as representatives of Hellenism with the former representing Stoic and the latter representing Platonist. Fourth, each of them contributed a considerable volume of work. In other words, unlike many other fragmented or short first century Koine Greek manuscripts that are currently available, their work resembles the corpus of the Pauline epistles. Consequently, the key anthropological terms used in their work exhibit a range of connotations. Thus, this selected corpus serves as a good reference in understanding the meanings of these terms in the first century's literature.

In the following part, I present the general usage of the four key terms, σῶμα (body), ψυχή (soul), πνεῦμα (τοῦ ἀνθρώπου) ([human] spirit), and καρδία (heart), in the work of Philo, Epictetus, and Plutarch. The purpose of this section is not to provide an exhaustive analysis of the key anthropological terms. Instead, it is to provide a general overview of their semantic range in first century Koine Greek literature.[83]

2.4.1 Σῶμα (body) in first century Koine

The occurrences of σῶμα (body) are 1698, 101, and 1019 times in the work of Plutarch, Epictetus, and Philo, respectively.[84] In most cases, the term simply denotes physical body. For instance, in Plutarch's work *Theseus* (6.2) the phrase τῇ τοῦ σώματος ῥώμῃ (in the strength of the body) describes the strength of the physical body of Θησέας (Theseus). In Epictetus' work *Dissertationes ab Arriano digestae* (1.1), people on earth are portrayed as: ἐπὶ γῆς γὰρ ὄντας καὶ σώματι συνδεδεμένους τοιούτῳ (for [we] exist on earth, and are bound to such a body).[85] In this text, σῶμα denotes physical body. Similarly, the term points to physical body in Philo's work. For instance, in *Legum allegoriae I* (1.3–4) the phrase στερεοῦ σώματος (of solid body) portrays an organic body that is capable of motion. This meaning of σῶμα as physical body is also extended to the connotation of a dead body, a corpse. For example, in *De Abrahamo* (258) σῶμα occurs in the following text: βραχέα τῷ σώματι ἐπιδακρύσας (after weeping a short time for the body). The term points to the corpse of Abraham's wife.

Intriguingly, σῶμα is also used by Philo to signify the cosmos as having a body. In his work *De opificio mundi* (36), his account of creation, the world (cosmos) is portrayed as having a σῶμα. The world before creation is depicted as: ἀσώματος κόσμος (a bodyless world); and the created world is portrayed by this phrase: τὸ γὰρ σῶμα φύσει στερεόν (for the body is by nature solid).

---

[83] In this section, all the reviewed Greek literature is directly cited from Thesaurus Linguae Graecae (TLG). Author, title, and section of the cited text are stated in the discussion. Separate citation will not be provided in parenthesis, footnote, and reference. Due to the format presented by TLG, in some cases the cited number is based on the Stephanus edition instead of the book section number.

[84] In this section, numbers of occurrences, unless stated otherwise, are based on the TLG statistical database.

[85] The English translation of all the cited Greek texts in this section is my own rendering.

In summary, the denotation of σῶμα is not limited to physical body in the first century Koine Greek literature: the word is also used in a meta-phorical sense to describe the cosmos having a body.[86]

2.4.2 Ψυχή (soul) in first century Koine

Ψυχή (soul) occurs 1141 times in Plutarch's work. The key meanings of ψυχή are as follows. First, the term is employed to depict the centre of the inner life of a human being. For instance, Plutarch writes in *Marcius Coriolanus* (38.3) that: ἀνόμοιον αἰσθήσει πάθος ἐγγινόμενον τῷ φανταστικῷ τῆς ψυχῆς συναναπείθει τὸ δόξαν, ὥσπερ ἐν ὕπνοις ἀκούειν οὐκ ἀκούοντες καὶ βλέπειν οὐ βλέποντες δοκοῦμεν (dissimilar to sensation, an experience taking place in the imagination of the soul assists in persuading the opinion [of people], as in sleep we think that we hear, but we do not hear, and see, but do not see). The term ψυχή is described as the seat of human imagination, leading to creating different sensations (vision and sound). Second, ψυχή denotes physical life. In *Comparatio Pelopidae et Marcelli* (3.5), the parallel between life and soul in: ἀφειδήσαντες τοῦ βίου καὶ τῆς ψυχῆς (taking no care for the life and the soul) is used in the context of portraying death. Third, ψυχή is used to describe the seat of emotion and thought. For example, the term denotes humans' inner courage in *Pyrrhus* (15.4): τόλμη δὲ καὶ ῥώμη τῆς ψυχῆς (but in boldness and in bodily strength of the soul). Fourth, the term depicts the invisible soul, which together with the physical body forms a human life. In portraying the impact of a plague Plutarch writes in his work *Pericles* (38.1): διαχρωμένην τὸ σῶμα σχολαίως καὶ ὑπερείπουσαν τὸ φρόνημα τῆς ψυχῆς (the body being tardily killed and the mind of the soul failing). The two aspects of a human life are represented by σῶμα (body) and ψυχή (soul).

In Epictetus, ψυχή (soul) occurs 63 times. First, the term denotes the seat of emotion and thought. For instance, ψυχή is associated with under-standing and apprehension in *Dissertationes ab Arriano digestae* (1.5): καὶ νὴ Δία ἐπι αὐτῆς τῆς ψυχῆς ἂν μὲν ᾖ οὕτως διακείμενος, ὥστε μηδενὶ παρακολουθεῖν μηδὲ συνιέναι μηδέν (and indeed with regard to the soul itself, but if someone would be in such state, with the result of neither fol-lowing nor understanding anything). Ψυχή is also portrayed in *Dissertationes ab Arriano digestae* (3.3) as being attracted to the appearance of good: οὕτως ἔχει καὶ ἐπὶ τῆς ψυχῆς. Τὸ ἀγαθὸν φανὲν εὐθὺς ἐκίνησεν ἐφ' αὐτό, τὸ κακὸν ἀφ' αὐτοῦ. Οὐδέ ποτε δ' ἀγαθοῦ φαντασίαν ἐναργῆ ἀποδοκιμάσει ψυχή (thus, it is also in the condition of the soul. When good appears, it imme-diately rouses itself after it, the bad, away from it. A soul never rejects the manifested presentation of good). Second, the term depicts the inner life

---

[86] Schweizer (1971b:1036–1041) also discusses the semantic range of σῶμα (body) in the first century Koine Greek, indicating that physical body and the living body of the cosmos are common meanings in that era.

or invisible part of a human, which is a constituent of a human being. For instance, Epictetus writes in *Dissertationes ab Arriano digestae* (3.7): ὅτι μὲν γὰρ τρία ἐστὶ περὶ τὸν ἄνθρωπον, ψυχὴ καὶ σῶμα καὶ τὰ ἐκός (that for there are three things concerning the human being, soul, body, and the external things). Ψυχή (soul), σῶμα (body), and τὰ ἐκός (the external things) are considered to be the three constituents of a human.

In Philo's work, ψυχή occurs 1833 times. First, the term is used to depict the inner life of a human being, which is the seat of reason, emotion, and desire. In *De specialibus legibus* (4.92), Philo states: διερευνησάμενοι φύσιν ψύχῆς καὶ τριττὸν εἶδος ἐνιδότες αὐτῇ, τὸ μὲν λόγου, τὸ δὲ θυμοῦ, τὸ δ' ἐπιθυμίας (examining closely the nature of soul and observing its three parts: the one of reason; the one of anger; the one of desire). Second, Philo uses ψυχή to denote a part of the human person which connects a person to God. In his discussion of Abraham (and Moses' comment on Abraham), Philo argues in *De posteritate Caini* (27) that: ὄντως γὰρ ἀτρέπτῳ ψυχῇ πρὸς τὸν ἄτρεπτον θεὸν μόνη πρόσοδός ἐστι (truly, for the unchangeable soul is the only way of access to the unchangeable God). Third, Philo even goes further by describing ψυχή as the dwelling place for God's Spirit. In *De virtutibus* (217), Philo states that: τοῦ θείου πνεύματος, ὅπερ ἄνωθεν καταπνευσθὲν εἰσῳκίσατο τῇ ψυχῇ (the spirit of God, breathed down from above, dwelt in the soul).

In summary, in first-century Koine ψυχή denotes the seat of reason, emotion, desire, the inner life of a human person, part of the constituent of a human being, and the inner or invisible part of a human being in which God's Spirit dwells.[87]

2.4.3 Πνεῦμα (spirit) in first century Koine

Πνεῦμα occurs 313 times in the work of Plutarch. There are several meanings expressed by πνεῦμα. First, the term denotes wind in the air. For instance, πνεῦμα is used in *Numa* (2.2) to describe the wind brought by a descending cloud: καὶ νέφους ἐπὶ τὴν γῆν ἐρείσαντος ἅμα πνεύματι καὶ ζάλῃ (and a cloud pushing wind and rain together upon the earth). This meaning is very common in Plutarch's work.[88] Second, πνεῦμα signifies breath. This can be illustrated by the usage of πνεῦμα in a phrase that occurs in *Demosthenes* (6.3): πνεύματος κολοβότης (shortness of breath). The phrase is used to describe the shortness of breath suffered by Demosthenes.

---

[87] Dihle (1974:616–617) also provides a discussion of the usage of ψυχή in first-century Koine Greek literature. Dihle states that "the impalpable essential core of man, the bearer of thought, will and emotion, the quintessence of human life" are the key meanings of ψυχή in the post-classical age (Dihle 1974:616).

[88] For instance, πνεῦμα denotes wind in the following works of Plutarch: *Aristides* 6.3; *Camillus* 34.4; *Pelopidas* 9.1; *Caesar* 52.1; *Cato Minor* 70.3; *Pyrrhus* 15.3; and *Romulus* 1.2.

Πνεῦμα occurs only twice in Epictetus' work. First, the word denotes a matter that God infuses into human eyes, enabling the capability of vision. In the following text from *Dissertationes ab Arrano digestae* (2.23), πνεῦμα is closely associated with eyes in this rhetorical question: εἰκῇ οὖν σοι θεὸς ὀφθαλμοὺς ἔδωκεν, εἰκῇ πνεῦμα ἐνεκέρασεν αὐτοῖς οὕτως ἰσχυρὸν καὶ φιλότεχνον (therefore, did God give you eyes without purpose, mix in them a spirit so strong and inventive without purpose?). However, the relation between πνεῦμα (spirit) and ὀφθαλμός (eye) is unclear. Second, πνεῦμα appears in an obscure passage in *Dissertationes ab Arrano digestae* (3.3): καὶ ὅταν τοίνυν σκοτωθῇ τις, οὐχ αἱ τέχναι καὶ αἱ ἀρεταὶ συγχέονται, ἀλλὰ τὸ πνεῦμα (and whenever someone is suffering dizziness, the skills and the virtues are not in trouble, but the spirit [is]), in which πνεῦμα is portrayed as something that could be disturbed, and that could be restored into a more settled state.

Πνεῦμα occurs 149 times in the work of Philo. The term carries different senses. First, πνεῦμα means air. In his discussion of creation, Philo states in *De opificio mundi* (29) that God created the incorporeal matter of water and of air: εἶθ' ὕδατος ἀσώματον οὐσίαν καὶ πνεύματος (forming the bodiless thing of water and air). Second, πνεῦμα signifies wind. In *De opificio mundi* (58), strong wind is depicted in the phrase νηνεμίας καὶ βίας πνευμάτων (stillness and powers of winds). Third, the term points to soul or life. For instance, the clause ὅτι πνεῦμά ἐστιν ἡ ψυχῆς οὐσία (that spirit is the substance of life), occurring in *Quod deterius potiori insidiari soleat* (81), demonstrates that Philo equates πνεῦμα (spirit) and ψυχή (life) in his explanation of the Genesis account.[89] Fourth, πνεῦμα is employed to denote human spirit that dwells inside a person. In *De gigantibus* (24), the human spirit of Moses is portrayed: τὸ Μωυδέως πνεῦμα, ὃ ἐπιφοιτᾷ τοῖς ἑβδομήκοντα πρεσβυτέροις (the spirit of Moses, which comes habitually to the seventy elders).

In summary, in first century Koine Greek literature πνεῦμα denotes air; wind; breath; a matter that gives human eyes vision; state of mind; life or soul; and human spirit.[90]

2.4.4 Καρδία (heart) in first century Koine

In Plutarch's work, καρδία occurs 51 times, and carries three main meanings. First, the word is used in a physiological sense, denoting the human organ, the heart. For instance, in *Quomodo adolescens poetas audire debeat* (30A), καρδία denotes the physical heart in the following sentence:

---

[89] Philo explains the meaning of πνεῦμα in Genesis 2.

[90] For further discussion of the meaning of πνεῦμα in first-century Koine Greek, see the work of Kleinknecht (1968:334–339), who combines the Koine Greek era and the Classical Greek era together under the section "πνεῦμα in the Greek World" to discuss the semantic range of πνεῦμα, stating that the term denotes wind, breath, life, and soul in the ancient Greek world.

ἡ καρδία πηδᾷ μόνον (the heart throbs alone). In the context, καρδία is used to describe the heart of Ἕκτορί (Hector) beating. Second, καρδία is used to portray emotion or the seat of emotion. In *Quomodo quis suos in virtute sentiat profectus* (84D) Plutarch quotes the words of Ἀλκιβιάδης (Alcibiades), τὴν καρδίαν στρέφεσθαι καὶ δάκρυα ἐκπίπτειν (the heart turns and tears fall out), to describe a heart being 'moved,' which points to emotion. Third, the term is associated with the mind. In *Quaestiones convivales* (647E*), the word occurs in the text, ὅτι τῇ καρδίᾳ τὸν θυμὸν ἐνστρατοπεδεύειν ᾤοντο (that [people] were thinking that the mind encamped in the heart). Thus, καρδία is employed to portray the mind.

Καρδία occurs once in Epictetus' work. In *Dissertationes ab Arriano digestae* (1.27), καρδία appears in this sentence to describe a broken heart of a person who is trembling: τὸν δὲ τρέμοντα καὶ ταρασσόμενον καὶ ῥηγνύμενον ἔσωθεν τὴν καρδίαν ἄλλῳ τινὶ δεῖ προσευκαιρεῖν (but the one who trembles and is troubled and is shattered within the heart, it is necessary for the person to find leisure in something else). In light of this, the meaning of καρδία is associated with emotion.

Καρδία occurs 39 times in the work of Philo. The word carries a range of meanings. First, it denotes the physical heart. In *De opificio mundi* (118), καρδία is listed with other body organs: τὰ δ' ἐντὸς λεγόμενα σπλάγχνα στόμαχος, καρδία, πνεύμων, σπλήν, ἧπαρ, νεφροὶ δύο (and the inward parts within are called stomach, heart, lungs, spleen, liver, and two kidneys). Second, καρδία means mind. In *Quod Deus sit immutabilis* (20), καρδία is employed to portray evil people thinking wickedness in this clause: καὶ πᾶς τις διανοεῖται ἐν τῇ καρδίᾳ ἐπιμελῶς τὰ πονηρὰ πάσας τὰς ἡμέρας (and everyone is carefully intending in the heart the evil things all the days). Third, Philo uses καρδία as an equivalent to ἡγεμονικόν (a dominant power of humans). For instance, in *De specialibus legibus* (1.213–214) Philo mentions that: οὔτε δὲ καρδίαν οὔτε ἐγκέφαλον, τοῦ ἡγεμονικοῦ τῷ ἑτέρῳ τούτων ἐνδιαιτωμένου (neither heart nor brain, as the dominant part of humans dwells in one of these [organs]).

In summary, καρδία carries the following meanings in first century Koine Greek: heart as an organ; the seat of emotion; mind; and a dominant power of humans.[91]

This section provides an overview of the semantic range of the key anthropological terms, σῶμα (body), ψυχή, (soul) πνεῦμα (spirit), and καρδία (heart), by investigating their occurrences in the first century Koine Greek literature, in particular, the work of Plutarch, Epictetus, and Philo.

---

[91] Behm also discusses the semantic range of καρδία in the ancient Greek world. Behm combines the Koine Greek era and the Classical Greek era together under the section "καρδία among the Greeks" and states that καρδία denotes heart "in a physiological sense as the central organ" and metaphorically, "the central organ of intellectual life, the seat of reason, from which feeling, willing and thinking proceed" in the ancient Greek world (Behm 1965:608–609).

3

Σῶμα (Body) in 1 Corinthians

3.0 Introduction

The social and corporate dimensions of σῶμα (body) in 1 Corinthians have been thoroughly researched and well-established by scholars.[1] The phrase τὸ σῶμα τοῦ Χριστοῦ (the body of Christ) is widely accepted as denoting the church. In this chapter I intend to re-examine σῶμα in 1 Corinthians by employing the basic principles of discourse analysis.[2] I would like to show that the key thematic meaning of σῶμα intended by Paul in 1 Corinthians is indeed communal, and thus demonstrate the value of discourse analysis as a sound methodological approach for the investigation of other anthropological terms.

I cannot provide a detailed analysis of all individual occurrences of σῶμα, and a traditional focus on the "lexical meaning" and the "sentence

---

[1] Dunn (2006:533–564) provides a detailed discussion, including an analysis of the corporate connotations of the phrase "the body of Christ." Gundry (1976:223–244) maintains the communal aspect of this phrase and rejects Bultmann's individualistic understanding. Both Dunn and Gundry provide an overview of scholarship addressing this Pauline phrase. Carter makes a recent contribution and asserts that the body of Christ is a metaphor to portray the church. This metaphor "subverts social distinctions because such distinctions have no place" in the church (Carter 2008:93–115).

[2] From this point onwards, the English translation, body, for the term σῶμα is not provided in this chapter.

51

meaning" is not my primary concern. Instead, the "thematic meaning" is my centre of attention.[3] According to discourse analysis, an author sometimes employs a word throughout a discourse to convey a meaning that cannot be identified by solely investigating the sentence and lexical meanings of the word. This thematic meaning can only be ascertained by investigating the context of the entire discourse in which a word occurs. By applying the basic principles of discourse analysis, I demonstrate that Paul does employ σῶμα to elucidate the social and corporate identity of the Corinthian community. This is the key thematic meaning of σῶμα in 1 Corinthians.

In terms of the general methodology described in § 1.4 above, we are here following Stage I in this research, analysing a single anthropological term, σῶμα, within a single discourse, 1 Corinthians. I first identify the discourse structure, and then ascertain the thematic meaning of σῶμα by examining the linguistic context of individual semantic units (at the paragraphic-sentential-clausal level) and the entire discourse, and by examining the sociolinguistic aspect.[4]

3.1 Discourse structure

The discourse structure refers to "the pattern an author uses to organize [the entire] text" (Westfall 2005:28). A discourse is composed of different semantic units that are unified and connected through various linguistic devices, enabling cohesion. This leads to a coherent flow and forms the core message, known as the macrostructure.[5] In the following section, I initially elucidate the major semantic units in 1 Corinthians by investigating the discourse markers, and then identify the macrostructure towards ascertaining the thematic meaning of σῶμα.

3.1.1 Discourse markers

In composing a discourse, an author sometimes uses linguistic devices to indicate the beginning or end of a semantic unit, and thus the change of topic. These devices are called discourse markers.[6] Whilst there are various discourse markers, conjunctions are one of the most commonly used (Pickering 1980:9). However, not every conjunction is a discourse marker. Given the frequency of conjunctions in any given discourse, including the Pauline epistles (for instance, there are 1044 conjunctions in 1 Corinthians), it is vital and more practical for me to focus on

---

[3] For an explanation of lexical meaning, sentence meaning, and thematic meaning, see § 2.3.2.3.

[4] For a description of the analytical steps, see § 2.3.3.3.

[5] For a detailed discussion of cohesion and coherence, see § 2.3.2.2.

[6] For an explanation of discourse markers, see § 2.3.2.2.

special conjunctive formulas.[7] In 1 Corinthians, there are two special conjunctive formulas, περὶ δὲ (now concerning) and verb-δέ-pronoun,[8] which mark the boundary of a semantic unit. As well as conjunctions, a summary statement can also act as a discourse marker.[9] In 1 Corinthians, Paul uses a specific summary statement to begin the first topic of church division, referring to Chloe's report (1:11). In two subsequent statements, to begin two new topics, Paul refers back to the oral report and uses the verb ἀκούω (to hear) (5:1; 11:8). As such, although there may be various discourse markers in this epistle, an analysis of the two conjunctive formulas and the specific summary statement is enough to identify the major semantic units.

3.1.1.1 *Περὶ δὲ (now concerning)*

The expression περὶ δὲ (now concerning) occurs six times in 1 Corinthians (7:1, 25; 8:1; 12:1; 16:1, 12).[10] This phrase is rare in the Pauline epistles, and otherwise only occurs twice in 1 Thessalonians (4:9; 5:1). Περὶ δὲ can be interpreted as "as for" (Moule 1959:62–63), and contains three elements: a conjunction δέ (now/but), a preposition περί (concerning), and a word or a phrase in the genitive case.[11] Notably, the word order in this phrase, placing περί (concerning) before δέ (now/but), has attracted some discussion.[12] Despite a few objections, it is widely believed that this phrase refers to a letter written by the Corinthians to Paul.[13] Regardless, most scholars agree

---

[7] A formula is defined as a phrase or a clause with the combination of specific grammatical particles. This combination is used repeatedly in a discourse or multiple discourses by the same author to mark a new topic.

[8] The Greek conjunction δέ means now or but.

[9] For further examples of discourse marker, see § 2.3.2.2.

[10] From this point onwards, the English translation, now concerning, for the term περὶ δὲ, is not provided in this chapter.

[11] For example, a genitive pronoun, ὧν (which/things), in 1 Cor 7:1; a genitive articular noun, τῶν παρθένων (the virgins), in 1 Cor 7:25; a genitive substantival adjective, τῶν εἰδωλοθύτων (the food offered to idols), in 1 Cor 8:1; and a genitive articular noun, τῆς λογείας (the contribution), in 1 Cor 16:1.

[12] Mitchell (1989:235–236) briefly discusses the peculiar word order in this phrase, which she calls a formula, and focuses on the function of δέ (now/but).

[13] Many scholars hold that περὶ δὲ refers to the questions written by the Corinthians to Paul (Barrett 1994:154; Fitzmyer 2008:273, 314; Ciampa and Rosner 2010:272, 330; Horsley 1998:95, 115; Fee 1987:274; Collins 1999:309). Hurd (1983:63–65) argues that the first occurrence in 7:1 reads περὶ δὲ ὧν ἐγράψατε (now concerning the things you wrote), and the subsequent occurrences are simply an abbreviation, omitting ὧν ἐγράψατε (things you wrote). However, Mitchell counters this interpretation and argues that in "a wide variety of ancient Greek texts" περὶ δὲ is "simply a topic marker, a shorthand way of introducing the next subject of discussion" (Mitchell 1989:233–234; 236–250). Thiselton (2000:617) also supports this view.

that περὶ δὲ (now concerning) is a linguistic device in 1 Corinthians, used to introduce new topics.[14]

In 7:1, after discussing the topic of sexual immorality, Paul begins to address the topic of marriage using the prepositional phrase περὶ δὲ (now concerning). In 7:20, Paul suddenly digresses to the topic of slavery, and in 7:25, again using περὶ δὲ (now concerning) returns to the topic of marriage. Then in 8:1, Paul proceeds to the topic of food and idols using the same phrase. In 12:1, Paul also uses περὶ δὲ (now concerning) to begin a lesson on spiritual gifts, and in 16:1, περὶ δὲ (now concerning) introduces the topic of contribution. Finally, in 16:12, Paul begins to address the topic of Apollos, again using περὶ δὲ (now concerning). Therefore, I concur with the view that περὶ δὲ (now concerning) is a discourse marker employed by Paul to introduce new topics in 1 Corinthians.[15]

3.1.1.2 Verb-δέ-pronoun

In 1 Corinthians, the occurrence of a particular independent clause exhibits an unusual pattern. This combines a first person singular indicative verb, the conjunction δέ (now/but), and a second person plural personal pronoun ὑμεῖς (you) and its case variants, and occurs seven times in the epistle.[16] If those occurrences with the verb θέλω (I want) are put aside, this particular combination only occurs four times: Παρακαλῶ δὲ ὑμᾶς (but I urge you), in 1:10; Ἐπαινῶ δὲ ὑμᾶς (but I praise you), in 11:2; Γνωρίζω δὲ ὑμῖν (but I make known to you), in 15:1, and Παρακαλῶ δὲ ὑμᾶς (but I urge you), in 16:15. Notably, all four of these occur when a new topic is introduced. In 1:10, following Παρακαλῶ δὲ ὑμᾶς (but I urge you), Paul begins to address the topic of church division. Similarly, in 11:2, following Ἐπαινῶ δὲ ὑμᾶς (but I praise you), Paul begins a teaching on the Lord's Supper. In 15:1, following Γνωρίζω δὲ ὑμῖν (but I make known to you), Paul begins to address the issue of resurrection. Lastly, in 16:5, following Παρακαλῶ δὲ ὑμᾶς (but I urge you), Paul begins to discuss the household of Stephanus. Many scholars notice that these four independent clauses are rhetorical devices in 1 Corinthians, used

---

[14] Orr and Walther (1976:227) call this a transitional phrase that introduces a new inquiry posed by the Corinthians. Collins, Hays, and Fee call this phrase a "formula," and Collins specifically calls this a "textual marker" (Collins 1999:257, 288; Hays 1997:110; Fee 1987:274). Mitchell (1989:234; 1993:191) calls this phrase a topic marker. Lee (2010:36) calls this a boundary marker. For both Collins and Hays, περὶ δὲ is a classic formula in Hellenistic letters used to identify a topic for consideration. There is a debate about the specific function of this phrase. It is regarded as a linguistic device introducing a topic either raised by the letter from the Corinthians to Paul (Wegener 2004:439) or raised by Paul himself.

[15] However, 1 Cor 7:25 is an exception, wherein Paul returns to a previous topic after a short digression, rather than introducing a new topic.

[16] I call this combination the "verb-δέ-pronoun" clause.

to introduce new topics.[17] However, none of the work reviewed identifies this verb-δέ-pronoun clause as a discourse marker.[18] I contend that this is a valid discourse marker because it is too coincidental to have four occurrences of this particular clause at the beginning of four new topics.

On the other hand, θέλω δὲ ὑμᾶς (but I want you to) occurs three times (7:32; 10:20; 11:3). In 7:32, Paul includes his own perspective in the middle of a discussion on marriage. In 10:20, Paul expresses the implication of partaking in idolatry. In 11:3, Paul presents a theological statement that he uses to discuss the issue of head coverings.[19] Notably, all three of these do not begin new topics,[20] and instead signify a shift in emphasis or act as a point of reference.

3.1.1.3 Summary statement: Report from Chloe's people

Paul begins the first topic, church division, using the phrase Παρακαλῶ δὲ ὑμᾶς (but I urge you, 1:10), which is a special conjunctive formula. He then immediately mentions the report from Chloe's people: "For members of Chloe's household have made it clear to me, my brothers and sisters,

---

[17] Bailey (1983:160–161) contends that the phrase Παρακαλῶ δὲ ὑμᾶς (but I urge you, 4:16) has a similar function as the phrases Ἐπαινῶ δὲ ὑμᾶς (but I praise you, 11:2) and Γνωρίζω δὲ ὑμῖν (but I make known you, 15:1). These mark the boundary of a topic.

[18] Many scholars perceive these clauses as transitional sentences, introducing a new topic. For example, Collins interprets Παρακαλῶ δὲ ὑμᾶς (but I urge you) in 1:10 as a standard formula in friendly Hellenistic letters to introduce an important theme. Also, "I commend you" in 11:2 introduces a new topic, and "I want you to know, brothers and sisters, the gospel I have proclaimed to you" in 15:1 is a disclosure formula that establishes a transition. Collins does not identify the verb-δέ-pronoun as a pattern or a formula (Collins 1999:76, 404, 533). Fee similarly interprets 1:10 as an immediate transition, and 15:1 as introducing some new concerns. Fee also does not identify the verb-δέ-pronoun clause (Fee 1987:52, 719). Both Barrett and Fitzmyer interpret the beginning of new topics in 1:10; 11:2; 15:1, and do not identify the combination clause (Barrett 1994:41, 247, 335; Fitzmyer 2008:140, 404, 544). Mitchell (1993:1) interprets the function of 1:10 as introducing the topic of ecclesial unity, which is the central theme in 1 Corinthians.

[19] Many scholars interpret this phrase as having a transitional function or as emphasising the issue. Thus, this phrase is not used to begin a new topic. For instance, Wimbush (1987:49–50) argues that this phrase signifies a shift in 7:32, enabling the inclusion of Paul's own perspective in the middle of a discussion about marriage. Ciampa and Rosner (2010:349) argue that the phrase in 7:32 is used to transit the discussion of marriage from an eschatological perspective to a Christological perspective. Fee (1987:472) suggests that the phrase in 10:20 places the previous discussion of the Lord's Table and Israel's history into right perspective.

[20] Collins (1999:295) argues that all three occurrences, together with other occurrences of θέλω (I want, 7:7; 10:1; 12:1; 14:5; 16:7), simply express Paul's wish. This phrase provides Paul with an opportunity to clarify his wish by referring back to the previous argument.

that there are quarrels among you"* (1:11).[21] Paul later states "It is actually reported that sexual immorality exists among you"* (5:1a). This short statement has two functions. First, it provides a succinct introduction to the discussion of πορνεία (fornication) in 5:1b–6:20. Second, the word ἀκούεται (it is reported) links back to ἐδηλώθη (it was declared) in 1:11. Thus, the topic of sexual immorality in 5:1–6:20 is a part of Chloe's report.[22]

Similarly, the statement in 11:18, "For in the first place, when you come together as a church I hear there are divisions among you, and in part I believe it"* begins a teaching on the Lord's Supper. The use of ἀκούω (to hear) in this short statement, links back to Chloe's report,[23] and points to a forthcoming new topic regarding σχίσμα (division). Notably, the previous discussion of head coverings in 11:2, begins with the verb-δέ-pronoun clause: Ἐπαινῶ δὲ ὑμᾶς (but I praise you). In 11:17, Paul begins the topic of the Lord's Supper with: "Now in giving the following instruction I do not praise you."* The contrast between ἐπαινῶ (I praise) and οὐκ ἐπαινῶ (I do not praise) is striking. This contrast, together with the specific summary statement including ἀκούω (to hear), is used by Paul to begin a new topic. Thus, the two summary statements in 5:1 and 11:18 are discourse markers.

3.1.2 Semantic units

As I have previously described, a discourse can be divided into smaller segments, which are called semantic units.[24] Based on the three identified discourse markers, I divide 1 Corinthians into 13 segments: the letter-opening, 11 major semantic units, and the letter-closing (see table 3.1).

---

[21] Scripture quoted by permission. All scripture quotations that are marked by an asterisk (*) are taken from the NET Bible® copyright ©1996-2016 by Biblical Studies Press, L.L.C. All rights reserved.

[22] Both Thiselton (2000:385) and Collins (1999:209) favour this interpretation, although various scholars are silent on this connection (Conzelmann, Horsley, Fitzmyer, Barrett, Orr and Walther). Ciampa and Rosner (2010:199) argue that the report in 5:1 has been publicly circulated. Fee (1987:199) suggests that the connotation of ὅλως is 'actually' instead of 'universally'.

[23] The scholars that hold this view include Fitzmyer (2008:432), Collins (1999:421), Fee (1987:537), and Hurd (1983:82). Thiselton (2000:849) maintains that Chloe's people are the source of the report in 11:18 (referring back to 1:10; 5:1). Fitzmyer (2008:432) mentions that it is an oral report, but does not mention Chloe.

[24] For further discussion of semantic units, see § 2.3.2.2.

Table 3.1. Semantic units of 1 Corinthians[a]

Semantic Unit		A	B	C	D	E	F	G	H	I	J	K	
Discourse Marker		V+δέ+ ὑμᾶς in 1:10	SS in 5:1	περί +δέ in 7:1	περί +δέ in 8:1	V+δέ + ὑμᾶς in 11:2	SS in 11:18	περί +δέ in 12:1	V+δέ+ ὑμᾶς in 15:1	περί +δέ in 16:1	περί +δέ in 16:12	περί +δέ in 16:15	
New Topic	Letter-opening (1:1–9)	Church Division 1:10–4:21	Sexual Immorality 5:1–6:20	Marriage 7:1–40	Food and Idols 8:1–11:1	Head Coverings 11:2–16	The Lord's Supper 11:17–34	Spiritual Gifts 12:1–14:40	Resurrection 15:1–58	Contribution 16:1–11	Apollos 16:12–14	Stephanus 16:15–18	Letter-closing (16:19–24)

[a] V + δέ is an abbreviation for the combination of a first person singular indicative verb and δέ (now/but). SS is an abbreviation for "summary statement," accompanied by the verb ἀκούω, which alludes to Chloe's report.

Each major semantic unit contains a specific topic: Unit A: Church Division (1:10–4:21), Unit B: Sexual Immorality (5:1–6:20), Unit C: Marriage (7:1–40), Unit D: Food and Idols (8:1–11:1), Unit E: Head Coverings (11:2–16), Unit F: The Lord's Supper (11:17–34), Unit G: Spiritual Gifts (12:1–14:40), Unit H: Resurrection (15:1–58), Unit I: Contribution (16:1–11), Unit J: Apollos (16:12–14), and Unit K: Stephanus (16:15–18). Table 3.2 outlines the perspectives of other scholars regarding the major semantic units in 1 Corinthians.[25]

---

[25] Table 3.2 does not present the full outline of each scholar. Rather, it presents the scholars that identify the same or similar unit as each of my units.

Table 3.2. Outline of 1 Corinthians by scholars[a]

	Unit A 1:10–4:21[b]	Unit B 5:1–6:20[c]	Unit C 7:1–40	Unit D 8:1–11:1[d]	Unit E 11:2–16	Unit F 11:17–34	Unit G 12:1–14:40	Unit H 15:1–58[e]	Unit I 16:1–11	Unit J 16:12–14	Unit K 16:15–18
MyOutline	Church Division	Sexual Immorality	Marriage	Food and Idols	Head Coverings	The Lord's Supper	Spiritual Gifts	Resurrection	Contribution	Apollos	Stephanus
Outline of Scholars	BR CR CZ FE FM HY HL OW TR TT	CR CZ FE FM HY HL OW TR TT BL CL MC →	BR CZ CR FE FM HY HL OW TR TT	BL BR CR CL FE FM HY HL MC OW TR BL CR	BR FE HL MC OW TR CL TT FM	BR FE HL MC OW TR	BR CL FE FM HL MC OW TR	BL BR CR CL FE HY HL MC OW TR TT	FE TR BL CR CL (16:1–24) CZ FM HL (16:1–12) MC OW TT	FE TR	

[a] In table 3.2, the abbreviations of the commentators are as follows: Bailey is abbreviated as BL; Barrett, BR; Ciampa and Rosner, CR; Collins, CL; Conzelmann, CZ; Fee, FE; Fitzmyer, FM; Hays, HY; Horsley, HL; Mitchell, MC; Orr and Walter, OW; Terry, TR; Thiselton, TT. For outlines, see Bailey 2011:7–9; Barrett 1994:28–29; Ciampa and Rosner 2010:24; Collins 1999:viii–x; Conzelmann 1975:vii–viii; Fitzmyer 2008:viii–x; Fee 1987:21–23; Hays 1997:xi–xiv; Horsley 1998:7–9; Mitchell 1993:184–186; Orr and Walther 1976:x–xv; Terry 1995:38–43; Thiselton 2000:vi–xiii.

[b] According to Terry, Ciampa and Rosner, and Bailey, this semantic unit ends in 4:17, and the second semantic unit begins in 4:18.

[c] For Fitzmyer, 5:1–7:40 contains two sub-segments (5:1–6:20 and 7:1–40), and 7:1–14:40 contains four sub-segments (7:1–40, 8:1–11:1, 11:2–34, and 12:1–14:40). For Conzelmann, 7:1–15:28 contains three minor divisions (7:1–40, 8:1–11:34, and 12:1–15:18). For Hays, 7:1–15:58 contains four sub-segments (7:1–40, 8:1–11:1, 11:2–14:20, and 15:1–58).

[d] For Ciampa and Rosner, 8:1–14:40 contains two sub-segments (8:1–11:1 and 11:2–14:40). For both Orr and Walther, and Barrett, 11:2–34 contains two sub-segments (11:2–16 and 11:17–34). For Mitchell, 11:2–14:40 contains three sub-segments (11:2–16, 11:17–34, and 12:1–14:40). For Thiselton, 11:2–14:40 contains two sub-segments (11:2–34 and 12–14).

[e] According to Mitchell (1993:xi), 15:1–57 is one unit, given that 15:58 is the concluding statement of the letter body (1:10–15:58).

Although my outline is slightly different from the outlines of various scholars, the main issue concerns whether a particular topic is considered a major segment or a minor sub-division. For example, C. K. Barrett divides 5:1–6:20 into three major segments: "Sexual Immorality" in 5:1–13, "Litigation" in 6:1–11, and "The Root of the Trouble" in 6:12–20. He also regards 11:2–16 and 11:17–34 as one major segment, titled "The Christian Assembly" (Barrett 1994:28–29). Nonetheless, of the work reviewed, Gordon Fee, Ralph Bruce Terry, and Richard Horsley propose a nearly identical outline to mine.[26]

There are several important points concerning various proposed outlines. First, one of the most comprehensive and recent discourse analyses of 1 Corinthians was conducted by Terry, in *A Discourse Analysis of First Corinthians* (Terry 1995). Even though many scholars have undertaken work on the epistle, a comprehensive study of 1 Corinthians, applying the principles of discourse analysis, is rare. Therefore, it is important to compare my proposed semantic units with Terry's. As shown above in tables 3.1 and 3.2, the two outlines are remarkably similar.[27]

Second, neither Terry nor Kenneth Bailey regard 4:21 as the end of the first semantic unit. Terry argues that the first unit ends in 4:17, proven by the chiastic structure of the unit.[28] Bailey contends that 4:17 serves as a critical point, where Paul introduces his "ways in Christ" to the Corinthians, and then elaborates on these in subsequent parts. [29] However, the context informs us that it is more likely for the first unit to include 4:18–21. In the absence of any clear discourse markers, Paul's travel plan in 4:18–21 can be interpreted as either part of the first segment "Church Division" or the second segment "Sexual Immorality." In 4:21, Paul mentions that he might discipline the Corinthians: ἐν ῥάβδῳ ἔλθω πρὸς ὑμᾶς (shall I come to you with a rod of discipline). This can refer to dissension in relation to either

---

[26] Fee (1987:21–23) proposes the same segmentation, but the titles are slightly different.

[27] Following are the topics of the semantic units proposed by Terry (1995:38–43): (A) Church division 1:10–4:17; (B) Fornication 4:18–6:20; (C) Marriage 7; (D) Idol food 8:1–11:1; (E) Head coverings 11:2–16; (F) The Lord's Supper 11:17–34; (G) Spiritual gifts 12–14; (H) The Resurrection 15; (I) Contribution 16:1–11; and (J) Apollos 16:12. Terry calls these "ten discourses;" however, I call the divisions "semantic units" and use "discourse" to refer to the whole epistle. An exception is 2 Corinthians due to the multi-letter theory, whereby 2 Cor 1–9 is considered a single discourse. This will be further discussed in chapter 5. There are only two minor differences between my outline and Terry's outline: Terry interprets 4:17 as the end of the first unit, and does not consider the discussion of Stephanus a semantic unit.

[28] According to Terry (1995:43), the first segment comprises two chiasms. The first chiasm is: A Division (1:10–17), B Wisdom (1:18–2:26), and A' Division (3:1–4). The second chiasm is: C Servanthood (3:5–15), D Wisdom and Division (3:16–23), and C' Servanthood (4:1–17). Notably, "Travel Plans" in 4:18–21 is perceived by Terry as part of the second segment, which avoids "disturbing" the chiasms.

[29] Bailey's argument is three-fold. First, Παρακαλῶ οὖν ὑμᾶς (Therefore, I urge you, 4:16) marks the boundary of a topic, which is the same function as the two other phrases (11:2; 15:1). Second, οὖν (4:16) concludes a segment and Διὰ τοῦτο (Because of this, 4:17) is prospective. Third, evidence from some earlier manuscripts shows a division between 4:16 and 4:17 (Bailey 1983:160–161, 179).

church division or to sexual immorality. It is possible for Paul to mention his disciplinary authority before addressing the issue of sexual immorality. Nonetheless, it is more probable for Paul to do so as a concluding remark for his discussion of division. As informed by the context, in response to sexual immorality there is an explicit articulation of a disciplinary action stated in 5:5. Therefore, it is likely that the disciplinary warning in 4:21 is connected to the issue of church division, rather than that of sexual immorality.

Third, most scholars, with the exception of Fee and Terry, do not perceive the discussion of Apollos as a separate segment, and instead interpret this as only part of the final unit in 16:1–24 (see table 3.2). However, the discourse marker περὶ δὲ (now concerning) in 16:12 strongly indicates that the discussion is a major concern in the epistle, despite its brevity. In addition, the mention of Apollos in the first unit plays an important role in Paul's argument against the communal schism.[30]

Fourth, none of the reviewed outlines separate the discussion of Stephanus. Together with the discussion of Apollos, it is considered part of the final unit. Whilst the five imperatives in 16:13–14, which denote a general encouragement,[31] are consistent with a typical concluding segment in the Pauline epistles,[32] the clause Παρακαλῶ δὲ ὑμᾶς (but I urge you) in 16:15 is a discourse marker. In fact, this clause begins the first semantic unit (1:10). The occurrence of the same clause near the beginning and the end of the epistle is an inclusio. Despite its brevity, the discussion of Stephanus is a valid semantic unit. The following discussion of discourse coherence will show that this inclusio, together with the mention of Stephanus, are significant in terms of the understanding of the epistle.

Nevertheless, these differences are comparatively minor when considering the outlines of the whole discourse. In summary, the semantic units that I outline, based on the three identified discourse markers, are fundamentally similar to those suggested by scholars. The discrepancy is two-fold:

---

[30] Ker (2000:96) contends that the discussion of Apollos in 16:12, although brief, is significant. In addition, Mihaila (2009:181–193) states that περὶ δὲ in 16:12 introduces a new topic. He argues that the mention of Apollos earlier in the epistle is important to the discussion of communal disunity, and the later mention of Apollos in 16:12 should be studied in light of this.

[31] The five consecutive imperative verbs in 16:13–14 are Γρηγορεῖτε (Be alert), στήκετε (stand firm), ἀνδρίζεσθε (be brave), κραταιοῦσθε (be strong), and γινέσθω (be done).

[32] For example, Collins (1999:599), Fee (1987:827), Fitzmyer (2008:623), Horsley (1998:224), and Thiselton (2000:1333–1334) consider 16:13 as the formal closing of the epistle. Some of these scholars perceive the five seriatim imperatives as signifying the hortatory part of the conclusion. Thiselton rightly argues that this is a Pauline style, as this short series of exhortation occurs in other Pauline epistles, including Romans (16:17–19), 2 Corinthians (13:11), Philippians (4:8–9), and 1 Thessalonians (5:12–22).

whether a topic is considered a major segment or a minor sub-division, and the title of the topic.

3.1.3 Discourse coherence

Overall, a discourse is not a random compilation of thoughts and sentences. Instead, different elements in a discourse, including various semantic units, are joined through cohesive linguistic devices.[33] Although the epistle is Paul's response to the questions from the Corinthians, as well as the oral reports, these semantic units are purposefully arranged in a coherent manner. Bailey (1983:154) remarks that the questions from the Corinthians are worked into Paul's outline, in order to fit his agenda and convey his intended message. In the following part, I explicate several cohesive linguistic devices to demonstrate that the communal relationship, both among the Corinthians and between Paul and the Corinthians, is the coherent theme connecting various semantic units.

3.1.3.1 Inclusio

As previously mentioned, the clause Παρακαλῶ δὲ ὑμᾶς, ἀδελφοί (but I urge you, brothers), occurs in 1:10 and 16:15. In 1:10, the subordinate clause following παρακαλῶ (I urge) is used to urge the Corinthians to be united, τὸ αὐτὸ λέγητε πάντες (you all say the same thing). In 16:15, the subordinate clause following παρακαλῶ (I urge) is used to urge the Corinthian to submit to Stephanus.[34] The repetition of the clause παρακαλῶ δὲ ὑμᾶς (but I urge you) at both the beginning and the end of the epistle should not be treated as mere coincidence.[35] In addition to this repeated clause, Stephanus and the Corinthians are also mentioned in both Unit A and Unit K. In Unit A, Paul contends that he has only baptised a few people, including Stephanus: "I also baptized the household of Stephanus. Otherwise, I do not remember whether I baptized anyone else"* (1:16).[36] In Unit K, Paul urges the Corinthians to submit to Stephanus: "to submit to people like this"* (16:16).

---

[33] For a detailed discussion of cohesion and coherence, see § 2.3.2.2.

[34] Both subordinate clauses are introduced by ἵνα (so that).

[35] Thiselton (2000:1337) perceives this phrase as a replication of the παρακαλῶ (I urge) formula in 1:10. However, he does not consider it a form of inclusio. Instead, the formula serves to introduce a request based on an institutional relationship. Similarly, Collins (1999:604) argues that the clause in 16:15 serves to make a request. Mitchell (1993:294) argues that παρακαλῶ ὑμᾶς (I urge you) in 1:10 is a rhetorical device that introduces an important theme in this epistle, but does not comment on the exact same replication in 16:15. In short, based on the comments, this occurrence is seemingly a mere coincidence. However, it would be too happenstance to have Παρακαλῶ δὲ ὑμᾶς (but I urge you), a verb-δέ-pronoun clause, occurring in both the first and the last chapter. Thus, it is more prudent to consider this occurrence as a form of inclusio.

[36] Paul first mentions Crispus and Gaius in 1:14 as the people that he has baptised. He then names Stephanus afterwards (1:15). Some scholars argue that this is not a lapse of memory (Collins 1999:84; Fee 1987:62–63; Thiselton 2000:141). Dahl (2004:92)

In addition to these similarities, there are also two contrasting elements. First, at the beginning of Unit A, Paul rebukes the Corinthians for their communal disunity: "there be no divisions (σχίσματα) among you … there are quarrels (ἔριδες) among you" (1:10–11). Conversely, in Unit K, Paul commends Stephanus' service, who and his household "devoted themselves to ministry for the saints"* (16:15). The rebuke and the praise form a sharp contrast. Second, at the end of Unit A, Paul's emotional expression is stark: "What do you want? Shall I come to you with a rod of discipline or with love and a spirit of gentleness?"* (4:21). However, in Unit K, Paul expresses joy regarding Stephanus' presence: "I was glad about the arrival of Stephanus"* (16:17).

These similarities and contrasts between Unit A and Unit K, together with the use of inclusio, are cohesive linguistic devices that create a coherent flow and enable the audience to perceive and understand a particular topic. Notably, Nils Dahl (2004:92) argues that the disunity in the community is related to the opposition to Paul and Stephanus. However, Bailey (1983:490–491) suggests an alternative understanding to the inclusion of Stephanus in 16:15, and argues that Paul uses the voluntary service of Stephanus as an example to show the Corinthians the right attitude of living within a community. These two hypotheses are not mutually exclusive. The use of inclusio and contrastive elements prove that the mention of Stephanus is not a random insertion, and instead is used by Paul to silence the opponents of Stephanus, and concurrently show the community the right attitude through the example of Stephanus.

3.1.3.2 Prominence

Prominence is another linguistic device to demonstrate the coherence of a discourse by highlighting an important point through the repetition of a theme (thematic prominence) or the repetition of a word (lexical cohesion).[37] In 1 Corinthians, I observe both thematic prominence and lexical cohesion.

Thematic prominence

The 11 major semantic units in 1 Corinthians address various issues raised either by the Corinthians or by Paul through the verbal reports. However, they are arranged by Paul to purposefully convey the importance of corporate unity and communal relationship, which is the central theme. Before discussing this central theme in light of thematic prominence, it is

---

argues that the omission of Stephanus is a deliberate act, since Paul does not want to involve Stephanus in the discussion of disunity. Pascuzzi (2009:824) suggests that it is an attempt to avoid calling attention to how many he had actually baptised. Stephanus is also considered to be holding a form of leadership in the Corinthian community (Hurd 1983:49; Ciampa and Rosner 2010:858).

[37] For discussion of discourse prominence, see § 2.3.2.2.

vital to attend to two discussions currently going on in scholarly work on 1 Corinthians. Both relate to the structural outline of the letter.

First, some scholars divide the epistle into two main parts: oral reports (1–6) and written questions (7–16).[38] Other scholars separate the topic of schism (1–4) from the oral and written reports (5–16).[39] Regardless, Paul is thought to arrange his letter by separating his response to the oral reports from his response to the written questions. The strongest objection to this kind of neat division is how Paul commences Unit F. Unit F (11:17–34) is situated in the division (7–16), which most scholars presume to be the apostle's answer to the questions raised in writing. As previously discussed, the summary statement in 11:18, "For in the first place, when you come together as a church I hear there are divisions (σχίσματα) among you", begins the topic of the Lord's Supper. Whether the report, suggested by ἀκούω (to hear) is from Chloe's people or not, it is obvious that Paul does not respond to a written question from the Corinthians here.[40] As such, it is more probable that the apostle arranges the letter in his own way to convey a particular point, rather than following this kind of neat grouping.

The second issue is related to the first one. If Paul deliberately separates the oral reports from each other and places the discussion of schism in the front, what is his purpose? There are two different suggestions. One is that Paul has to defend his apostolic authority before he can address the questions raised.[41] Alternatively, it is suggested that the epistle is centred on one key theme: ecclesial unity. Thus, it is important for Paul to set the tone at the beginning of the letter.[42] These two seemingly opposite suggestions are not necessarily mutually exclusive.[43] I argue that Paul addresses the communal disunity whilst asserting his apostolic authority. In other words, the letter is written to attend to two main issues: the communal relationship within the Corinthian community, and the relationship between Paul and the Corinthians. I attempt to show below that this is the thematic prominence displayed in the epistle.

---

[38] Scholars who support a three-part division include Conzelmann (1975:vii–viii), Thiselton (2000:vi–xiii), and Orr and Walther (1976:x–xv).

[39] The scholars who support a two-part division include Barrett (1994:28–29), Fitzmyer (2008:viii–x), and Fee (1987:21–23).

[40] Burk (2008:106) also holds this view, who argues that the oral reports are signified in 1:11, 5:1, and 11:18; and Paul deals with the written questions in 7:1 onwards.

[41] Fee 1987:47–49; Dahl 2004:94–95.

[42] Mitchell 1993:1, 301–2.

[43] According to Fee (1987:47), many people regard the schism mentioned in the first four chapters is behind every issue discussed in the subsequent part of the epistle. Fee repudiates this idea based on two observations. First, no factional parties are mentioned in chapters 5–16. Second, there is no evidence in the epistle that Apollos and Cephas are the rallying points for these parties. Hence, the argument of Fee is different from that of Mitchell who suggests that disunity is the key issue discussed in the whole letter.

In 1 Corinthians, some discussions are noticeably a common concern for the whole Corinthian community, including the issues of church division (A), the Lord's Supper (F), spiritual gifts (G), and contribution (I). Some are less obvious, such as the discussions of sexual immorality (B) and head coverings (E). The rest, including the discussions of marriage (C), food and idols (D), resurrection (H), Apollos (J), and Stephanus (K), are comparatively obscure in terms of their communal focus. Nonetheless, I argue that all of the semantic units are connected by one central theme as explained below.

In his discussion of the schism (A), Paul urges the whole community, as indicated by πάντες (all) in 1:10, to be united by the same mind (ἐν τῷ αὐτῷ νοΐ). The concern is for the entire community, emphasising communal relationship and corporate unity. However, the relationship between Paul and the community is also clearly a focal point in his discussion, which is demonstrated by the account of factionalism (1:12–14) and the Corinthians' challenge to Paul's authority (4:1–3).

In dealing with the case of sexual immorality (B), Paul commands the Corinthians to deal with the fornicator when they assemble (συναχθέντων, 5:4), suggesting that the whole community should act together to deal with this issue. Most importantly, by using the metaphor of yeast Paul warns the Corinthians about the adverse effect of this situation on the whole community, as indicated by the phrase "the whole batch of dough" (ὅλον τὸ φύραμα, 5:6). Hence, the problem of sexual immorality is not confined to an individual person. Rather, it has an effect on the entire community.[44]

The discussion of marriage (Unit C) seems to be unrelated to the entire community. However, Paul noticeably connects this discussion with the previous one at the beginning of Unit C: "But because of immoralities, each man should have relations with his own wife and each woman with her own husband"* (7:2).[45] The ultimate concern for Paul to discuss marriage is sexual immorality, a practice which could spread like yeast in a community as discussed in Unit C.[46] Furthermore, Paul addresses those who are single

---

[44] Kim (2008:57) provides a convincing argument regarding the connection between sexual immorality and the Corinthian community, arguing that the issue is related to the power conflicts among the Corinthians, since some people exercise their freedom irresponsibly at the expense of the whole community.

[45] The word πορνεία only occurs five times in the letter: 5:1 (twice); 6:13; 6:18; and 7:2. The word occurs four times in Unit C (5:1–6:20) and one time in Unit D (7:1–40)

[46] Various scholars commonly consider that this segment is related to the issue of sexual immorality depicted in the preceding context (Ciampa and Rosner 2010:266; Orr and Walther 1976:207; Fitzmyer 2008:274; Fee 1987:277–278). Some scholars, including Bailey, Mitchell, and Collins, consider 7:1–40 as part of the semantic units of 5:1–6:20 (see table 3.2).

(7:8) and married (7:10). Therefore, the discussion in this unit is relevant to every member in the community.[47]

In Unit D, Paul discusses the issue of food and idols. This is an issue which impacts the whole community, and is related to the conflict among the Corinthians. Unit D is written in the form of chiasm. The issue of food and idols is discussed in 8:1–13 (D1) and 10:1–11:1 (D3),[48] with the topic of freedom appearing in the centre of the chiastic structure, 9:1–27 (D2).[49] There are three basic observations about the entire Unit D. First, the issue is a concern for the entire community. For example, Paul mentions that τινὲς (some, 8:7) are accustomed to idol worship in D1, but his emphatic call in D3 addresses the whole community: "So then, my dear friends, flee from idolatry" (10:14). Second, the conflict between two parties within the community is subtly portrayed throughout the unit. In D1, Paul begins his discussion in 8:1 by mentioning "the wise": οἴδαμεν ὅτι πάντες γνῶσιν ἔχομεν (we know that "we all have knowledge")*. Then, he attends to the underlying conflict between "the weak" (τοῖς ἀσθενέσιν, 8:9) and "the wise" (σὲ τὸν ἔχοντα γνῶσιν, 8:10).[50] The wise (also known as the strong) believe that they

---

[47] Some scholars argue that this issue is of a communal concern. For example, Scroggs (1972:283–303) argues that the passage is to counter a group of "Corinthian extremists" who insist on the practice of sexual abstinence among the married. Fee (1987:269–270) also supports the view regarding the extremists. In addition, Paul's teaching on marriage, for Scroggs (1972:297), hinges on the apostle's concern for the larger community of the church over the smaller community of the family given the imminent advent of Christ. On the other hand, Mitchell (1993:121–122) contends that marital relationship is a component of the larger community group based on contemporary Greek philosophical background. Thus, she concludes that the issue of marriage also contributes to the contention within the community. Although the text itself does not provide a clear illustration that this issue is directly related to the unity of the church, Mitchell's proposed theory is possible.

[48] In 8:1–13, Paul deals with the general principle of food offered to idols.

[49] Ciampa and Rosner 2010:367; Terry 1995:43; Bailey 1983:229. In Bailey's structural analysis of this segment, he demonstrates the parallelism employed in the text, which is more complex than a simple chiasm.

[50] This is a common view held by various scholars, with which I concur. The wise are also known as "the strong." For Mitchell (1991:237) the concern of food and idols is a divisive issue. There are two groups in the community, "the Strong" and "the Weak" (Thiselton 2000:606; Fee 1987:358–362; Conzelmann 1975:140–141). Murphy-O'Connor (2010:88, 97) argues that the phrase πάντες γνῶσιν ἔχομεν (we all have knowledge, 8:1) denotes "the Strong," and suggests that the Weak are under the oppression of the Strong. Fee (1987:358–359) further argues that Paul uses his own example regarding the discussion of freedom to illustrate the problematic attitudes held by both groups. However, some scholars, including Horsley (1998:115) and Hurd (1983:123–125), reject the presence of the Strong and the Weak, as Hurd argues that while some Corinthians were less secure in their new faith than others, there is nevertheless no proof in the text indicating that they formed a group.

possess the true knowledge, and they despise the weak. Third, D2 seems to be out of place. There are two views regarding the purpose for Paul to write D2. Some argue that Paul uses his own example in D2 to teach the truth of exercising freedom.[51] Therefore, his teaching, on the one hand, rebukes the attitude of the wise people whom he mentions in D1; and on the other hand, instructs the weak regarding the truth of idol worship detailed in D3. Conversely, some argue that Paul uses D2 to defend his apostolic authority.[52] The two views are considered by some as mutually exclusive.[53] Nonetheless, I argue that these two views coexist, based on two reasons. The theme of freedom depicted in D2 re-emerges in D3, as indicated by the occurrence of ἐλευθερία (freedom) in 10:29. This shows that D2 is not an unrelated digression. Rather, it is in the centre of a chiasm, and it provides an example for the Corinthians to learn the truth of exercising freedom in relating to food offered to idols. However, Paul also uses this opportunity to further defend his apostolic authority that is challenged by some Corinthians, a topic that he has previously mentioned (4:1–3).[54] In summary, the discussion of food and idols concerns the entire community that is in conflict. Paul also uses this discussion to reaffirm his apostolic authority in facing the opposition from the community.

In Unit E, Paul discusses the issue of head covering. The two verbs in 11:5, προσευχομένη (praying) and προφητεύουσα (prophesying), likely imply that the situation is related to a Christian assembly instead of a private incident. This claim is based on observing the wider context. In this letter, both verbs, προσεύχομαι (to pray) and προφητεύω (to prophesy) almost exclusively occur in 1 Cor 11 and 1 Cor 14.[55] In 1 Cor 14, they appear in the discussion of exercising spiritual gifts and division in the church. Therefore, it is likely that Paul coherently employs them on both occasions, chapters 11 and 14, to express the key issue of church division that concerns the whole community, with reference to their worship assembly.[56]

---

[51] Thiselton 2000:662–3; Collins 1999:328–9; Ciampa and Rosner 2010:396.

[52] Barrett 1994:200; Orr and Walther 1976:240; Fee 1987:392–393; Willis 1985:270–272.

[53] For example, Collins (1999:328) and Robertson and Plummer (1929:176) argue that the text is the discussion of Paul's personal example, and reject the notion that Paul defends his apostleship in this segment. Conversely, Fee (1987:392–393) argues that Paul devotes this segment to defend his apostolic authority rather than providing personal example, since the Corinthians challenge Paul's apostolicity by questioning his teaching (as he forbids them to attend pagan temples).

[54] Fitzmyer (2008:353) also includes both views in his interpretation of chapter 9.

[55] The occurrence of προφητεύω: 11:4 (twice); 13:9; 14:1, 3 (four times), 24, 31, 39. The occurrence of προσεύχομαι: 11:4 (twice), 13; 14:13 (five times). Both verbs exclusively occur in chapters 11 and 14, with the one exception of προφητεύω also appearing in 13:9.

[56] Mitchell (1991:262–263) further argues that the issue of head coverings and women's authority is a reflection of factionalism.

In Unit F, the word συνερχομένων (coming together, 11:18, 20) points to the gathering of the community at the Lord's Supper. This focus of communal gathering is further accentuated by the repetition of συνέρχομαι (to come together, 11:17, 18, 20, 33, 34).[57] The underlying issue in this unit points to communal schism as indicated by σχίσματα ἐν ὑμῖν (divisions in you, 11:18). Thus, the issue involves the entire community.

In Unit G, the discussion of exercising spiritual gifts is set in the background of Christian gathering, ὅταν συνέρχησθε (whenever you gather), in 14:26). The Corinthians are urged to do all things in right order (14:40). In other words, this is the concern of the whole community when they gather together in worship.

In Unit H, the discussion of the resurrection seems to be purely theological. However, the argument presented by Paul alludes to factionalism. Paul challenges the wrong view held by the Corinthians: "how are some of you saying (πῶς λέγουσιν ἐν ὑμῖν τινες) there is no resurrection of the dead?"* (15:12). The phrase ἐν ὑμῖν τινες (some of you) is particularly intriguing. This indicates that the wrong view of resurrection is not embraced by the whole community. Instead, there are some members proclaiming it. In addition, the previous context touches on Pauls' apostleship: "For I am the least of the apostles...I worked harder than all of them"* (15:9–10). Therefore, it is highly possible that the phrase ἐν ὑμῖν τινες (some of you) points to the faction that challenges Paul's apostolic authority, and this faction also proclaims a wrong belief of resurrection.[58] Thus, the schism within the community and the relationship between Paul and the Corinthians are two underlying issues in the discussion of resurrection.

When Paul discusses the contribution (I), he asks the Corinthians to follow the direction he gives to "the churches of Galatia"* (16:1). In other words, his discussion refers to the notion that the collection involves the whole Christian community.

Concerning Apollos (J), the appearance of his name in 16:12 forms an inclusio, since Paul first introduces him in 1:12 and then mentions his name in the context of schism (3:5–8). As such, there is a connection between 16:12 and the issue of division (Fitzmyer 2008:622–623; Fee 1987:824–825; Conzelmann 1975:297.) Some argue that the absence of Apollos among the

---

[57] Horsley (1998:158) argues that the word is employed in other Greek literature to denote the uniting of different factions.

[58] Mitchell (1993:287) argues that Paul mentions the gospel in 15:1 to encourage the community to be united by citing their common foundation—Christ's gospel. Hence, the passage in 15:9–11 serves as an exemplary function, illustrating Paul's humility. On the other hand, 15:9–10 can also be understood from the perspective of the schism. According to Fee (1987:719), the seemingly unnecessary account of Paul's apostleship in this text alludes to the underlying conflict between the apostle and the community. Paul asserts his apostleship by invoking his relationship with the Risen Christ to tackle the conflict in the community. This theory is considerably sound when the context of the whole letter is considered.

Corinthians (or his reluctance to visit the community as indicated in 16:12) is his own attempt to avoid either escalating the disunity in the community (Barrett 1994:392; Mitchell 1993:293) or being exploited by the factionalists. Thiselton is more specific as he argues that Apollos is disgusted by the disunity (Thiselton 2000:1332). Regardless of the reason for Apollos' absence, there is a general understanding that Apollos' visit is connected to the problem of the communal schism.

As I have previously discussed, the discussion of Stephanus (K) forms an inclusio. Paul uses the selfless service offered by Stephanus as an example to illustrate the desirable attitude in the life of a community. This attitude is required to tackle communal schism.

In summary, the theme of communal relationship and corporate unity is the thematic prominence shown across all the semantic units. All the units discuss topics that concern the entire Corinthian community. Amongst these units, some specifically point to the strained relationship between Paul and the Corinthian community (A, H, J, and K).

Lexical cohesion

In terms of another form of prominence, σῶμα is the fourth most frequent noun in the letter, displaying a strong pattern of lexical cohesion (see Appendix 1). The word is repeated 46 times in 1 Corinthians.[59] The high occurrence rate signifies the importance of σῶμα in this epistle. Figure 3.1 shows that σῶμα occurs in six semantic units, with an exceptionally frequent occurrence in Units B, G, and H.

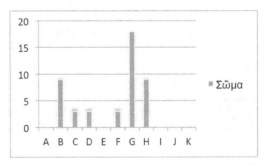

Figure 3.1. The occurrences of σῶμα in semantic units of 1 Corinthians.

---

[59] The occurrences of σῶμα in 1 Corinthians are as follows: 5:3; 6:13 (twice), 15, 16, 18 (twice), 19, 20; 7:4 (twice), 34; 9:27; 10:16, 17; 11:24, 27, 29; 12:12 (thrice), 13, 14, 15 (twice), 16 (twice), 17, 18, 19, 20, 22, 23, 24, 25, 27; 13:3; 15:35, 37, 38 (twice); 40 (twice), 44 (thrice). Σῶμα occurs 74 times in all the authentic Pauline epistles.

In this and subsequent frequency graphs, the horizontal axis shows semantic units, chapters, verses, or other divisions of text; the vertical axis shows number of occurrences.

By providing (in § 3.2.1.1) a detailed analysis of the individual occurrences of σῶμα in each semantic unit and its overall occurrence in the entire discourse, I demonstrate that σῶμα is used to connote communal and corporate unity, which is its thematic meaning.

3.1.3.3 Macrostructure

A macrostructure denotes the core message of a discourse, which is intended by the author for the audience. It is a short abstract that can be summarised by the audience after reading a particular discourse.[60] From the coherence displayed by various linguistic devices, including the inclusio and the thematic prominence, I argue that the macrostructure of 1 Corinthians can be understood as follows: In response to the written questions of the Corinthians and the oral reports, Paul asserts his apostolic authority in facing an opposition from some Corinthians, and calls for corporate unity by reproaching the schism within the community and highlighting the importance of communal relationship among the Corinthians.

3.2 Σῶμα (Body) in 1 Corinthians

The following part analyses the occurrence of σῶμα in each semantic unit, and then examines its overall occurrence in the entire discourse in light of the sociolinguistic aspect, the macrostructure, and the discourse flow.

3.2.1 Σῶμα (body) in semantic units

Table 3.3 shows the occurrences of σῶμα in all the major semantic units.

Table 3.3. The occurrences of σῶμα in 1 Corinthians

Major Semantic Unit		A 1:10–4:21	B 5:1–6:20	C 7:1–40	D 8:1–11:1	E 11:2–16	F 11:17–34	G 12:1–14:4	H 15:1–58	I 16:1–11	J 16:12–14	K 16:15–18	
Topic	Letter-opening (1:1–9)	Church Division	Sexual Immorality	Marriage	Food and Idols	Head Coverings	The Lord's Supper	Spiritual Gifts	Resurrection	Contribution	Apollos	Stephanus	Letter-closing (16:19–24)
Occurrence of Σῶμα	0	0	9	3	3	0	3	18	9	0	0	0	0

---

[60] For discussion of macrostructure, see § 2.3.2.2.

3.2.1.1 Σῶμα *(body) in Unit B*

Σῶμα occurs nine times in Unit B. The word is distributed unevenly throughout the unit, with all but one of the occurrences congregating in the unit's third division. The term's overall occurrences connote a strong corporate and communal reference.

In Unit B, Paul discusses the case in which a man in the Corinthians community commits incest (5:1–13). Then, he digresses to comment on a legal dispute (6:1–8) before resuming the topic of sexual immorality (6:9–20).[61] Instead of focusing on a specific case (as in 5:1–13), the discussion in 6:9–20 involves the general issue of prostitution. Paul warns the Corinthians against visiting prostitutes. In this discussion, σῶμα occurs in one big cluster, with eight occurrences appearing in 6:13–20. Table 3.4 shows the distribution of σῶμα in Unit B.[62] In this table (and the subsequent tables, tables 3.5 to 3.9), an asterisk is used to symbolize an individual occurrence of σῶμα.

Table 3.4. Σῶμα in Unit B "Sexual Immorality" (1 Cor 5:1–6:20)[a]

5:1–13 Sexual Immorality	6:1–8 Lawsuit	6:9–20 Sexual Immorality
*		* ** ***
		* *

[a] One of the most intriguing observations is the use of chiasm in Units B, C, and D. There is a short digression in each major semantic unit, in which Paul discusses a specific topic before returning to the main theme. For example, the lawsuit in Unit B and the slavery in Unit C are both obvious digressions. Terry (1995:43) also notes this chiastic structure.

---

[61] Deming (1996:289–312) provides an insightful explanation of this digression. He argues that 1 Cor 5–6 centres on a single case of sexual immorality. The failed attempt by some Corinthians to resolve this case in the public courts leads to strife and moral confusion within the community. Therefore, the three divisions, 5:1–13, 6:1–8, and 6:9–20, can be understood as a coherent segment. Deming's argument is helpful in understanding the transition from 5:1–13 to 6:1–8. However, Paul clearly discusses a general scenario in 6:9–20: sexual immorality with the practice of visiting prostitutes. Hence, it is likely that Paul arranges his discussion as follows. Both the single case (5:1–13) and the general practice (6:9–20) of sexual immorality would destroy a Christian community, which is exemplified by the strife-fueled court case (6:1–8).

[62] These sub-divisions are created for showing how σῶμα is *spatially* distributed in a major semantic unit. The division is determined by dividing the semantic unit according to its context. For example, the discussion of Sexual Immorality in 5:1–13 temporarily digresses to the discussion of a Lawsuit in 6:1–8 before returning to the topic of Sexual Immorality in 6:9–20. Therefore, it is appropriate to divide the semantic unit into three parts: 5:1–13, 6:1–8, and 6:9–20. The creation of this sub-division is for visual enhancement, aiming to illustrate the occurrences of the clustered σῶμα.

According to the concept of lexical cohesion, when two or more occurrences of similar lexical items appear in close proximity, these lexical items likely belong to the same semantic domain.[63] As shown in table 3.4, σῶμα occurs eight times within eight verses, appearing as a cluster in the last sub-division (6:13–20). The clustered occurrence of σῶμα suggests that the word connotes a similar, if not identical, meaning throughout, as explained below.

Paul begins his argument in 6:13 by explaining this principle: "The body (σῶμα) is not for sexual immorality, but for the Lord, and the Lord for the body (τῷ σώματι)"*. He further explains this principle in 6:15 by stating that τὰ σώματα ὑμῶν μέλη Χριστοῦ ἐστιν (your bodies are members of Christ) and it is wrong that make them members of a prostitute (τὰ μέλη τοῦ Χριστοῦ ποιήσω πόρνης μέλη). Then, Paul contrasts the two different scenarios in: "anyone who is united with a prostitute is one body with her"* (6:16) and "But the one united with the Lord is one spirit with him"* (6:17). Paul continues his argument in 6:19 by stating that your body (τὸ σῶμα ὑμῶν) is the temple of the Holy Spirit who is in you. Finally, he concludes the argument in 6:20 by giving a hortatory statement: "glorify God with your body (τῷ σώματι ὑμῶν)."*

In this cluster, σῶμα is first employed to denote the physical body (6:13). Then, the term is used as a metaphor, depicting the community in which the people are the members of Christ, as illustrated by τὰ σώματα ὑμῶν (your bodies, 6:15).[64] The plural form τὰ σώματα (the bodies) highlights each individual member. The term undergoes further shift in 6:16, pointing to sexual union as suggested by the phrase ὁ κολλώμενος...ἓν σῶμά (the joining of σῶμα during conjugation).[65] Sexual union is compared with a spiritual union in 6:17. Then, σῶμα is used to depict the physical body again in 6:18, before shifting to a new dimension in the following verse: τὸ σῶμα ὑμῶν (your body, 6:19), denoting the temple of the Holy Spirit.[66]

The term σῶμα seems to connote different meanings in each individual occurrence. However, the word is commonly employed to elucidate relationship: sexual relationship between two people (their physical bodies), and spiritual relationship between believers and Christ. The latter form of relationship peculiarly resembles a sexual one.[67] In Unit B, the reference to

---

[63] For the discussion of lexical cohesion, see § 2.3.2.2.

[64] Fee (1987:253) contends that this is an abrupt change of direction.

[65] Horsley (1998:92) argues that the shift changes from physical body to sexual union.

[66] Jewett (1971:262) comments on the σῶμα-temple language, and argues that Paul establishes the principles of exclusive corporal relationship.

[67] I agree with the analysis of D. Martin (1995:174–177) who argues that ethical immorality is not the main reason why Paul argues against visiting prostitutes. Instead, the greater concern is the symbolic message conveyed by this kind of immoral sexual union. I focus on the resemblance between sexual union and Christ-believers relationship in a positive sense. On the contrary, Martin focuses

relationship is the shared meaning of the occurrences of σῶμα. Of interest, sexual intercourse performed by an individual is used to explain a communal Christ-believers relationship. In this relationship, σῶμα carries a metaphorical sense, portraying a relationship between Christ and his believers, as a corporate community.[68]

The following part focuses on two exegetical issues. The solution to both issues further illuminates this corporate and communal connotation of σῶμα in Unit B. The first exegetical problem is the replacement of σῶμα by ἡμᾶς (us) in 6:14. In 6:13, σῶμα connotes the physical body that God cares for (ὁ κύριος τῷ σώματι). In 6:14, Paul discusses the future resurrection in which ἡμᾶς (us) is employed: καὶ ἡμᾶς ἐξεγερεῖ διὰ τῆς δυνάμεως αὐτοῦ (and he will raise us by his power)*. If the connection between σῶμα in 6:13 and the discussion of resurrection in 6:14 is considered, taking into account the coherent flow, the parallel between σῶμα and ἡμᾶς (us) becomes apparent. In 6:14, instead of using σῶμα as in the previous verse, Paul argues that God will raise the physical body of the believers: ἡμᾶς ἐξεγερεῖ (he shall raise us).[69] In other words, ἡμᾶς (us) replaces the word σῶμα (body in singular). As such, the use of this plural pronoun expresses a subtle nuance. The focus of the resurrection is not on "individual" believers. Rather, the resurrection of the community (signified by a plural personal pronoun) is Paul's emphasis.[70] If the community is truly Paul's focus, the σῶμα that denotes the physical body in its own sentence (6:13) carries an undertone which alludes to the corporate and communal reference as illuminated by ἡμᾶς (us) in the immediate context (6:14).

The second exegetical issue is the interpretation of the combination of a singular σῶμα and a plural ὑμῶν (your) in this passage. In this cluster, there

on the negative implication behind this kind of union. He argues that this is a dichotomy deliberately set up by Paul. Christians are part of Christ's body. And πορνεία (fornication) represents the κόσμος, the very essence of this world that is antithetical to God's kingdom. The copulation between a man and a prostitute becomes the conjoining of Christ and this κόσμος, which is totally inappropriate.

[68] May (2004:143) argues that the σῶμα language in 20–6:12 is unequivocally communal. Both May (2004:140) and Mitchell (1993:120) consider that communal identity is the focal concern in 20–6:12.

[69] Ciampa and Rosner (2010:255) also note this replacement.

[70] Jewett (1971:260) argues that σῶμα defines ἡμᾶς (us) as a corporal entity, emphasizing the union between a person with another person or God. On the other hand, Thiselton (2000:464) suggests that ἡμᾶς (us) points to single in-Christ corporeity, illustrating the bodily resurrection. Fee (1987:256) repudiates the interpretation of Robinson (1952:29) who argues that σῶμα means the whole person in light of ἡμᾶς (us). Both Fee (1987:256) and Thiselton (2000:466) argue for the bodily identity denoted by σῶμα, pointing to either the physical union (as suggested by Jewett) or the single bodily entity of Christ-believers (as argued by Thiselton). However, both scholars suggest that the term alludes to some form of communal union and oneness. Their view is similar to what I hold: the corporate connotation behind the overall occurrence of σῶμα in this cluster.

are three occurrences in which σῶμα is combined with a personal plural possessive pronoun (6:15, 6:19, and 6:20). Two of the three occurrences have the combination of a singular σῶμα and ὑμῶν (your). They occur in 6:19 (τὸ σῶμα ὑμῶν, your body) and 6:20 (τῷ σώματι ὑμῶν, in your body).[71] Not only does this combination depart from the normal expected grammatical rule, this combination will also re-emerge in other Pauline passages in our study. Therefore, this combination requires further investigation.

In Koine Greek grammar, the combination of a singular noun and singular personal possessive pronoun, and the combination of a plural noun and plural personal possessive pronoun follow the basic rule of agreement.[72] Unless the noun is abstract in nature, the combination of a singular noun and a plural personal possessive pronoun is abnormal, since it violates the rule of agreement.[73] I call this abnormal construct the "abnormal singular construct." Previous scholarship has either overlooked or been unable to satisfactorily explain a particular grammatical construct in the Pauline epistles, namely the combination of a singular anthropological noun and plural personal possessive pronoun.[74] This abnormal grammatical construct is carefully explicated in my recent article, "The Distributive Singular in Paul: The Adequacy of a Grammatical Category".[75] The key findings are summarised as follows:

In the Pauline epistles, there are 212 occurrences of this abnormal singular construct, and most of them contain an abstract noun.

---

[71] Of interest, the textual variant in 6:19 provokes further observation. Although a number of ancient and reliable manuscripts (P⁴⁶, ℵ, A*, B, D, F) argue for the reading of a singular σῶμα, a plural reading, τὰ σώματα (the bodies), is found in a number of prominent manuscripts (Aᶜ, L, Ψ, 33, 1881). If the singular reading is the original, which is widely understood to be the case, then the plural reading could well be a "correction" intended by some scribes when they copied manuscripts. In other words, the singular construct was considered to be so abnormal that some scripts rectified it with a plural σῶμα as they believed the plural was supposed to be the correct reading. This is further demonstrated by the corrected version of the Codex Alexandrinus, A, in around c. 400. In other words, the peculiarity regarding the use of a singular σῶμα is highlighted as the construct was probably considered to be wrong by some scribes. It is possible that an attempt was made to harmonize the text (an abnormal singular construct) with another text in the preceding context in which τὰ σώματα ὑμῶν (your bodies) is used (6:15). However, this is only a conjecture. Of all the reviewed works, only a few mention this variant. For example, Robertson and Plummer (1929:129) notice the textual variant, but no explanation is provided.

[72] In Koine Greek grammar, singular possessive pronoun combining with a plural noun is acceptable, for example, οἱ ὀφθαλμοί μου (my eyes) in Luke 2:30.

[73] Chen 2015:105–107.

[74] In examining the phrase μετὰ τοῦ πνεύματος ὑμῶν (with your spirit, Gal 6:18), Fee (1994:469) notes that scholarship has been unable to provide a satisfactory explanation for this abnormal grammatical construct.

[75] Chen 2015:104–130.

Nonetheless, amongst the 212 occurrences, 37 have a concrete noun and 26 contain an anthropological term.[76] In explaining this peculiar construct some modern scholars define the singular anthropological term as the distributive singular, which is defined as "the use of singular in reference to a plurality of objects" (Winer 1877:218). Some of the scholars adopt Turner's analysis, an analysis that supports Winer's definition. Turner provides a comprehensive analysis and cites copious examples, including a number of Pauline passages, to advocate Paul's use of the distributive singular (Turner 1963:23-24).[77] However, my work has shown the inadequacy of Turner's analysis. For example, out of the 29 examples of καρδία (heart) cited by Turner, there are only three valid examples of the abnormal singular construct. Even if all three abnormal constructs were explained by the distributive singular, Turner's analysis could hardly prove that the distributive singular is Paul's common grammatical expression.[78] Furthermore, by studying the occurrences of the 37 concrete nouns as well as the 26 anthropological terms in the abnormal singular construct, I have shown that the distributive singular is not a good and valid explanation to account for this abnormal construct in Paul's letters. Instead, the abnormal construct could be explained by the following grammatical categories: normal singular (denoting corporate and social dimensions); the epistolary plural; and some type of metaphor.[79]

In light of the above discussion, the distributive singular must not be the presumed explanation of any abnormal singular construct in Paul's letters. In 6:19–20, the abnormal singular contruct seems to contradict the preceding phrase in 6:15, in which τὰ σώματα ὑμῶν (your bodies) occurs. Why is σῶμα used in the plural form instead of the singular form? This can be explained by two reasons. First, the predicate nominative in 6:15 is a plural noun, μέλη (members). The two phrases, τὰ σώματα ὑμῶν (your bodies) and μέλη τοῦ Χριστοῦ (members of Christ), are joined by a singular copula verb ἐστιν (is). Therefore, it would be grammatically natural for the nominative to use a plural noun, and in this case, τὰ σώματα (the bodies) to highlight the parallel. Second, 6:15 emphasises the fact that each member of the Corinthian community, suggested by the plural σώματα, is also a member of Christ, suggested by the plural μέλη (members). However, this abnormal construct in 6:19–20 is not widely mentioned by many commentators.[80] Among those who discuss it, Fee (1987:263) advocates the use of

---

[76] Chen 2015:112–113. There is one occurrence that contains multiple anthropological terms in 1 Thess 5:23, and this will be further discussed in chapter 6.

[77] Chen 2015:107–108.

[78] Chen 2015:108.

[79] Chen 2015:112–130.

[80] This construction is not mentioned in the work of Barrett, Collins, Thiselton, Conzelmann, Orr and Walther, Robertson and Plummer, Ciampa and Rosner.

the distributive singular for σῶμα without providing any reason. Apart from critical commentaries, this construct is mentioned in several monographs, in which some support the use of the distributive singular.[81]

In terms of the singular σῶμα in 6:19–20, the use of the distributive singular can be refuted on three grounds. First, previous analysis of the macrostructure reveals that the central theme in the epistle is the corporate unity and communal relationship of the Corinthians. Therefore, it is likely that Paul employs a singular form of σῶμα to emphasise the corporate unity and communal aspect.[82] According to the context, the discussion in 6:12–20 concerns the immoral conjugal union between the Corinthians and prostitutes. In 6:19, Paul asks a rhetorical question: ἢ οὐκ οἴδατε ὅτι τὸ σῶμα ὑμῶν ναὸς τοῦ ἐν ὑμῖν ἁγίου πνεύματός (Or do you not know that your body is the temple of the Holy Spirit who is in you)*. Putting the textual variant aside, σῶμα in this verse can be viewed in two different perspectives. The term denotes either the physical body, pointing to the physical union between a man and a woman, or a metaphor, alluding to the Christian community.[83] As per earlier discussion, the connotation of relationship is the same semantic domain shared by the occurrences of σῶμα in Unit B. In terms of the wider context, in chapter 3, Paul compares himself to a builder. The apostle constructs a building by laying a good foundation; and the building is a metaphor which connotes the Corinthian community. In concluding his argument, Paul asks a rhetorical question in 3:16: Οὐκ οἴδατε ὅτι ναὸς θεοῦ ἐστε καὶ τὸ πνεῦμα τοῦ θεοῦ οἰκεῖ ἐν ὑμῖν; (Do you not know that you are God's temple and that God's Spirit lives in you?)*. The physical temple (the tabernacle or the temple in Jerusalem), which is now represented by the church, is being realised in the Christian community in which God dwells through his Holy Spirit. The clause in 3:16 is strikingly similar to the clause in 6:19, ἢ οὐκ οἴδατε ὅτι τὸ σῶμα ὑμῶν ναὸς τοῦ ἐν

---

[81] By referring to other Pauline passages, Robinson (1952:29–30) argues that one should not place too much emphasis on this combination because of the inconsistency demonstrated in Paul's usage. He suggests that this combination can be a purely grammatical variation, and cites the example of καρδία (heart) in Paul's work. He also suggests that this can be a collective singular with an emphasis on the mass in contrast to the individualization. Gundry (1976:220) also supports the use of the collective singular in 6:19–20, but he repudiates Robinson's theory. Gundry argues that the collective singular does not negate individualization.

[82] Although this is not a common view, commentators do not always have a definite conclusion on this matter. For example, Thiselton considers the passage, the peculiar syntax of τὸ σῶμα ὑμῶν (your body) in particular, and indicates that it refers to an individual dimension. However, Thiselton argues for the corporate aspect of σῶμα based on his comparison of 6:19 and 3:16. For both Thiselton and Conzelmann, the community focus in 3:16 has shifted to an individual application (Thiselton 2000:316, 474; Conzelmann 1975:112).

[83] Fee (1987:264) suggests that Paul takes the imagery of the church (denoted by σῶμα) in 3:16 and applies it as a depiction of an individual person in 6:19.

ὑμῖν ἁγίου πνεύματός (Or do you not know that your body is the temple of the Holy Spirit who is in you)*. Since both of them occur in the same discourse, it is natural to consider that they are connected. Paul's concern in 3:16 is for the community. Although Paul discusses sexual union, when considering the above-mentioned connection in the wider context, his core concern is for the community in which God dwells instead of the individual physical body.[84]

Although many commentators hold the view that σῶμα in chapter 6 points to the individual physical body,[85] several scholars argue for the corporate and communal connotation of σῶμα. For example, Kempthorne (1968:568–574) contends that the σῶμα refers to the corporate Body; the peculiar singular construct provides this corporate allusion.[86] He also notices that the phrase in 6:19 echoes another phrase in 12:27 in the later part of the epistle: Ὑμεῖς δέ ἐστε σῶμα Χριστοῦ καὶ μέλη ἐκ μέρους (Now you are Christ's body, and each of you is a member of it)* (ibid. 573). Murphy-O'Connor (1979:53–54) argues that the singular σῶμα is a true singular which denotes the identity of the community. The main reason is because both the immediate context (6:19), οὐκ ἐστὲ ἑαυτῶν (you are not of your own)*, and the wider context (3:23), ὑμεῖς δὲ Χριστοῦ (but you [are] Christ's), elucidate the authentic humanity that Christ embodies. Thus the focus is on the community instead of individuality. Newton (1985:57) also suggests that τὸ σῶμα ὑμῶν (your body) is in parallel with ναός τοῦ ἐν ὑμῖν ἁγίου πνεύματός (the temple of the Holy Spirit in you). Both phrases point to a corporate understanding. Fitzmyer (2008:270) also argues that Paul urges the community of Corinth to have a corporate honoring of God in 6:20.[87] I agree with the view of Kempthorne and Murphy-O'Connor. By considering the wider textual context, it is more reasonable to argue that Paul first addresses the issue of sexual immorality (6:12–18); he then shifts his

---

[84] Conzelmann (1975:112) argues the opposite: the focus of community in 3:16 is now transferred to the individual.

[85] For example, Fee (1987:263–264), Collins (1999:249–250), and Fitzmyer (2008:269–270) support this view. Thiselton (2000:474) defines the singular form of σῶμα as the distributive singular.

[86] He explains that the term is used in parallel with the temple, which points to the corporate dimension. Furthermore, the genitive pronoun can be interpreted as appositional, meaning "the Body that you are members," with the allusion to the corporate Body of Christ. He deduces his argument from a similar usage in contemporary Greek literature. Finally, he claims that the phrase τὸ ἴδιον σῶμα (one's own body) in the preceding verse does carry a corporate allusion (Kempthorne 1968:568–574).

[87] Fitzmyer suggests that σῶμα in 6:19 connotes the physical body, and σῶμα in 6:20 points to a corporate reference. Although Fitzmyer is ambiguous and inconsistent in his conclusion, he pinpoints this corporate connotation by arguing that the plural ὑμῶν (your) is used to encourage the Corinthians to honour God in a "corporate" manner, and the singular form emphasises the individual conduct of honouring.

focus by providing a teaching regarding the impact of sexual immorality on the Christian community (6:19–20). The concluding remark of this passage (6:20), δοξάσατε δὴ τὸν θεὸν ἐν τῷ σώματι ὑμῶν (Therefore glorify God with your body)*, should also be understood accordingly. To sum up, the immediate context of 6:12–20 concerns immoral conjugal union; the ultimate concern of the apostle, however, is in fact for the community which is denoted by the true singular σῶμα.

Second, this combination only occurs in 6:19 and 6:20 in the whole discourse. In the only two occurrences of σῶμα combining with ὑμῶν (your) in other authentic Pauline epistles, σῶμα is in plural form.[88] There is no credible evidence that shows that the distributive singular for σῶμα in the abnormal singular construct is Paul's common practice (Chen 2015:114–118). I argue that the usage of a singular σῶμα is a deliberate act with a particular purpose.

Third, in the preceding context, 6:14 in particular, the replacement of σῶμα by ἡμᾶς (us) suggests the synonymous nature of the two words. If ἡμᾶς (us) is deliberately employed by Paul to convey the communal focus in 6:14, it would be natural for him to use the singular σῶμα in 6:19–20 to highlight the same point. Since the concept of coherence is prominent according to discourse analysis, σῶμα, in place of ἡμᾶς (us), is employed by the apostle to help his readers to perceive the corporate connotation highlighted in his written message.

One of the most recent and revolutionary explanations regarding this combination is given by Gupta. Although in favour of the distributive singular, he suggests two speculative possibilities. First, Paul attempts to create a "more direct engagement with the readers by addressing the whole but communicating vividly to the individual." Second, Paul draws attention "to the corporate while speaking particularly about each individual." After considering the singular/plural oscillation in the context, Gupta (2010:531) argues that 6:19 demonstrates Paul's concern for both the embodied person and the corporate body. Of interest, Gupta's conclusion repudiates his own assumption of the distributive singular. According to his interpretation, σῶμα appears as a true singular noun instead of a distributive singular noun, since he speculates that the singular σῶμα highlights the corporate connotation of a community and the plural pronoun emphasises the individual within the community. Thus, Gupta's identification of the distributive singular is incorrect while his speculative conclusion of the use of the singular σῶμα is accurate.

---

[88] This combination only occurs two times in the authentic Pauline epistles apart from 1 Corinthians. Furthermore, σῶμα is always in its plural form (Rom. 8:11, 12:1). If we take the first and the third person plural possessive pronouns into consideration, there is only one occurrence (Rom 1:24) of a plural form of σῶμα combining with a plural possessive pronoun.

In short, there are different sentence meanings behind each individual σῶμα in this semantic unit. However, the overall occurrence of σῶμα (as a cluster) demonstrates a corporate and communal connotation in Unit B.

3.2.1.2 Σῶμα (body) in Unit C

Σῶμα occurs three times in Unit C, and its distribution is shown in table 3.5.

Table 3.5. Σῶμα in Unit C "Marriage" (1 Cor 7:1–40)

7:1–19 Marriage	7:20–24 Slavery	7:25–40 Marriage
*		*
*		

Σῶμα occurs twice in close proximity in a sub-segment regarding marriage. In 7:4, by employing the phrase τοῦ ἰδίου σώματος οὐκ ἐξουσιάζει (she/he does not have authority of her/his own body) twice, Paul sets forth that a person should not deprive his or her marriage partner of conjugal rights. Σῶμα appears in 7:34; the context concerns a comparison between virgins/unmarried women and married women. On both occasions, the term simply alludes to sexual relations.

3.2.1.3 Σῶμα (body) in Unit D

Σῶμα occurs three times in Unit D, with two of its occurrences forming a cluster as shown in table 3.6. The clustered σῶμα displays a strong corporate and communal connotation, as explained below.

Table 3.6. Σῶμα in Unit D "Idolatry" (1 Cor 8:1–11:1)

8:1–13 Food and Idol	9:1–27 Freedom	10:1–11:1 Food and Idol
	*	*
		*

In Unit D, Paul warns the Corinthians against idolatry. He employs σῶμα in 9:27 to illiustrate self-discipline in the metaphor of boxing, as this metaphor appears in the wider context in which Paul discusses the use of freedom. More importnatly, he urges them not to partake in idol feasts (10:1–11:1). In 10:16, the phrase τοῦ σώματος τοῦ Χριστοῦ (the body of Christ) is introduced to portray the Eucharistic bread shared by the Corinthians. Then, Paul states in 10:17 that ἓν σῶμα οἱ πολλοί ἐσμεν (we who are many are one body)*. Obviously, σῶμα does not depict the physical body. In the clause ἓν σῶμα οἱ πολλοί ἐσμεν, there are two predicate nominatives: ἓν σῶμα (one body) and οἱ πολλοί (many). The two predicate nominatives are appositional in nature, with the implied ἡμεῖς (we) as the subject and ἐσμεν (are) as the verb. The contrastive nature between ἕν and πολλοί is employed here to denote the unity of the community.[89] Therefore, σῶμα in 10:17 carries a corporate reference, as the believers of the Corinthian community are portrayed as ἓν σῶμα (one body), highlighting the corporate unity.[90]

The close proximity between the phrase ἓν σῶμα (one body) and the previous phrase τὸ σῶμα τοῦ Χριστοῦ (the body of Christ) indicates a connection between the two. The bread shared by the community is described as the body of Christ, and intriguingly, the community is in return the one body.[91] This corporate and communal aspect is also accentuated by the two words in the context: κοινωνία (fellowship, 10:16) and μετέχομεν (we partake, 10:17). Both words emphasise the communal participation. The focus of community is again highlighted by the usage of σῶμα in this semantic unit. This concurs with the previous analysis of the macrostructure of 1 Corinthians.

3.2.1.4 Σῶμα (body) in Unit F

Σῶμα occurs three times in Unit F, appearing in a cluster (11:24–29) as shown in table 3.7. The corporate and communal connotation behind σῶμα is also evident, as detailed below.

---

[89] Collins (1999:380) also argues that unity is depicted by this phrase, and indicates that this motif is reiterated in chapter 12. Fee (1987:469) suggests the parallel between the clause ἓν σῶμα οἱ πολλοί ἐσμεν (we who are many are one body) and the following clause οἱ γὰρ πάντες ἐκ τοῦ ἑνὸς ἄρτου μετέχομεν (for we all share the one bread) is constructed in a chiastic structure. This parallel connects the common bread with the church community.

[90] As well argued by Murphy-O'Connor (2009:178–179), this σῶμα shows that Paul is conscious of the unity of the community that he alludes to the multiplicity of its members only in subordinate clauses.

[91] According to Fee (1987:469), the bread represents Christ's death. The eating of the bread symbolises that believers becomes partners in the redeemed community. Thiselton (2000:762) makes a similar comment, and argues that the communal aspect must not be minimised in this passage because communal participation in the identity and redemptive work of Christ is the focus. Of interest, Conzelmann (1975:172) sees the underlying emphasis of this passage is to encourage unity. Since Mitchell (1993:254–256) asserts that unity is the key theme of 1 Corinthians, she argues that raising the contrast between the cult meal and Eucharist is a means for Paul to deal with the Corinthian factions. The focus of community depicted in this segment is the common conclusion made by various scholars. As well summarised by Fitzmyer (2008:391), the connection of κοινωνία (fellowship) and σῶμα establishes the corporate sense of the ecclesiastical meaning of the phrase τοῦ σώματος τοῦ Χριστοῦ (the body of Christ).

Table 3.7. Σῶμα in Unit F "The Lord's Supper" (1 Cor 11:17–34)

11:17–22 The Problem	11:23–25 The Lord's Word	11:26–34 The Solution
	*	* *

The topic of this semantic unit is the Lord's Supper. The famous saying of Christ, τοῦτό μού ἐστιν τὸ σῶμα (this is my body), is quoted by Paul in 11:24 as he urges the Corinthians to be prudent in partaking in the Lord's Supper. The phrase does not seem to highlight any communal connotation, since it is uttered by Christ to elucidate his redemptive death. However, Paul provides an intriguing statement in 11:29: for the one who eats and drinks without discerning the body (μὴ διακρίνων τὸ σῶμα) eats and drinks judgement against himself.[92] The identification of τὸ σῶμα (the body) is not as straightforward as it seems to be. Some argue that σῶμα in 11:29 points to the Eucharistic bread; with the community being urged to discern (διακρίων) the sacred bread for Eucharist from the ordinary bread for normal feast. Or it denotes the body of Christ in the church, the presence of Christ in the church more specifically, as some argue.[93] As indicated by συνέρχεσθε (you come together)* in 11:17, the Lord's Supper is observed when the community gathers around. Given the wider textual context of this segment, the problem faced by the Corinthians does not merely concern the discernment of the Eucharistic bread; there are divisions. When Paul addresses the issue faced by the Corinthians gathered for Eucharist, he mentions "For in the first place, when you come together as a church I hear there are divisions (σχίσματα) among you" (11:18). The issue is clearly σχίσμα (division) instead of wrongly identifying the nature of the bread. As such, the clause διακρίων τὸ σῶμα (discern the body) does not illustrate the Eucharistic body, nor does it concern the presence of Christ. Rather, the clause should be understood as Paul urging the Corinthians to discern the gathering as the body of Christ, the church.[94] The focal point is not merely

---

[92] Some manuscripts have the reading τὸ σῶμα τοῦ κυρίου (the body of the Lord), including ℵ², C³, D, F, G and 1881c. Many important manuscripts, including the manuscripts of the Alexandrian text-type, support the absence of τοῦ κυρίου (the Lord), including P⁴⁶, ℵ, B, C, 33, 1739, and 1881.

[93] Fitzmyer (2008:446–447) provides a detailed account of how both views are understood by major commentators. He argues that the term means to take stock of oneself when receiving the body and blood of Christ. However, he fails to pinpoint the exact connotation of the term. Surburg (2000:212) combines the two views together, and argues that σῶμα connotes both the sacramental body and the ecclesiastical body.

[94] Many scholars adopt this view: Ciampa and Rosner 2010:555; Collins 1999:439; Robertson and Plummer 1929:252; Orr and Walther 1976:274; Horsley 1998:162; Hays 1997:200; Stanley 1876:203. Fee (1987:563) and Kim (2008:62) provide an

on the Eucharist. It emphasises unity, in contrast with σχίσμα (division).[95] In other words, σῶμα in Unit F alludes to the corporate unity and communal relationship.

3.2.1.5 Σῶμα (body) in Unit G

The most frequent occurrences of σῶμα in 1 Corinthians occur in Unit G "Spiritual Gifts." Σῶμα occurs nineteen times within three chapters, with eighteen of them forming a huge cluster in 12:12–27 as shown in table 3.8.

Table 3.8. Σῶμα in Unit G "Spiritual Gifts" (1 Cor 12:1–14:40)

12:1–31 Spiritual Gifts	13:1–13 Love	14:1–40 Spiritual Gifts
* ********** *** * * * **	*	

Within this cluster, the contrast between τὸ σῶμα ἕν (the body [is] one) and μέλη πολλά (many members) is repeated. For example, the clause τὸ σῶμα ἕν ἐστιν καὶ μέλη πολλὰ ἔχει (the body is one and yet has many members)* in 12:12 is followed by the clause τὸ σῶμα οὐκ ἔστιν ἕν μέλος ἀλλὰ πολλά (the body is not a single member, but many)* in 12:14. Then, he reiterates the concept in 12:20 by stating: δὲ πολλὰ μὲν μέλη, ἕν δὲ σῶμα (there are many members, but one body)*. Finally, Paul states his concluding remark of this segment in 12:27: Ὑμεῖς δέ ἐστε σῶμα Χριστοῦ καὶ μέλη ἐκ μέρους (Now you are Christ's body, and each of you is a member of it)*. The emphasis on ἕν (one) unequivocally highlights the corporate and communal essence connoted by σῶμα. Not only is the Corinthian community reminded of their identity being the body of Christ, the community is also urged to remember their unity. In the following part, the occurrences of σῶμα in 12:12–27 will be examined individually.

Paul commences the discussion of spiritual gifts by writing: "Now concerning the spiritual gifts" (12:1). Then he continues on the topic of gifts with the argument in 12:4–11: "Now there are different gifts, but the same Spirit."* He also provides a list of various spiritual gifts. Then, Paul compares the variety of gifts operating within the faith community with σῶμα. The clause Καθάπερ γὰρ τὸ σῶμα ἕν ἐστιν καὶ μέλη πολλὰ ἔχει in

---

insightful argument, suggesting that Paul rebukes the ideology of the powerful and the rich who abuse the poor. The body of Christ, as Kim notes, points to the living Christ crucified, who deconstructs the powers and reconstructs the community.

[95] Collins (1999:438–439) holds a similar view, and mentions that various Church Fathers quote 11:28 in their work to encourage ecclesial unity.

12:12 (For just as the body is one and yet has many members)* echoes a previous utterance in 10:17 in Unit D, ἓν σῶμα οἱ πολλοί ἐσμεν (we who are many are one body)*. The unity of a community portrayed by ἓν σῶμα (one body) re-emerges. ῝Εν σῶμα (one body) is further elaborated in 12:13, in which the contrastive elements, including Jews and Gentiles, slaves and the free, are employed to heighten the unity as portrayed by the clause, πάντες εἰς ἓν σῶμα ἐβαπτίσθημεν (we were all baptized into one body). Whether βαπτίζω (to baptise) denotes water baptism (pointing to the initial rite of entering into a Christian community) or common experience in the Holy Spirit (pointing to immersion as a metaphor), the unity of the Corinthian community is highlighted by the phrase πάντες εἰς ἓν σῶμα (baptized into one body) in either case.[96] Son rightly connects the phrase ἓν σῶμα (one body) in 12:12–20 to the earlier portrayal of the sexual union between a man and a prostitute. The sexual union between a man and a woman described in chapter 6 is in analogical parallel with the spiritual union between Christ and the church in chapter 12, since they both employ the phrase ἓν σῶμα (one body) to denote this union. The use of ἓν σῶμα (one body) marks the phenomenon that individual believers become corporately the body of Christ created by the Holy Spirit (Son 2001b:107–122). Then, he concludes that the usage of ἓν σῶμα illustrates the existence of a person: the existence of an individual person "extends beyond his individual boundaries to form a corporate unity (body) with others and with Christ" (ibid. 121). I concur with Son's conclusion, as it is obvious that σῶμα in 12:13 denotes the faith community and the use of ἓν σῶμα (one body) highlights the corporate connotation.

Scholarship offers a rich discussion of the meaning of σῶμα in 1 Corinthians 12.[97] Some focus on the function of σῶμα in the text, determining whether Paul uses it to promote unity or diversity.[98] Others focus on the communal aspect of σῶμα.[99] In the following discussion, I argue that

---

[96] For example, Collins (1999:604–605) and Barrett (1994:289) adopt the understanding of water baptism; Fee (1987:462–463) supports the metaphorical sense of the term. On the other hand, Neyrey (1986:157) notes that the body language in chapter 12 denotes wholeness and unity, whereas the Holy Spirit portrayed in this chapter functions to unify the cornucopia of gifts given to the body's diverse members.

[97] Jewett (1971:202–250) provides a detailed account of the views held by various scholars.

[98] This resembles Grice's utterer's meaning, which is the intended meaning of an author, and is implicated in the utterance of the author (Grice 1991:65).

[99] For example, Käsemann (1971:114–115) repudiates the understanding of σῶμα as an individual human self, and advocates that the concept behind the term points to the notion of believers being incorporated into the kingdom of Christ. Nonetheless, he also argues that the physical aspect of the human body must not be denied, since Christ uses our bodies to glorify God. The view of Käsemann on σῶμα is largely communal based, which is in accord with my own conclusion.

the word is employed to denote both the communal aspect and the call for unity despite the diversity.

As discussed above, the use of σῶμα in 12:12–14 is metaphorical, denoting the community. Paul temporarily switches the denotation of σῶμα to create an illustration. In 12:15–17, the word is employed to denote the physical body, describing the relationship of different organs, including foot, hand, ear, and eye with the body. The prepositional phrase ἐκ τοῦ σώματος (from the body) is repeated four times within the two verses, illustrating that organs, despite the differences, are part of the body. Paul temporarily shifts the denotation of σῶμα from a metaphorical one, illustrating a faith community (12:12–14), to an ontological one, signifying the physical body (12:15–17) as a means to vividly explain the concept of unity. Paul argues that it is necessary to have differences in order to carry out different functions (as he explains in 12:17), and asks two rhetorical questions (If the whole body were an eye, what part would do the hearing? If the whole were an ear, what part would exercise the sense of smell?). Following this explanation, Paul subtly shifts the denotation of σῶμα back to denote a community in 12:18. In 12:18, the clause, "But as a matter of fact, God has placed each of the members in the body just as he decided"* no longer concerns the physical body. The subject is now changed to God. Σῶμα in 12:18 refers back to the faith community (body is not a single member, but many) mentioned in 12:14. Then, in 12:19 Paul uses a similar rhetorical question as in the case of 12:17. However, the content is no longer related to the physical body: εἰ δὲ ἦν τὰ πάντα ἓν μέλος, ποῦ τὸ σῶμα; (if they were all the same member, where would the body be?)*. Of interest, the phrase εἰ δὲ... ποῦ (but if... where) is the exact wording used in 12:17. Nonetheless, σῶμα in 12:19 denotes the community, and μέλος (member) refers to the individual Christians within it. Following a thorough exposition, Paul summarises his argument in 12:20 by reiterating δὲ πολλὰ μὲν μέλη, ἓν δὲ σῶμα (So now there are many members, but one body)*. The expression πολλὰ μέλη, ἓν σῶμα (many members, one body)* has been repeated three times in a similar manner (12:12, 14, 20).

Subsequently, Paul focuses on the specifics regarding the members of the one body. In 12:22, Paul introduces an argument regarding "those members that seem to be weaker"*. However, the connotation of σῶμα throughout its occurrences in 12:22–23 remains unchanged. The term clearly denotes the community in which there are weaker members (μέλη τοῦ σώματος ἀσθενέστερα, in 12:22), less honourable members (ἀτιμότερα εἶναι τοῦ σώματος, in 12:23a), and less respectable members (τὰ ἀσχήμονα ἡμῶν, in 12:23b).[100] Despite the varieties, Paul argues in 12:24 that ὁ θεὸς συνεκέρασεν τὸ σῶμα (God has blended together the body)*. The purpose of

---

[100] Fitzmyer (2008:480) defines the triple comparison, ἀσθενέστερα (weaker), ἀτιμότερα (less honourable), and ἀσχήμονα (less presentable) in 12:22–23, as the alpha-privative adjectives, one of positive degree and two of comparative degree.

God's arrangement, according to the apostles, is explained in 12:25 by the ἵνα clause, ἵνα μὴ ᾖ σχίσμα ἐν τῷ σώματι (so that there may be no division in the body)*. This phrase echoes the almost exact same phrase μὴ ᾖ ἐν ὑμῖν σχίσματα (so that there may be no divisions among you) in 1:10, located in the first verse of the first semantic unit (Unit A).[101] The significance of this echo is as follows. First, the word σχίσμα (division) does not occur in the Pauline epistles except here.[102] Second, the position of the almost exact same phrase in both the beginning and the end of the epistle is not a mere coincidence. It is in accordance with how σῶμα is presented in the whole discourse. In Unit A, Paul addresses the issue of church division, the σχίσμα (division). Various topics are then discussed by Paul in different semantic units. However, in the midst of these semantic units the concept of community alluded to by σῶμα is gradually developed. When it comes to the seventh major semantic unit (Unit G), the key concept of ἓν σῶμα (one body) is thoroughly elaborated. This concept is the key to address the issue of σχίσμα (division).

Following his discussion on the concept of many members within one body and the purpose of God's arrangement, Paul proceeds to provide a powerful summative statement in 12:27, Ὑμεῖς δέ ἐστε σῶμα Χριστοῦ καὶ μέλη ἐκ μέρους (Now you are Christ's body, and each of you is a member of it)*. The community, despite having different μέλη (members), is one body of Christ. The phrase σῶμα Χριστοῦ (body of Christ) in this summative statement unequivocally denotes the faith community, emphasising its corporate nature. The phrase is followed by a detailed description of different offices and gifts operated in the church (12:28–31), before the apostle pinpoints the most important gift of all: love (13:1–13). Σῶμα no longer occurs after 12:27 except one time in 13:3, in which the term is employed to denote the physical body. Paul argues that "If I give away everything I own, and if I give over my body in order to boast, but do not have love, I receive no benefit."* Σῶμα in 13:3 does not carry any communal and corporate reference.

In conclusion, the nineteen occurrences of σῶμά in this semantic unit, 12:12–27 in particular, are mainly employed by Paul to elucidate the faith

---

[101] The only minor difference between the two phrases is that σχίσμα (division) is singular in 12:25 and plural in 1:10.

[102] Some scholars suggest that the usage of σχίσμα (division) alludes to the presence of a political element as the word is used in the Hellenistic era to denote political fissure. Welborn (1987:85–111) argues that the word is used to portray a cleft in political consciousness. Fitzmyer (2008:141) notes that the verb derived from σχίσμα (division) is employed by contemporary historians to portray the conflicts between city and states in the Greco-Roman world. Mitchell (1993:68–77) suggests that the four phrases, τὸ αὐτὸ λέγειν (to say the same thing), μὴ ᾖ ἐν ὑμῖν σχίσματα (there may be no divisions in you), ἦτε δὲ κατηρτισμένοι ἐν τῷ αὐτῷ νοΐ (you would be united in the same mind), and ἐν τῇ αὐτῇ γνώμῃ (in the same purpose), all carry a heavy political sense in contemporary Greek literature.

community of Christ, highlighting the communal relationship and calling for corporate unity.

3.2.1.6 Σῶμα (body) in Unit H

As shown in table 3.9, there are nine occurrences of σῶμα in Unit H. Again, a cluster can be observed. Although the term clearly carries anthropological connotations, the nuance of the corporate aspect of σῶμά in Unit H must not be overlooked, as explained below.

Table 3.9. Σῶμα in Unit H "Resurrection" (1 Cor 15:1–58)

15:1–32 Resurrection	15:33–34[a] Bad Company	15:35–58 Resurrection
		* ** * *
		* * *
		*

[a]15:33–34 displays a digression in the discussion of the resurrection. In the first subdivision, Paul addresses the issue of resurrection: how can some of you say there is no resurrection of the dead? (15:12). Then, he digresses, and warns the Corinthians against "bad company" (15:33). Finally, he resumes the discussion of resurrection: "But someone will say, 'How are the dead raised? With what kind of body will they come?'"(15:35). This digression becomes the centre of the chiasm in 1 Cor 15.

The last cluster of σῶμα in 1 Corinthians occurs in Unit H, in which Paul discusses the topic of resurrection. This cluster is big, with σῶμα occurring nine times in a relatively short range, 15:35–44. In 15:35, Paul responds to the question which inquires about the nature of the resurrected σῶμα. By employing the analogy of a seed, Paul explains the nature of this σῶμα in 15:37–38. Then, σῶμα is used in 15:40 to portray heavenly bodies (celestial objects) and earthly bodies (creatures on earth). Finally, in 15:44, Paul distinguishes between σῶμα ψυχικόν (natural body) and σῶμα πνευματικόν (spiritual body). Σῶμα ψυχικόν (natural body) denotes the physical body that a believer has on earth; and σῶμα πνευματικόν (spiritual body) denotes the body that believers have when ἐγείρεται (it is raised). Paul does not elaborate on the nature of σῶμα πνευματικόν (spiritual body) despite providing the comparison between the two kinds of body.[103] More importantly,

---

[103] There has been an ongoing attempt to understand this ambiguous phrase σῶμα πνευματικόν (spiritual body). Several decades ago, there was definition by Schweizer (1968:389–415) in light of ancient Gnosticism, and argument by Conzelmann (1975:282–287) according to the antithesis of ψυχικόν-πνευματικόν (natural-spiritual). For the last ten years, various scholars have been contributing to this discussion. For examople, Dunn (2002:4–18), in his lengthy comments on Thiselton's view, suggests that σῶμα πνευματικόν (spiritual body) is a body that will not be subject to death and decay, a body that is beyond the reach of corruption

he aims to repudiate the denial of future resurrection. Paul concludes this major semantic unit by highlighting the immortality that is brought forth by the resurrection. Hence, the individual occurrence of σῶμα in this unit does not denote the corporate and communal connotation.

Nonetheless, there is one particular nuance worth noting. Paul, in 15:35, anticipates a question asked by some people who respond to his teaching of resurrection: πῶς ἐγείρονται οἱ νεκροί; ποίῳ δὲ σώματι ἔρχονται; (How are the dead raised? With what kind of body will they come?)*. Of interest, the singular σῶμα is used with a third person plural verb, ἔρχονται (they come). None of the reviewed commentators notice this nuance.[104] Thiselton (2000:1261) and Fee (1987:780) do discuss the possible parallel between νεκροί (the dead) and σώματι (body). If these two words are indeed in parallel, then the contrast of comparing a plural οἱ νεκροί (the dead) and a singular σώματι (body) becomes even more peculiar. Despite failing to notice this nuance and providing a clear explanation, Horsley (1998:209) argues that σῶμα is the principle of continuity, referring to a social-political life of resurrection in which it requires embodied people.

I argue that Paul leaves traces of a corporate connotation in his usage of σῶμα, despite his teaching focusing on the resurrected body. This can be supported by the wider textual context. The discussion of resurrection does not begin in Unit H. Paul briefly mentions the future resurrection in Unit B: "The body (τὸ σῶμα) is not for sexual immorality, but for the Lord, and the Lord for the body (τῷ σώματι). Now God indeed raised the Lord and he will raise us (ἡμᾶς) by his power."* The corporate connotation of σῶμα is subtly alluded to in this verse, indicated by the replacement of σῶμα with ἡμᾶς (us). In light of the discourse coherence previously discussed, it is possible that Paul subtly adopts the corporate connotation and communal aspect of σῶμα underlined in Unit B and 'mildly' employs it in his discussion of resurrection in Unit H. In other words, Paul leaves some kind of trails in his usage of σῶμα in Unit H, which carries an undertone of this corporate connotation.

---

and atrophy. Endsjø (2008:417–436) provides one of the most recent contributions. Although he does not analyse this phrase, his focuses on the wider issue to explain why the Corinthians refuse to believe in the general resurrection of the dead. His study is based on some ancient Greek stories of resurrection, which can provide further insights into understanding σῶμα πνευματικόν (spiritual body). However, I do not provide a detailed analysis to uncover the meaning of this phrase. My focus aims to ascertain the thematic meaning of σῶμα in 1 Corinthians. In other words, rather than providing a thorough analysis of the sentence meaning of σῶμα πνευματικόν (spiritual body), I focus on discourse coherence indicated by the recurrent theme of σῶμα and resurrection in 1 Corinthians.

[104] They include Collins, Orr and Walther, Robertson and Walther, Ciampa and Rosner, Fitzmyer, Murphy-O'Connor, Conzelmann, Thiselton, Fee, and Horsley.

3.2.2 Sociolinguistic aspect

The sociolinguistic aspect involves an investigation of the relationship between the author and the audience to ascertain whether the relationship can provide any further insights regarding the content of a discourse. Notably, in analysing the form of the Pauline epistles, Luther Stirewalt Jr. (2003:113) argues that Paul combines the forms and functions of personal and official letter writing of the Greco-Roman era so that he addresses the community as the corporate body that worshipped, confessed, educated, and disciplined together. In the following part, I explore the different forms of relationship between Paul and the Corinthians.

3.2.2.1 Apostle and teacher

Paul begins his letter by stating that he is κλητὸς ἀπόστολος Χριστοῦ Ἰησοῦ (called to be an apostle of Christ Jesus)*, a phrase that asserts his authority as an apostle over the Corinthians. When he commences his first major semantic unit, he begins with Παρακαλῶ δὲ ὑμᾶς (but I urge you) in 1:10. This phrase is a common literary device in Hellenistic letters. However, Hellenistic rulers or people with authority would not use such a polite expression. Instead, they would directly command their audience. In light of this, Paul appears to be "distinctly polite" whilst refraining from commanding the audience (Conzelmann 1975:31). As previously mentioned in the macrostructure, Paul does not simply deal with the schism within the community; otherwise, he could have used a more assertive approach by formally commanding the Corinthians. The apostle also calls for unity between some members of the community and himself. His polite tone fits his message which attempts to "deconstruct the ideologies of powers" (Kim 2008:38), which is the cause of the schism, by demonstrating an enormous humility. This is evident in his appeal to the Corinthians in 2:1–6, in which he describes his arrival at the Corinthian community "in weakness and in fear and with much trembling" (2:3). This portrayal is far from the authoritarian tone delivered by an ancient ruler.

As an apostle, Paul carries the role of a teacher. Winter (2001:32–39) provides some valuable insights regarding the teacher-student relationship in the first century. He argues that teachers in the first century "competed among themselves for students" (ibid. 36). Furthermore, students displayed loyalty to their teachers, since they were "encouraged to be extremely zealous" in showing their loyalty (ibid. 39). This finding sheds light on the unrest described in 1:12–17. Some members in the community attempt to display exceptional loyalty and zeal towards their own teacher (such as Apollos, Cephas, or another teacher) by rejecting Paul's authority. This contributes to the internal schism and the rejection of Paul's apostolic ministry.

3.2.2.2 Brother in Christ

The vocative ἀδελφοί (brothers) occurs 20 times in this letter.[105] Among all the authentic Pauline letters, this is the most frequent occurrence.[106] This provides insights into the socio-dynamic relationship between Paul and his readers, reflecting his underlying intention. He could have heavily exerted his apostleship in the epistle. Instead, he appeals to the Corinthians as "brothers," a more egalitarian address. In responding to issues of division and the rejection of his authority, the use of the vocative ἀδελφοί (brothers) emphasises the communal relationship over authority. In a community of Christ, everyone is equal. This attitude is the solution to the fractures and strife that trouble the community.

3.2.2.3 Parent-founder

Paul addresses the Corinthians by calling them "my dear children" (4:14), which reflects another dimension of their relationship. In Paul's time, the key elements of the parent-child relationship were authority, imitation, affection, and education (Mihaila 2009:177). The imitation element is evident in 4:16 and 11:1 when Paul calls for their imitation to "correct the Corinthians' behaviour, and to regain their allegiance" (Fiore 2003:241). Furthermore, the authority element is evident when Paul portrays himself as the builder in 3:10, "asserting for himself a place of priority" (Polaski 1999:110). Paul expects the Corinthian community to respect and obey him (Holmberg 1980:78). The expression of these elements allows Paul to address the challenges to his apostolicity. On the other hand, the affection element enables Paul to convey his care for the Corinthian community, a display of love, which is the key solution to a divided community.[107]

In summary, when considering the sociolinguistic aspect, it is not difficult to see how Paul uses various relational expressions to call for unity, a unity not merely prescribed to resolve the schism within the community. The apostle also calls for unity between the community and himself.

---

[105] The occurrences of the vocative ἀδελφοί (brothers) are as follows: 1:10, 11, 26; 2:1; 3:1; 4:6; 7:24, 29; 10:1; 11:33; 12:1; 14:6, 20, 26, 39; 15:1, 31, 50, 58; 16:15. In NT scholarship, some scholars do not consider the vocative to be a real case and treat many vocatives in NT texts as nominatives of direct address (Wallace 1996:56; Porter 1994:86–88). I acknowledge this divided opinion. However, whether vocative is identified as a valid case (the position that I hold) or a nominative for direct address, its usage still illustrates Paul's egalitarian approach.

[106] The vocative ἀδελφοί (brothers) occurs ten times in Romans and three times in 2 Corinthians. 1 Thessalonians is the only other epistle that dsplays an unusually frequent occurrence of the vocative, in which it occurs 14 times (with only five chapters).

[107] The topic of love is beautifully expressed in 1 Cor 13.

3.3 Thematic meaning of σῶμα

The dominant occurrences of σῶμα in various semantic units in 1 Corinthians connote social and corporate dimensions. I, therefore, argue that the key thematic meaning of σῶμα intended by Paul in the epistle is communal. The thematic meaning of this anthropological term is in accordance with the macrostructure of the epistle and the sociolinguistic aspect. The macrostructure shows that the central theme of the epistle concerns communal relationship and corporate unity (within the community), and the relationship between Paul and the community. The sociolinguistic aspect also confirms that various expressions by the apostle call for this communal relationship. The following section addresses the discourse flow, and how σῶμα fits into the epistle.

3.3.1 The flow of discourse

As I have previously discussed, a narrative discourse displays a flow, involving the progress of various stages towards a climax or a peak episode. This peak is defined as "a zone of turbulence" (Longacre 1983:38), and is characterised by a shift in the occurrence of a grammatical device, including a lexical device.[108] This discourse flow also occurs in non-narrative texts, wherein the peak is known as an expository climax. Through the application of statistical models, Terry determines that the climax in 1 Corinthians occurs in chapters 12–15.[109]

In this chapter, drawing on the analysis of σῶμα found in various semantic units, I observe a similar "flow." In Unit A, church division is a key issue, and appears as the first "episode." The communal connotations of σῶμα in subsequent "episodes," ἒν σῶμα (one body) in 1 Cor 12 finally emerges as the "climax." This climax or peak is characterised by a shift in the proportion of use of two grammatical devices: the unusually frequent occurrence of σῶμα (nineteen occurrences in Unit G), and the exceptionally frequent occurrence of the vocative ἀδελφοί (brothers), with the vocative mostly

---

[108] For further discussion of discourse flow, see § 2.3.2.2.

[109] The large number of verbless clauses starting from 1 Cor 12 and the change of text type in 1 Cor 15 (from hortatory to persuasive, indicated by a sudden lack of imperatives) indicate a "zone of grammatical turbulence" (Terry 1995:120–121). Similarly, in an analysis of James, the peak of the letter (4:7–10) is identified by illustrating a zone of grammatical turbulence (Terry 1992:121–123). Other scholars also demonstrate discourse flow and the peak episode in other expository writings. For instance, in an examination of Malachi, Taylor and Clendenen propose a "more unified, verifiable, and satisfying" structure by adopting Longacre's theory of discourse structure. They argue that the "third address" (3:7–24) is the climax of the book, pointing out its unique textual arrangement (Taylor and Clendenen 2004:229–231). The recent discourse analysis of Romans by Lee (2010:442–443) also shows the existence of flow and a peak episode in the letter.

occurring in Units G and H. The discourse then proceeds to its dénouement, the mentioning of σῶμα in the topic of the resurrection with a subtle communal nuance pointing to the communal aspect (15:35). Despite the seemingly diverse topics discussed in 1 Corinthians covered in this epistle, there is a central, yet covert theme running throughout the whole discourse. The flow of discourse can be observed by examining the usage of σῶμα throughout the epistle, as shown in figure 3.2.

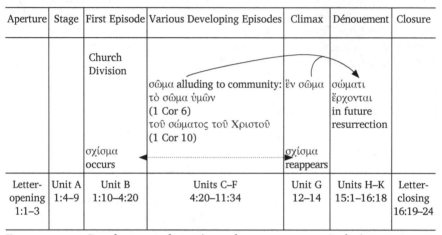

Aperture	Stage	First Episode	Various Developing Episodes	Climax	Dénouement	Closure
		Church Division	σῶμα alluding to community: τὸ σῶμα ὑμῶν (1 Cor 6) τοῦ σώματος τοῦ Χριστοῦ (1 Cor 10)	ἓν σῶμα	σώματι ἔρχονται in future resurrection	
		σχίσμα occurs		σχίσμα reappears		
Letter-opening 1:1–3	Unit A 1:4–9	Unit B 1:10–4:20	Units C–F 4:20–11:34	Unit G 12–14	Units H–K 15:1–16:18	Letter-closing 16:19–24

Key: ──────▶ : Development of prominent theme; ◀·······▶ : Inclusio

Figure 3.2. The flow of discourse of 1 Corinthians based on σῶμα.

3.4 Conclusion

By applying the basic principles of discourse analysis, I have analysed the usage of σῶμα in 1 Corinthians. I have not provided a detailed analysis of all individual occurrences of σῶμα. Also, the lexical meaning or sentence meaning have not been my primary concern. Instead, I have focused on the thematic meaning, which is conveyed by an author through the recurrent use of a word throughout a discourse.

Through an exploration of the discourse structure, the overall occurrences of clustered σῶμα in various semantic units, and the sociolinguistic aspect, I conclude that social and corporate connotations are present in the thematic meaning of σῶμα in 1 Corinthians. This communal interpretation is particularly illustrated by the body of Christ and ἓν σῶμα (one body), and well-established and widely accepted in Pauline scholarship. Thus, I demonstrate the value of discourse analysis in ascertaining and verifying this understanding of σῶμα in 1 Corinthians.

4

Anthropological terms
in Philippians

4.0 Introduction

In this chapter, I conduct Stage II of our analysis — multiple anthropo-logical terms within a single discourse: the key anthropological terms in Philippians. I investigate the terms ψυχή (soul), πνεῦμα (spirit), καρδία (heart), and σῶμα (body) to ascertain the presence of any social and corporate connotations. As in chapter 3, I initially identify the discourse structure of Philippians, which provides a framework for analysing the anthropological terms.

4.1 Discourse structure

To examine the discourse structure of Philippians and elucidate its major semantic units, I investigate the discourse markers, exploring the discourse coherence, and ascertaining the macrostructure of the epistle. However, before proceeding it is important for us to review a significant issue, regarding the integrity of Philippians.

4.1.1 The unity of Philippians

The application of discourse analysis assumes that each Pauline epistle is one single discourse. Since the integrity of Philippians has been challenged, it is important to review the issue of unity.

The partition theory, also known as the compilation theory, originated in nineteenth-century German scholarship.[1] This theory suggests that Philippians is the result of the redaction of two or more Pauline letters. For example, early proponent J. E. Symes, in his 1914 work, argues that the epistle comprises five letters (Jones 1918:xlii). This theory became prominent in the mid-twentieth century, and Philippians was considered a combination of two or three letters because of inherent irregularities.[2]

This theory was later vigorously repudiated by modern scholars on three grounds. First, there is no textual tradition, from manuscripts to patristic allusions, supporting the circulation of different portions of Philippians.[3] Second, the method of redaction makes the epistle more convoluted, which

---

[1] Reed (1997:125–131) provides a detailed account of the history of this theory.

[2] The main irregularities used to support the partition theory are as follows. First, there is an unusual disjuncture in 3:1. Τὸ λοιπόν ἀδελφοί μου χαίρετε ἐν κυρίῳ (Finally, my brothers and sisters, rejoice in the Lord) can be interpreted as "Finally, brothers, farewell in the Lord." Since a similar phrase also appears at the end of the Corinthian epistle (2 Cor. 13:11), this phrase in 3:1 is interpreted as marking the end of a letter. However, 3:1 occurs in the middle of Philippians instead of the end. This anomaly is further supported by the sudden change of tone, from a joyful tone in 3:1 to a harsh tone in 3:2 (Beare 1959:3–5). Second, 4:10–20 is an expression of thanks that is abruptly included at the end of Philippians. Since this content is alienated from its previous context, this is interpreted as a separate letter (Beare 1959:149–150; Murphy-O'Connor 1996:216–217). Third, there is external evidence proving that Paul sent multiple letters to the Philippians. In Polycarp's letter (ΠΡΟΣ ΦΙΛΙΠΠΗΣΙΟΨΣ B), he mentions to the Philippians the letters sent by Paul, τοῦ μακαρίου καὶ ἐνδόξου Παύλου ... ὑμῖν ἔγραψεν ἐπιστολάς (the blessed and glorifed Paul... he wrote letters to you) in 3:2. The plural ἐπιστολάς (letters) indicates more than one letter (Harrison 1936:329; Hansen 2009:17). Therefore, based on these irregularities and on the external evidence of more than one letter from Paul to the Philippians, the current form of Philippians is the result of redaction, which combines several letters into one. For example, Beare (1959:4–5) argues that Philippians comprises a letter of thanks (4:10–20), a letter despatched with Epaphroditus on his return to Philippi (1:1–3:1; 4:2–9, 21–23), and a letter of interpolation containing two warnings (3:2–4:1).

[3] According to Hansen (2009:17), although Polycarp does mention ὑμῖν ἔγραψεν ἐπιστολάς (he wrote letters to you), the plural ἐπιστολάς (letters) can be otherwise explained: the plural noun was sometimes employed in Greek for an important letter; the plural noun might refer to other Pauline letters; or the plural might refer to another letter sent to the Philippians, as alluded to in Philippians 3:2.

violates the spirit of redaction.[4] Third, the thematic unity of Philippians is well illustrated by common themes that appear throughout.[5] Many modern NT scholars support the unity of Philippians, including Moisés Silva, Gordon Fee, Bonnie Thurston, Ralph Martin, and Walter Hansen.[6]

If Philippians comprises several letters, it would not be possible to apply some basic principles of discourse analysis. For example, the notion of coherence depends on the epistle being one single discourse with a perceptible flow intended by the author. Nonetheless, given that most modern scholars soundly support the unity of Philippians, I also confidently support the unity and integrity of the epistle. The findings of an analysis, regarding the thematic prominence, lexical cohesion, and discourse flow, provide further proof of unity.

4.1.2 Discourse markers

I identify four discourse markers that demarcate the semantic units in Philippians: change of verb mood, use of the vocative, formulas,[7] and lexical cohesion. Due to the transitional role of these discourse markers, they may indicate the boundary of a major or minor semantic unit.[8]

4.1.2.1 Change of verb mood

The change of verb mood is a linguistic clue for marking the boundary of a semantic unit. The imperative mood is generally used for command and

---

[4] For example, Hawthorne (1983:xxix–xxxii) questions why the supposed compilation makes the epistle so convoluted, given that redaction usually aims to create a neat piece of work.

[5] For example, Jewett (1970:40–53) identifies six indicators of the unity of Philippians. He suggests that the most powerful indicator is the strong connection between the epistolary thanksgiving in 1:3–11 and the subsequent sections. Garland (1985:141–173) compares the phrase in 3:1 with the phrase in 4:4, Χαίρετε ἐν κυρίῳ πάντοτε· πάλιν ἐρῶ, χαίρετε (Rejoice in the Lord always. Again I say, rejoice). He argues that χαίρετε (rejoice), when combined with ἐν κυρίῳ (in the Lord), always means rejoice instead of good-bye in the epistle. Other common themes that appear throughout the epistle include the encouragement to stand firm, the call to humility, and Paul's joyful confidence in the Philippians (Garland 1985:157).

[6] For details of their arguments, see Silva 1992:14–15; Fee 1995:398–400; Thurston and Ryan 2005:30–33; Hansen 2009:15–19; Martin 1989:10–21. Despite this support for the unity of Philippians, the partition theory has advocates in modern scholarship. For example, Reumann (2008:12–13) suggests that the epistle combines three letters in C.E. 90–100.

[7] As mentioned in chapter 3, a formula is the combination of specific grammatical or lexical forms which is used repeatedly in a discourse or multiple discourses by the same author to mark a new topic. For example, the special conjunctive phrase περὶ δὲ (now concerning), and the special conjunctive formula verb-δέ-pronoun, are considered two formulas that function as discourse markers in 1 Corinthians.

[8] A major semantic unit is a new topic discussed in a discourse. Within each major semantic unit there may be sub-divisions that are called minor semantic units.

exhortation although it can sometimes be employed to express a request or a concession (Robertson 1934:946–947; Blass and Debrunner 1961:195). The occurrence of the imperative is approximately ten times less than that of the indicative and slightly less than that of the subjunctive in the NT.[9] The investigation into the occurrence of the imperative mood, given its smallness in number, may indicate whether there is a significant change of discussion within a discourse.[10]

There are 26 imperative verbs in Philippians.[11] Table 4.1 shows the spatial distribution of individual occurrences.

Table 4.1. The occurrences of imperative in Philippians

	Chapter 1	Chapter 2	Chapter 3	Chapter 4
Imperative as indicated by *	* *	****** **	*** ** *	******** **

As shown in table 4.1, the imperative verbs appear in three main clusters: 1:27–2:18; 2:29–3:2; 4:1–9. They occur throughout the segment of 1:27–2:18, with eight imperative verbs occurring within 22 verses. Nine imperative verbs are found within nine verses in 4:1–9. The imperatives also appear in high density within four verses in 2:29–3:2.

In 1:27–2:18, Paul encourages the Philippians by providing an example of Christ.[12] The focus of this segment is different from the previous one (1:12–26) in which Paul discusses his imprisonment. Hence, 1:27–2:18 is a semantic unit marked by the use of imperatives. In 4:1, the conjunction

---

[9] The significance of the imperative mood is also detailed by Fantin (2010:6–8) who argues that the mood is generally neglected in scholarship (Wallace 1996:447).

[10] The first person plural subjunctive, which is also called the hortatory subjunctive, is a common usage in exhortation (Wallace 1996:464). However, the hortatory subjunctive only occurs once in Philippians (3:15). Hence, I do not include the subjunctive.

[11] 1:27 (twice); 2:2, 5, 12, 14, 18 (twice), 29 (twice); 3:1, 2 (thrice), 17 (twice); 4:1, 3, 4 (twice), 5, 6 (twice), 8, 9, 21. There is no imperative used in the letter-opening (1:1–2) and the letter-closing (4:21–23).

[12] The segment 2:5–11 is widely considered an early Christian hymn. For instance, Martin (1997:24–41) provides a detailed literary analysis of 2:5–11 in the history of NT studies, in which he cities different reasons why the section is regarded by many as a hymn. Hansen (2009:122–127) also provides his argument for the hymnal structure of this section. However, not everyone is convinced by the hymnal nature although Martin does not deny the poetic essence of the passage (Fee 1995:192–194). The focus of my analysis is not to determine whether it is a hymn. Instead, the focus is on a topic in Unit D (2:19–30) as shown later in 4.1.3, which is undoubtedly the example of Christ.

Ὥστε (therefore) is employed to conclude the previous discussion as Paul proceeds to discuss a new topic: the issue of Euodia and Syntyche in 4:2. 4:2–9, therefore, is likely to be a semantic unit. Finally, the concentrated imperatives in 2:29–3:2 are an indicator of a shift between two semantic units. Prior to 3:1, the discussion focuses on Timothy and Epaphroditus. The discussion is then shifted to mention τοὺς κύνας (the dogs) in 3:2.

Given these observations, it is possible to identify the boundaries of a few semantic units, namely 1:27–2:18, 4:2–9, and two semantic units divided by 3:1.[13]

4.1.2.2 Vocative

The second discourse marker is the usage of vocative. The following part examines the usage of the vocative ἀδελφοί (brothers),[14] which occurs six times in Philippians: 1:12; 3:1, 13, 17; 4:1, 8. Most of these occurrences are used to begin a new topic.

In 1:12, Paul addresses the Philippians using the vocative: ἀδελφοί. He then discusses his own imprisonment in 1:12–26.[15] Therefore, ἀδελφοί, combined with the special conjunctive formula (verb-δέ-pronoun), which was discussed in chapter 3,[16] begins a new topic.

In 3:1, ἀδελφοί is combined with Τὸ λοιπόν (finally).[17] In 3:1, Paul begins to warn the Philippians against a problematic group by calling them dogs, evil workers, and the mutilated (3:2). Hence, the vocative marks this new discussion. This is also supported by the use of imperatives as mentioned above.

Both ἀδελφοί in 3:13 and 3:17 appear in the middle of Paul's argument regarding the warning against τοὺς κύνας (the dogs) by citing himself as an

---

[13] These identified units will be further confirmed when other discourse markers are reviewed.

[14] From this point onwards, the English translation, brother, for the term ἀδελφοί, is not provided in this chapter.

[15] White (1972:15–16) argues that the vocative is used in the Roman era as a marker to mark major transitions of the body of a letter. He provides some interesting examples, including γινώσκειν σε θέλω, μῆτηρ (I want to know you, mother) and φανερόν σοι ποιῶ, ἄδελφε (I make known to you, brother), which demonstrate a striking resemblance to Paul's utterance in 1:12. This vocative use is also discussed by Mullins (1964:44–50) who cites various examples in the Oxyrhynchus Papyri.

[16] Ἀδελφοί in 1:12, appearing in the formula γινώσκειν δὲ ὑμᾶς βούλομαι (but I wish you to know), is widely discussed by commentators (Fee 1995:106; Hansen 2009:65–66). Sanders (1962:348–362) provides numerous examples in Pauline letters by citing passages in Romans, 1 Corinthians, 2 Corinthians, Philippians, and 1 Thessalonians, showing that Paul frequently marks the beginning of a new discussion by employing this specific formula: the combination of a verb in the first person present tense, the conjunction δέ (but/and), the recipients denoted by ὑμᾶς (you), and the vocative ἀδελφοί.

[17] The function of τὸ λοιπόν (finally) as a marker will be discussed later.

example, his relationship with Christ in particular. The two vocatives, then, clearly do not function as a marker commencing a new topic. Rather, they are employed to make an emotional statement.[18] Paul proclaims that "I do not consider myself to have attained this...reaching out for the things that are ahead" (3:13), and he urges the Philippians to imitate him (3:17).

In 4:1, ἀδελφοί is combined with ὥστε (therefore). Without coupling with an infinitive, ὥστε (therefore) is usually an inferential particle. Resembling ὥς τέ (as so), it simply means "and so" (Moule 1959:144). As previously mentioned, 4:1 concludes the previous discussion, with ἀδελφοί marking the end of the topic discussed in chapter 3.

In 4:8, ἀδελφοί is used together with τὸ λοιπόν (finally). The clauses in 4:8–9 conclude the discussion of Euodia and Syntyche before moving to the last topic in the letter, in which the gift sent by the Philippians to Paul through Epaphroditus is the focus. This gift demonstrates the concern of the Philippians for Paul: τὸ ὑπὲρ ἐμοῦ φρονεῖν (to think for me) in 4:10.

An analysis of ἀδελφοί indicates that the vocatives in 1:12; 3:1; 4:1; 4:8 are discourse markers, delineating the boundaries of several semantic units.

4.1.2.3 Formulas

The formulaic praise in 1:3 and the use of τὸ λοιπόν (finally) in 3:1 and 4:8 are additional formulas which function as discourse markers, marking either the beginning or the end of several semantic units, as explained below.

Paul commences his first discussion, expressing his concern for the Philippians in his prayer (1:3–11). The clause Εὐχαριστῶ τῷ θεῷ μου (I give thanks to my God) in 1:3 appears to be a formula, marking the first discussion of a letter.[19]

Τὸ λοιπόν (finally) is an inferential conjunction formed by the combination of the article, τὸ (the), and the adverb, λοιπός (remaining).[20] The phrase means "from now" or "therefore."[21] The phrase is found in 3:1 and 4:8. There is little doubt that τὸ λοιπόν (finally) in 3:1 is one of the most discussed conjunctions in Philippians. The debate of the unity of the letter

---

[18] The use of vocative can sometimes express great emotion; for examples, see Matt 4:10; Mark 1:24; Luke 4:34; Acts 5:3; 1 Cor 15:55 (Wallace 1996:67–68).

[19] For example, the same clause in Rom 1:8 and Phlm 1:4 serves as a marker, commencing the first discussion in its respective letter.

[20] I call this conjunctive a formula due to the fact that it is peculiarly formed by the combination of an article and an adverb instead of any conjunctive particles.

[21] Both Turner (1963:336) and Thrall (1962:25–30) set forth that the conjunction has been weakened in Hellenistic Greek to a mere connective particle meaning "so." In the post-classical Greek, the conjunction usually serves as a transitional particle, either introducing a new line of thought or a logical conclusion (Blass and Debrunner 1961:235).

hinges on the peculiar location of this conjunction.[22] However, there is little dispute among those who support and repudiate the partition theory regarding the function of τὸ λοιπόν (finally) being as a marker which initiates a new topic in Philippians.[23]

As previously discussed, τὸ λοιπόν (finally) in 4:8 is used with ἀδελφοί to conclude the discussion commenced in 4:1 by providing a general exhortation.[24]

4.1.2.4 Lexical cohesion

Most commentators observe the frequency of χαίρω (to rejoice) throughout Philippians, which illustrates the motif of joy.[25] I particularly examine the unusual occurrence of a cluster of χαίρω (to rejoice), with two χαίρω appearing in close proximity, throughout the epistle.[26] The word is the

---

[22] As mentioned above, those who favour the partition theory argue that the conjunction means "finally," drawing a comparison between Philippians and 2 Corinthians in which Paul uses λοιπόν (remaining) to mark the end of his letter. This theory is vigorously repudiated by many modern scholars. For instance, some of them (Silva 1992:167) point out that τὸ λοιπόν (finally) does not always mean "finally", nor does it mark the end of a letter (1 Cor 1:16; 4:2; 7:29; and 1 Thess 4:1).

[23] Banker (1996:112) defines the function of this conjunction as a topic introducer in 3:1, and Fee (1995:286) identifies it as a framing device to highlight the section of 3:1 to 4:1. Hawthorne (1983:123–124) considers this conjunction marks a new section. The most insightful observation of all, however, is given by Reed (1996:83), who argues for the single-letter theory of Philippians by providing an intriguing observation regarding the hesitation formula used in the Hellenistic letters. By citing several examples he argues that λοιπόν (remaining) may be used as a discourse marker either at the beginning, middle, or end of a Hellenistic letter. When it is used in the middle of a letter, the word often concludes a previous narrative or list of commands with the final request, and usually commences a topic that is with respect to the future.

[24] Hawthorne (1983:185) argues that τὸ λοιπόν (finally) does not denote the end of the letter. Instead, it elucidates the imperative λογίζεσθε (consider) as the last imperative of all the imperatives in the section beginning at 4:1. On the other hand, Fee (1995:413–415), arguing that Philippians is a letter of friendship, suggests that Paul adds another set of exhortations. Similar to Hawthorne's view, τὸ λοιπόν (finally) signifies the final vocative in the hortatory dimension.

[25] The motif of joy, which is signified by the frequent occurrence of both χαίρω (to rejoice) and χαρά (joy), is widely observed in scholarly works, including modern critical commentaries (Thurston and Ryan 2005:33; Hawthorne 1983:17–19; Fee 1995:52–53; Reed 1997:333; Jewett 1970:52; Bockmuehl 1998:58–59; Silva 1992:46).

[26] Apart from χαίρω (to rejoice), the corresponding noun χαρά (joy), and corresponding verb συγχαίρω (to rejoice together), are considered. Halliday (2002:8) provides a succinct explanation, stating that the clearest form of lexical cohesion is demonstrated by two or more occurrences, in close proximity, of the same lexical item.

fourth most frequent verb in Philippians (see Appendix 2). Figure 4.1 shows the spatial distribution of these clusters.

#	**	#	#	*~ *~	*#*	# **	*
1:4	1:18	1:25	2:2	2:17, 18	2:28, 29; 3:1	4:1, 4	4:10

Key: *: Occurrence of Χαίρω; #: Occurrence of Χαρά; ~: Occurrence of Συγχαίρω; : Cluster

Figure 4.1. The occurrences of χαίρω in Philippians.

As well as illustrating thematic prominence, which will be discussed later, the clusters also function as discourse markers.[27] These clusters are found in 1:18; 2:17–18; 2:28–3:1; 4:4. Except in 1:18, all of these occur in the transitions between major semantic units as identified earlier.[28] This confirms their transitional function.[29] Although the cluster in 1:18 does not begin a new discussion, it is combined with ἀλλὰ καί (but and) in the middle of the topic of Paul's imprisonment, focusing on Paul's σωτηρία (salvation). Thus, the cluster marks the minor semantic unit in which Paul articulates his hope of release from prison.[30]

---

[27] According to Levinsohn (2000:19–20), repetition can sometimes be an indicator of a point of departure, signifying a switch in topic in a discourse. Moreover, he demonstrates that points of departure of this kind occur more frequently in non-narrative texts by citing texts from James, Titus, and Galatians (Levinsohn 2000:69–74).

[28] Based on my earlier analysis, the following semantic units are identified: 1:12–26; 1:27–2:18; 3:1–4:1; 4:2–9.

[29] The reason behind their transitional function will be explained in the following discussion of prominence in this chapter. Thurston and Ryan (2005:112) also note the transitional nature of χαίρω by suggesting that the word appears at major point of transition.

[30] The combination of ἀλλὰ (but) and καί (and) denotes a strong addition with an emphatic force. Turner (1963:330), Blass and Debrunner (1961:233) argue that ἀλλὰ-καί (but-and) provides an additional force to the previous discussion; and Robertson (1934:1185–1186) suggests the continuative and connective nature of the combination found in Phil. 1:18. Hawthorne (1983:39), Thurston and Ryan (2005:62) all define the conjunctive particles ἀλλὰ-καί (but-and) in 1:18f as progressive, moving the letter on to a new topic. Thurston and Ryan notice that the use of future tense, χαρήσομαι (I shall rejoice), accentuates this progressive force. Nevertheless, the conjunctive particles are not widely considered to be marking the boundary of a major discussion. Instead, the new topic introduced in 1:18f–26 is part of the major segment, 1:12–26. Banker (1996:16), Hansen (2009:65–76), and Thurston and Ryan (2005:38) all consider 1:18b–26 as only one of the minor units within the major segment 1:12–26. My conclusion concurs that the combination of

Conversely, the single occurrence of χαίρω (to rejoice) in 4:10 occurs at the beginning of the segment in which gifts are sent by the Philippians to Paul through Epaphroditus. In combination with δέ (but/and), χαίρω (to rejoice) marks the beginning of a new topic.[31]

4.1.3 Semantic units

Through the four identified discourse makers, the letter can be divided into: the letter-opening, seven major segments, and the letter-closing. As shown in table 4.2 the boundaries of some units are marked by more than one discourse marker.[32]

χαίρω (to rejoice) and ἀλλὰ-καί (but-and) begins a minor semantic unit in 1:18, in the middle of the major discussion of Paul's imprisonment.

[31] Although δέ (but/and) can be an adversative conjunction, it is more commonly a transitional or continuative particle, which is almost equivalent to καί (and) (Turner 1963:331; Dana and Mantey 1928:244). Robertson (1934:1183–1184), however, sets forth that δέ (but/and) can also be used to introduce a new topic, which is in harmony with the preceding discussion. As previously mentioned, there is general support (from scholars who support or repudiate the partition theory) that 4:10–20 is a major topic of discussion.

[32] Georgakopoulou and Goutsos (2004:95) suggest that the transitional function may be realised by more than one discourse marker.

Table 4.2. Semantic units of Philippians

Semantic Unit	A 1:3–11	B 1:12–26	C 1:27–2:18	D 2:19–30	E 3:1–4:1	F[a] 4:2–9	G 4:10–20
Discourse Markers							
DM 1: Change of Verb Mood			Imperative within 1:27–2:18			Imperative within 4:2–9[b]	
DM 2: Vocative		ἀδελφοί (1:12)			ἀδελφοί (3:1 and 4:1)	ἀδελφοί (4:8)	
DM 3: Formulas	Εὐχαριστῶ τῷ θεῷ (1:3)				τὸ λοιπόν (3:1)	τὸ λοιπόν (4:8)	
DM 4: Lexical Cohesion			Clustered χαίρω[c] (2:17–18)	Clustered χαίρω (2:28–3:1)			χαίρω with δέ (4:10)
New Topic	Letter-opening (1:1–2)	Paul's Concern for Philippians	Paul's Imprisonment	Christ's Example	Timothy and Epaphroditus	Paul's Example	Euodia and Syntyche	Philippians' Concern for Paul	Letter-closing (4:21–23)

[a] Although ἀδελφοί and τὸ λοιπόν occur in 4:8, the idea expressed in the sentence in which these markers are situated is completed in 4:9. Hence, the unit ends in 4:9 instead of 4:8.

[b] Since it is clear that 3:1–4:1 belongs to the same semantic unit, we consider 4:2 as the beginning of Unit F.

[c] "Clustered χαίρω" in the table is the abbreviation for the cluster in which χαίρω and its associated nouns (χαρα and συγχαίρω) appear.

As shown above, each of the major semantic units contains a topic: Unit A (Paul's Concern for Philippians), Unit B (Paul's Imprisonment), Unit C (Christ's Example), Unit D (Timothy and Epaphroditus), Unit E (Paul's Example), Unit F (Euodia and Syntyche), and Unit G (Philippians' Concern for Paul).

Table 4.3. Outline of Philippians by scholars[a]

	Semantic Unit A	Semantic Unit B	Semantic Unit C	Semantic Unit D	Semantic Unit E[b]	Semantic Unit F[c]	Semantic Unit G
My Outline	Paul's Concern for Philippians 1:3–11	Paul's Imprisonment 1:12–26	Christ's Example 1:27–2:18	Timothy & Epaphroditus 2:19–30	Paul's Example 3:1–4:1	Euodia & Syntyche 4:2–9	Philippians' Concern for Paul 4:10–20
Outline of Scholars	BK	BK	BL	BM	BK	BK	BK
	BL	BL	BM	FE	FE	HS	BL
	CD	BM	FE	HS	HS	HT	BM[d]
	FE	CD	HS	HT	LF	LF	CD
	HS	FE	HT	MC	MS	MS	HS
	HT	HS	MS	MS	SV	MT	HT
	LF[e]	HT	MT	MT	PL	OS	LF
	MC	LF	PL	SV	TR	RE	MS
	MS	MC	RE[f]	RE	WT	RM	OS
	MT	MS	RM	RM			RE
	OS	MT	TR	TR			PL
	RE	SV		WT			RM
	RM	OS					TR
	TR	PL				FE	
	WT	RE				SV	
		TR					

[a] In table 4.3, the abbreviations of the commentators are as follows. Banker is abbreviated as BK; Black, BL; Bockmuehl, BM; Craddock, CD; Fee, FE; Hansen, HS; Hawthorne, HT; Lightfoot, LF; Marchal, MC; Marshall, MS; Martin, MT; Osiek, OS; Peterlin, PL; Reed, RE; Reumann, RM; Silva, SV; Thurston and Ryan, TR; Witherington, WT. For detailed outlines, see Banker 1996:16–19; Black 1995:43–44; Bockmuehl 1998:46; Craddock 1985:ix–x; Fee 1995:54–55; Hansen 2009:12; Hawthorne 1983:xlix; Lightfoot 1913:71; Marchal 2006:119–152; Marshall 1992:v–vii; Martin 1989:58; Osiek 2000:8–9; Peterlin 1995:v–vii, 9; Reed 1997:289; Silva 1992:18; Thurston and Ryan 2005:38; Witherington 1994:ix–x. Although Reumann (2008:6) maintains the partition theory, he proposes a structural outline based on logical and thematic development.

[b] For Fee, this segment ends in 4:3, rather than 4:1. For Lightfoot, 3:2 begins this segment.

[c] Some scholars consider this segment as two separate divisions. For instance, Thurston and Ryan regard 4:2–3 and 4:4–9 as two major segments. For Hawthorne, this segment starts in 4:1. According to Lightfoot, 4:2–3 and 4:4–9 are two sub-divisions. Together with 3:1 and 3:2–4:1, they belong to 3:1–4:9. For Martin, this segment commence in 4:1. Fee considers this segment commences in 4:4. In this segment, 4:4–9 and 4:10–20 are two sub-divisions, with 4:21–23 being the closing remark. For Silva, 4:2–23 belong to one segment, which is consisted of three sub-divisions: 4:2–9; 4:10–20; and 4:21–23.

[d] 4:10–20, for Bockmuehl, is a sub-division of 4:4–23.

[e] According to Lightfoot, 1:1–2, 1:3–11, and 1:12–26 are three sub-divisions of a bigger unit (1:1–26).

[f] According to Reed (1997:210–211), 1:27–2:18 is Paul's petition to the Philippians, and the segment can be sub-divided into 1:27–30 and 2:1–18.

As shown in table 4.3, the semantic units that I outline are similar to those proposed by various scholars.[33] In particular, my outline is nearly identical to the outlines of John Banker, Jeffrey Reed, and Walter Hansen. Two of the most comprehensive and recent discourse analyses of Philippians were conducted by Banker and Reed. When comparing their approach with mine, the point of focus is different. Banker (1996:15–19) focuses on thematic grouping based on different constituents, Reed focuses on letter format,[34] and I focus on discourse markers. Nonetheless, all three approaches derive a similar conclusion. Arguably, this is due to the fact that all three approaches are based on the same underlying principles of discourse analysis.[35]

4.1.4 Discourse coherence

As I have previously mentioned, the concept of coherence is arguably "of central importance to discourse analysis" (Schiffrin 1987:21). Different elements in a discourse, including various semantic units, are connected through various cohesive linguistic devices to form a coherent message. In the following part, I review several linguistic devices, such as inclusio and prominence, to demonstrate that communal relationship, both among the Philippians and between Paul and the Philippians, is the central theme.

4.1.4.1 Inclusio

There are several occurrences of inclusio in Philippians. First, κοινωνία (fellowship), which occurs in Unit A, reappears in the last unit (Unit G) in the form of κοινωνέω (to share). At the beginning of the letter, Paul expresses his prayer of thanksgiving regarding his partnership with the Philippians: ἐπὶ τῇ κοινωνίᾳ ὑμῶν εἰς τὸ εὐαγγέλιον (upon your fellowship in the gospel) in 1:5. The thanksgiving prayer in Unit A sets the tone of the letter with

---

[33] The main difference hinges upon whether a particular topic is considered to be a major segment or a minor sub-division.

[34] Reed (1997:178–179) argues that the letter is written based on ancient letter format. According to Reed, Philippians is fundamentally epistolary, combining with personal and paraenetic functions of language. Hence, his analysis incorporates the comparisons between the parallels exhibited between ancient letters and Philippians, and illustrates how Philippians adopts different formulas used in ancient letters (Reed 1997:178–295).

[35] According to discourse analysis, an author divides the whole discourse into segments by means of thematic grouping. These segments (key topics) are usually marked by linguistic clues known as discourse markers, and all the segments are connected coherently. Therefore, the three approaches are not contradictory. Their differences rest on how each study begins its analysis. Banker begins by focusing on the thematic grouping to identify the key topics in the epistle; Reed examines the coherent structure indicated by how an ancient letter flows; and I identify the discourse markers to ascertain the thematic groups (such as, the key topics within a discourse).

the occurrence of κοινωνία (fellowship) denoting partnership. Then, Paul reiterates this partnership at the end of the letter in a stronger expression: οὐδεμία μοι ἐκκλησία ἐκοινώνησεν... εἰ μὴ ὑμεῖς μόνοι (no church shared with me...except you alone) in 4:15.

Second, the phrase τὸ αὐτὸ φρονῆτε (to think the same) in 2:2 is repeated in 4:2 as τὸ αὐτὸ φρονεῖν (to think the same). Paul emphasises the communal oneness of the Philippians, first in a general sense (for the whole community in 2:2), then in a specific manner (regarding the issue of the two women in 4:2).

Third, στήκω (to stand firm) in 1:27 re-emerges in 4:1. The word only occurs twice in the letter, in both cases in the imperative mood. At the beginning of Unit C, Paul urges the Philippians to communal unity by stating: στήκετε ἐν ἑνὶ πνεύματι (stand firm in one spirit, 1:27). Near the end of Unit E, Paul reiterates a similar concept by encouraging them to unite together: στήκετε ἐν κυρίῳ (stand firm in the Lord) in 4:1.

Fourth, the word συναθλέω (to strive together) occurs in 1:27 and 4:3. In both cases, συναθλέω (to strive together) is associated with εὐαγγέλιον (gospel). In 1:27, the word depicts the Philippians striving together. In 4:3, the word depicts Paul striving together with the Philippians.

Lastly, the phrase χάρις...Ἰησοῦ Χριστοῦ (grace...of Jesus Christ) occurs in both the letter-opening (1:2) and the letter-closing (4:23).

As shown in my examination, many of the occurrences of inclusio point to the corporate and relational aspect, which is a prominent theme in the epistle.[36] The letter is centred in the relationship, friendship in particular, between Paul and the Philippians, and among the Philippians. This key theme will further be explored as follows.

4.1.4.2 Prominence

As I have previously mentioned (§ 2.3.2.2), prominence is the repetition of a theme (thematic prominence) or a word (lexical cohesion) throughout a discourse to enable and facilitate coherence. In the following part, I demonstrate the centrality of friendship and corporate unity in Philippians through thematic prominence and lexical cohesion.

---

[36] Both Hansen and Garland discuss the use of inclusio in Philippians. Garland (1985:160–161) provides a list of words that show the use of inclusio in Philippians, for instance, σωτηρία (salvation) in 1:28) and σωτήρ (savior) in 3:20, παράκλησις (advocate) in 2:1 and παρακαλέω (I encourage) in 4:2. Of importance, the rare words in 1:27, including πολιτεύεσθε (live as a citizen), στήκετε (stand firm), and συναθλοῦντες (striving together), reappear later in the epistle: πολίτευμα (citizenship) in 3:20, στήκετε (stand firm) in 4:1), συνήθλησάν (strived together) in 4:3. For Garland, this demarcates 1:27–4:3 as a single unit. Hansen (2009:48–50) identifies six references to κοινωνία (fellowship) in 1:5, 7; 2:1; 3:10; 4:14, 15, highlighting the motif of partnership throughout the epistle.

Thematic prominence

The two inter-related themes highlighted by thematic prominence are friendship and corporate unity.

The friendship theme, between Paul and the Philippians, appears in all the semantic units. In Unit A, Paul expresses his affection and care for the Philippians in the following clauses: "for your every remembrance of me" (1:3);[37] "it is right for me to think this about all of you" (1:7a); "because I have you in my heart" (1:7b);[38] and "I long for all of you" (1:8). The friendship is also evident from the use of κοινωνία (fellowship) language: "all of you being my partakers (συγκοινωνούς) in the grace" (1:7b).

In Unit B, the focus shifts to Paul's imprisonment (1:12–26). Nonetheless, the relationship between Paul and the Philippians remains in the background. Paul explains the reason behind the possibility of his σωτηρίαν (salvation) from his δεσμός (imprisonment) by stating: "because of your prayer" (1:19).

In Unit C, Paul uses Christ as an example (2:1–4) to urge for unity: "Have this attitude in yourselves which also [was] in Christ Jesus" (2:5). However, the relational tone can be detected in the description of the Philippians' obedience to Paul. The apostle exhorts the Philippians' obedience both "in my presence" and "in my absence" (2:12). Furthermore, Paul expresses his delight in the Philippians: "for my boasting on the day of Christ" (2:16). Lastly, the unit ends with the announcement of the shared joy: "I rejoice (χαίρω) and rejoice together (συγχαίρω) with all of you...be glad (χαίρετε) and rejoice together (συγχαίρετέ) with me" (2:17–18).

In Unit D, the relationship is reflected by the sending of Timothy (from Paul to the Philippians) and Epaphroditus (originally from the Philippians to Paul).

In Unit E, Paul uses himself as an example to urge the Philippians to imitate him (3:17). As previously mentioned, Paul employs ἀδελφοί twice (3:13 and 3:17) to express his emphatic emotion in his encouragement.

Although Euodia and Syntyche are the focal point in Unit F, the relational tone between Paul and the Philippians can be detected. Paul urges the Philippians to help the two women: ἐρωτῶ καὶ σέ, γνήσιε σύζυγε, συλλαμβάνου αὐταῖς (I say also to you, true fellow worker, help them) in 4:3. Paul addresses the Philippians as γνήσιε σύζυγε (true fellow worker),[39] while the women are portrayed as αἵτινες ἐν τῷ εὐαγγελίῳ συνήθλησάν μοι

---

[37] This phrase could refer to the Philippians' care for Paul (Reumann 2008:102–103; Thurston and Ryan 2005:49). However, either interpretation would still point to the friendship between Paul and the Philippians.

[38] The phrase διὰ τὸ ἔχειν με ἐν τῇ καρδίᾳ ὑμᾶς (because I have you in my heart) will be discussed in detail later in this chapter.

[39] A detailed discussion of the identity of γνήσιε σύζυγε (true fellow worker) will be provided later in this chapter.

μετά (they strived together with me in the gospel). Later in this chapter, the analysis reveals that Unit F is the peak in Philippians, and displays unusual grammatical and syntactic phenomena. The relationship, in particular unity, between Paul, Euodia, Syntyche, and the Philippians is strongly highlighted in this climactic unit.

Finally, in Unit G, Paul's relationship with the Philippians is again highlighted in the following clauses: I rejoiced greatly in the Lord at last that you renewed your concern for me (τὸ ὑπὲρ ἐμοῦ φρονεῖν) in 4:10; and to share with (συγκοινωνήσαντές) me in the trouble in 4:14.

In summary, in my analysis aspects of the relationship between Paul and the Philippians are highlighted through thematic prominence. Many scholars specify this relationship as friendship,[40] with some drawing on research by Stanley Stowers and Luke Johnson.[41] In the mid-1980s, Stowers provided important insights regarding the epistle.[42] In his research on ancient letters in the Greco-Roman era, Stowers (1986:60) identifies a particular form of letter called letters of friendship. He argues that some NT letters, including Philippians, follow this letter form. In addition, Johnson (2010:328–329) identifies and explains the use of friendship rhetoric in Philippians. In a recent commentary, Hansen explains why Philippians is parallel with Hellenistic letters of friendship and summarises ten arguments for that claim (Hansen 2009:8–11). Overall, the insights provided by Stowers and Johnson correspond with the thematic prominence highlighted in my analysis.

Lexical cohesion

The second form of prominence is known as lexical cohesion. The repetition of an identical or similar lexical item or the repetition of several lexical items with the same topic is employed to highlight a coherent theme. In Philippians, there are four key patterns of lexical cohesion. The following

---

[40] See Fitzgerald, John T., ed. 1996. *Friendship, Flattery, and Frankness of Speech: Studies on Friendship in the New Testament World.* Supplements to Novum Testamentum 82. Leiden, Netherlands: Brill. In this work, the contributions by Reumann (1996:83–106), Berry (1996:107–124), Malherbe (1996:125–139), and Fitzgerald (1996:141–160) provide valuable discussion of the matter.

[41] For example, Fee, Hansen, and Reed refer to Stower in their works (Fee 1995:5; Hansen 2009:6–10; Reed 1997:169–171), and Fowl refers to Johnson in his work (Fowl 2005:218).

[42] Both Stowers and Johnson conclude that Philippians is a letter of friendship. Alexander (1989:87–101) suggests that Philippians follows the format of the Hellenistic family letter. However, not everyone agrees that Philippians is a letter of friendship or family. Bockmuehl (1998:35) rejects this and cites similar disagreement by some Greek patristic commentators. Peterlin (1995:2) suggests that defining Philippians as a family letter is part of the reason why the epistle is treated as an informal correspondence.

part demonstrates how these patterns illustrate corporate unity and communal relationship.

The first pattern of lexical cohesion is demonstrated by the repetition of the words relating to κοινωνία (fellowship) throughout the epistle. There are six references to κοινωνία (fellowship) in the letter, elucidating the motif of partnership:[43] τῇ κοινωνίᾳ ὑμῶν (your fellowship) in 1:5; συγκοινωνούς μου (my partakers) in 1:7;[44] εἴ τις κοινωνία (if there is fellowship) in 2:1; κοινωνίαν [τῶν] παθημάτων αὐτοῦ (the fellowship of his sufferings, 3:10); καλῶς ἐποιήσατε συγκοινωνήσαντές μου τῇ θλίψει (you did well, taking part in my trouble) in 4:14; and οὐδεμία μοι ἐκκλησία ἐκοινώνησεν...εἰ μὴ ὑμεῖς μόνοι (no church shared with me...except you alone) in 4:15. Four out of the six references point directly to the partnership between Paul and the Philippians (1:5, 1:7, 4:14, and 4:15). Not only is partnership mentioned throughout the letter through the lexical cohesion of κοινωνία (fellowship), it is also reiterated as a form of inclusio (1:5 and 4:15).

Second, words with the prepositional prefix συν- (a prefix indicating "together with") occur with striking frequency.[45] The prefix is used for both verbs and nouns, including συγκοινωνούς (partakers) in 1:7, συναθλοῦντες (striving together) in 1:27, σύμψυχοι (fellow-souled) in 2:2, συγχαίρω (I rejoice together) in 2:17, συγχαίρετέ (you rejoice together) in 2:18, συνεργὸν (fellow worker) in 2:25, συστρατιώτην (fellow-soldier) in 2:25, συμμορφιζόμενος (sharing the same form) in 3:10, σύμμορφον (share the likeness) in 3:21, σύζυγε (fellow worker) in 4:3, συλλαμβάνου (help) in 4:3, συνήθλησάν (they strived together) in 4:3, συνεργῶν (fellow workers) in 4:3, and συγκοινωνήσαντές (taking part) in 4:14. Apart from συμμορφιζόμενος (sharing the same form) in 3:10 and σύμμορφον (share the likeness) in 3:21, twelve words with this prefix are employed to depict a communal and corporate reference.[46] Nine out of these twelve words elucidate the relationship between Paul and the Philippians, with only three of them

---

[43] Hansen (2009:48–50) provides a thorough analysis of this motif of partnership connoted by the six references of κοινωνία. Fitzgerald (2007:289) suggests that κοινωνία is an expression of friendship in the ancient world. More importantly, he argues that reconciliation of friendship is the key of the use of friendship language.

[44] Nongbri (2009:803–808) argues for a variant reading of 1:7, in which μου (my) is possibly placed after τῆς χάριτος (the grace) in the original letter. Thus through the support to Paul, the Philippians become partakes of the benefaction, which χάρις (grace) denotes, that the apostle has originally received from God. In other words, Paul is a broker of divine benefaction.

[45] From this point onwards, the explanation of the prepositional prefix συν- (as a prefix indicating together with) is not provided in this chapter.

[46] Συλλαμβάνω in 4:3 means "help" in its middle voice. However, the connotation behind the word carries the essence of corporate unity and communal relationship (Bauer 1979:777).

illustrating the relationship among the Philippians.[47] This demonstrates that the theme of unity is not limited to portray unity among the Philippians, since the same theme is also used to portray the unity between the apostle and the Philippians. Regarding words with the prefix συν-, there is one particular nuance that invites curiosity, which centres on the use of σύζυγε (fellow worker). In 4:3, the Philippians are addressed by Paul as σέ (you), in the singular form, instead of the plural ὑμᾶς (you), before calling them his γνήσιε σύζυγε (true fellow worker). The majority of the commentators consider γνήσιε σύζυγε (true fellow worker) to be an unnamed person in the community.[48] However, σύζυγε (fellow worker), a masculine singular noun, might also refer to the whole church as if addressing one person (Craddock 1985:70).[49] A pronoun is used to refer to the identified subject in the previous context. In this case, the immediate masculine subject is ἀδελφοί μου ἀγαπητοί (my beloved brothers) in 4:1. Furthermore, this unit is the climax of the letter (as discussed later) which highlights the issue of communal unity. Using a singular σέ (you) to address the whole community that is represented by ἀδελφοί is a natural utterance. Thus the use of the singular masculine noun σύζυγε (fellow worker) as well as singular σέ (you) in the same verse further accentuates the corporate entity of the Philippian community. The unusual grammatical choice is not unique in Unit F, since this unit also displays many unusual grammatical phenomena, indicating the climactic point of Paul's argument, which will be detailed later in this chapter.

Third, as previously mentioned, χαίρω (to rejoice) and its cognates, χαρά (joy) and συγχαίρω (to rejoice together), occur 16 times in Philippians. Whilst this repetition in clustered form is perceived as a discourse marker, it

---

[47] Words with the prefex συν- illustrate the corporate unity and communal relationship between Paul and the Philippians, and occur in 1:7; 2:17, 18, 25 (twice); 4:3 (three times), 14. Words with same connotation are used to depict the same theme among the Philippians, and occur in 1:27 (twice); 4:3.

[48] See Martin 1989:152–153; Marshall 1992:109; Fowl 2005:178–179; Bockmuehl 1998:240–241; Lightfoot 1913:158–159; Thurston and Ryan 2005:141; Osiek 2000:113; Beare 1959:145; Hansen 2009:284–285; Reumann 2008:628–630. Many of these commentators would provide a list of people whom they conjecture to be the possible identity of this person, mostly with uncertainty except a few. For instance, Fee (1995:393–395) provides an interesting argument suggesting that this person is Luke. Some argue that it refers to a person with the proper name, Σύζυγε (Vincent 1897:131). The problem of this view is that this name is not found in either other Greek literature or early church writings (Marshall 1992:109). It is also suggested that Σύζυγε is Paul's wife since ἡ σύζυγος means wife in some Greek literature (Bauer 1979:775–756; Lightfoot 1913:159). However, this view is refuted because of the masculine gender attached to its modifier, γνήσιε (true) (Bockmuehl 1998:240–241).

[49] Hawthorne (1983:180) considers this possibility to be the best deduction as he argues that Paul sees the entire Philippian church as a unit, as a single individual.

is also a form of prominence. Joy is therefore a prominent theme,[50] and, in particular, also highlights the relationship between Paul and the Philippians. In 1:4, Paul prays for the Philippians: μετὰ χαρᾶς (with joy). In 1:19, Paul rejoices due to his possible release: διὰ τῆς ὑμῶν δεήσεως (because of your prayer). In 1:25, Paul prefers to live (παραμενῶ πᾶσιν ὑμῖν) with a purpose: εἰς τὴν ὑμῶν προκοπὴν καὶ χαρὰν τῆς πίστεως (for your progress and joy of the faith). In 2:2, Paul calls for unity among the Philippians, which would fill him with joy (2:2). In two clauses, the relationship between Paul and the Philippians is accentuated: χαίρω καὶ συγχαίρω πᾶσιν ὑμῖν (I rejoice and I rejoice together with all of you) in 2:17; and ὑμεῖς χαίρετε καὶ συγχαίρετέ μοι (you rejoice and you rejoice together with me) in 2:18. When Paul sends Epaphroditus back to the Philippians, χαρῆτε (you may rejoice) in 2:28 and χαρᾶς (joy) in 2:29 portray the joy. In 4:1, Paul calls the Philippians his χαρὰ καὶ στέφανός (joy and crown). In 4:10, Paul rejoices because of the Philippians' concern: Ἐχάρην...μεγάλως (I rejoiced greatly). Given these occurrences, the repetition of χαίρω (to rejoice) and its cognates clearly emphasises the theme of friendship and relationship. As previously discussed, the clustered χαίρω (to rejoice) functions as a discourse marker, and the reason for this is now evident. When Paul shifts topic, he highlights his relationship with the Philippians through the use of χαίρω (to rejoice), which probably reminds the audience of the joyous and positive affection shared between them.

Fourth, other words can be used as "thematically equivalent synonyms or even figurative expressions" to portray the same thematic meaning (Lemke 1995:89). The anthropological terms employed in Philippians belong to the same lexical set, which facilitates lexical cohesion, and illustrate corporate and communal dimensions, both in relation to the Philippians and between Paul and the Philippians. These key terms occur in ἐν τῇ καρδίᾳ ὑμᾶς (in your heart) in 1:7; ἑνὶ πνεύματι (in one spirit) in 1:27; μιᾷ ψυχῇ (in one soul) in 1:27; κοινωνία πνεύματος (fellowship of spirit) in 2:1; σύμψυχοι (fellow-souled) in 2:2; ἰσόψυχον (like-minded, or literally, same-souled) in 2:20; παραβολευσάμενος τῇ ψυχῇ (risking the soul) in 2:30; τὸ σῶμα τῆς ταπεινώσεως ἡμῶν (our humble body) in 3:21a; τῷ σώματι τῆς δόξης (to the body of glory) in 3:21b; and μετὰ τοῦ πνεύματος ὑμῶν (with your spirit) in 4:23. The remainder of this chapter will focus on the thematic meanings of these anthropological terms, and will detail the corporate and communal connotations.

Table 4.4 summarises these four patterns of lexical cohesion, which function as thematic equivalent synonyms to portray the theme of corporate unity and communal relationship.

---

[50] Heil (2010:2–3) argues that a connotation of joy envelopes the letter. The cause of rejoicing is in being conformed to Christ, which indicates unity among and between the Philippians, Paul, Timothy, and Epaphroditus.

Table 4.4. Lexical cohesion: Thematic equivalent synonyms

Letter-opening	Unit A	Unit B	Unit C	Unit D	Unit E	Unit F	Unit G	Letter-closing
	ἐν τῇ καρδίᾳ ὑμᾶς 1:7 P&PH		ἑνὶ πνεύματι 1:27 PH μιᾷ ψυχῇ 1:27 PH κοινωνία πνεύματος 2:1 PH σύμψυχοι 2:2 PH	ἰσόψυχον 2:20 P&PH Παραβολ-ευσάμενος τῇ ψυχῇ 2:30 P&PH	τὸ σῶματῆς ταπεινώ-σεως ἡμῶν 3:21a PH τῷ σώματι τῆς δόξης 3:21b PH			μετὰ τοῦ πνεύματος ὑμῶν 4:23 PH
	κοινωνίᾳ 1:5 P&PH συγκοινω-νούς 1:7 P&PH		κοινωνία 2:1 PH		κοινωνίαν 3:10 P&C	σύζυγε 4:3 P&PH	ἐκοινώνη-σεν 4:15 P&PH	
			συναθλ-οῦντες 1:27 PH σύμψυχοι 2:2 PH συγχαίρω 2:17 P&PH συγχαίρετέ 2:18 P&PH	συνεργὸν 2:25 P&PH συστρατι-ώτην 2:25 P&PH		συλλαμβά-νου 4:3 PH συνήθλη-σάν 4:3 P&PH συνεργῶν 4:3 P&PH	συγκοινω-νήσαντές 4:14 P&PH	
1:1–3	1:3–11	1:12–26	1:27–2:18	2:19–30	3:1–4:1	4:2–9	4:10–20	4:21–23

Key: P&PH: between Paul and the Philippians; P&C: between Paul and Christ; PH: amongst the Philippians

In summary, both the inclusio and the prominence (thematic prominence and lexical cohesion) indicate that the coherent theme of the discourse centres on the communal, relational, and corporate unity, both among the Philippians and between Paul and the Philippians.[51]

---

[51] Some commentators contend that the epistle has mixed themes and multiple purposes. For example, Hawthorne (1983:xlviii) asserts that Paul has many things in mind, from expressing his deep affection for the Philippians, informing them

4.1.5 Macrostructure

Many commentators perceive disunity among the Philippians to be the key issue that Paul addresses, with the conflict between Euodia and Syntyche especially prompting Paul to write this letter.[52] Nonetheless, I thus far show that the focal point, which is illustrated by the discourse coherence, centres on the friendship between Paul and the Philippians, despite the discord between Euodia and Syntyche. If the conflict between the two women was vital, then the thematic prominence of friendship would have been surpassed. Therefore, I propose that the macrostructure can be expressed as follows. The friendship between Paul and the Philippians is under stress

---

of the erroneous teaching they might encounter, to thanking them for the gift of money. Hawthorne concludes that the letter follows no logical progression with swift changes of topic and tone. Hansen (2009:25–30) and Fee (1995:29–33) propose that there is more than one key issue in Philippians, pointing to the multipurpose nature of the epistle. Acknowledging the multifaceted issues addressed by Paul, Fee (1995:38–39) argues that the epistle still follows a basic chronological scheme. However, other commentators contend that the epistle does have a single purpose, with a coherent theme. Peterlin (1995:227) concludes that disunity is the core issue addressed by Paul, and argues that there are numerous allusions to disunity in the Philippian church. Conversely, S. Winter (1997:213) argues that Paul seeks to foster his own relationship with the Philippians, and contends that the major texts in the epistles do not attempt to encourage community harmony among the Philippians. These two pieces of research were conducted in the 1990s, and although arriving at opposite conclusions, they both attempt to prove that Philippians is not Paul's random collection of thoughts.

[52] Most commentators support this view (Silva 1992:222; Hawthorne 1983:179; Martin 1989:152; Thurston and Ryan 2005:142; Hansen 2009:282; Bockmuehl 1998:238; Beare 1959:142–143; Fee 1995:391–393). However, S. Winter (1997:166) argues that the conflict is between the two women and Paul. First, the same construction in 2 Cor 4:13; 12:18, τὸ αὐτὸ πνεῦμα (the same spirit), refers to Paul and either the Corinthians or his associates. Second, Paul addresses an unnamed helper, γνήσιε σύζυγε (true fellow worker) in Phil 4:3 and asks her to help the two women who were working with Paul. Hence, τὸ αὐτὸ φρονεῖν (to think the same) should be understood as an encouragement to resume their cooperation with Paul. Third, had Paul promoted reconciliation between the two women, he would have used παρακαλῶ (I urge) once not twice. The repeated use indicates an urge for cooperation with the apostle, and is the same demand specific to two individuals. Winter's alternative conclusion may be valid, except that in one argument he treats γνήσιε σύζυγε (true fellow worker) as female, which contradicts the masculine vocative, γνήσιε (true). Nevertheless, the immediate context can be explained either way. The repetition of παρακαλῶ can be interpreted as Paul refusing to take sides and treating the two women equally. Or as Paul addressing the two women individually, appealing for reconciliation with Paul. However, the wider context heavily emphasises the friendship between Paul and the Philippians. Thus, Winter's argument concurs with the macrostructure. It is most certain that the tone of unity, within the community and between Paul and the community, underlies the coherence of the whole discourse.

due to an undefined conflict between Euodia and Syntyche. As a result, by invoking his friendship with the Philippians, Paul calls for unity within the community and between himself and his friends, and reconciliation between Euodia and Syntyche.

4.2 Anthropological terms in Philippians

As previously mentioned, the key anthropological terms produce a pattern of lexical cohesion, involving a prominence, which highlights corporate and communal unity. In the following part, I analyse the occurrences of the key anthropological terms in each semantic unit, and then examine their overall occurrences in the entire discourse in light of the sociolinguistic aspect, the macrostructure, and the discourse flow.

4.2.1 Anthropological terms in semantic units

The anthropological terms that occur in each semantic unit are: καρδία (heart) in 1:7 and 4:7; ψυχή (soul) in 1:27 and 2:30; the words derived from ψυχή (soul): σύμψυχοι (fellow-souled) in 2:2 and ἰσόψυχον (like-minded, or literally, same-souled) in 2:20; πνεῦμα (spirit) in 1:27, 2:1, and 4:23; and σῶμα (body) in 3:21. In addition, φρονέω (to think) is also examined. Although φρονέω is not an anthropological term, its cognate φρήν (mind) is (Bertram 1974:220–221).[53] The plural form, φρένες, means diaphragm, and the singular form is used metaphorically to depict "inner part" or "mind,"[54] functioning as a parallel of νοῦς (mind), which is an anthropological term.[55] As such, φρονέω (to think) is also examined.

4.2.1.1 Καρδία (heart) in Units A and G

Καρδία (heart) occurs twice in Philippians: 1:7 (Unit A); and 4:7 (Unit G). Καρδία (heart) in Unit A denotes the corporate and communal aspect; while the one in Unit G does not carry this connotation.

---

[53] Kümmel (1963:43) also considers φρένες (diaphragm), the plural form of φρήν (mind), an anthropological term.

[54] According to Bertram (1974:220), the word is used by Homer to depict inner part, mind, and understanding.

[55] Bertram (1974:229) states that this usage is adopted by the works of Josephus. My findings are consistent with Bertram's observation. For instance, in his work *Jewish Antiquities* (10.114) Josephus uses the phrase ἐξεστηκότατων φρενῶν αὐτόν (disordered in his minds) to describe how οἱ ἀσεβεῖς (the godless people) consider Jeremiah. The genitive noun τῶν φρενῶν (the minds) does not denote diaphragm. Instead, it denotes mind, as the context depicts how the godless people believe that Jeremiah is out of his mind.

Τῇ καρδίᾳ ὑμᾶς (in the heart) in Unit A

In Unit A, Paul expresses his affections towards the Philippians through various utterances as mentioned. One of the expressions is: διὰ τὸ ἔχειν με ἐν τῇ καρδίᾳ ὑμᾶς (because you have me in the heart) in 1:7b. The articular infinitive clause consists of διά (because), which indicates cause (Turner 1963:142–143). Hence, the clause explains the cause of a preceding idea. In 1:7a, Paul makes known his concern for the Philippians: τοῦτο φρονεῖν ὑπὲρ πάντων ὑμῶν (to think this about all of you). His reason is then explained in 1:7b. Grammatically speaking, the infinitive clause can be understood as either "I have you in the heart" or "You have me in your heart." The word order suggests the former is a more appropriate reading, since με (me) has a closer proximity to the infinitive phrase, διὰ τὸ ἔχειν (because to have), than ὑμᾶς (you) (Wallace 1996:196).[56] Therefore, the reason why Paul thinks of the Philippians is because the apostle has the Philippians in his heart.[57] The following context also supports this reading, since Paul's expression, ἐπιποθῶ πάντας ὑμᾶς (I long for you all) in 1:8, aligns with the interpretation of "I have you in my heart." Paul employs καρδία (heart) to express affection in 1:7 in the context that highlights the friendship between Paul and the Philippians.

Τὰς καρδίας ὑμῶν (your hearts) in Unit G

The phrase τὰς καρδίας ὑμῶν (your hearts) appears as a normal plural construct in 4:7. Paul uses the phrase to encourage the Philippians to make known their requests to God instead of being anxious (4:6). The term is likely to be used in contrast with τὰ νοήματα (the minds, 4:7), portraying emotion.[58] The plural noun emphasises all the individuals of the Philippian community.[59] The term does not highlight the strong corporate and communal aspect in this occurrence.

---

[56] Reed (1991:9–10) also argues that the SO word order is more prominent in the non-copulative infinitive, including in Phil 1:7.

[57] This understanding is also held by a number of scholars (Martin 1989:66; Hansen 2009:52; Fee 1995:90; Bockmuehl 1998:63; Silva 1992:56; Thurston and Ryan 2005:50).

[58] Καρδία (heart) and νοῦς/νόημα (mind) in this verse are considered to be denoting two different aspects: emotion and thought/volition (Hawthorne 1983:185; Vincent 1897:137). Fee (1995:411) understands καρδία (heart) as the centre of one's being. Lightfoot (1913:161) considers it as the seat of thought as well as of feeling.

[59] Hansen (2009:294–295) argues that the plural of καρδία (heart) highlights all individuals in the community.

4.2.1.2 Ψυχή *(soul) in Units C and D*

Ψυχή (soul) occurs twice in Philippians (1:7; 2:30). Other words related to ψυχή (soul) are also found in the epistle, σύμψυχοι (fellow-souled) in 2:2 and ἰσόψυχον (like-minded, or literally, same-souled) in 2:20. The following part explores the usage of ψυχή (soul), and its cognates, which have corporate and communal connotations.

Μιᾷ ψυχῇ (in one soul) and σύμψυχοι (fellow-souled) in Unit C

Ψυχή (soul) occurs at the beginning of Unit C (1:27–2:18) in the following clause: στήκετε ἐν ἑνὶ πνεύματι, μιᾷ ψυχῇ συναθλοῦντες (stand firm in one spirit, striving together in one soul) in 1:27. I argue that the phrase μιᾷ ψυχῇ (in one soul), based on its context, denotes corporate unity and communal relationship.

Referring to the context of Unit C, Paul begins the semantic unit by urging the Philippians to conduct their life worthy of Christ's gospel by uniting together as a community (1:27–30). This unity, according to Paul, can only be achieved by being humble (2:1–4); and Christ is a perfect example of humility (2:5–11). Paul then ends this unit by invoking his friendship with the Philippians (2:12–17).

From the immediate context, ψυχή (soul) is not used to connote a human soul (in an ontological sense) as the apostle urges the community to strive "in one soul." Instead, the singular ψυχή (soul), emphasised by μία (one), is used in a metaphorical sense to portray the communal unity.[60] This unity is further accentuated by a verb with the prefix συν-: συναθλοῦντες (striving together) to emphasise togetherness. The clause μιᾷ ψυχῇ συναθλοῦντες (striving together in one soul) is also connected to its previous clause στήκετε ἐν ἑνὶ πνεύματι (stand firm in one spirit). As discussed later, some scholars consider the two clauses to be in parallel, with ψυχή (soul) and πνεῦμα (spirit) being synonymous.[61] Putting aside this suggestion for the moment, it is obvious that unity is highlighted through the use of ἑνὶ (one, masculine gender), μιᾷ (one, feminine gender), and συν-. In other words, the corporate unity and communal oneness is highlighted. Moreover, this corporate and communal reference is also supported by the preceding and the following context of μιᾷ ψυχῇ συναθλοῦντες (striving together in one soul) as explained below.

In the preceding context, through the conjunction ὅτι (that) the verb στήκετε (stand firm) is linked back to ἀκούω (I hear), while ἀκούω (I hear)

---

[60] Many commentators regard ψυχή (soul) to be used in a metaphorical sense. For instance, the term is understood as denoting social life (Jewett 1971:352); communal sharing (Hansen 2009:8); "unity and oneness" (Fee 1995:164); "attitude and life principle" (Thurston and Ryan 2005:69); "mental harmony" (Silva 1992:94); or "single minded" (Marshall 1992:35; Beare 1959:67).

[61] I provide a detailed analysis of πνεῦμα (spirit) in 1:27 later in this chapter.

is connected to the preceding main verb πολιτεύεσθε (conduct yourselves) through ἵνα (so that). In other words, μιᾷ ψυχῇ συναθλοῦντες τῇ πίστει τοῦ εὐαγγελίου (striving together in one soul in the faith of the gospel) is syntactically associated with the main clause ἀξίως τοῦ εὐαγγελίου τοῦ Χριστοῦ πολιτεύεσθε (conduct yourselves worthy of the gospel of Christ).[62] The main command stated in 1:27 is "Conduct your lives." Πολιτεύομαι means "live," "conduct oneself," or "lead one's life," with a connotation alluding to the life as a citizen (Bauer 1979:686). This word is likely chosen by Paul to elucidate that the Philippians are like citizens within the Christian community in the kingdom of God. Hence, it is coherent to regard ψυχή (soul) as relating to social life (possibly as a citizen) instead of connoting a human soul.[63] In other words, the communal aspect depicted by πολιτεύεσθε (conduct yourselves) in the preceding context is further elaborated by the corporate unity emphasised by μιᾷ ψυχῇ (in one soul).

In the following context, the focus on corporate unity continues. Before asking the Philippians to imitate Christ (2:5) and detailing Christ's example of humility (2:6–11), Paul encourages the Philippians to fill him with joy by being united: ἵνα τὸ αὐτὸ φρονῆτε, τὴν αὐτὴν ἀγάπην ἔχοντες, σύμψυχοι, τὸ ἓν φρονοῦντες (so that you may think the same thing, having the same love, fellow-souled, be of one mind) in 2:2. Not only is the ἵνα (so that) clause a clear exhortation to corporate unity, the striking occurrence of σύμψυχοι (fellow-souled) also reminds the readers of the earlier occurrence of μιᾷ ψυχῇ (in one soul). The lexical meaning of the adjective σύμψυχος (fellow-souled) is harmonious or united in spirit (Bauer 1979:781).

Given the context of ψυχή in 1:27, I conclude that ψυχή (soul) connotes the corporate reference, highlighting the corporate unity. The Philippian community is portrayed metaphorically as a human person, and is urged to be united as if a single communal being with one ψυχή.

Surprisingly, at the end of Unit C (2:12-17), Paul invokes his friendship with the Philippians, despite focussing on unity among the Philippians throughout the unit.[64] He begins by discussing their obedience with and without his presence (2:12) and finishes in 2:17–18 by expressing: I rejoice (χαίρω) and I rejoice together (συγχαίρω) with all of you, and in the same way, rejoice (χαίρετε) and rejoice together (συγχαίρετέ) with me. The request, χαίρετε καὶ συγχαίρετέ (rejoice and rejoice together), seems out of place given the focus on corporate unity. Perhaps Paul is comforting those who are worried about his imprisonment (Hansen 2009:190). Or perhaps Paul is asking the Philippians to share his joy due to the advance of the gospel (Fee 1995:256) or due to his sacrifice (Beare 1959:94). However, taking

---

[62] See figure 4.2 for the syntactical chart of 1:27.

[63] Zerbe (2009:198) argues that the majority of the people in the Philippian Christian community did not hold Roman citizenship. Thus they would understand Paul's suffering and struggle.

[64] Fee (1995:256) also notes the unusual way to end this segment.

into consideration the repetition of the prefix συν- in the same verse, it seems that Paul wants to highlight the partnership between himself and the community.[65] Thus, perhaps the overt call for corporate unity, stated in previous clauses in 1:27 and in 2:2, is actually a subtle call for unity between Paul and the Philippians. The repetitive use of the prefix συν- throughout the epistle reflects the patterns of lexical cohesion, as previously discussed. Overall, the heavy emphasis on partnership and friendship by Paul denotes a particular point, which will be further addressed in an examination of discourse flow.

Τῇ ψυχῇ (in the soul) and ἰσόψυχον (like-minded/same-souled) in Unit D

Ψυχή (soul) occurs at the end of Unit D (2:19–30) in the following clause: παραβολευσάμενος τῇ ψυχῇ (risking [his] soul, 2:30). Whilst ψυχή (soul) denotes the life of Epaphroditus, the usage alludes to relationship.

In Unit D, Paul discusses Timothy and Epaphroditus. In the second half of the unit, he mentions the need to send Epaphroditus back to the Philippians. The clause παραβολευσάμενος τῇ ψυχῇ (risking [his] soul) which modifies the preceding clause διὰ τὸ ἔργον Χριστοῦ μέχρι θανάτου ἤγγισεν (because of the work of Christ he came close to almost die), portrays the near death experience of Epaphroditus. Hence, ψυχή (soul) simply means life, Epaphroditus' physical life.[66] Nonetheless, if the wider textual context is considered, there is a nuance worth noting. The following ἵνα clause indicates that the noble act of Epaphroditus is closely related to Paul's discussion of friendship. The clause ἵνα ἀναπληρώσῃ τὸ ὑμῶν ὑστέρημα τῆς πρός με λειτουργίας (so that he could make up for your inability to serve me) illustrates the relational aspect of Epaphroditus' action. Risking his life is not merely an individual act of sacrifice. Instead, it is deeply related to the Philippian community as indicated by ἀναπληρώσῃ τὸ ὑμῶν ὑστέρημα (he could make up for your inability). In other words, the clause παραβολευσάμενος τῇ ψυχῇ (risking [his] soul) alludes to the deep friendship between Epaphroditus (who represents the Philippians) with Paul.[67]

Based on an analysis of the wider textual context, the allusion to friendship becomes more evident. As previously mentioned, the theme depicted in Unit D contributes to the thematic prominence of relationship in the letter. The relationship between Paul (who is going to send Timothy to the

---

[65] Hawthorne (1983:106) specifies this as friendship that the apostle shares together with his friends at Philippi.

[66] The sense of ψυχή (soul) in 2:30 is widely understood as physical life (O'Brien 1991:343; Hawthorne 1983:119; Beare 1959:99; Reumann 2008:432; Fee 1995:283; Martin 1989:123; Hansen 2009:208–209; Thurston and Ryan 2005:105).

[67] Thurston and Ryan (2005:105) argue that the participle, παραβολευσάμενος, is used in the papyri to describe someone who exposes himself to danger for the sake of friendship. Thus, it highlights the theme of friendship.

Philippians) and the Philippians (who have previously sent Epaphroditus to Paul) dominates the discussion in this unit. Of interest, Paul employs ἰσόψυχον (like-minded, or literally, same-souled) to portray Timothy in the early part of Unit D: For I have no one who is like-minded (ἰσόψυχον) who will genuinely be concerned for the things concerning you in 2:20. The lexical meaning of ἰσόψυχος is like-minded (Bauer 1979:381), which points to Timothy in this text. This like-mindedness actually refers to the concern of Paul (and Timothy) for the Philippians. A comparison of ἰσόψυχος (like-minded) in the early part of Unit D and ψυχή (soul) in the latter part of Unit D is meaningful. On the one hand, Timothy, who is like-minded (ἰσόψυχος) with Paul, is genuinely concerned for the Philippians. On the other hand, Epaphroditus, who represents the Philippians, risks his life (ψυχή) for the sake of his friendship with Paul. Although ἰσόψυχος (like-minded) and ψυχή (soul) do not share an identical meaning in their own sentences, both words are used in the context of the relational aspect. Putting different elements together, μιᾷ ψυχῇ (in one soul) plus σύμψυχοι (fellow-souled) in Unit C, and ἰσόψυχος (like-minded,or literally, same-souled) plus ψυχή (soul) in Unit D, all point in the same direction: the corporate unity and friendship.

4.2.1.3 *Πνεῦμα (spirit) in Units C and D*

The term πνεῦμα (spirit) occurs five times in Philippians. Two of these occurrences denote the divine Spirit: τοῦ πνεύματος ᾽Ιησοῦ Χριστοῦ (the Spirit of Jesus Christ) in 1:19; and πνεύματι θεοῦ (Spirit of God) in 3:3. The remaining three occurrences, including ἑνὶ πνεύματι (in one spirit) in 1:27; κοινωνία πνεύματος (fellowship of spirit) in 2:1; and τοῦ πνεύματος ὑμῶν (your spirit) in 4:23, show that the term carries the corporate and communal reference.

῾Ενὶ πνεύματι (in one spirit) and κοινωνία πνεύματος (fellowship of spirit) in Unit C

In 1:27, πνεῦμα (spirit) neither connotes the human spirit in an ontological sense nor denotes the Holy Spirit. Resembling ψυχή (soul) in 1:27, πνεῦμα (spirit) is used as a metaphor, depicting the Philippians united together as a corporate entity, as if a single communal being, having one πνεῦμα (spirit). The rationale behind this argument is as follows.

First, the phrases ἑνὶ πνεύματι (in one spirit) and μιᾷ ψυχῇ (in one soul) are synonymous, portraying corporate and communal aspects.[68] As shown in figure 4.2, μιᾷ ψυχῇ συναθλοῦντες (striving together in one soul) is a

---

[68] This view is also held by a number of scholars. Banker (1996:71) argues that the two phrases are idiomatic, both mean unitedly. For Hawthorne (1983:56–57), the two expressions are equivalent in meaning. Silva (1992:94) also suggests that πνεῦμα (spirit) and ψυχή (soul) are in the form of parallelism. Beare (1959:67), Peterlin (1995:56–57), and Thurston and Ryan (2005:69) hold that the two clauses depict unity of heart and purpose.

subordinate clause of στήκετε ἐν ἑνὶ πνεύματι (stand firm in one spirit). The participle συναθλοῦντες (striving together) modifies its main verb στήκετε (stand firm). Συναθλοῦντες (striving together) is a post-verbal present participle that follows the present imperative στήκετε (you must stand firm), which can well be a participle of means (Wallace 1996:628–629). "Stand firm in one spirit by means of striving together in one soul" as Paul states. The subordinate clause is used to augment the meaning of the main clause. Thus it is logical to see that ἑνὶ πνεύματι (in one spirit) and μιᾷ ψυχῇ (in one soul) are in parallel, synonymously pointing to communal unity. Just as ψυχή (soul) is not used to connote a human soul, since Paul urges the community to strive "in one soul," neither should πνεῦμα (spirit) be regarded as depicting a human spirit.[69] Instead, they both are used to portray the community as one united corporate being, which is further highlighted by the lexical cohesion of corporate entity through the use of ἑνὶ (one), μιᾷ (one), and the prefix συν-.

---

[69] The term denotes "a common spirit" behind the ideas of "Christian harmony" instead of the Holy Spirit (Hawthorne 1983:96); "mental harmony" and "singleness of purpose" (Silva 1992:94); "single mind" (Marshall 1992:35); "common attitude" (Thurston and Ryan 2005:69); "communal disposition" (Vincent 1897:33); "collective spirit of the Philippians" (Reed 1997:300); or "inward unity" (Beare 1959:67).

Key:

Subject | **Main Verb** | Object
⟋_____ : Subordinate Clause
|_____ : Modifier or Adjectival/Adverbial Word/Phrase
[   ]: Implied/Ellipsis
X: Not required

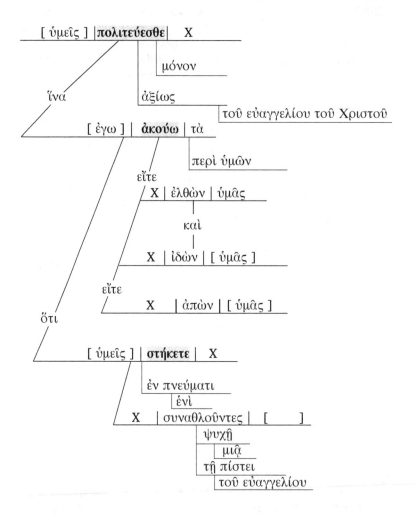

Figure 4.2. Syntactical structure of Philippians 1:27.

Second, I refute the idea that πνεῦμα (spirit) connotes the Holy Spirit. Many scholars interpret the spirit as the Holy Spirit.[70] Two key arguments support their interpretation. First, the locative phrase ἑνὶ πνεύματι (in one spirit), in 1 Cor 12:13 and Eph 2:18, refers to the Holy Spirit, and is never used in the Pauline epistles to describe oneness or unity. Second, given the occurrence of a similar clause στήκετε ἐν κυρίῳ (stand firm in the Lord, 4:1), πνεῦμα (spirit) should be understood as parallel with κυριός (Lord). However, I identify two problems with these two arguments:

First and foremost, as discussed in chapter 2, the meaning of a word must be determined by its textual context, both at the sentential level and the discourse level. In ascertaining the meaning of the phrase ἑνὶ πνεύματι (in one spirit), whilst there is value in consulting other discourses from Paul (the same phrase in 1 Cor 12:13 and Eph 2:18)[71] and referring to a similar clause in the same epistle (stand firm in the Lord in 4:1), the immediate textual context must be given utmost priority. Therefore, its subordinate clause, μιᾷ ψυχῇ συναθλοῦντες (striving together in one soul), and its preceding main clause, ἀξίως τοῦ εὐαγγελίου τοῦ Χριστοῦ πολιτεύεσθε (conduct yourselves worthy of the gospel of Christ) must be considered. As previously argued, πνεῦμα (spirit) is best understood as a metaphor portraying corporate unity, which is illustrated by its parallel μιᾷ ψυχῇ (in one soul) and the citizenship of a community denoted by πολιτεύεσθε (conduct yourselves).

Second, there are some differences between Phil 1:27 and the other two texts. The phrase ἑνὶ πνεύματι (in one spirit) in 1 Cor 12:13 occurs in an independent clause, appearing in the discussion concerning the gifts of the Holy Spirit (1 Cor 12). The phrase ἑνὶ πνεύματι (in one spirit) in Eph 2:18 occurs in a subordinate clause, appearing in the context that mentions the Trinity: δι᾽ αὐτοῦ ἔχομεν τὴν προσαγωγὴν οἱ ἀμφότεροι ἐν ἑνὶ πνεύματι πρὸς τὸν πατέρα (through him, we both have access to the Father by means in Spirit), with the αὐτοῦ (him) referring to Christ. In both cases, the Holy Spirit is an obvious interpretation for πνεῦμα. Nonetheless, the clause στήκετε ἐν ἑνὶ πνεύματι (stand in in one spirit) in Phil 1:27 is syntactically connected to a subordinate clause with another anthropological term, and its context (Unit C, 1:27–2:18) does not contain any discussion of the Holy Spirit. Furthermore, if πνεῦμα (spirit) denotes the Holy Spirit, then πνεῦμα (spirit) would be a personal noun (instead of an object) by definition. The combination of a preposition ἐν (in) and a dative personal noun is used to depict means or instrument (Wallace 1996:373–375).[72] If the subordinate clause is considered, which contains the participle of "means," the text

---

[70] See Fee 1995:163–166; Martin 1989:83; Bockmuehl 1998:99; Osiek 2000:49; Reumann 2008:266. Bockmuehl, Osiek, and Reumann quote the arguments provided by Fee in their work.

[71] Whether Ephesians is an authentic Pauline letter is disputed.

[72] Fee (1995:165) argues that it is definitely a locative, a dative denoting sphere. Nonetheless, the Holy Spirit is a divine being instead of an object.

would read: "Stand firm by means of one Spirit, by means of striving together in one soul." The two "means" ("one Spirit" and "striving together in one soul") would become parallel in meaning. This would almost equate the Holy Spirit with striving in one soul, an unnatural interpretation.[73] On the other hand, if the dative noun is interpreted as an agent,[74] it would be even more problematic. Στήκετε (stand firm) is clearly understood as an action taken by the Philippians instead of the Holy Spirit.[75] In contrary, it is much more natural to regard πνεῦμα (spirit) and ψυχή (soul) as in parallel: "Stand firm unitedly (as if one corporate being) together by striving unitedly (as if one corporate being) for the faith of the gospel."

One minor argument supporting the meaning of the Holy Spirit rests on the phrase κοινωνία πνεύματος (fellowship of spirit, 2:1) in the following context. Since πνεῦμα (spirit) in 2:1 connotes the Holy Spirit, as widely argued,[76] it is natural for πνεῦμα (spirit) in 1:27 to have the same denotation? (Fee 1995:165). However, this interpretation is not entirely unambiguous.[77] The strongest argument supporting the meaning of the Holy Spirit is the occurrence of a similar phrase in Paul's final benediction in 2 Cor 13:13: ἡ κοινωνία τοῦ ἁγίου πνεύματος (the fellowship of the Holy Spirit).[78] However, this argument is contestable. Πνεῦμα (spirit) in Phil 2:1 is anarthrous, but πνεῦμα (spirit) in 2 Cor 13:13 is articular. Given this, F. F. Bruce interprets the indefinite πνεῦμα (spirit) in Phil 2:1 as "spiritual" instead of the Holy Spirit (Bruce 1965:167). I agree with Bruce's interpretation. The anarthrous genitive noun πνεύματος (of spirit), together with κοινωνία (fellowship), should be interpreted as "spiritual fellowship." This interpretation does not contradict the context in which corporate unity is emphasised. Furthermore, if πνεῦμα (spirit) denotes the Holy Spirit, then it would likely

---

[73] The clause στήκετε ἐν κυρίῳ (stand firm in the Lord) in 4:1 does not have this problem, since it stands without any subordinate clause attaching to it. "Stand firm by means of the Lord" is an appropriate interpretation.

[74] The function of the Holy Spirit, according to Martin (1989:83), gears towards the definition of agent.

[75] Unlike the passage in 1 Cor 12:13, the main verb, ἐβαπτίσθημεν (we were baptized), is in passive voice. Therefore, understanding the Spirit (ἐν ἑνὶ πνεύματι) as the agent or instrument doing the action is natural: "We were baptised by the agent/means of the one Spirit."

[76] This view is supported by many commentators (Lightfoot 1913:107; Osiek 2000:52; Vincent 1897:54; Reumann 2008:302; Hansen 2009:110; Martin 1989:86–87; Fee 1995:181; Marshall 1992:42; Fowl 2005:80; Beare 1959:71; Hawthorne 1983:66; Witherington 1994:61–62).

[77] As well argued by Bockmuehl (1998:106), the connotation of πνεῦμα (spirit) in 1:27 and 2:1 are ambiguous.

[78] An argument cited by scholars, including Bockmuehl (1998:107) and Reumann (2008:302). Κοινωνία πνεύματος (fellowship of spirit) is not found elsewhere in other Pauline works. The similar phrase in 2 Cor 13:13, ἡ κοινωνία τοῦ ἁγίου πνεύματος (the fellowship of the Holy Spirit), is its closest form.

have been in dative case to form a parallel with the preceding phrase in the same verse: Εἴ τις οὖν παράκλησις ἐν Χριστῷ...εἴ τις κοινωνία πνεύματι (therefore, if there is some comfort in Christ...if there is some fellowship *in spirit*). Furthermore, the genitive singular πνεύματος (of spirit) is almost always articular or coupled with a relevant modifier, such as ἁγίου (holy) and θεοῦ (of God) when used by Paul to denote the Holy Spirit.[79]

Τοῦ πνεύματος ὑμῶν (your spirit) in letter-closing

The phrase μετὰ τοῦ πνεύματος ὑμῶν (with your spirit) in 4:23 in the letter-closing is part of the benediction which ends the letter. The singular πνεῦμα (spirit) occurs in the abnormal singular construct. I present a detailed analysis of this Pauline benediction, together with the exact same benediction occurring in Galatians and Philemon, in chapter 6. Nonetheless, an overview of the findings is as follows. The phrase μετὰ τοῦ πνεύματος ὑμῶν (with your spirit) is synonymous with μεθ' ὑμῶν (with you). The singular πνεῦμα (spirit) is not a distributive singular noun. Rather, πνεῦμα (spirit) is a normal singular, pointing to one united corporate being despite the presence of many members denoted by a plural ὑμῶν (your).

4.2.1.4 Σῶμα (body) in Unit E

Σῶμα (body) occurs twice in Unit E: τὸ σῶμα τῆς ταπεινώσεως ἡμῶν σύμμορφον τῷ σώματι τῆς δόξης αὐτοῦ (our humble body into the likeness of his glorious body) in 3:21. In discussing a future resurrection, the two occurrences of the singular σῶμα (body) denote the body of the Philippians. The phrase τὸ σῶμα ἡμῶν (our body) is another abnormal singular construct found in the epistle.[80] In light of the context, σῶμα (body) should not be automatically treated as a distributive singular. In the immediate context, believers are portrayed as: "a group of citizens (πολίτευμα) in heaven"

---

[79] Πνεύματος (of spirit), the singular genitive noun, occurs 36 times in Paul's letters. 29 of them clearly denote the Holy Spirit. Among them, 19 are articular (Rom 8:2, 5, 6, 23, 27; 15:30; 1 Cor 2:10, 14; 12:7, 8; 2 Cor 1:22; 3:8; 5:5; 13:13; Gal 3:14; 5:17, 22; 6:8; Phil 1:19), and eight are coupled with a relevant modifier: ἁγίου (holy) in Rom 5:5; 8:11; 15:13; 1 Cor 6:19; 1 Thess 1:6; θεοῦ (God's) in Rom 15:19; αὐτοῦ (Christ's) in Rom 8:11; κυρίου (Lord's) in 2 Cor 3:18. In other words, only 3 of 29 occurrences of the anarthrous πνεύματος (of spirit) denote the Holy Spirit (Rom 7:6; 1 Cor 2:4, 13). The occurrences of πνεύματος (of spirit) that do not denote the Holy Spirit (either obviously or contestable) are found in Phil 2:1; 1 Cor 5:4; 2 Cor 3:6, 7:1; Gal 6:18; Phil 4:23; and Phlm 1:25.

[80] Many scholars do not comment on the singular use of σῶμα (body) in 3:21 (Hawthorne 1983:172; Beare 1959:138–140; Vincent 1897:120–1; Marshall 1992:104; Silva 1992:215; Bockmuehl 1998:236; Fowl 2005:175; Martin 1989:148; Hansen 2009:272–273; Fee 1995:382–383; Osiek 2000:106; Thurston and Ryan 2005:134).

in 3:20,[81] which contrasts with another group: "the enemies of the cross of Christ" in 3:18. The singular πολίτευμα denotes a group of heavenly citizens, pointing to the believing community.[82] Therefore, the singular σῶμα (body) in 3:21 can be interpreted as a deliberate act to highlight the corporate unity. In addition, this reflects the wider context, in which communal relationship is the focus. This nuance suggests that Paul is not interested in the resurrection and transformation of an individual believer.[83] Rather, he is chiefly concerned with all the individuals, as indicated by ἡμῶν (our), in the community, as signified by the singular σῶμα (body).

4.2.1.5 Φρονέω *(to think) in Philippians*

Φρονέω (to think) occurs ten times in Philippians. As previously mentioned, its corresponding noun φρήν denotes mind (which literally means diaphragm in its plural form). In the epistle, φρονέω (to think) appears in most semantic units (A, C, E, F, and G).[84]

In Unit A, Paul portrays his thought for the Philippians: ἐμοὶ τοῦτο φρονεῖν ὑπὲρ πάντων ὑμῶν (for me to think this about all of you) in 1:7. In Unit C, Paul urges the Philippians to unite: τὸ αὐτὸ φρονῆτε...τὸ ἓν φρονοῦντες (to think the same thing...be of one mind) in 2:2 by showing humility (τῇ ταπεινοφροσύνῃ) in 2:3[85] as shown by Christ: Τοῦτο φρονεῖτε ἐν ὑμῖν ὃ καὶ ἐν Χριστῷ Ἰησοῦ (have the same mind in you as it was in

---

[81] According to Bauer (1979:686), the lexical meaning of πολίτευμα is commonwealth, usually denoting a colony of foreigners or relocated veterans.

[82] Krentz (2008:258) argues that πολίτευμα (citizenship/a group of citizens) is used in 3:20 to portray the Philippians as a heavenly, eschatological colony inside Philippi. This colony concept is supported by archaeological findings, which suggest that Philippi went through "at least 500 years of successive colonization" (Zerbe 2009:198). Doble argues (2002:18) that πολίτευμα (citizenship/a group of citizens) in 3:20 points to a community living in allegiance to its acknowledged authority. By explaining σῶμα (body) in light of πολίτευμα (citizenship/a group of citizens), Doble (2002:26) asserts that σῶμα τῆς ταπεινώσεως (the humble body) refers to the embodied selves of the community, with their citizenship (1:27; 3:20) being characterised by humility. I agree with Doble regarding the communal dimension of σῶμα (body), given that the usage here is coherent with the citizenship alluded to in πολιτεύεσθε (conduct yourselves, 1:27). As previously argued, communal unity is the key message portrayed by πολιτεύεσθε (conduct yourselves) and ἑνὶ πνεύματι (in one spirit) and μιᾷ ψυχῇ (in one soul).

[83] Otherwise, the text would have been written as follows: τὰ σώματα τῆς ταπεινώσεως ἡμῶν...τοῖς σωμάσιν τῆς δόξης αὐτοῦ (our humble bodies...into the bodies of his glory).

[84] Φρονέω (to think) occurs in 1:7; 2:2 (twice), 5; 3:15 (twice), 19; 4:2, 10 (twice). Its corresponding word ταπεινοφροσύνη (humility) occurs in 2:3.

[85] Doble (2002:6–11) regards all the words relating to φρονέω (to think) as pointing to the mindedness, with the community-mindedness highlighted with the combination of ταπ- (humble-) and φρον- (think-).

Christ Jesus) in 2:5. In Unit E, Paul encourages the mature to have the same mind (τοῦτο φρονῶμεν) in 3:15, indicating communal unity.[86] This word is also used to describe the mindset of the enemies: οἱ τὰ ἐπίγεια φρονοῦντες (thinking the earthly things) in 3:19. In Unit F, Paul urges Euodia and Syntyche to be united: τὸ αὐτὸ φρονεῖν (to think the same) in 4:2. Lastly, in Unit G, the friendship between Paul and the Philippians is addressed: τὸ ὑπὲρ ἐμοῦ φρονεῖν, ἐφ᾽ ᾧ καὶ ἐφρονεῖτε (to think for me, you were concerned for me) in 4:10.

Given these occurrences, φρονέω (to think) is predominately used to elucidate corporate unity and communal friendship, which is a central theme highlighted by the inclusio, as previously discussed: τὸ αὐτὸ φρονῆτε (you would think the same) in 2:2; τὸ αὐτὸ φρονεῖν (to think the same) in 4:2. Neither phrase means to share an identical thought and opinion.[87] Rather, they are used to engender unity, a unity in purpose through humility.[88] Overall, my analysis shows that corporate and communal aspects are connoted in the thematic meaning of φρονέω (to think), according to its common pattern and usage, which certainly transcends its lexical meaning, "think".

4.2.2 Sociolinguistic aspect

As previously discussed, the sociolinguistic aspect involves examining the relationship between the author and the audience to see whether further insights can be gained for understanding the discourse. In Philippians, instead of calling himself an apostle to exert his apostolic authority, Paul begins his letter by calling himself a δοῦλος (slave/servant) of Christ in 1:1.[89] This illustrates a "friendlier relationship" between the apostle and the recipients.[90] This kind of relationship is further indicated by other expressions.

---

[86] Φρονέω (to think) is used to describe those who do not share the same mind: εἴ τι ἑτέρως φρονεῖτε (if you think otherwise) in 3:15.

[87] As well argued by Hawthorne (1983:67), to demand drab uniformity of thought and everyone holding in common a particular opinion would only contribute to disunity.

[88] The phrase can also be understood as "unity of mind" (Silva 1992:161), "unison of thought" (Lightfoot 1913:108), "like-minded" (Hansen 2009:111).

[89] Paul's self-designation, a δοῦλος (slave/servant) of Christ, carries a positive connotation, alluding to his noble status and his leadership, which is different from an ordinary slave with a low status in the Greco-Roman world. For the discussion of this positive connotation, see § 2.3.2.3.

[90] Agosto (2005:102) argues that Paul calls himself both an apostle and a servant of Christ in Romans and Galatians. Comparatively speaking, the absence of stating his apostleship in Philippians reflects this friendlier relationship between Paul and the Philippians. Brown (2001:725) presumes that this self-designation would resonate with the Philippians in a way that it would not have resonated among the Galatians. The reason was due to a possible connection between the Philippians

In addition to ἀδελφοί, he addresses the Philippians by using various words with the prefix συν- instead of calling them φίλος (friend): συγκοινωνούς (partakers) in 1:7; σύζυγε (fellow worker) in 4:3; and συνεργῶν (fellow workers) in 4:3. For Epaphroditus, a representative of the Philippians, Paul refers to him as συνεργὸν (fellow worker) in 2:25 and συστρατιώτην (fellow soldier) in 2:25. As reiterated, the use of words with the prefix συν- indicates that Philippians is a letter of friendship.[91] In other words, the relationship between Paul and the Philippians is friendship and partnership.[92]

However, there are two important issues in identifying this relationship as mere friendship. First, Paul does not use φίλος (friend) to address his friends in Philippi. Second, the gift-giving segment in the epistle does not fit with the Greco-Roman friendship category.

Paul's hesitation to address the Philippians as φίλος (friend) invites discussion. For instance, Witherington presents a sound argument. He argues that Paul is the mentor of the Philippians. Their relationship is "friendly and affectionate," to the extent that Paul does not need to "pull rank" to persuade them (Witherington 1994:120–121). Thus, he appeals to them on the basis of this close relationship. It is likely that the friendship language is only a means adopted by Paul to achieve a particular goal.

The friendship described in the letter is at odds with the Greco-Roman practice, in particular Paul's response to the gift received from the Philippians (4:15–19). In the Greco-Roman world, gift-giving invites social reciprocity in which the receiver should repay the gift to the giver who is socially more superior as if repaying a debt, in order to form a lasting relationship (Peterman 1997:88). Nonetheless, the writing of Paul does not reflect that he is indebted to the Philippians. In fact, he expresses that he shares a deeper partnership with them, which transcends the normal exchange embedded in Greco-Roman gift-giving (ibid. 158–159). The letter is not simply a friendship letter, expressing affection. Instead, Paul has a particular purpose about which he desires to persuade the Philippians by using the partnership and friendship language.[93]

---

and the family of Caesar, whom Paul met during his imprisonment in Rome during the composition of Philippians.

[91] Fitzgerald (2007:293–294) details the elements in ancient Greek friendship. By referring to different Greek literature, Fitzgerald demonstrates that the language used in Philippians is friendship language. Likewise, Stowers (1991:111–113) shows how μιᾷ ψυχῇ (in one soul), the κοινωνία (fellowship) language, and words with the prefix συν- are ancient friendship language. White (1990:211) also provides a similar analysis as Stowers', showing how the language in Philippians fits the idea of friendship in the Hellenistic moralist tradition.

[92] Lyons and Malas (2007:61–66) argue that the six key characteristics in Greco-Roman friendship (unity, partnership, equality, moral excellence, frankness, and loyalty) are detected in Philippians.

[93] Zerbe (2009:199–200) argues that merely treating the epistle as a letter of friendship with a nice, warm tone overlooks the political and subversive tone. He

The answers to these two issues, together with the findings of the discourse analysis, provide further insights regarding the following question: Why does Paul emphasise his deep partnership and friendship with the Philippians when the letter primarily concerns communal disunity? Does he use his friendship as a platform to persuade those who are in conflict to be united? Or, is Paul in fact part of the cause of this disunity? Although the text itself does not overtly name the connection between Paul and the conflict, it is a plausible argument. I agree with Witherington that Paul is a mentor and teacher of the Philippians. However, the heavy friendship and partnership language is not employed to simply appeal to a troubled community. Rather, it is highly likely that Paul appeals to the Philippians in a friendly and affectionate way for unity, a unity between the apostle and the community, vis-à-vis reconciliation. In other words, the disunity among the Philippians is somehow related to the apostle himself. This argument will be tested in the following discussion.

4.3 Thematic meaning of anthropological terms

In the previous analysis, I demonstrated that the coherent theme displayed in Philippians centres on friendship (between Paul and the community), communal relationship and corporate unity (within the community). My analysis of the key anthropological terms shows the corporate and communal reference illustrated by the use of various terms: καρδία (heart); ψυχή (soul), including σύμψυχοι (fellow-souled) and ἰσόψυχον (same-souled); πνεῦμα (spirit); and σῶμα (body). Although each of the anthropological terms carries a specific meaning in its sentence, many of their occurrences share a common thematic meaning. The terms are usually used in a metaphorical sense; and their occurrences form a coherent pattern within the discourse. Their common thematic meaning points to the corporate and communal aspect. This thematic meaning is the intended meaning of Paul who uses various terms to appeal for unity.

4.3.1 The flow of discourse and peak

As discussed in chapter 2 and demonstrated in chapter 3, as well as other discourse analyses, a discourse, including an epistle, usually displays a flow of progress.[94] The peak of a discourse usually reveals the core message of a discourse; and it can be identified by several features. As previously mentioned, peak is "a zone of turbulence," in which an epistolary climax

---

also suggests that Philippians is primarily about practicing Messianic citizenship. Although citizenship is the language that Paul uses, I arguably assert that the epistle addresses a deeper issue, which is the relational challenge between Paul and the Philippians.

[94] For further discussion of discourse flow, see § 2.3.2.2 and § 3.2.1.5.

appears and is then followed by a dénouement, the release of tension. Peak is signified by a shift of the proportion of use of a particular grammatical device, or a shift to specific grammatical element. In addition, in order to prevent the audience from missing the utmost important point the narrator employs extra words, including parallelism, paraphrase, and tautologies to highlight the key climactic event (Longacre 1983:39).[95]

The peak or climax of a discourse usually exhibits several characteristics. First, it normally appears towards the end of a discourse. Second, it is marked by a shift in the occurrence of a grammatical device. Third, specific persons might be emphasised, usually those involved in a conflict situation. Fourth, the theme of the climax is developed in earlier episodes before reappearing more fully in the peak. Fifth, extra words, serving either as parallelism or synonym, highlight the climactic event. Finally, a resolution is presented, signifying the dénouement.

In Philippians, Unit F matches all the characteristics of a peak. First, it is situated near the end of the epistle, appearing as the second-last major semantic unit. Second, there is a significant shift in the use of imperatives. Eight imperatives are used in only eight verses. Unlike the imperative verbs in previous segments, the frequency and their close proximity is striking.[96] Third, the unit does show a shift to specific participants. The communal unity issue discussed in the earlier semantic units is now specified as the problem surrounding two persons, Euodia and Syntyche, with a conflict element alluded to by the expression, τὸ αὐτὸ φρονεῖν (to think the same).[97] Fourth, the concepts of στήκετε (stand firm) and τὸ αὐτὸ φρονεῖν (to think the same) are fully "developed" and clearly expressed in 4:1–3. The general exhortation to the Philippians, στήκετε ἐν ἑνὶ πνεύματι, μιᾷ ψυχῇ συναθλοῦντες (stand firm in one spirit, striving together in one soul) in 1:27, is now specified in the pre-peak episode, στήκετε ἐν κυρίῳ (stand firm in the Lord) in 4:1, since Paul is about to focus on the two women. In addition, the general encouragement to the Philippians, τὸ αὐτὸ φρονῆτε (you should think the same) in 2:2, in an earlier episode (Unit C) is now "fully developed" into a specific expression, τὸ αὐτὸ φρονεῖν (to think the same) in 4:2 in the peak, pointing to the two women. Fifth, the clustered use of the prefix συν- is found in the same verse (4:3): σύζυγε (fellow worker); συλλαμβάνου (help); συνήθλησάν (they strived together); and συνεργῶν (fellow workers). This highlights the relationship between Paul and the

---

[95] As previously mentioned, peak also occurs in non-narrative discourses, including expository and hortatory discourses. For an explanation of peak, see § 2.3.2.2.

[96] As previously mentioned, there are also eight imperatives throughout Unit C (1:27–2:18). However, these eight imperatives are spread across 22 verses, and as such, the intensity and frequency is less than in Unit F.

[97] In 4:2, the repetition of the verb, παρακαλῶ (I urge), is commonly perceived as a means to heighten Paul's exhortation and to emphasise the equal importance of both women (Hawthorne 1983:178; Silva 1992:222; Thurston and Ryan 2005:140).

Philippians. The issue of unity moves from within the community to the relationship between Paul and the Philippians.[98] Arguably, this repetition is not mere coincidence. I contend that the repetitive use of the prefix συν- as a cluster, in 4:3, underscores the climactic point in 4:2–3. This displays a form of synonym by including other words with similar connotations to emphasise the climax.

Finally, regarding the resolution offered to the issue, the occurrence of συλλαμβάνου αὐταῖς (help them) in 4:3 is most intriguing. Among all the imperatives occurring in Unit F, the clause συλλαμβάνου αὐταῖς (help them) in 4:3 unmistakably stands out. Apart from the intransitive imperative verb χαίρετε (rejoice) in 4:4, which does not require an accusative noun as an object in the clause, συλλαμβάνω (to help) is the only transitive verb in this unit that does not follow the Object-Verb word order.[99]All the other imperatives display an OV structure, including μηδὲν μεριμνᾶτε (be anxious of nothing) in 4:6, τὰ αἰτήματα ὑμῶν γνωριζέσθω (make your requests known) in 4:6, ταῦτα λογίζεσθε (consider these things) in 4:8, and ταῦτα πράσσετε (practice these things) in 4:9.[100] The common OV order is the norm, or known as "unmarked" in linguistic terms.[101] By contrast, the clause συλλαμβάνου αὐταῖς (help them) displays a VO word order.[102] Being a "marked" structure, the clause signifies its prominence in this climactic unit. In this climax, "Help them!" is the resolution offered by Paul, a prominent exhortation made in the peak. As previously mentioned, συλλαμβάνω (to help) also alludes to the connotation of "togetherness." Moreover, the Philippians are addressed by Paul with the singular σέ (you) in 4:3, instead of a plural ὑμᾶς (you), before calling them as his γνήσιε σύζυγε (true fellow worker). The use of σέ (you, in singular form) further accentuates the single corporate entity of the Philippian community.

---

[98] Although one of the lexical meanings of συλλαμβάνω is "help," the word connotes "togetherness" in regard to this particular meaning. Futhermore, when συλλαμβάνω is employed to denote help or support, the case of the respective noun is dative, instead of accusative (Bauer 1979:777).

[99] It is abbreviated as VO hereafter. Similarly, Object-Verb is abbreviated as OV.

[100] Since the subject of an imperative verb is not stated as it is implied by the verb itself, the normal rule of word order, as VSO as the unmarked word order scheme, cannot be applied (Reed 1997:380).

[101] The term "unmarked" denotes the usual norm of the grammatical or syntactical structure used in a text. The opposite is "marked," as the writer wants to highlight an important point by altering the "normal" grammatical or syntactical structure. Therefore, a "marked" structure indicates emphasis.

[102] Regarding the discussion of word order in the NT, Voelz (2005:425–427) gives a brief account of how Semitic language impacts on the word order of some of the NT books. On the other hand, Terry (1995:137–154) provides a very detailed analysis. He shows that VSO is rare in hortatory writings (epistles) by conducting an analysis of several selected NT epistles with only 2.8% of all the different word orders (although this word order is more frequent in the gospels).

The dénouement is marked by Χαίρετε ἐν κυρίῳ πάντοτε· πάλιν ἐρῶ, χαίρετε (rejoice in the Lord always, I shall say again, rejoice) in 4:4. As argued, the transitional role of the clustered χαίρω (to rejoice) is now employed to signify a new sub-division. The climax is wound down, followed by exhortatory encouragements illustrated by the intensive use of imperative.[103]

---

[103] According to Longacre (1983:22), dénouement can be considered as part of the peak episode, occurring right after the climactic moment.

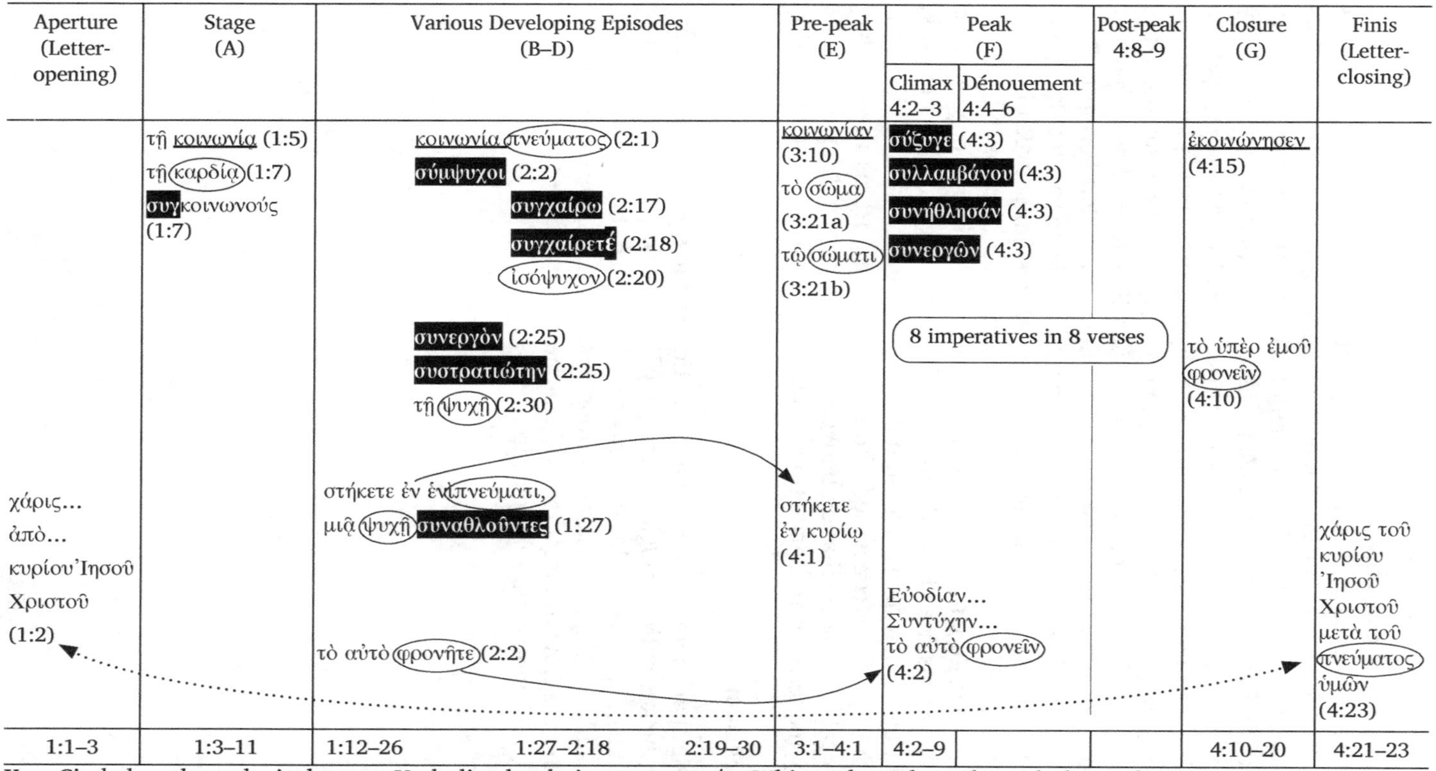

Aperture (Letter-opening)	Stage (A)	Various Developing Episodes (B–D)	Pre-peak (E)	Peak (F) Climax 4:2–3 / Dénouement 4:4–6	Post-peak 4:8–9	Closure (G)	Finis (Letter-closing)
χάρις... ἀπὸ... κυρίου Ἰησοῦ Χριστοῦ (1:2)	τῇ κοινωνίᾳ (1:5) τῇ καρδίᾳ (1:7) συγκοινωνούς (1:7)	κοινωνία πνεύματος (2:1) σύμψυχοι (2:2) συνχαίρω (2:17) συνχαίρετέ (2:18) ἰσόψυχον (2:20) συνεργόν (2:25) συνστρατιώτην (2:25) τῇ ψυχῇ (2:30) στήκετε ἐν ἑνὶ πνεύματι, μιᾷ ψυχῇ συναθλοῦντες (1:27) τὸ αὐτὸ φρονῆτε (2:2)	κοινωνίαν (3:10) τὸ σῶμα (3:21a) τῷ σώματι (3:21b) στήκετε ἐν κυρίῳ (4:1)	σύζυγε (4:3) συνλαμβάνου (4:3) συνήθλησάν (4:3) συνεργῶν (4:3) 8 imperatives in 8 verses Εὐοδίαν... Συντύχην... τὸ αὐτὸ φρονεῖν (4:2)		ἐκοινώνησεν (4:15) τὸ ὑπὲρ ἐμοῦ φρονεῖν (4:10)	χάρις τοῦ κυρίου Ἰησοῦ Χριστοῦ μετὰ τοῦ πνεύματος ὑμῶν (4:23)
1:1–3	1:3–11	1:12–26 / 1:27–2:18 / 2:19–30	3:1–4:1	4:2–9		4:10–20	4:21–23

Key: Circled: anthropological terms; Underlined: relating to κοινωνία; White-coloured words: with the prefix συν-
→ : Inclusio and development of prominent theme; ⋯⋯► : Inclusio

Figure 4.3. The flow of discourse of Philippians.

The flow of discourse is shown in figure 4.3. From the flow of discourse, the dominant and coherent theme is corporate unity. The community is metaphorically portrayed as a single corporate being, which is depicted as having a πνεῦμα (spirit) or a ψυχή (soul), and having a mind with the capacity of τὸ αὐτὸ φρονεῖν (to think the same). The members of this being are σύμψυχοι (fellow-souled), whom Paul calls σύζυγε (fellow worker). They are regarded as his συνεργοί (fellow workers) and συγκοινωνοί (partakers). Paul urges them, as a corporate being, by this exhortation: συγχαίρετέ (rejoice together). And in his benediction, the apostle calls for the grace of Christ to be with this corporate being which is portrayed as πνεύματος ὑμῶν "your (in plural form) spirit (in singular form)". Furthermore, Paul considers himself as part of this community as demonstrated by many words with the prefix συν-, highlighting the partnership between him and the community. The climax reveals that the issue that disturbs the unity is the rife between Euodia and Syntyche. However, the constant approach for Paul to invoke his friendship throughout the letter, including in the peak, subtly illustrates that the relational unity between Paul and the Philippians is what the apostle is concerned about. By appealing to his friends, Paul explicitly calls for reconciliation between the two women. Nonetheless, he implicitly requests for reconciliation between the Philippians and himself.

4.4 Conclusion

I conclude that there is a common thematic meaning in Philippians, connoted by the key anthropological terms, καρδία (heart), ψυχή (soul), πνεῦμα (spirit), and σῶμα (body). Based on my investigation of the discourse structure, the anthropological terms in various semantic units, the sociolinguistic aspect, and the flow of discourse, the common thematic meaning is corporate unity and communal relationship.

5

Καρδία in Romans and
2 Corinthians 1–9

5.0 Introduction

In this chapter, I would like to address Stage III of this study—a single anthropological term within multiple discourses. I investigate the term καρδία (heart),[1] and its possible social and corporate connotations in the Pauline epistles. Καρδία occurs 37 times in the Pauline epistles,[2] with 71% of its occurrences located in Romans and 2 Corinthians.[3] As in previous

---

[1] From this point onwards, the English translation, heart, for the term καρδία is not provided in this chapter.

[2] If καρδία is compared with other Pauline anthropological terms, its occurrence is relatively infrequent; for example, σάρξ (flesh) occurs 71 times, and σῶμα (body), 74 times. Comparatively less attention is paid to the study of καρδία in the NT. The most comprehensive works are by Behm (1965:611–613), Bauer (1979:403), and Jewett (1971:305–333). Many scholars quote the dictionary definition found in the TDNT, which defines καρδία as the seat of emotion, volition, and reason.

[3] Καρδία occurs 15 times in Romans (41%), five times in 1 Corinthians (14%), 11 times in 2 Corinthians (30%), one time in Galatians (3%), twice in Philippians (5%), three times in 1 Thessalonians (8%), and no times in Philemon. The percentages indicate the occurrences in a given epistle over the total occurrences in all seven Pauline epistles. The number of occurrences of καρδία per chapter in a given epistle is as follows: 0.9 in Romans, 0.3 in 1 Corinthians, 0.8 in 2 Corinthians, 0.2 in Galatians, 0.5 in Philippians, 0.6 in 1 Thessalonians, and 0 in Philemon. Thus

chapters, I first identify the discourse structure of a particular epistle, which provides a framework for analysing καρδία according to its occurrences in various semantic units and in the entire discourse.

5.1 Καρδία in Romans

In the first section of this chapter I examine καρδία in Romans, by identifying the discourse structure of the epistle, and then ascertaining the thematic meaning of καρδία in this discourse.

5.1.1 Discourse structure of Romans

As in previous chapters, an analysis of the discourse structure elucidates the major semantic units in Romans by investigating the discourse markers, examining the discourse coherence, and ascertaining the macrostructure.

5.1.1.1 Discourse markers

The four discourse markers that illuminate the semantic units in Romans are change of verb mood, lexical cohesion, formulas, and the use of the vocative.

Lexical cohesion

In Romans, some key words are unusually frequent when compared with their overall occurrences in the Pauline epistles (see Appendix 3). These words, which are useful in identifying different major topics, include δικαιόω (to justify), ἁμαρτία (sin), πίστις (faith), Ἰσραήλ (Israel), Ἰουδαῖος (Jew), and θάνατος (death).[4]

First, justification and sin are two key motifs in Romans. Δικαιόω (to justify) and ἁμαρτία (sin) occur 15 and 48 times respectively.[5] Their occurrences are concentrated in the first half of the letter: 100% of the occurrences

---

Romans and 2 Corinthians have the highest number of occurrences of καρδία per chapter.

[4] For δικαιόω (to justify), ἁμαρτία (sin), and Ἰσραήλ (Israel), more than half of their occurrences in Pauline letters are found in Romans alone. The following are the percentage of their occurrences in Romans when compared with that in all of the Pauline letters: δικαιόω (to justify), 60%; ἁμαρτία (sin), 81%; Ἰσραήλ (Israel), 69%. For πίστις (faith), Ἰουδαῖος (Jew), and θάνατος (death), nearly half of their occurrences are found in Romans. The percentage of their occurrences in Romans when compared with that in all of the Pauline letters are as follows: πίστις (faith), 44%; θάνατος (death), 49%; Ἰουδαῖος (Jew), 44%.

[5] The occurrences of δικαιόω (to justify): 2:23; 3:4, 20, 24, 26, 28, 30; 4:2, 5; 5:1, 9; 6:7; 8:30 (twice), 33.

of δικαιόω and 96% of the occurrences of ἁμαρτία are found in Rom 1–8. See figure 5.1.

Second, in the discussion of justification (Rom 1–8), there are three sub-topics. The first topic is illustrated by the occurrences of Ἰουδαῖος (Jew) and Ἕλλην (Greek),[6] which are clustered in Rom 1–3. In these chapters, Paul argues that both the Jews and the Gentiles are sinful, under God's judgment, and in need of the gospel.[7] The second topic focuses on faith as illustrated by the frequent occurrences of πίστις (faith), which are clustered in 3:22–4:20.[8] In these chapters, Paul discusses the role of faith in justification.[9] The third topic is illustrated by the occurrences of θάνατος (death) that are clustered in chapters 5–8. In these chapters, Paul explains the following relations: sin and death (5:12), the Law and death (7:13), the Holy Spirit and freedom from the principle of death (8:2).[10] The following figures show the clustered occurrences of Ἰουδαῖος (Jew) and Ἕλλην (Greek), πίστις (faith), and θάνατος (death). See figures 5.2, 5.3, 5.4.

Third, the discussion of justification (1–8) is followed by the topic of the salvation of Israel (9–11). This is reflected by the lexical cohesion of the word Ἰσραήλ (Israel) with all of its occurrences appearing in 9–11. See figure 5.5.

---

[6] Ἕλλην primarily means a Greek person; however, it is also employed in a broader sense, denoting a Gentile (a non-Jewish person).

[7] This is illustrated by the occurrences of Ἰουδαῖος (Jew) and Ἕλλην (Greek) in 1:16; 2:9, 10; 3:9. These reappear in Rom 9–10 after being absent for several chapters.

[8] The occurrences of πίστις (faith) are as follows: 1:8; 12, 17 (thrice); 3:3, 22, 25, 26, 27, 28, 30 (twice), 31; 4:5, 9, 11, 12, 13, 14, 16, 19, 20.

[9] Paul's discussion of this topic is exemplified by 3:24–25.

[10] These three relations can be understood as three sub-topics within Rom 5–8. The divisions can further be proved by the lexical cohesion of νόμος (law) and πνεῦμα (spirit). In Rom 7:1–25, the occurrences of νόμος (law) and πνεῦμα (spirit) are 23 and 1, respectively. However, the occurrences of νόμος (law) and πνεῦμα (spirit) in 8:1–29 are 5 and 21, respectively. Although both segments discuss the issue of death, there is a shift of focus from νόμος (law) in chapter 7 to πνεῦμα (spirit) in chapter 8. Regarding νόμος (law) in 8:2, ὁ γὰρ νόμος τοῦ πνεύματος (for the law of the spirit) and τοῦ νόμου τῆς ἁμαρτίας (the law of sin), the word does not denote the OT Law. The word denotes principle, which is one of the meanings of νόμος (law) in Koine Greek (Bauer 1979:542). According to Gosnell (2009:262), the reference of νόμος (law) in 7:1–8:2 alternates between a sense of written regulation, and a sense of some other overriding, controlling entity.

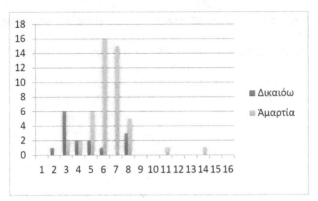

Figure 5.1. The occurrences of δικαιόω and ἁμαρτία in Romans.

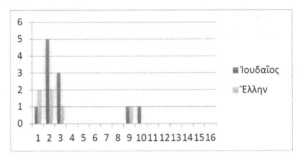

Figure 5.2. The occurrences of Ἰουδαῖος and Ἕλλην in Romans.

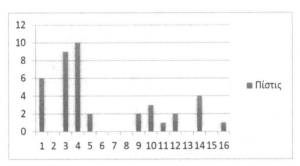

Figure 5.3. The occurrences of πίστις in Romans.

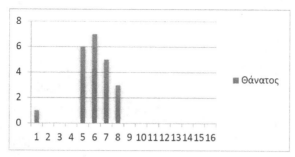

Figure 5.4. The occurrences of θάνατος in Romans.

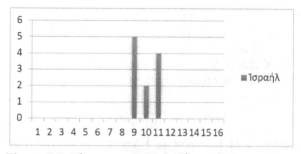

Figure 5.5. The occurrences of Ἰσραήλ in Romans.

As shown in this examination, the lexical cohesion of various key words indicates that Rom 1–11 is divided into two major discussions: justification (1–8) and the salvation of Israel (9–11). In the discussion of justification, there are three sub-topics: the sinfulness of both the Jews and the Gentiles (1–3), the role of faith in justification (3–4), and the freedom from death in Christ (5–8).

Change of verb mood

There are 62 imperative verbs in Romans.[11] Approximately 90% of them occur in Rom 11–16. The contrast between the early part and the latter part of the epistle is evident as shown in figure 5.6.

---

[11] The occurrences of the imperative verbs are as follows: 3:4; 6:11, 12, 13 (twice), 19; 11:9, 10 (twice), 18, 20 (twice), 22; 12:2 (twice), 14 (thrice), 16, 19, 20 (twice), 21 (twice); 13:1, 3, 4, 7, 8, 14 (twice); 14:1, 3 (twice), 5, 13, 15, 16, 20, 22; 15:2, 7, 10, 11 (twice); 16:3, 5, 6, 7, 8, 9, 10 (twice), 11 (twice), 12 (twice), 13, 14, 15, 16, 17. The imperative form of ἀσπάζομαι (to greet) occurs 16 times in Rom 16.

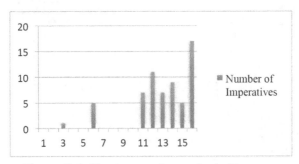

Figure 5.6. The imperative verbs in Romans.

Since Rom 11 is part of the major topic of the salvation of Israel (9–11) and Rom 16 is the final greeting of the epistle, Rom 12–15 appears to be a semantic unit.[12] This is further confirmed by the formula in Rom 12:1, which is discussed below. Since the imperative is frequently used for exhortation, Rom 12–15 is a hortatory segment.

Formulas

There are two types of formulas in Romans: formulaic praise and verb-conjunction-ὑμᾶς-ἀδελφοί.[13] Most of these formulas demarcate a major semantic unit.[14]

First, the phrase εὐχαριστῶ τῷ θεῷ (I give thanks to God) in 1:8 occurs after the initial greeting.[15] It marks the discussion of the gospel and its power as summarised in 1:16.[16] Second, also in the category of formulaic

---

[12] According to the statistics, there are 59 imperatives directed to the Romans. Since 49 of them occur in Rom 12–16, 83% of the imperatives (directed to the Romans) are found in these five chapters. On the other hand, there is also a display of lexical cohesion in Rom 16, since ἀσπάζομαι (to greet) occurs 16 times in 16:1–16. This signifies that this segment is a semantic unit in which Paul gives his final greeting to the Romans.

[13] Translation: verb-conjunction-you-brothers.

[14] The clauses οὐ θέλω δὲ ὑμᾶς ἀγνοεῖν (but I do not want you to be ignorant) in 1:13 and οὐ γὰρ θέλω ὑμᾶς ἀγνοεῖν (for I do not want you to be ignorant) in 11:25 are excluded. As demonstrated in the analysis of 1 Corinthians in § 3.1.1.2, the clause, θέλω δὲ ὑμᾶς (but I want you), does not function as a discourse marker.

[15] As discovered, this kind of formulaic praise/prayer occurs in both 1 Corinthians and Philippians, functioning as a boundary marker that begins the major discussion of Paul's epistles. This formula and its functions are also noted by Dunn (1988a:28). Jewett (2007:118) calls this the thanksgiving formula.

[16] Scholars widely consider 1:16–17 as the key theme that Paul seeks to expound in the main body of the epistle. For example, Dunn (1988a:46) describes these verses as the launching pad that provides the primary thrust and direction for the rest of the letter. For Jewett (2007:136), these verses set the tone for the entire letter. Similarly, Cranfield (1975:87) considers 1:16b–17 as the theological theme

praise, the doxological expression αὐτῷ ἡ δόξα εἰς τοὺς αἰῶνας, ἀμήν (The glory be to him forever, amen) in 11:36 marks the end of the topic of the salvation of Israel. Third, in the other type of formula, Παρακαλῶ οὖν ὑμᾶς, ἀδελφοί (Therefore I urge you, brothers) in 12:1 begins the hortatory segment, a segment that contains a multitude of imperatives, with the exhortation centring on Christian living in a community.[17] Fourth, this exhortation is concluded in 15:30–33, in which Παρακαλῶ δὲ ὑμᾶς, ἀδελφοί (but I urge you, brothers) in 15:30,[18] combined with the subsequent blessing (15:33), marks the end of this semantic unit.[19] Finally, the formula Παρακαλῶ δὲ ὑμᾶς, ἀδελφοί (but I urge you, brothers) in 16:17 introduces a warning from Paul. However, it occurs in the middle of the final greeting and the final remarks. Thus, in this case the formula demarcates a minor unit.[20]

Vocative

Apart from the occurrences of vocative ἀδελφοί (brother)[21] that forms part of the formulas (in 12:1; 15:30; 16:17), there are five occurrences of ἀδελφοί in Romans: 7:1, 4; 8:12; 10:1; 15:14. Some of them are discourse markers.

---

that is detailed in the main body of the epistle, and Schlatter (1995:25) argues that Rom 1–8 is the theological treatise that supports the thesis stated in these verses. Schreiner (1998:58) widely claims that virtually all scholars acknowledge that these verses are decisive for the interpretation of Romans.

[17] According to Dunn (1988b:708), οὖν (therefore) refers this exhortation back to the previous context (Rom 5–11), a view shared by Schreiner (1998:639). Byrne (1996:361) also supports this view, arguing that this segment concerns how the audience should "live out as a community" in response to the gospel explained in the preceding context.

[18] There is a textual variant regarding the word ἀδελφοί (brothers) in 15:30. Quite a number of manuscripts support the presence of this vocative, including manuscripts of the Alexandrian text-type (ℵ, A, C, 33, 1739) and other important manuscripts (D, F, ψ, and 1881). Only P[46] and B support the absence of ἀδελφοί. Hence, it is more likely that Paul included ἀδελφοί in 15:30 in the original manuscript.

[19] Jewett (2007:934) regards this expression in 15:30 as the typical request formula; and in this context it connects back to the preceding arguments in chapters 1–15.

[20] Dunn (1988b:902) observes that there is a discontinuity as 16:17–24 is not connected with the previous context. Jewett (2007:988) also notices the abrupt placement of this exhortative formula. Moo (1996:928) considers that 16:17 marks the shift of discussion. Byrne (1996:456) states that this segment remains an oddity in Paul's letter to Rome. Some scholars attempt to explain this strangeness. For example, Schreiner (1998:801) argues that this indicates Paul's own inscription. Despite various suggestions, this study argues that 16:17 marks a new minor discussion within the segment, in which Paul gives his final remarks.

[21] From this point onwards, the English translation, brother, for the term ἀδελφοί, is not provided in this chapter.

In 7:1, ἀδελφοί marks the minor unit in which Paul focuses on the discussion of the Law, a topic within the major unit in Rom 5–8. In 7:4, ἀδελφοί appears in the middle of the discussion of the Law, and it is followed by the pronoun μου (my). Hence, it functions as an emphatic address instead of a boundary marker.[22] In 8:12, ἀδελφοί does not function as a boundary marker, since it appears in the middle of the discussion of the Holy Spirit. In 10:1, the vocative appears in the middle of the topic of the fate of Israel, and commences a sub-topic that focuses on the salvation of the Israelites, as illustrated by the phrase αὐτῶν εἰς σωτηρίαν (for their salvation). Thus, it begins a minor unit. Finally, ἀδελφοί in 15:14 marks a new semantic unit, in which Paul reiterates his travel plan to Rome.[23]

5.1.1.2 Semantic units

Through the four identified discourse makers, the letter can be divided into: the letter-opening, the subsequent seven major semantic units, and the letter-closing. Table 5.1 shows that each of the nine major semantic units contains a topic: Unit A (The gospel and its power), Unit B (Sinfulness of both Jews and Gentiles), Unit C (Justified by faith), Unit D (Freedom from sin and death), Unit E (Salvation of Israel), Unit F (Exhortation on Christian living in community), and Unit G (Final greetings and remarks). Table 5.2 compares the semantic units identified in this study with those suggested by other scholars.[24]

---

[22] The emphatic address, as argued by Wallace (1996:68–69), is demonstrated by the use of the vocative preceded by ὦ (oh). However, in Koine and Semitic usage, Blass and Debrunner (1961:81) observe that the omission of ὦ (oh) is common in the NT. The use of ἀδελφοί μου (my brothers) as a comparatively emphatic address lacks substantial evidence. The suggestion is a conjecture that needs to be verified.

[23] In identifying units within a discourse, it is pertinent to consider both formal markers (for example, vocative ἀδελφοί and formulaic expressions in this case) and content/semantic criteria (for example, lexical cohesion occurs in a particular part of a text). Occasionally, there may be conflict between these markers, which would require careful discernment. In this case, vocative "brother" does appear in 7:4, but the "Law" topic, in terms of semantics, is not interrupted in any way by it. For discussion of discourse markers, see § 2.3.2.2.

[24] Table 5.2 does not present the full outline of each scholar. Rather, it presents the scholars that identify the same or similar unit as each of my units.

Table 5.1. Semantic units of Romans

	A	B	C	D			E		F	G	
Major Units	1:8–17	1:18–3:20	3:21–4:25	5–8			9–11		12:1–15:33	16:1–24	
Minor Units				D1 5–6	D2 7	D3 8	E1 9	E2 10–11		G1 16:1–16	G2 16:17–23
Discourse Markers	Letter-opening (1:1–7)	Formula: εὐχαριστῶ τῷ θεῷ 1:8 — Lexical cohesion: Ἰουδαῖος and Ἕλλην	Lexical cohesion: πίστις	Lexical cohesion: θάνατος	Vocative ἀδελφοί 7:1 — Lexical cohesion: νόμος (23) vs. πνεῦμα (1)	Lexical cohesion: νόμος (5) vs. πνεῦμα (21)		Vocative ἀδελφοί 10:1 — Formula: αὐτῷ ἡ δόξα εἰς τοὺς αἰῶνας, ἀμήν 11:36	Formula + Vocative: παρακαλῶ οὖν ὑμᾶς, ἀδελφοί 12:1 — Formula + Vocative: Παρακαλῶ δὲ ὑμᾶς, ἀδελφοί 15:30	Lexical cohesion: ἀσπάζομαι	Formula + Vocative: παρακαλῶ δὲ ὑμᾶς, ἀδελφοί, 16:17 — Letter-closing (16:25–27)
		100% of the occurrences of δικαιόω / 96% of the occurrences of ἁμαρτία					100% of the occurrences of Ἰσραήλ		90% of the imperatives		
		Justification							Exhortation		
New Topic	The gospel and its power	Sinfulness of both Jews and Gentiles	Justified by faith	Freedom from sin & death			Salvation of Israel		Exhortation on Christian living in community	Final greeting and remarks	

Table 5.2. Outline of Romans by scholars[a]

My Outline	Semantic Unit A 1:8–17[b]	Semantic Unit B 1:18–3:20	Semantic Unit C 3:21–4:25[c]	Semantic Unit D 5–8	Semantic Unit E 9–11	Semantic Unit F 12:1–15:13	Semantic Unit G 15:14–33[d]	Semantic Unit H 16:1–23
Outline of Scholars	Byrne Cranfield Stuhl.	Deibler Fitzmyer Käsemann Sanday Schreiner Stuhl.	Fitzmyer Hultgren Käsemann Schreiner	Barrett Byrne Cranfield Fitzmyer Hultgren Jewett Käsemann Moo Schreiner	Barrett Byrne Cranfield Deibler Dunn Hultgren Jewett Käsemann Moo Sanday Schlatter Schreiner Stuhl.	Byrne Cranfield Deibler Dunn Fitzmyer Jewett Käsemann Moo Sanday Schlatter Schreiner Stuhl.	Byrne Deibler Dunn Fitzmyer Käsemann Moo Sanday Schlatter Schreiner Jewett Stuhl.	Byrne Dunn Fitzmyer Käsemann Moo Schlatter Schreiner
	Dunn Fitzmyer Hultgren Stuhl.							
		Byrne Cranfield Jewett Moo						

[a] For detailed outlines, see Barrett 1991:14–15; Byrne 1996:27–28; Cranfield 1975:28–29; Deibler 1998:23–34; Dunn 1988a:vii–xi; Fitzmyer 1993:viii–xii; Hultgren 2011:v–viii; Jewett 2007:vii–ix; Käsemann 1980:ix–xi; Moo 1996:33–35; Sanday and Headlam 1902:xvlvii–l; Schlatter1995:v–vi; Schreiner 1998:25–27; Stuhlmacher 1994:14–16. In this table, Stuhlmacher is abbreviated as Stuhl., and Sanday and Headlam as Sanday.

[b] 1:1–7 and 1:8–17 are considered by Byrne to be two sub-segments of 1:1–17. According to Cranfield, 1:8–16a is one segment, and 1:16b–17 is another.

[c] 3:21–4:25 is considered by Fitzmyer to be two segments: 3:21–31; 4:1–25.

[d] For Dunn and Moo, 15:14–16:27 is divided into three sub-segments: 15:14–33; 16:1–23; 16:25–27. According to Sanday and Headlam, the epilogue is composed of 15:14–33, 16:1–16, 16:17-20, 16:21–23, and 16:25–27. For Byrne and Schlatter, 15:14–16:27 is a major segment which is subdivided into 15:14–33 and 16:1–27. Schreiner considers 15:14–16:23 as one major segment which is divided into 15:14–33 and 16:1–23. However, for Jewett and Stuhlmacher, 15:14–16:23 is one major segment with many sub-segments in it.

The proposed outline in this study is similar to the structural outlines proposed by various scholars. In the following part I examine the discourse coherence and macrostructure of the major semantic units.

5.1.1.3 Discourse coherence

The two major cohesive linguistic devices, inclusio and prominence, are the central focus in ascertaining the coherent message of Romans. I would like to show that the letter is highly community focused.

Inclusio

An inclusio occurs in Units A and F. In Unit A, Paul begins his first discussion with a prayer Πρῶτον μὲν εὐχαριστῶ τῷ θεῷ μου (I thank my God through Jesus Christ for all of you)* in 1:8.[25] Then, Paul discloses his true intention and expresses his desire to visit Rome with a specific purpose: ἵνα τινὰ καρπὸν σχῶ καὶ ἐν ὑμῖν καθὼς καὶ ἐν τοῖς λοιποῖς ἔθνεσιν (so that I may have some fruit even among you, just as I already have among the rest of the Gentiles)* in 1:13. Of interest, a corresponding utterance occurs near the end of the letter, forming an inclusio. In 15:28, καρπός (fruit) re-emerges as Paul reiterates his intention: τοῦτο οὖν ἐπιτελέσας καὶ σφραγισάμενος αὐτοῖς τὸν καρπὸν τοῦτον, ἀπελεύσομαι δι' ὑμῶν εἰς Σπανίαν (Therefore after I have completed this and have safely delivered this bounty to them, I will set out for Spain by way of you.)* This inclusio reveals the purpose of this letter: Paul needs the support from the Romans to bring the gospel to τοῖς λοιποῖς ἔθνεσιν (the rest of the Gentiles). In other words, Romans is not a letter for Paul to merely express his doctrinal belief, the salvation of individual believers.[26] Rather, it focuses on the faith community. As argued by Byrne, Paul aims to use Romans to invoke "sympathy" to his approach of including the Gentiles "as equal citizens in the eschatological people of God." Nonetheless, for Byrne, Paul ultimately hopes that "the Gentile Christians in Rome will be in the same relationship to himself as the communities he has personally founded" (Byrne 1996:19). I concur with Byrne's view, and further argue that Paul is concerned about different communities, including the Gentiles in Spain.[27]

[25] Scripture quoted by permission. All scripture quotations that are marked by an asterisk (*) are taken from the NET Bible® © 1996–2016 by Biblical Studies Press, L.L.C. All rights reserved.

[26] Although different scholars have different views on the ultimate purpose of Romans, they commonly do not consider Romans as Paul's doctrinal letter. Rather, the letter is deeply connected with the Christian community in Rome. For Jewett (2007:74–75, 932), this epistle is an ambassadorial letter of Paul to seek support from the Romans in order to launch a successful mission to Spain. Since there is little Jewish population in Spain, Paul cannot rely on the Jewish God-fearers in that region to do his work. Hence, he needs the support of the Christians in Rome. On the other hand, Käsemann (1980:405) argues that the letter is carefully crafted to reflect the importance of Israel in salvation history in order to win over the Jewish Christians, who constitute the minority in the largely Gentile Christian congregation in Rome. According to Smiga (1991:272–273), the letter is Paul's request to the Romans for supporting his need in Jerusalem in light of the lack of support from the Roman community in facing an upcoming challenge in Jerusalem. Despite the difference in these views, they commonly indicate Paul's focus on the communal and relational aspect. Paul is not primarily concerned about the salvation plan for individuals. This focus is in accordance with my view.

[27] Jewett (2007:74–80) provides a detailed explanation of this "Spanish mission." He demonstrates how various texts in Romans, including 1:14 and 16:1–2, point to

This emphasis on the Gentiles is also observed in another inclusio. In the letter-opening, Paul proclaims that he receives grace and the apostleship: εἰς ὑπακοὴν πίστεως ἐν πᾶσιν τοῖς ἔθνεσιν (the obedience of faith among all the Gentiles)* in 1:5. A similar phrase re-emerges in the letter-closing: εἰς ὑπακοὴν πίστεως εἰς πάντα τὰ ἔθνη (for the obedience of faith among all the Gentiles) in 16:26. Paul calls himself an apostle of the Gentiles in this letter (11:13), and he highlights in this inclusio that the Gentiles are of his concern.

The connection of these two foci, faith community and Gentiles, will be explained in the section on sociolinguistics aspect.

Prominence

In the following part I demonstrate the emphasis on the communal aspect in Romans through two forms of prominence, thematic prominence and lexical cohesion, which generate the coherence of a discourse.

Thematic prominence

Throughout the letter, Paul focuses on different communities in various semantic units. In Unit A, Paul expresses his desire to visit the Romans. Paul describes himself as a debtor Ἕλλησίν τε καὶ βαρβάροις (both to the Greeks and to the barbarians)* in 1:14, and articulates his intention to proclaim the gospel. This gospel is the power of God for salvation Ἰουδαίῳ τε πρῶτον καὶ Ἕλληνι (to the Jew first and also to the Greek)* in 1:16. In other words, Paul's central concern is about the salvation of these three communities: Ἰουδαῖος (Jew), Ἕλλην (Greek), and βάρβαρος (barbarian).[28] Dunson also advocates a similar view. He connects 1:16–17 with other passages in Romans (3:21–5:2; 9:30–10:17), and demonstrates that Paul employs the "faith-righteousness relationship" to articulate the power of the gospel to break down the partition between

---

this purpose. However, Barclay (2008:96–97) contends that Jewett's explanation is based on a shaky hypothesis. Barclay argues that the contextual hypotheses, such as the role of Phoebe in this Spanish mission and the Spanish cultural situation, are immensely attractive but are speculative. Nonetheless, Barclay does not negate the "missional" instead of the "doctrinal" purpose, in writing Romans. For Barclay, the substantiation of this purpose does not require Jewett's contextual hypotheses. [28] Jewett (2007:146) similarly argues that the phrase παντὶ τῷ πιστεύοντι (to everyone who believes) does not denote individual believers. Instead, it refers to different cultural groups in the schema of God's salvation. Dunson (2011:27) connects 1:16–17 with other passages in Romans (3:21–5:2 and 9:30–10:17), demonstrating that the "faith-righteousness relationship" is employed by Paul to articulate the power of the gospel to dissolve the division between the Jew and the Gentiles, emphasising the communal aspect instead of the individualistic aspect.

the Gentiles and the Jews, highlighting the importance of the communal aspect.[29]

In Unit B, Paul points out that both the Greeks and the Jews are equally in need of salvation. The phrase Ἰουδαῖος τε πρῶτον καὶ Ἕλληνος (Jew first and also Gentile) is repeated three times in this semantic unit: 2:9; 2:10; 3:9.[30] Both groups are depicted as sinful: προῃτιασάμεθα γὰρ Ἰουδαίους τε καὶ Ἕλληνας πάντας ὑφ᾽ ἁμαρτίαν εἶναι (for we have already charged that Jews and Greeks alike are all under sin)* in 3:9. Hence, Paul is not concerned with the sinfulness of individual human beings. Instead, the two communities, Ἰουδαῖος (Jew) and Ἕλλην (Greek), are his centre of discussion.

In Unit C, Paul details his argument regarding justification by faith. He begins his argument by seemingly focusing on individuals λογιζόμεθα γὰρ δικαιοῦσθαι πίστει ἄνθρωπον (For we consider that a person is declared righteous by faith)* in 3:28. However, he immediately refers to the two communities, the Jews and the Gentiles: ἢ Ἰουδαίων ὁ θεὸς μόνον; οὐχὶ καὶ ἐθνῶν; (Or is God the God of the Jews only? Is he not the God of the Gentiles too?)* in 3:29. Then, Paul cites Abraham as an example (4:1–12). However, his argument soon focuses on Abraham's descendants (4:13–25). The quotation, πατέρα πολλῶν ἐθνῶν τέθεικά σε (I have made you the father of many nations)* in 4:17, highlights Paul's concern for the ἔθνος (Gentile).

In Unit D, Paul discusses the topic of freedom from sin and death. Whilst no specific community is mentioned in this semantic unit, there are two main observations that show that Paul's discussion centres on Christians, particularly the Christian community in Rome. First, there are various expressions that denote Christians, including ὅσοι ἐβαπτίσθημεν εἰς Χριστὸν Ἰησοῦν (as many as were baptized into Christ Jesus)* in 6:3, νυνὶ δὲ ἐλευθερωθέντες ἀπὸ τῆς ἁμαρτίας (But now, freed from sin)* in 6:22, and ὑμεῖς δὲ οὐκ ἐστὲ ἐν σαρκὶ ἀλλὰ ἐν πνεύματι (You, however, are not in the flesh but in the Spirit)* in 8:9. Second, Paul uses ἀδελφοί four times (7:1, 4; 8:12, 29). This word generally emphasises kinship among believers. However, in this context it specifically refers to the Christian community in Rome, based on its first occurrence in 1:13 to address the Romans before re-emerging in 7:1.[31]

---

[29] Dunson (2012:178) provides a detailed discussion of this issue in his most recent work, and concludes that for Paul, individual experiences suffer a fundamental deficiency apart from being embedded into community.

[30] The three occurrences of Ἰουδαῖος (Jew) and Ἕλλην (Greek) are different in case: genitive in 2:9; dative in 2:10; and accusative in 3:9.

[31] Jewett (2007:430) suggests that the word includes all members of the communities, including women. Furthermore, there is a dispute whether the word is employed to address the Jewish Christians in Rome. For various arguments concerning this suggestion, see Moo 1996:411–412.

In Unit E, Paul's discusses Israel's fate as illustrated by the frequent occurrences of Ἰσραήλ (Israel).[32] Moreover, the relationship between the two communities, Ἰσραήλ (Israel) and ἔθνος (Gentile), is highlighted.[33] Of interest, the expressions such as, Ὑμῖν δὲ λέγω τοῖς ἔθνεσιν (Now I am speaking to you Gentiles)* in 11:13, μὴ κατακαυχῶ τῶν κλάδων (do not boast over the branches)* in 11:18, and μὴ ἦτε [παρ'] ἑαυτοῖς φρόνιμοι, ὅτι πώρωσις ἀπὸ μέρους τῷ Ἰσραὴλ γέγονεν ἄχρι οὗ τὸ πλήρωμα τῶν ἐθνῶν εἰσέλθῃ (you may not be conceited: A partial hardening has happened to Israel until the full number of the Gentiles has come in)* in 11:25, may subtly reflect the tension between the Gentile Christians and the majority of the Jewish non-believers.[34] Regardless of the presence of this tension, the key theme of Unit E is clearly the salvation of Israel, its corporate solidarity instead of an individual Israelite.[35]

In Unit F, Paul discusses Christian living. Nonetheless, he focuses on the communal aspect, the Christians in Rome in particular. This is demonstrated by this encouragement: καθάπερ γὰρ ἐν ἑνὶ σώματι πολλὰ μέλη ἔχομεν, τὰ δὲ μέλη πάντα οὐ τὴν αὐτὴν ἔχει πρᾶξιν, οὕτως οἱ πολλοὶ ἓν σῶμά ἐσμεν ἐν Χριστῷ, τὸ δὲ καθ' εἷς ἀλλήλων μέλη (for just as in one body we have many members, and not all the members serve the same function, so we who are many are one body in Christ, and individually we are members who belong to one another)* in 12:4–5. Furthermore, the call to love is reiterated in this unit: 12:9; 13:8; 13:10; and 14:15.[36] In addition to this general call, Paul

---

[32] Staples (2011:372–374) provides a brief account of the various identifications of Ἰσραήλ (Israel).

[33] The word ἔθνος means nation, it also denotes a Gentile. This word frequently occurs in this semantic unit: 9:24, 30; 10:19; 11:11, 12, 13 (twice), 25.

[34] For Jewett (2007:678), this tension is contributed by the prejudice of the Gentile Christians, who are the majority members of the audience, towards the Jews and Jewish Christians in the community. Käsemann (1980:305) suggests that there are disagreements in the community due to the arrogance displayed by the Gentile Christians. Dunn (1988b:669) and Moo (1996:691) also support this view. Conversely, Byrne (1996:339) and Schreiner (1998:595) hold a different view. Byrne argues that these expressions do not illustrate such a tension. Rather, it is Paul's tactic to strike a balance between the inclusion of the Gentiles and the inclusion of the Jews in his preaching; and Schreiner argues that these expressions highlight Paul's role as the apostle to the Gentiles. The validity of this communal tension arguably does not negate the fact that Paul is concerned for both the Gentiles and the Jews.

[35] Abasciano and Schreiner disagree with each another concerning the nature of Rom 9–11. Abasciano (2006:353–358) argues that the segment centres on the corporate election of Israel, whilst Schreiner argues for both corporate election and individual election. For Schreiner (2006:376–377), these two kinds of election are inseparable. Despite their differences, both scholars affirm the corporate aspect in Rom 9–11, the same argument that I hold.

[36] Kim (2010:318) further contends that the connection between 11:16–24 and the exhortation in 12–15 hinges on the subject of love: the main thrust of Paul's teaching in Romans 12–15 is the kind of love that creates and sustains unity between the

deals with the issue of food in 14:1–15:13, which troubles the Christian community in Rome. Scholars commonly argue that the central focus of this segment is on community.[37] Dunson and Moxnes further argue that the key concern is the unity of the faith community.[38]

In Unit G, the final semantic unit, the concern for community is evident in Paul's greetings to various individuals in the church in Rome (16:3–16).[39]

As shown above, the thematic prominence in this epistle is the focus of different communities, a common theme being reiterated throughout various semantic units.

Lexical cohesion

The second form of prominence is lexical cohesion. In addition to the lexical cohesion previously discussed, the occurrences of καρδία also display signs of lexical cohesion. The term occurs in patterns, pointing to the communal response of different communities towards God. This is detailed in the second section of this chapter.

5.1.1.4 Macrostructure

Based on the analysis presented above, I argue that the macrostructure of Romans is as follows. God's salvific plan includes the salvation of both the Jews and the Gentiles. Through the gospel, both groups are freely justified by God in Christ through faith. As being set free from sin and death by the work of the Holy Spirit, the members of the Christian community should live by the principle of love.

5.1.2 Occurrence of Καρδία in Romans

Of all the Pauline epistles, καρδία occurs most frequently in Romans, 15 times in total.[40] In the following section I analyse the occurrences of καρδία

Jewish and the Gentile believers in the churches of Rome. On the other hand, this "universalistic love ethic" of Paul, according to Yinger (1998:94–95), is an argument intended by Paul to deal with a communal conflict alluded in 12:14–21.

[37] Many commentators support this view (Moo 1996:746–747; Jewett 2007:738; Byrne 1996:361–362; Schreiner 1998:649; Fitzmyer 1993:637; Dunn 1988b:705; Stuhlmacher 1994:185; Schlatter 1995:227).

[38] Dunson (2011:37) argues that the communal function of faith explained in the earlier part of the epistle is the base for the exhortation to unity within the diversity in the Christian community. According to Moxnes (1994:217–219), the passage in 12:1–2 speaks of collective conversion, and the text in 12:3–16 encourages the unity in the community.

[39] Schreiner (1998:789) suggests that the greetings reflect the warm relationships that characterized the Christian community.

[40] The occurrences of καρδία are as follows: 1:21, 24; 2:5, 15, 29; 5:5; 6:17; 8:27; 9:2; 10:1, 6, 8, 9, 10; 16:18.

in various semantic units, and then examine its overall occurrences in the entire discourse in light of the sociolinguistic aspect, the macrostructure, and the discourse flow.

5.1.2.1 *Καρδία in semantic units*

As demonstrated in the previous analyses of 1 Corinthians and Philippians, the thematic meaning of an anthropological term cannot be solely determined by referring to the immediate textual context at the sentential level, since this is insufficient in ascertaining its meaning expressed through the discourse coherence. Hence, I focus on understanding καρδία by recognizing its occurrences as a pattern within and across various semantic units. In other words, the sentential meaning of καρδία in each individual occurrence is not my primary concern. In Romans, καρδία occurs in Units B, D, E, and G. Its thematic meaning indicated by its overall occurrences points to the corporate and communal aspect as explained below.

Καρδία in Unit B

In Unit B, καρδία denotes a corporate reference. The term occurs in 1:21, 1:24, 2:5, and 2:15. In all of these occurrences, καρδία is either associated with the Gentiles or the Jews. For both groups, the term denotes their darkened unrepentant hearts. Forming a pattern, καρδία reflects the enmity between the Gentiles, as a corporate entity, and God. The term also reflects the disobedience of the Jews, as another corporate entity, towards God.

In 1:21, the two concepts, ἐματαιώθησαν ἐν τοῖς διαλογισμοῖς αὐτῶν (they became futile in their thoughts)* and ἐσκοτίσθη ἡ ἀσύνετος αὐτῶν καρδία (their unintelligent heart was darkened) are identical in meaning. Hence, καρδία and διαλογισμός (thought) are likely in parallel. Since διαλογισμός (thought) is related to the mind, it is reasonable to consider that καρδία either alludes to or denotes mind.[41] Most importantly, καρδία

---

[41] Schreiner (1998:87) also suggests this parallel, and concludes that καρδία denotes mind. However, most commentators express their understanding of καρδία without mentioning this parallel. Fitzmyer (1993:128) argues that καρδία denotes mind in Romans, which designates the responsive and emotional reactions of the intelligent and planning self. Some scholars hold a similar view. Although they argue that elsewhere in Romans καρδία generally denotes inner life, they assert that καρδία here refers to the faculty of thought and understanding in light of its modifier ἀσύνετος. Hence, the intellectual aspect is highlighted (Cranfield 1975:118; Dunn 1988a:60; Morris 1988:85). Conversely, some scholars stress the neutrality of καρδία as the home of either evilness or goodness (Sanday and Headlam 1902:45; Barrett 1991:37). Notably, in comparing Romans and Matthew, Brodie (2009:528) suggests that Matthew assimilates some of the ideas in Romans. Regarding the darkness of heart in 1:21, he argues that Matthew adopts this theme and reshapes it as the darkness in the body in 6:22–23, illustrating the lost sight of God. Jewett (2007:332) emphasises the Hebraic nature of καρδία, and argues that this is the

describes the negative response of the Gentiles, as a group, towards God, as indicated in the immediate context: οὐχ ὡς θεὸν ἐδόξασαν (They did not glorify him as God)* in 1:21.

In 1:24, the genitive form of καρδία modifies ἐπιθυμία (desire). The genitive can well be the genitive of production (the desires produced by the hearts).[42] Καρδία denotes the seat of emotion or thought, which produces desire.[43] In this text, ἐπιθυμία (desire) signifies sinful desire as illustrated by the context,[44] and points to ungodly sexual lust (1:24). Καρδία also carries the same function as that in 1:21, pointing to the enmity between the Gentiles and God as evident in the context: παρέδωκεν αὐτοὺς ὁ θεὸς (God gave them over)* in 1:24.

There is one peculiar phenomenon in 1:21 and 1:24, which requires a careful investigation. A singular καρδία is modified by a plural possessive pronoun αὐτῶν (their) in 1:21, ἡ ἀσύνετος αὐτῶν καρδία (their unintelligent heart), but a plural καρδία is modified by a plural possessive pronoun

---

source of both διαλογισμοί (thoughts) and ἐπιθυμίαι (desires). This understanding is vastly different from the portrayal of a human being having a rational part and a sensual part within Hellenistic anthropology. Jewett's view is similar to Stacey's. According to Stacey (1956:196–198), the Pauline usage of καρδία is a continuum of the Hebrew word לֵב, and καρδία is almost synonymous with the Koine Greek concept of νοῦς (mind), citing the occurrence of καρδία in 1:21 and νοῦς (mind) in 1:28. Similarly, Moo (1996:107) traces καρδία back to the OT Hebrew word לֵב, denoting the thinking, feeling, and willing ego of humans in their relationship with God. Byrne (1996:74) compares ἀσύνετος καρδία (unintelligent heart) with the OT usage, quoting Ps 76:5 in the LXX, and suggests that καρδία in Pauline literature points to the inward self of human beings as thinking, willing and feeling subjects. The problem with the above analyses, which traces καρδία back to לֵב, is two-fold. First, it is a pure diachronic approach. Second, if the audience are mostly Gentile Christians, as many commentators claim, it would be strange for Paul to use a Hebraic concept (which would be alien to the Gentile audience) to convey a point. It is obvious that καρδία in 1:21 is closely linked to διαλογισμός (thought), which is generated by the mind. The two words are simply in parallel. This observation is deduced from the immediate context without tracing the word back to its so-called OT equivalent.

[42] For this category of genitive, refer to Wallace 1996:104–105.

[43] Most commentators, including Cranfield, Fitzmyer, Schreiner, Byrne, Dunn, Moo, Käsemann, Stuhlmacher, Schlatter, Sanday and Headlam, do not discuss the nature of this genitive as they focus on desire. By citing the example in Ps 21:3, Jewett (2007:167) argues that the phrase ταῖς ἐπιθυμίαις τῶν καρδιῶν αὐτῶν (the desires of their hearts) is a Hebrew expression: the means the motivational centre of humankind.

[44] Ἐπιθυμία (desire) can be employed to denote both good desires and evil desires as the word is not always negative as many assume. Ἐπιθυμία (desire) also refers to longing (Bauer 1979:293). In fact, Paul uses the word four times (Rom 1:24; 6:12; Gal; 5:24, 1 Thess 2:17), one of those is used to describe his longing to see the Thessalonians: τὸ πρόσωπον ὑμῶν ἰδεῖν ἐν πολλῇ ἐπιθυμίᾳ (in our great desire to see you in person)*.

in 1:24, τῶν καρδιῶν αὐτῶν (their hearts). As previously mentioned, καρδία occurs 36 times in all the Pauline epistles. The plural forms of καρδία occur 15 times, with 11 of them modified by personal possessive pronouns. All of these pronouns are plural.[45] The singular forms of καρδία occur 22 times, with nine of them modified by personal possessive pronouns.[46] However, only three of these possessive pronouns are in plural form: αὐτῶν καρδία (their heart) in Rom 1:21; τὴν καρδίαν αὐτῶν (their heart) in 2 Cor 3:15; and ἡ καρδία ἡμῶν (our heart) in 2 Cor 6:11.[47] As previously explained, the singular noun must not be automatically defined as the distributive singular to explain the abnormal singular construct (see § 3.2.1.1).

The text in 1:21 states that ἡ ἀσύνετος αὐτῶν καρδία (their unintelligent heart) is darkened. In 1:24, the text discusses ταῖς ἐπιθυμίαις τῶν καρδιῶν αὐτῶν (the desires of their hearts). Semantically, καρδία is closely associated with unintelligence or desires. In both cases, καρδία is connected to ἀσύνετος (unintelligent) and ἐπιθυμία (desire), words depicting mind and emotion. Both cases display an agreement in number. In ἡ ἀσύνετος... καρδία (the unintelligent...heart), the singular substantival adjective is correlated with the singular καρδία. In ταῖς ἐπιθυμίαις τῶν καρδιῶν (the desires of hearts), the plural noun is modified by the plural καρδία. It would be a relatively forced interpretation to argue that καρδία in 1:21 is a distributive singular noun. Rather, it is more convincing to perceive it as the

---

[45] Pauline texts with the plural forms of καρδία include Rom 1:24[⊘]; 2:15[⊘]; 5:5[⊘]; 8:27; 16:18; 1Cor 4:5; 2 Cor 1:22[⊘]; 3:2[⊘],3; 4:6[⊘]; 7:3[⊘]; Gal 4:6[⊘]; Phil 4:7[⊘]; 1 Thess 2:4[⊘]; 3:13[⊘]. The symbol ⊘ indicates the presence of a possessive pronoun (all the pronouns are in plural form). Amongst them, first and second person plural possessive pronouns occur in Rom 5:5 (ταῖς καρδίαις ἡμῶν, our hearts); 2 Cor 7:3 (ταῖς καρδίαις ἡμῶν, our hearts); Gal 4:6 (τὰς καρδίας ἡμῶν, our hearts); Phil 4:7 (τὰς καρδίας ὑμῶν, your hearts); 1 Thess 2:4 (τὰς καρδίας ἡμῶν, our hearts); and 1 Thess 3:13 (ὑμῶν τὰς καρδίας, your hearts).

[46] Pauline texts with the singular forms of καρδία include Rom 1:21[⊕]; 2:5[#],29; 6:17; 9:2*; 10:1, 6*, 8*, 9*, 10; 1 Cor 2:9; 7:37a*,37b; 14:25*; 2 Cor 2:4; 3:15[⊕]; 5:12; 6:11[⊕]; 8:16; 9:7; Phil 1:7; 1 Thess 2:17. The symbol * indicates the presence of a singular possessive pronoun; ⊕ indicates the presence of a plural possessive pronoun; and [#] denotes the presence of a singular reflexive pronoun.

[47] In Pauline disputed letters, intriguingly, all the plural forms of καρδία are modified by plural possessive pronoun without any exception. For singular forms of καρδία, if a personal possessive pronoun is present, then it is always a plural possessive pronoun. The singular forms of καρδία in the disputed letters occur in Eph 1:18[⊛]; 4:18[⊛]; 5:19[⊛]; 6:5[⊛]; Col 3:22; 1 Tim 1:5; and 2 Tim 2:22. The symbol ⊛ indicates the presence of a personal possessive pronoun, and all of them are in plural form. All the plural forms of καρδία are always modified by plural possessive pronouns: ταῖς καρδίαις ὑμῶν (your hearts) in Eph 3:17; τὰς καρδίας ὑμῶν (your hearts) in Eph 6:22; αἱ καρδίαι αὐτῶν (their hearts) in Col 2:2; ταῖς καρδίαις ὑμῶν (your hearts) in Col 3:15; ταῖς καρδίαις ὑμῶν (your hearts) in Col 3:16; τὰς καρδίας ὑμῶν (your hearts) in Col 4:8; ὑμῶν τὰς καρδίας (your hearts) in 2 Thess 2:17; ὑμῶν τὰς καρδίας (your hearts) in 2 Thess 3:5.

normal singular, given the singular use of the substantival adjective despite the presence of a plural pronoun αὐτῶν (their).[48]

In the discussion of the wrath of God, καρδίαν (2:5) is directly modified by the adjective ἀμετανόητον (unrepentant), a hapax legomenon in the NT.[49] Ἀμετανόητον καρδίαν (unrepentant heart) is conjoined with σκληρότητά (hardness) by καί (and), forming a parallel to indicate that "hardness" is synonymous with "unrepentant heart."[50] Cranfield (1975:145) provides a valuable insight and valid argument by suggesting that another cognate of σκληρότης (hardness), σκληροκαρδία (hard heart) (a word that occurs only once in Matthew), pointing back to the OT with reference to the unrepentant Israel. The singular form of καρδία in 2:5 is qualified by σου (your, in singular form), a pronoun which points to the Jews as a corporate entity, instead of an individual.[51] The sentence meaning of καρδία in 2:5 is likely associated with volition, since unrepentance can be regarded as an attitude, alluding to volition. Nonetheless, the corporate entity is well illustrated by καρδία, as the term is used to portray the disobedience of a people group, the Jews.

In 2:29, καρδία is associated with περιτομή (circumcision), in which Paul makes a sharp contrast between περιτομή καρδίας ἐν πνεύματι (circumcision of heart in spirit) in 2:29 and ἐν σαρκὶ περιτομή (circumcision in flesh) in 2:28, by defining the difference between ἐν τῷ κρυπτῷ Ἰουδαῖος (a Jew who is one inwardly)* in 2:29 and ἐν τῷ φανερῷ Ἰουδαῖός (a Jew who

---

[48] Many major commentators, including Barrett, Cranfield, Byrne, Moo, Dunn, do not mentioned this nuance regarding the singular use of καρδία, let alone the combination between καρδία and αὐτῶν (their). Byrne (1996:74) and Dunn (1988a:60) refer to the similarity between 1:21 and Psalm 75:6 (76:5, LXX). However, in the LXX a plural ἀσύνετος (unintelligent) is linked with a singular dative καρδία: οἱ ἀσύνετοι τῇ καρδίᾳ (the unintelligent ones in heart). Paul may be alluding to the LXX, it is certainly not a direct quotation though.

[49] A hapax legomenon is a word that occurs only once in the NT.

[50] Bauer (1979:756) defines the word as hardness of heart, a usage commonly found in other Greek literature. As such, 2:5 could be rendered as τὴν σκληρότητά (τῆς καρδίας) σου καὶ ἀμετανόητον καρδίαν (your hardness of heart and unrepentant heart). Σκληρότητά (hardness) and ἀμετανόητον (unrepentant) are in parallel, both describing καρδία.

[51] This view can further be supported by the Shema text in Deut 6. In Deut 6:4–6 (LXX), the text reads: Ἄκουε, Ισραηλ κύριος ὁ θεὸς ἡμῶν κύριος εἷς ἐστιν καὶ ἀγαπήσεις κύριον τὸν θεόν σου ἐξ ὅλης τῆς καρδίας σου...καὶ ἔσταιτὰ ῥήματα ταῦτα, ὅσα ἐγὼ ἐντέλλομαί σοι σήμερον, ἐν τῇ καρδίᾳ σου (Listen, Israel: The Lord our God is one Lord, and you shall love the Lord your (singular) God with all your (singular) heart...and these words that I am commanding you (singular) today must be kept in your (singular) heart). The interplay between ἡμῶν (our) and σου (your, singular), as well as the usage of a singular καρδία treat the Israelites as "one", as the nation Ισραηλ (Israel) is in the text instead of using the plural proper noun, Ισραηλῖται (Israelites).

is one outwardly)* in 2:28.[52] Of interest, the description of "the circumcision of hardened hearts" also occurs in Deut 10:16 and Jer 4:4, portraying the stubborn Israelites.[53] The notion of having the heart circumcised is contrasted with ἐν σαρκὶ περιτομή (circumcision in flesh). In the context, 2:5 in particular, the unrepentant attitude of the ancient Israelites is in view. Therefore, καρδία in 2:29 indicates a contrastive attitude. In other words, the two occurrences of καρδία, in 2:5 and 2:29, are associated with volition according to their sentence meanings. However, they both are employed to convey a message to reflect the corporate disobedience of the Jews.

Καρδία in Unit D

In Unit D, there is a shift regarding the community with which καρδία is associated. The occurrences of καρδία in this unit (5:5; 6:17; 8:27) are associated with believers. Καρδία denotes the hearts of the believers, which receive God's love, obey teaching, and are searched by the Holy Spirit. Again, the pattern of καρδία indicates a corporate reference.

In the discussion of justification, Paul argues in 5:5 that the hope of believers is not in vain because ἡ ἀγάπη τοῦ θεοῦ ἐκκέχυται ἐν ταῖς καρδίαις ἡμῶν διὰ πνεύματος ἁγίου τοῦ δοθέντος ἡμῖν (the love of God has been poured out in our hearts through the Holy Spirit who was given to us)*. Contextually, ἐκκέχυται ἐν ταῖς καρδίαις ἡμῶν (poured out in our hearts) and τοῦ δοθέντος ἡμῖν (who was given to us) share a similar meaning. The concept (the love of God being poured out in our hearts) can also be interpreted as the love of God given to us.[54] Of interest, of all the Pauline epistles, the verb ἐκχύννω (to pour out) only occurs in Romans.[55] In 5:5,

---

[52] The genitive of καρδία can be understood as an objective genitive, a view supported by Moo. It is a contrast that Paul sets up: the dative of σαρκὶ (flesh) illustrates περιτομή (circumcision) done in the flesh, comparing with περιτομή (circumcision) done in καρδία (Moo 1996:174).

[53] Dunn notes this similarity. Jewett argues that the concept of περιτομὴ καρδίας (circumcision of heart) is a popular OT and rabbinic idea. The understanding of Dunn regarding καρδία as the experiencing and motivating centre of human is also similar to the idea of Jewett (2007:448) of καρδία being the centre of human with the emphasis on intentionality. Jewett does give a strong argument that καρδία in this text is a continuum of the Hebraic concept (Dunn 1988a:91, 124; Jewett 2007:333, 448).

[54] The love of God is interpreted as the Spirit of God (Byrne 1996:167), a view that Cranfield (1975:261–263) repudiates.

[55] Cranfield (1976:262–263) observes that the verb ἐκχέω (to pour out), as well as its Hellenistic form ἐκχύννω, is normally used in the LXX to describe the pouring of the wrath of God. For Cranfield, this usage can be demonstrated in Rev 16, in which nine times ἐκχέω (to pour out) is employed to portray the pouring of the Seven Bowls of God's wrath. Thus, God's love as the subject of ἐκχύννω (to pour out) is unusual.

καρδία is the object, or the recipient of the pouring. Based on the context, it is a reasonable conjecture to argue that God's love is directed to 'people,' instead of the seat of emotion, will, and reason.[56] Therefore, ταῖς καρδίαις ἡμῶν (in our hearts) and ἡμῖν (in you) are synonymous, denoting the whole person instead of illustrating mere emotion and volition. More importantly, the phrase ταῖς καρδίαις ἡμῶν (in our hearts) denotes a specific group of people: believers.

In 6:17, καρδία is linked to the imperative verb ὑπηκούσατε (obey). Paul discusses how believers are free from the slavery of sin and obedience ἐκ καρδίας to God's teaching. The uncommon occurrence of ἐκ καρδίας (from heart), the only occurrence in Paul's work, has invited some discussion.[57] Cranfield asserts that the phrase is in contrast to outward obedience, as ἐκ καρδίας (from heart) elucidates inward obedience. Dunn (1988a:343) also proposes this kind of inward–outward contrast, and argues that καρδία denotes deep motivation. Contextually, the meaning of καρδία as "motivation" lacks substantial support, since there is no such contrast presented in the textual context of both the preceding and the following texts. Jewett fails to consider the Deuteronomy quotation as he simply defines καρδία as "the centre of man" in Rom 10 (Jewett 1971:333). However, I argue that the word denotes a positive orientation of the audience towards God's teaching, as indicated by the context. In 6:17, καρδία is neither modified by other adjective and pronoun, nor associated with nouns that depict volition, emotion, and reason. However, based on the context I propose that the term reflects the positive attitude expressed by a group, the believers in general, and the Roman Christians in specific,[58] towards God and God's teaching. The sentence meaning of καρδία denotes volition. However, the usage of καρδία indicates a corporate aspect.

In 8:27, καρδία occurs in the middle of the passage in which Paul discusses the help of the Holy Spirit offered to believers. In portraying the role and the work of the Holy Spirit, Paul writes: ὁ δὲ ἐραυνῶν τὰς καρδίας οἶδεν

---

[56] Some scholars do not specify the meaning of καρδία, and they simply interpret the text as God's love for "people" (Fitzmyer 1993:398; Stuhlmacher 1994:80; Byrne 1996:171; Sanday and Headlam 1902:125; Moo 1996:304–305). Others argue that καρδία denotes the inner life of an individual (Schlatter 1995:122), including human experience (Schreiner 1998:257), and the seat of thought, volition and emotion (Jewett 2007:356; Dunn 1988a:253).

[57] Cranfield (1975:324) rejects Bultmann's interpretation of ἐκ καρδίας (from heart) as a non-Pauline insertion (the phrase does not occur elsewhere in Paul's work). He argues that the phrase is a good Greek expression which can be found in other contemporary Greek literature and 2 Pet 1:22. I agree with Cranfield. It is not persuasive to repudiate Paul's authorship of a text merely based on the occurrence of a rare linguistic construction. For example, there are approximately 87 hapax legomena in Romans alone.

[58] Schreiner (1998:334), Jewett (2007:418), and Moo (1996:400) also support that Roman Christians are in view in 6:17.

τί τὸ φρόνημα τοῦ πνεύματος (And he who searches our hearts knows the mind of the Spirit)*. The masculine participle ὁ ἐραυνῶν (he who searches) points to God who does the searching of καρδία. God is also the one who knows τὸ φρόνημα τοῦ πνεύματος (the mind of the Spirit).[59] To ascertain the meaning of καρδία in 8:27, it is essential to refer to the immediate context. The text in 8:26 states that προσευξώμεθα καθὸ δεῖ οὐκ οἴδαμεν (we do not know how we should pray)* in 8:26. Both the phrase οὐκ οἴδαμεν (we do not know) in 8:26 and the word οἶδεν (he knows) in 8:26 refer to "knowledge." Hence, it is reasonable to interpret καρδία as the mind. The text can be interpreted as follows. The human mind is unable to know what to pray for (8:26), but God is able to search our mind (8:27).[60] Most importantly, the teaching in 8:26 is about the help of Holy Spirit offered to believers as indicated by the plural pronoun ἡμῶν (our) in the clause τὸ πνεῦμα συναντιλαμβάνεται τῇ ἀσθενείᾳ ἡμῶν (the Spirit helps us in our weakness)* in 8:26 and the plural noun ἁγίων (saints) in the clause ὅτι κατὰ θεὸν ἐντυγχάνει ὑπὲρ ἁγίων (intercedes on behalf of the saints according to God's will)* in 8:27. Therefore, καρδία is once again used in the context to denote a corporate entity, believers.

Καρδία *in Unit E*

In Unit E, καρδία first portrays Paul's heart (9:2; 10:1), depicting his grief and his desire concerning the welfare of the Israelites, his own people. Then, the term is employed to denote the heart of the Israelites (10:6, 8, 9, 10). The corporate entity that is associated with καρδία is shifted from Christians (Unit D) to the Jews (Unit E). The term is once again used to describe the response of a particular community towards God. In this case, the context of καρδία is related to the Israelites, as they, a corporate entity, are invited to accept the salvific grace of God.

In this unit, Paul first discusses the negative response of the Israelites towards Christ and his salvation, and then describes his feelings by expressing this: λύπη μοί ἐστιν μεγάλη καὶ ἀδιάλειπτος ὀδύνη τῇ καρδίᾳ μου

---

[59] Dunn (1988a:479) repudiates the argument that the Holy Spirit is the subject of ἐραυνῶν (searching). I agree with Dunn on the basis of the usage of the masculine participle. Had the Holy Spirit been the acting subject of the participle, τὸ ἐραυνῶν (the one (neuter in gender) who searches) would have been used. Byrne (1996:266–270) renders the participle as "Searcher of hearts", suggesting God as the subject.

[60] Dunn (1988a:479) argues that καρδία denotes the seat of inner life, the centre where ambitions, values, and motives are rooted by referring to the OT texts in which the searching of heart is mentioned (for example, Ps 44 and Ps 139). However, he does not explain how he derives "motive" in his definition. I contend that the understanding of καρδία in 8:27 depends on the previous verse in which the verb οἶδα (to know) could provide clues. The meaning of καρδία in this text, in my opinion, is quite ambiguous, and the meaning of "mind" is by far the best conjecture.

(I have great sorrow and unceasing anguish in my heart)* in 9:2. Although καρδία is directly linked with ἀδιάλειπτος (unceasing), combined with λύπη (grief) in the previous phrase the text is centred on Paul's emotion, his grief and pain in specific.[61] Then, καρδία in the phrase ἡ μὲν εὐδοκία τῆς ἐμῆς καρδίας (the good pleasure of my heart) (10:1) elucidates Paul's longing[62] for the salvation of his own people, vis-à-vis the Israelites. Paul wishes to see his own people receiving God's salvation in Christ. This desire comes from his καρδία.[63] Regardless whether it is a genitive of possession or a genitive of source, καρδία in both texts is clearly associated with "desire."[64]

Καρδία occurs four times in 10:5–13. In 10:6 and 10:8, the text in which καρδία occurs are both quotations from the LXX. The exact phrase μὴ εἴπῃς ἐν τῇ καρδίᾳ σου (Do not say in your heart)* in 10:6 appears in Deut 8:17 and 9:4 (LXX). Both texts in the LXX are employed to warn the Israelites against boasting about their wealth and righteousness. The phrase in 10:8 resembles the phrase in Deut 30:14 (LXX): ἔστιν σου ἐγγὺς τὸ ῥῆμα σφόδρα ἐν τῷ στόματί σου καὶ ἐν τῇ καρδίᾳ σου καὶ ἐν ταῖς χερσίν σου αὐτὸ ποιεῖν (For the thing is very near you–it is in your mouth and in your mind so that you can do it)*. The passage is the teaching that reminds the Israelites to obey God's commandments. In all three LXX texts, καρδία is a translation of לֵב. The most captivating notion of these LXX texts is the combination of

---

[61] Byrne (1996:286) observes that the two nouns, λύπη (grief) and ὀδύνη (anguish), are used together in Isa 35:10 and 51:11 (LXX). Fitzmyer (1993:544) makes the same observation. This usage illustrates the lament nature of the text, portraying painful emotion (Moo 1996:557). In this verse, the association between ὀδύνη (anguish) and καρδία could have been written as ὀδύνη τῆς καρδίας (anguish of the heart). Rather, a dative is used. I suggest that the two phrases conjoined by καί are likely in parallel—λύπη μοί (grief in me) and ὀδύνη τῇ καρδίᾳ (anguish in the heart) with λύπη (grief) and ὀδύνη (anguish) expressing the same emotion. Thus, μοί (in me) and τῇ καρδίᾳ (in the heart) are synonymous—"in me" can also be expressed as "in my heart". As such, καρδία illustrates Paul himself as a person whilst emphasizing on the emotional aspect.

[62] Εὐδοκία can be defined as good will, good pleasure, or wish (Bauer 1979:319; Moulton and Milligan 1930:260). However, when εὐδοκία is combined with καρδία (as in Rom 10:1), the word connotes "wish" (Bauer 1979:404).

[63] Of interest, following the initial discussion of καρδία in 1:24, most commentators do not analyse the meaning of καρδία in the subsequent texts in which καρδία occurs (Dunn 1988a:73; Moo 1996:111; and Schreiner 1998:92); or they simply refer it back to 1:21 (Morris 1988:88). It seems that a definition of καρδία is assumed, and the same definition is imposed on all the occurrences of καρδία. This imposition reflects a problematic approach of semantic study as discussed in chapter 2.

[64] The genitive form of καρδία modifies εὐδοκία (good pleasure). The genitive can be a genitive of possession, meaning that the desire that belongs to καρδία. It can also be a genitive of source or a genitive of production. Wallace suggests that the genitive of production is not common in the NT. However, the two categories of genitive are very similar (Wallace 1996:104–105).

στόμα (mouth) and καρδία.[65] Στόμα and καρδία are explicitly used in Deut 30:14 (LXX). Although στόμα does not appear in Deut 8:17 and 9:4 (LXX), the word εἴπῃς (you say), the aorist form of λέγω (to say), is likely an allusion to στόμα. Of interest, Paul adopts the combination of στόμα and καρδία in his own argument.[66] The two phrases in Rom 10:9 display this usage: ὁμολογήσῃς ἐν τῷ στόματί σου (confess with your mouth); and πιστεύσῃς ἐν τῇ καρδίᾳ (believe in your heart). Therefore, to ascertain the meaning of καρδία in Rom 10, its "partner," στόμα, must also be considered. As shown below, the meaning of καρδία in Rom 10 is unique, and it deserves special attention.

In terms of the στόμα-καρδία motif, the two nouns can either be regarded as conceptually synonymous or deliberately contrastive.[67] Unless Paul's quotation of Deuteronomy is considered totally disjunctive,[68] as if Paul simply adopting the words in Deuteronomy without any intention of referring to their original meanings,[69] we should assume the original text is of significant influence on

---

[65] From this point onwards, the English translation, mouth, for the term στόμα, is not provided in this chapter

[66] In this passage, Paul's own interpretation of the Deuteronomy is marked by τοῦτ᾽ ἔστιν (that is), a phrase that occurs three times in 10:6–8. Dunn (1988b:602) argues that Paul deliberately quotes from Deuteronomy instead of simply using the language. Barrett (1991:185) asserts that Paul uses the text in Deuteronomy, but provides a fresh interpretation, by attempting to link the text to Christ, an understanding that is not present in the mind of the Deuteronomic writer. Even though the original text in Deut 30 concerns the law, Cranfield (1979:524) argues that Paul does consider the Law and Christ as two closely related entities. Therefore, such a new interpretation of an OT text is not a mere arbitrary practice. Robinson (1979:125) also repudiates the quotation of Deuteronomy as arbitrary, and argues that the salvific purpose of God is now accomplished despite the failure of people in obeying the law. Stuhlmacher (1994:155) articulates that Christ has put an end to the death-producing verdict of the Law.

[67] Cranfield (1979:527) considers that the two words interpret each other, denoting the same concept. Byrne (1996:321) holds the same view, and considers the contents of confessing and believing (Jesus is Lord and God's raising Jesus from the dead) echo the early Christian creedal formulas. However, Fitzmyer (1993:592) regards the two words as representing two different dimensions, depicting an antithesis between inward-outward. For Fitzmyer, στόμα denotes outward confession, and καρδία denotes inward faith. Dunn (1988b:608–609) also highlights this contrast, and argues that στόμα points to the recitation of creed, and καρδία, the affective belief. Moo (1996:657) shares a similar view, asserts that verbal confession is an outward manifestation of inner response. He also observes a nuance in the word order. Στόμα-καρδία in 10:9 is a direct quotation of Deut. 30; but καρδία-στόμα in 10:10 is Paul's conclusion set by Paul. For Moo, this word order indicates that Paul regards that believing in the heart is more crucial.

[68] In his analysis of Rom 10:5–10, Hays (1989:5–21) provides a detailed account regarding the scholarship of Paul's interpretation of the OT.

[69] According to Sanday and Headlam (1902:289), Paul simply quotes the Deuteronomy text in a proverbial manner to express his message. In other words,

Paul's usage of καρδία in Rom 10. Hence, we need to conduct an investigation of καρδία in Deuteronomy. This approach is a helpful diachronic approach, examining the intertextual connection between two texts. It would be a problematic diachronic approach if the meaning of καρδία in any given Pauline epistle is ascertained by retrospectively examining the *general* Hebrew usage of לֵב. However, καρδία in Rom 10 is a specific quotation from the OT text with a purpose (as I assume). Therefore, it is important to briefly investigate how the Deuteronomy texts are connected with Rom 10.

The στόμα-καρδία motif in Deut 30 is not unique, as it is also mentioned in 6:6–7 and 11:18–19. Although the word στόμα does not occur in the two texts, λαλέω (the action of speaking) is used to allude to στόμα.[70] This motif appears in the context of the presentation of God's Law. The ancient Israelites are urged to remember, to speak about, to recite, to teach, and to keep the commandments of God. Notably, the well-known שְׁמַע "Hear" (6:4, BHS) precedes the teaching about the commandments: ἐν τῇ καρδίᾳ σου καὶ ἐν τῇ ψυχῇ σου (in your heart and in your soul) in 6:6 (LXX). Therefore, the Law must be incorporated in their lifestyle, and putting God's words into καρδία can be rendered as remembering or internalising God's commandments.[71] Overall, Deut 30:14 has a summative purpose, and the articulated noun τὸ ῥῆμα (the word) refers to all the commandments in the book.[72] Τὸ ῥῆμα (the word) is not far from στόμα, nor from καρδία.[73] Apparently, τὸ ῥῆμα (the word) is close to both στόμα and καρδία if the Israelites follow the instruction in Deut 6, wherein they become familiar with the word by talking about it and meditating upon it.[74]

---

the quotation is not Paul's interpretation of the OT text. However, Hays (1989:82) repudiates this view, and demonstrates by his analysis, showing that Paul uses Deut 30 as a metaphor for Christian proclamation.

[70] Driver (1896:92, 331) states this argument, and this study concurs with it.

[71] Christensen (2001:143) argues that the word לֵב in Deut 6 is used to urge the Israelites to internalize the law. Christensen seems to be stretching the point. However, Deuteronomy teaches the Israelites to memorise the commandments. Thus, it is reasonable to argue that the purpose of memorising the commandments is to internalise them, so that the law could be well-integrated into daily life. Nelson (2002:91, 350) defines this internalisation as meditation. However, καρδία-στόμα can be understood as a vocalised meditation.

[72] This is proposed by Nelson (2002:349), and I agree with his view. Since Deut 30:14 is clearly part of the summary of Deuteronomy, and it is a summary placed before the prologue.

[73] The key theme of Deut 30:11–14, according to Hays (1989:81), is the nearness of the word. The text teaches that the word is so close to you, simply in your mouth and in your heart. In light of this, the text in Rom 10, for Hays (1989:82–83), should be understood as follows: Just as how the word of God was present to Israel in Torah in the past, the same word of God is now present in the Christian gospel.

[74] It is more natural to interpret the notion of the word being close to both καρδία and στόμα is the result of talking and internalizing it. Driver also holds this view (Driver 1896:331).

Given this brief analysis of Deuteronomy, στόμα and καρδία are seemingly not used synonymously. The two words or the concepts signified are not equivalent, and instead are in contrast. The law must be verbalised and memorised as part of the lifestyle of the Israelites. By doing so, the law would be near to καρδία and στόμα, as concluded in Deut 30.

There are three main views to understand the purpose for Paul to quote Deut 30. First, Paul considers the close relationship between the Law and Christ, and thus καρδία and στόμα are synonymous (as suggested by both Cranfield and Byrne). Second, the motif of καρδία and στόμα in the well-known OT text is a good representation of the external confession and internal belief, which highlights the totality, both outward and inward aspects, of faith (as argued by Fitzmyer). Third, Deuteronomy is used as a metaphor to illustrate the notion that God's word (in the gospel) is present in Christians, just as God's word (in the Torah) is present in the Israelites (as suggested by Hays). If Paul does follow the original denotation of this motif, then it is likely that Paul adopts the external-internal contrast in Rom 10, highlighting the notion of totality.

More importantly, I argue that the occurrences of καρδία in Rom 10 do not elucidate an individual. Just as the Israelites are addressed as a corporate entity in Deut 30, the Israelites are also addressed as a corporate body in need of salvation in Rom 10. The corporate reference is emphasised by the usage of καρδία.

Καρδία in Unit G

The last occurrence of καρδία occurs in Unit G. The term in 16:18 describes τῶν ἀκάκων (the innocent ones) who are deceived by the false teachers. It is commonly held that καρδία is linked to the mind because of the word ἄκακος (innocent).[75] The specific group that Paul focuses on in this usage of καρδία is the false teachers who deceive the simple-minded.

5.1.2.2 Sociolinguistic aspect

In Romans, Paul first calls himself δοῦλος Χριστοῦ Ἰησοῦ and κλητὸς ἀπόστολος (a slave of Christ Jesus, called to be an apostle)* in 1:1, before addressing the audience as ἀδελφοί.[76] As previously mentioned, the self-designation δοῦλος Χριστοῦ (slave of Christ), denotes Paul's leadership and his noble status.[77] Referring to the context of the audience, Brown (2001:732)

---

[75] Various scholars, including Cranfield, Moo, Byrne, and Dunn, argue that ἄκακος (innocent) refers to the "simple-minded" instead of the "innocent." Therefore, καρδία is likely linked to the mind. Cranfield (1979:801) suggests that the word points to the simple-minded people in the Christian community.

[76] For discussion of the sociolinguistic implications associated with ἀπόστολος (apostle) and ἀδελφοί, see § 3.2.2.1 and § 3.2.2.2.

[77] For the discussion of this self-designation, see § 2.3.2.3.

argues that this self-designation is the result of Paul's contextualisation of the Roman congregation. This designation is a "technical term," which highlights the high status enjoyed by imperial slaves, alluding to "Familia Caesaris" in the Roman congregation (ibid. 737). Thus, Paul uses δοῦλος Χριστοῦ Ἰησοῦ (slave of Christ Jesus) to emphasise "the obligation and power that accompany apostleship" (ibid. 733).

The purpose of Paul, according to Brown (ibid. 735–756), is to create a rhetorical tactic to gain sympathy from the audience regarding his mission as an apostle to the Gentiles, and as a result, inviting the audience to participate in this mission. Brown's insightful argument can further be supported by Paul's intriguing proclamation: εἰμι ἐγὼ ἐθνῶν ἀπόστολος (I am an apostle to the Gentiles)* in 11:13b. As previously discussed, the clause Ὑμῖν δὲ λέγω τοῖς ἔθνεσιν (Now I am speaking to you Gentiles)* in 11:13a indicates that the Christian community in Rome mainly consists of the Gentiles. Hence, the emphatic statement in 11:13b demonstrates the authority claimed by Paul, who is a Jew, over his audience, the Gentile Christians in Rome. This illustrates that the Gentile Christians are an essential focus in this letter. This focus is also illustrated by various explicit statements made by Paul (1:13; 15:16, 18).

As an apostle, Paul carries the role of teacher. As mentioned in the discussion of the sociolinguistic aspect there was a common loyalty displayed by students to their teachers in the first century.[78] Given that the Christian community was not founded by Paul, it is quite probable that the letter is employed by him as a means to assert his apostolic authority to "earn" the loyalty and respect from the Romans, which is largely consisted of Gentile believers. His purpose, however, is to urge the Romans to offer him help to partake in his gospel mission to Spain. This should be their obligation, Paul being their apostle chosen by God for the Gentiles.

As previously discussed in the section of discourse coherence, the faith community and the Gentiles are two focal points in Romans.

5.1.3 Thematic meaning of καρδία in Romans

From my analysis, the overall occurrences of καρδία in various semantic units indicate that the term is not randomly employed. Rather, it shows a particular pattern as shown in table 5.3.

---

[78] For a detailed discussion, see § 3.2.2.2.

Table 5.3. Καρδία in Romans

	A 1:8–17	B 1:18–3:20	C 3:21–4:25	D 5–8	E 9–11	F 12:1–15:33	G 16:1–24
Major Semantic Units							
Occurrence of Καρδία	*Letter-opening (1:1–7)*	αὐτῶν καρδία (1:21) τῶν καρδιῶν αὐτῶν (1:24) καρδίαν (2:5) ταῖς καρδίαις αὐτῶν (2:15) περιτομὴ καρδίας ἐν πνεύματι		ἐν ταῖς καρδίαις ἡμῶν (5:5) ἐκ καρδίας (6:17) τὰς καρδίας (8:27)	τῇ καρδίᾳ μου (9:2) τῆς ἐμῆς καρδίας (10:1) τῇ καρδίᾳ σου (10:6) ἐν τῇ καρδίᾳ σου (10:8) τῇ καρδίᾳ σου (10:9) καρδίᾳ (10:10)		*τὰς καρδίας (16:18)*
							Letter-closing (16:25–27)

Key: Different community groups represented by or associated with καρδία in the text are highlighted differently: double underlined for the Gentiles; highlighted in black for the Jews/Israelites; single underlined for Christians; italic for false teachers. There is no highlight for καρδία associated with Paul.

In each of the three units, καρδία is associated with different communities as shown in table 5.4: the Gentiles, the Christians, and the Jews.

Table 5.4. Pattern of καρδία in Romans

Unit B (1:18–3:20)	Unit D (5–8)	Unit E (9–11)
Gentiles and Jews	Christians	Jews/Israelites

The terms elucidate the community's response to God—the ignorance of the Gentiles and the rebellion of the Jews towards God (Unit B), the blessings of God received by the believers (Unit D), and the invitation to the Israelites to accept the salvific grace of God in Christ (Unit E). There is a subtle corporate aspect attached to καρδία in highlighting the relationship between God and each of these communities. Despite the notion that the sentence meaning of individual occurrence of καρδία varies, the thematic meaning connoted by καρδία, as illustrated by its recurrent discourse pattern in various semantic units, points to different corporate entities regarding their response to God and his salvation in Christ.

5.1.3.1 The flow of discourse and peak

As demonstrated in previous chapters, a discourse usually displays a flow of stages. In Romans, the letter-opening (1:1–7) is the aperture. Unit A is the stage that sets up the key theme, the gospel and its power, which is fully developed in the following episodes. Units B to D function as the developing episodes, in which the content and the power of the gospel are fully explained. Paul first explains the sinfulness of both the Jews and the Gentile, and their need of salvation. The thematic meaning of καρδία points to their negative response to God. Then, Paul discusses the blessings of the believers, both the Jews and the Gentiles. The thematic meaning of καρδία points to their positive relationship with God in Christ. In the pre-peak episode (Unit E), Paul discusses the salvific plan of Israel. The climax is situated in the peak (Unit F), which is followed by the post-peak (Unit G1), the closure (Unit G2), and finis (letter-closing) respectively. The discourse flow of Romans is shown in figure 5.8.

As previously explained, a peak usually reveals the core message of a discourse. The discourse peak usually appears near the end of a discourse. It is a turbulent zone with the occurrence of a shift in the proportion of use of one or more particular grammatical device. As previously mentioned, there is a concentrated occurrence of imperatives in Rom 12. Normally, the use of imperative is not of particular interest, since it usually signifies the expository nature of the text. However, the use of imperatives in Rom 12 is relatively unique. One of the most intriguing observations is the use of prohibitive imperative: μὴ (not) plus imperative. There is an unusually frequent occurrence of this device in chapter 12 as shown in figure 5.7.

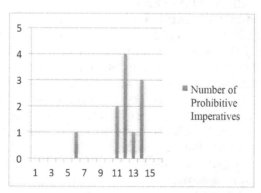

Figure 5.7. The prohibitive imperative verbs in Romans.

The peculiarity of this usage does not merely rest on the frequency. The syntax of these imperatives also captures a degree of interest. All four prohibitive imperative verbs in Rom 12 occur in four parallel constructions, and this phenomenon is absent elsewhere in Romans. These parallel constructions are as follows: μὴ συσχηματίζεσθε...ἀλλὰ μεταμορφοῦσθε (Do not be conformed...but be transformed)* in 12:2; εὐλογεῖτε...καὶ μὴ καταρᾶσθε (Bless...and do not curse)* in 12:14; μὴ τὰ ὑψηλὰ φρονοῦντες ἀλλὰ τοῖς ταπεινοῖς συναπαγόμενοι (Do not be haughty but associate with the lowly)* in 12:16; and μὴ νικῶ ὑπὸ τοῦ κακοῦ ἀλλὰ νίκα ἐν τῷ ἀγαθῷ τὸ κακόν (Do not be overcome by evil, but overcome evil with good)* in 12:21. Each individual prohibitive imperative is accompanied by a synonymous expression that is in the form of either an imperative or a verbal phrase as shown in table 5.5.

Table 5.5. Synonymous expression of the prohibitive imperatives in Rom 12

	Prohibitive Imperative	Synonymous Expression
12:2	μὴ συσχηματίζεσθε	μεταμορφοῦσθε
12:14	μὴ καταρᾶσθε	εὐλογεῖτε
12:16	μὴ γίνεσθε φρόνιμοι παρ' ἑαυτοῖς	τοῖς ταπεινοῖς συναπαγόμενοι
12:21	μὴ νικῶ ὑπὸ τοῦ κακοῦ	νίκα ἐν τῷ ἀγαθῷ τὸ κακόν

As mentioned in previous chapters, an author could employ extra words (including parallelism, paraphrase, and tautologies) in the discourse peak to draw the audience's attention to the climactic point. The influx of imperatives, the use of prohibitive imperatives, and the use of parallelism indicate that Rom 12 is the peak of Romans.

Rom 12 does not merely contain a general exhortation. As shown in both the aperture and the finis, Paul mentions the obedience of the Gentiles to God through faith. The Gentiles, as a corporate entity, are of Paul's concern, as indicated by the repetition of the word ἔθνη (Gentiles) in both the aperture (1:5) and the finis (16:26). The pre-peak unit can be a rhetoric device, answering the possible challenge: why does Paul, a Jew, focus on his ministry to the Gentiles instead of the Jews? Paul argues that despite his concern for his own people, the salvation of the Israelites only comes when τὸ πλήρωμα τῶν ἐθνῶν εἰσέλθῃ (the full number of the Gentiles has come in)* in 11:25. With Paul's overt intention to go to Spain through the Romans, I propose that Rom 12 is directed by Paul to the Roman Christians with a specific purpose. Paul urges the Romans to offer their bodies as a living sacrifice by serving one another in the Christ's community, the one body. However, this is also Paul's invitation to request them to partake in his ministry—his intention to bring the gospel to the Gentiles in Spain through the "help" of the Romans.[79]

---

[79] As previously mentioned, this is the view held by Jewett.

Aperture	Stage (A)	Various Developing Episodes (B–C)		Pre-peak (D)	Peak (E) Climax	Post-peak (F)	Closure (G)	Finis
εἰς ὑπακοὴν πίστεως ἐν **πᾶσιν** **τοῖς** **ἔθνεσιν** (1:5)	ἐσκοτίσθη ἡ ἀσύνετος αὐτῶν **καρδία** (1:21) ταῖς ἐπιθυμίαις τῶν **καρδιῶν** αὐτῶν (1:24) ἀμετανόητον **καρδίαν** (2:5) τὸ ἔργον τοῦ νόμου γραπτὸν ἐν ταῖς **καρδίαις** αὐτῶν (2:15) περιτομὴ **καρδίας** ἐν πνεύματι (2:29)	ἡ ἀγάπη τοῦ θεοῦ ἐκκέχυται ἐν ταῖς **καρδίαις** ἡμῶν (5:5) ὑπηκούσατε δὲ ἐκ **καρδίας** εἰς ὃν παρεδόθητε τύπον διδαχῆς (6:17) ὁ δὲ ἐραυνῶν τὰς οἶδεν τί τὸ φρόνημα τοῦ πνεύματος (8:27)	μὴ εἴπης ἐν τῇ **καρδίᾳ** σου (10:6) τὸ ῥῆμά... ἐν τῇ **καρδίᾳ** σου (10:8) πιστεύσῃς ἐν τῇ **καρδίᾳ** σου (10:9) **καρδίᾳ** γὰρ πιστεύεται εἰς δικαιοσύνην (10:10)	Recurrent prohibitive imperative verbs with parallelism in 12:2, 14, 16, 21			εἰς ὑπακοὴν πίστεως εἰς **πάντα** **τὰ ἔθνη** (16:26)
	ἵνα τινὰ **καρπὸν** σχῶ καὶ ἐν ὑμῖν καθὼς καὶ ἐν τοῖς λοιποῖς **ἔθνεσιν** (1:13)					τοῦτο οὖν ἐπιτελέσας καὶ σφραγισάμε- νος αὐτοῖς τὸν **καρπὸν** τοῦτον, ἀπελεύσομαι δι' ὑμῶν εἰς **Σπανίαν** (15:28)	
1:1–7	1:8–17	1:18–4:25		9:1–11:36	12:1–21 13:1– 15:13	15:14– 16:16	16:17–24	16:25– 27
	Intention to visit Rome	The Gospel of God for the Jews and the Gentiles		Salvation of Israel	Exhortation on Christian living in community	Various Teachings	Intention to visit Spainthru Rome	

Key: - - - - - - ▶ : Inclusio

Figure 5.8. The flow of discourse of Romans.

5.1.4 Summary

From my analysis, the sentence meaning of καρδία in Romans denotes mind, the seat of emotion and volition, or even the whole person. Nonetheless, the thematic meaning of the term carries a corporate dimension. The term occurs in clustered pattern in the epistle, associating with different communities, including the Gentiles, the Jews, and the Christians. To conclude, the thematic meaning of καρδία, as illustrated by its recurrent discourse pattern, points to the corporate response of different groups to God and his salvation in Christ. This corporate aspect that is associated with the usage καρδία highlights the relationship between God and each of those communities.

5.2 Καρδία in 2 Corinthians

In the second section of this chapter I focus on καρδία in 2 Cor 1–9. I initially identify the discourse structure of 2 Cor 1–9, and then ascertain the thematic meaning of καρδία in this discourse.

5.2.1 Discourse structure of 2 Corinthians

As previously mentioned, in applying discourse analysis I assume that each Pauline epistle to be one single discourse. Since the unity of 2 Corinthians has been challenged, it is important for us to briefly review the issue of integrity.

5.2.1.1 The unity of the letter

The unity of 2 Corinthians has been challenged.[80] Scholars are divided in their views. Some commentators advocate a multi-letter theory (Barrett 1973:23–44; Furnish 1984:35–54; Betz 1985:3–36; Thrall 1994:3–49; Roetzel 2007:24–35), but others support the unity (Martin 1986:xxxix–xl; Watson 1993:96; Witherington 1995:328, 333–336; Bruce 1996:171; Barnett 1997:24–25; McCant 1999:23; Keener 2005:151).[81] The reasons for supporting a multi-letter theory include: a sharp change of tone between 2 Cor 9 and 2 Cor 10–13 (Héring 1967:xi; Barrett 1973:24; Furnish 1984:31; Thrall 1994:5; Lambrecht 1999:8); chapters 8 and 9 being inconsistent (Betz 1985:139–44; Thrall 1994:36–43); 2:14–7:4 appearing as an interpolation, disconnected from the previous and the proceeding contexts;[82] and the non-Pauline literal style in 6:14–7:1, illustrated by the high occurrences

---

[80] For a detailed discussion of this issue, see Thrall 1994:3–49; Harris 2005:8–51.

[81] Apart from commentators, some NT scholars also advocate the unity of 2 Corinthians (Amador 2000:92–111; DeSilva 1993:41–70).

[82] Bornkamm and Weiss are proponents of this theory as noted by Furnish (1984:35) and Thrall (1994:20–23).

of hapax legomena (Lambrecht 1999:8).[83] Conversely, the reasons for supporting the unity include: the absence of text tradition challenging the unity (Lambrecht 1999:9; McCant 1999:23); the coherent flow of the letter (Hughes 1967:xxiii; Barnett 1997:24–25; Amador 2000:108–111; Keener 2005:151); the connectedness of chapters 8 and 9 (DeSilva 1993:41–70; Watson 1993:96; Witherington 1995:335–336); and 2:14–7:4 being the result of Paul's natural interruption during composition or digression (Martin 1986:xxxix–xl; Bruce 1996:171).

I do not intend to address the issue of unity. It is important to note that καρδία only occurs in 2 Cor 1–9. According to various multi-letter theories, 2 Cor 1–9 is usually considered to be a separate letter.[84] On the other hand, for those who consider the epistle a single letter, the topics discussed in 1–9 are distinctively different from those in 10–13.[85] Thus, my analysis focuses on the thematic meaning of καρδία in 2 Cor 1–9, treating the first nine chapters as a separate discourse. In the following section I examine the discourse structure of 2 Cor 1–9, its semantic units, its coherence, and then the thematic meaning of καρδία.

5.2.1.2 Discourse markers

Two discourse markers are helpful in identifying the major semantic units in 2 Cor 1–9: formulas and lexical cohesion.

Formulas

Two types of formulas are used in 2 Cor 1–9: formulaic praise and verb-ὑμᾶς-ἀδελφοί.[86] Most of these formulas demarcate a major semantic unit.

There are three formulaic praises in this discourse: Εὐλογητὸς ὁ θεὸς (Blessed is the God)* in 1:3; Τῷ δὲ θεῷ χάρις (But thanks be to God)* in 2:14; and Χάρις τῷ θεῷ (Thanks be to God)* in 9:15. Each of them marks the beginning or the end of a new topic of discussion. In 1:3 the formulaic praise marks the beginning of the first discussion after the initial greeting. In 2:14 the formula commences a discussion in which Paul articulates his apostolic ministry. Finally, the formula in 9:15 marks the end of a discussion of monetary collection (8:1–9:15).

Regarding the verb-ὑμᾶς-ἀδελφοί formula, there are two occurrences: 1:8 and 8:1. In 1:8 the formula Οὐ γὰρ θέλομεν ὑμᾶς ἀγνοεῖν, ἀδελφοί (For we do not want you to be unaware, brothers)* signifies a minor shift of the

---

[83] Thrall (1994:29–30) provides a brief discussion of this argument proposed by various commentators.

[84] For example, Furnish (1984:xi) names 2 Cor 1–9 as Letter D.

[85] For example, McCant (1999:7) divides the letter into three main parts: 1–7; 8–9; 10–13.

[86] Translation: verb-you-brothers. From this point onwards, this English translation is not provided in this chapter.

discussion: from the general suffering endured by all (1:3–7) to a more specific suffering endured by Paul (1:8–2:13).[87] In 8:1 the formula Γνωρίζομεν
δὲ ὑμῖν, ἀδελφοί (Now we make known to you)* commences a new topic of
collecting money from the Corinthians.

Lexical cohesion

One particular proper name appears to be unusually frequent in 2 Cor 1–9:
Τίτος (Titus).[88] This is the most frequent proper name in the letter apart
from Χριστός (Christ) (see Appendix 4). This becomes obvious when its
occurrences in the other Pauline epistles are examined. Τίτος occurs seven
times in 2 Cor 1–9.[89] The name occurs in clusters in 7:4–13, 8:6–23, and
12:28. In 7:2, Paul makes an emphatic call by using an imperative clause
Χωρήσατε ἡμᾶς (Receive us), and ends this segment by expressing his passion for the Corinthians (7:4). He then shifts the topic to the arrival of Τίτος
(7:6), discussing the report brought by Τίτος concerning the Corinthians
(7:5–16).[90] The shift signifies a change in topic. On the other hand, the mentioning of Τίτος in chapter 8 is related to the matter of money collection.

5.2.1.3 Semantic units

Through the two identified discourse makers, there are four major semantic
units identified in 2 Cor 1–9: Unit A (Paul's ministry to the Corinthians);
Unit B (Paul's apostolic ministry); Unit C (Paul's response to the report of
Titus regarding the Corinthians); and Unit D (Money collection from the
Corinthians). Table 5.6 shows the semantic units of 2 Cor 1–9, and table 5.7
compares the outline of this study and those suggested by other scholars.[91]

---

[87] A similar formula also occurs in Rom 1:13; 11:25; 1 Cor 10:1; 12:1; and 1 Thess
4:13. The verb in Romans and 1 Corinthians is θέλω, the verb in 2 Corinthians and
1 Thessalonians is θέλομεν.

[88] From this point onwards, the English translation, Titus, is not provided in this
chapter.

[89] The occurrences of Τίτος in 2 Corinthians are as follows: 2:13; 7:6, 13, 14; 8:6,
16, 23; 12:18 (twice).

[90] The theory that considers 7:5–16 as a separate letter is problematic due to the
following reasons. First, Καὶ γὰρ in 7:5 is a transitional conjunction that refers back
to its antecedent. In addition, there is a pattern of lexical cohesion displayed by
παράκλησις (7:4, 7, 13), which is accompanied by occurrences of παρακαλέω (7:6,
7, 13). The theme of consolation is repeated, and is extended from 7:4 to 7:5–16.
Hence, 7:5–16 is connected with the previous part instead of being an independent
letter. DeSilva (1998:3–6) opposes the theory of 2 Cor 1–7 being a compilation
of multiple letters, and provides a detailed account regarding its integrity by
investigating the common vocabularies shared within 1–7.

[91] Table 5.7 does not present the full outline of each scholar. Rather, it presents the
scholars that identify the same or similar unit as each of my units.

Table 5.6. Semantic units of 2 Cor 1–9

Major Units	A 1:3–2:13		B 2:14–7:4	C 7:5–16	D 8:1–9:15
Minor Units	A1 1:3–7	A2 1:8–2:13			
Discourse Markers DM1: Formulas	Εὐλογητὸς ὁ θεὸς καὶ πατὴρ (1:3)	Οὐ γὰρ θέλομεν ὑμᾶς ἀγνοεῖν, ἀδελφοί (1:8)	Τῷ δὲ θεῷ χάρις (2:14)		Γνωρίζομεν δὲ ὑμῖν, ἀδελφοί (8:1) Χάρις τῷ θεῷ (9:15)
DM2: Lexical Cohesion	Letter-opening (1:1–2)			Τίτος	
New Topic		Paul's ministry to the Corinthians	Paul's apostolic ministry	Paul's response to the report of Titus regarding the Corinthians	Money collection from the Corinthians

Table 5.7. Outline of 2 Cor 1–9 by scholars[a]

My Outline	Semantic Unit A 1:3–2:13[b]	Semantic Unit B 2:14–7:4[c]	Semantic Unit C 7:5–16[d]	Semantic Unit D 8:1–9:15
Outline of Scholars	Barnett Barrett Bruce Lambrecht Martin Matera Thrall Witherington	Barnett Barrett Bruce Harris Lambrecht Matera Roetzel Thrall	Bruce DeSilva Harris Hughes Keener Lambrecht Martin Matera Thrall Witherington	Bruce Harris Hughes Lambrecht Martin Matera McCant Plummer Thrall Watson Witherington

[a] For detailed outline, see Barrett 1973:51–52; Bruce 1996:175–176; DeSilva 1998:vii; Furnish 1984:xi–xii; Harris 2005:ix–xi; Hughes 1967:vii–viii; Lambrecht 1999:v–vi; Martin 1986:xxxvii–xxxviii; Matera 2003:vii–viii; McCant 1999:7; Plummer 1925:xx–xxi; Thrall 1994:xiii–xiv; Thrall 2000:ix–x; Watson 1993:vii–viii; Witherington 1995:viii–ix.

[b] The scholars shown in this column commonly consider 2:13 as the end of a major division. However, they disagree on the key divisions of 1:1–2:13. The major divisions identified by various scholars are as follows: Bruce (1:1–2:13); Witherington (1:3–7 and 1:8–2:16); Thrall and Matera (1:1–11 and 1:12–2:13); Lambrecht and Barrett (1:3–11 and 1:12–23); Martin (1:3–11, 1:12–14, and 1:15–2:13); Barnett (1:1–11 and 1:12–2:13).

[c] For Bruce, 2:14–7:1 and 7:2–16 are two major segments. For Roetzel, 2:14–7:4 is a separate letter.

[d] For Witherington, Bruce, and Martin, this segment begins in 7:2 instead of 7:5. According to DeSilva, this segment commences in 7:4.

My proposed segmentation is basically similar to that proposed by various scholars. In the following section I examine the discourse coherence and macrostructure of 2 Cor 1–9 based on the identified major semantic units.

5.2.1.4 Discourse coherence

Two forms of prominence, thematic prominence and lexical cohesion, are helpful in ascertaining the coherent message of 2 Cor 1–9. My examination below shows that the letter has a relational focus, emphasizing the relationship between Paul and the Corinthian community.

Thematic prominence

Paul's relationship with the Corinthians is a prominent theme conveyed in all three semantic units of 2 Cor 1–9.

In Unit A, Paul argues that he is sincere and has a pure motive towards the Corinthians. This is well illustrated by 1:12, in which Paul states: ὅτι ἐν ἁπλότητι καὶ εἰλικρινείᾳ τοῦ θεοῦ...ἀνεστράφημεν ἐν τῷ κόσμῳ, περισσοτέρως δὲ πρὸς ὑμᾶς (that with pure motives and sincerity which are from God...we conducted ourselves in the world, and all the more toward you)*.

In Unit B, Paul declares that his God-given ministry of reconciliation is for ministering to the Corinthians. Paul receives τὴν διακονίαν τῆς καταλλαγῆς (the ministry of reconciliation)* from God, and urges the Corinthians καταλλάγητε τῷ θεῷ (be reconciled to God)* in 5:18–20.

Unit C focuses on Paul's response to Titus' report concerning the Corinthians. The relational tone between Paul and the Corinthians is displayed by various expressions, including: εἰ καὶ ἐλύπησα ὑμᾶς ἐν τῇ ἐπιστολῇ (even if I made you sad by my letter)* in 7:8; νῦν χαίρω...ἐλυπήθητε εἰς μετάνοιαν (now I rejoice...you were made sad to the point of repentance)* in 7:9; and εἴ τι αὐτῷ ὑπὲρ ὑμῶν κεκαύχημαι (if I have boasted to him about anything concerning you)* in 7:14.

In Unit D, Paul requests the Corinthians to partake in monetary contribution, by appealing to them instead of commanding them: Οὐ κατ' ἐπιταγὴν λέγω (I am not saying this as a command)* in 8:8. He also expresses his affection for them, ἡμῶν ἐν ὑμῖν ἀγάπῃ (in the love from us that is in you)* in 8:7, and his boasting about them, ὑπὲρ ὑμῶν καυχῶμαι Μακεδόσιν (I keep boasting to the Macedonians about this eagerness of yours)* in 9:2.

Lexical cohesion

There are three patterns of lexical cohesion in 2 Cor 1–9. These demonstrate the relationship between Paul and the Corinthian community.

The first pattern is the repetition of διακονία (ministry). The word διακονία occurs 18 times in the Pauline epistles, and 11 of them occur in 2 Cor 1–9.[92] In chapters 1–7, the word portrays Paul's ministry, such as ἡ διακονία τοῦ πνεύματος (the ministry of the Spirit)* in 3:8 and τὴν διακονίαν τῆς καταλλαγῆς (the ministry of reconciliation)* in 5:18. The word reflects Paul's emphasis on his apostolic ministry to the Corinthians. In 2 Cor 8–9, διακονία pinpoints the ministry of monetary contribution to other Christian communities (8:4; 9:1, 12–13), since Paul encourages the Corinthians to participate in this ministry. The word highlights the relationship between the apostle and the Corinthians.

---

[92] The occurrences of διακονία (ministry) in 2 Cor 1–9 are as follows: 3:7, 8, 9 (twice); 4:1; 5:18; 6:3; 8:4; 9:1, 12, 13.

The second pattern is the repetition of καυχάομαι (to boast) and its cognates, καύχησις (boasting) and καύχημα (object of boasting). These three words, which belong to the same lexical set, occur ten times when combined together.[93] Καύχησις (boasting) is first introduced in 1:12, expressing Paul's boasting of his pure conscience towards the Corinthians. These words are employed in the context in which the relationship between the apostle and the Corinthians is highlighted. For example, Paul invites the Corinthians to boast about him (5:12), and Paul boasts about the Corinthians (7:14, 9:2).

The third pattern is the repetition of χάρις (grace). The word occurs 16 times in 2 Cor 1–9.[94] The distribution of χάρις, however, demonstrates an unusual pattern as the word congregates in chapters 8–9, with ten occurrences clustered in these two chapters. The word is related to the discussion of the collection.

5.2.1.5 Macrostructure

Based on the above findings, the macrostructure of 2 Cor 1–9 focuses on Paul's relationship with the Corinthians, and can be explained as follows. Paul defends his apostolic ministry towards the Corinthians. He first makes known his pure motives towards them (Unit A) before laying out his apostolic ministry among them (Units B and C): the ministry of reconciliation that has been given to him as Christ's ambassador. The discourse then proceeds to a seemingly disjunctive segment in Unit D. Nonetheless, the topic of monetary contribution (Unit D) is expressed by alluding to his apostolic authority illustrated by the phrase Οὐ κατ' ἐπιταγὴν λέγω (I am not saying this as a command)* in 8:8a.

5.2.2 Occurrence of Καρδία in 2 Cor 1–9

Καρδία occurs 11 times in 2 Corinthians, with all occurrences in chapters 1–9 as shown in the following figure.[95] Figure 5.9 shows the occurrences of καρδία in 2 Cor 1–13, and table 5.8 shows the detailed occurrences of καρδία in the semantic units of 2 Cor 1–9.

---

[93] The occurrences of καυχάομαι (to boast) in 2 Cor 1–9 are as follows: 5:12; 7:14; 9:2. The occurrences of καύχησις (boasting) are as follows: 1:12; 7:4, 14; 8:24. The occurrences of καύχημα (object of boasting) are as follows: 1:14; 5:12; 9:3.

[94] See 2 Cor 1:2, 12, 15; 2:14; 4:15; 6:1; 8:1, 4, 6, 7, 9, 16, 19; 9:8, 14, 15. The occurrences of χάρις (grace) are the second most frequent among the authentic Pauline epistles. The word occurs 24 times and ten times in Romans and 1 Corinthians respectively.

[95] The occurrences of καρδία are as follows: 1:22; 2:4; 3:2, 3, 15; 4:6; 5:12; 6:11; 7:3; 8:16; 9:7.

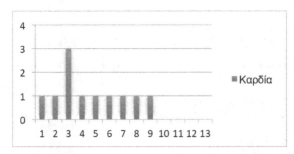

Figure 5.9. The occurrences of καρδία in 2 Corinthians.

Table 5.8. The occurrences of καρδία in 2 Cor 1–9

Semantic Units	A (1:3–2:13)	B (2:14–7:4)	C (7:5–16)	D (8:1–9:15)
	δοὺς τὸν ἀρραβῶνα τοῦ πνεύματος ἐν ταῖς καρδίαις ἡμῶν (1:22)	ἡ ἐπιστολὴ ἡμῶν ὑμεῖς ἐστε, ἐγγεγραμμένη ἐν ταῖς καρδίαις ἡμῶν (3:2)		ἐν τῇ καρδίᾳ Τίτου (8:16)
	ἐκ...συνοχῆς καρδίας ἔγραψα ὑμῖν (2:4)	ἐστὲ ἐπιστολὴ Χριστοῦ... ἐγγεγραμμένη... ἐν πλαξὶν καρδίαις σαρκίναις (3:3)		προῄρηται τῇ καρδίᾳ (9:7)
		ἀναγινώσκηται Μωϋσῆς, κάλυμμα ἐπὶ τὴν καρδίαν αὐτῶν κεῖται (3:15)		
		ὁ θεὸς...ὃς ἔλαμψεν ἐν ταῖς καρδίαις ἡμῶν (4:6)		
		τοὺς ἐν προσώπῳ καυχωμένους καὶ μὴ ἐν καρδίᾳ (5:12)		
		πρὸς ὑμᾶς...ἡ καρδία ἡμῶν επλάτυνται (6:11)		
		ἐν ταῖς καρδίαις ἡμῶν ἐστε (7:3)		
Topic	Paul's ministry to the Corinthians	Paul's apostolic ministry	Paul's response to Titus' report of the Corinthians	Money collection from the Corinthians

5.2.2.1 *Καρδία in semantic units*

To ascertain the thematic meaning of καρδία, it is essential to understand the term by recognizing its occurrence as a pattern across different semantic units. In 2 Cor 1–9, καρδία occurs in Units A, B, and D. My following analysis shows that its thematic meaning points to the corporate and communal aspect.

Καρδία in Unit A

Καρδία occurs twice in Unit A (1:22; 2:4). In 1:22, τὸν ἀρραβῶνα τοῦ πνεύματος (the pledge, which is the Spirit) is to be given ἐν ταῖς καρδίαις ἡμῶν (in our hearts).[96] The genitive noun τοῦ πνεύματος (the Spirit) is epex-egetical, appositional to τὸν ἀρραβῶνα (the pledge). The Holy Spirit is the pledge. The phrase is conjoined by καὶ to another phrase, ὁ καὶ σφραγισάμενος ἡμᾶς (the one who sealed us). The act of sealing is commonly perceived as corresponding with the giving of the Holy Spirit as a pledge.[97] Καρδία can either denote the inner person or is a synonym of ἡμᾶς (us).[98] The geni-tive construct ταῖς καρδίαις ἡμῶν (our hearts) is a normal plural construct, highlighting the individual hearts of the Corinthians.[99] Regardless whether καρδία means the inner self or is synonymous with ἡμᾶς (us), the important point is that the use of the plural pronoun ἡμῶν (our) emphasises the rela-tional aspect, namely Paul and the Corinthian community that receives the Holy Spirit.[100]

In 2:4, Paul employs καρδία to describe his emotion. Paul informs the Corinthians that he writes this letter out of πολλῆς θλίψεως καὶ συνοχῆς καρδίας...διὰ πολλῶν δακρύων, οὐχ ἵνα λυπηθῆτε ἀλλὰ τὴν ἀγάπην ἵνα γνῶτε (great distress and anguish of heart...not to make you sad, but to let you know the love)*. Καρδία is associated with or directly modified by συνοχή (anguish), δάκρυον (tear), λυπέω (to grieve), and ἀγάπη (love),

---

[96] Various scholars attempt to identify the meaning of ἀρραβών (pledge). For example, Kwon (2008:526–529) discusses whether the connotation is figurative or literal.

[97] Ἀρραβών (pledge) is frequently interpreted by considering another word σφραγίζω (to seal), since both words are commercial terms (Barrett 1973:79–80; Furnish 1984:137; Martin 1986:28; Harris 2005:207). The analysis of this passage usually considers the occurrence of all four participles: βεβαιῶν (confirming), χρίσας (anointing), σφραγισάμενος (sealing), and δούς (giving). Βεβαιόω (to confirm) and σφραγίζω (to seal) are compared and analysed. However, I do not intend to investigate the participles, but only focus on the two commercial terms that are joined by καί (and).

[98] Furnish (1984:138) argues that ταῖς καρδίαις ἡμῶν (our hearts) is synonymous with ἡμᾶς (us), by referring to the same phrase in Rom 5:5: ἡ ἀγάπη τοῦ θεοῦ ἐκκέχυται ἐν ταῖς καρδίαις ἡμῶν διὰ πνεύματος ἁγίου τοῦ δοθέντος ἡμῖν (the love of God has been poured out in our hearts through the Holy Spirit who was given to us)*. Conversely, Harris (2005:208) quotes BAGD and TDNT, and argues that καρδία refers to the indwelling-place of heavenly powers and beings and the centre in man to which God returns.

[99] There is no evidence in the context suggesting that καρδία denotes emotion, reason, and volition.

[100] Both Barnett (1973:113) and Thrall (1994:158) point out its communal aspect. Barnett argues that this phrase is understood as the Holy Spirit dwelling within us as individuals, and as congregation. Thrall contends that the anointing described in 1:21–22 points to the messianic community destined to reign with Christ.

words depicting emotion. Καρδία is qualified by both θλίψεως (distress) and συνοχῆς (anguish). Both genitives link to the preposition ἐκ (from), portraying Paul's emotion.[101] Nonetheless, the emotion depicted by καρδία is directly associated with the love of Paul for the Corinthians. In other words, in this context καρδία is employed in highlighting the relationship between Paul and the Corinthian community.[102]

Καρδία in Unit B

In 2 Cor 1–9, the occurrences of καρδία are concentrated in Unit B, with the term appearing seven times in this unit alone. Many of its occurrences occur in the context in which the contrast between the old covenant and the new covenant is underlined. In this unit, Paul defends his apostolicity against his opponents, and asserts his apostolic ministry to the Corinthian community. There is an ongoing attempt in scholarship to identify the opponents.[103] Although my analysis may shed light on the nature of the opponents, it is not my primary task to provide an exact identification. As explained below, the overall occurrences of καρδία in this unit carry a strong corporate reference.

Καρδία first occurs twice in 3:2–3. The context is related to the comparison between the old covenant and the new covenant. Moses is the minister of the old covenant (3:7), and Paul is the minister of the new (3:8). Paul states that the community is his letter: ἡ ἐπιστολὴ ἡμῶν ὑμεῖς ἐστε, ἐγγεγραμμένη ἐν ταῖς καρδίαις ἡμῶν (You yourselves are our letter, written on our hearts) in 3:2.[104] He reiterates this idea by asserting that the

---

[101] Martin (1986:36) concludes that this verse concerns the inner life of Paul who opens up to the Corinthians. However, I agree with Harris (2005:221) that 2:4 articulates the personal emotions that motivate Paul to write to the Corinthians.

[102] Thrall (1994:170) suggests that this relationship reflects a parental concern grounded in love. Roetzel (2007:135) considers the relationship between Paul and the Corinthians as a family. For Lambrecht (1999:31), Paul places extreme emphasis on love in the context.

[103] As previously mentioned, some scholars perceive 2:14–7:4 as a separate letter. There has been an attempt to reconstruct the historical setting of 2:14–7:4 in order to identify Paul's opponents. For example, Jewett (1971:27–31) develops the view of G. Friedrich, identifying the opponents as the divine-man-missionaries. His argument is based on on the criticism of F. C. Baur's Judaizers and D. Georgi's Pneumatic Teachers. Jewett executes this reconstruction by applying mirror-reading. Sumney (1990:95–112) criticises this method, and develops a new method to analyse 2 Corinthians. Blanton (2010:151) argues that the opponents are individuals striving to mediate the renewed covenant between God and humans, as he identifies the opponents as so-called agents of righteousness.

[104] There is a significant textual variant in 3:2, in which ὑμῶν (your) is the variant form of ἡμῶν (our). The variant ὑμῶν (your) is supported by ℵ, 33, 1175, 1881, and *pc*; with the majority of the manuscripts having ἡμῶν (our). Both Barrett (1973:96) and Thrall (1994:223) believe that the variant form is possibly due to the assimilation of 7:3, in which the phrase ἐν ταῖς καρδίαις ἡμῶν (on our hearts) occurs. Since Paul

community is Christ's letter: ἐγγεγραμμένη...ἐν πλαξὶν καρδίαις σαρκίναις (written...on tablets of human hearts)*, in contrast to ἐν πλαξὶν λιθίναις (on stone tablets)* in 3:3. The theme 'stone' is repeated in the following verses. Paul explains how Moses received the old covenant on Mount Sinai. In 3:7, the convenant is described as ἐν γράμμασιν ἐντετυπωμένη λίθοις (carved in letters on stone tablets)*. In 3:15, the Israeli community is depicted with the words κάλυμμα ἐπὶ τὴν καρδίαν αὐτῶν κεῖται (a veil lies on their heart) when they listen to the covenant. This portrayal refers to the OT texts, including Exod 34 and Jer 31:31–34. The juxtapositions between καρδία and λίθος (stone), as well as καρδίαις σαρκίναις (hearts of flesh) and λιθίναις (of stone), elucidate a deliberate contrast between "outward" and "inward." Hence, καρδία denotes the aspect of inwardness. Καρδία in this unit, including its two occurrences in 3:2–3, may mean the mind or inner self.[105] Importantly, I contend that καρδία portrays the mind of the Corinthian community. Similar to the usage of καρδία in 1:22, the community under the new covenant is compared with the Israeli community in the old covenant. The usage in 3:2–3 is not concerned with the heart of an 'individual.' Rather, it denotes the hearts of people who belong to the same community.

In 3:15, καρδία occurs in the context in which Paul draws on the OT text to argue his point. He refers to the event at Mount Sinai where Moses receives the old covenant from God on behalf of the ancient Israelites. The phrase τὴν καρδίαν αὐτῶν (their heart) refers to the Israelites.[106] This phrase is written in the abnormal singular construct, with the singular καρδία combining with the plural αὐτῶν (their). Regarding the combination of καρδία and possessive pronoun, as previously discussed, this abnormal singular

does not need commendation, for Barrett, the context is in favour of ὑμῶν (your). Scholars are divided in their opinions. Some regard ὑμῶν (your) as a better attested reading (Furnish 1984:181; Martin 1986:51; Thrall 1994:224). Some accept ἡμῶν (our) as the more appropriate one (Lambrecht 1999:41; Harris 2005:261). From the preceding sentence, Paul asks a rhetorical question, asking whether he needs a recommendation letter πρὸς ὑμᾶς ἢ ἐξ ὑμῶν (to you or from you). From this context, it would be more logical, I would argue, to view that the Corinthians are Paul's letter—ἡ ἐπιστολὴ ἡμῶν ὑμεῖς ἐστε...ἐγγεγραμμένη ἐν ταῖς καρδίαις ἡμῶν (you are our letter...written on our hearts).

[105] According to Lambrecht (1999:41), καρδία refers to the very core of the person where God's Spirit is active. Alternatively, Thrall (1994:226–227) argues that καρδίαις σαρκίναις (hearts of flesh) elucidates sensitive feeling and λίθινος (stone) denotes a lack of feeling or inferiority in mind. For Nguyen (2008:172), καρδία in 2:14–7:14 denotes the inward spiritual dimension of a Christian identity. However, in this unit Nguyen (2008:162–163, 205) renders καρδία as hearts/minds, where the inward work of the Holy Spirit takes place. Given the context, it is likely the sentence meaning of καρδία denotes mind, emphasising the inwardness of people.

[106] Again, many commentators do not notice the abnormal combination of a singular καρδία and a plural αὐτῶν (their). See Jewett 1971:329; Martin 1986:69; Furnish 1984:233; Thrall 1994:267; Lambrecht 1999:53.

construct is extremely rare in the Pauline epistles. It must not be automatically assumed that the distributive singular is the explanation to the abnormal construct. Based on the context, the most natural explanation for the singular καρδία in 3:15 is that the Israelites are regarded as having one heart, highlighting their corporate identity and their common mindset of rebellion. Paul argues that a veil lies over their heart, which points to their stubborn mind as a nation which hinders their ability to see the glory of the Lord (3:16–18). This corporate identity illustrated by the singular καρδία is further exemplified by the contrast between αὐτῶν (their) in 3:15, the Israelites, and ἡμεῖς (we) in 3:18, the Christian community. In the establishment of the old covenant, the Israelites are treated as one nation, one entity. Therefore, the corporate entity is highlighted by the use of a singular καρδία despite the plural αὐτῶν (their).

In 2 Cor 4, Paul continues to defend his apostolic ministry. The light of the gospel is described as ἔλαμψεν ἐν ταῖς καρδίαις ἡμῶν πρὸς φωτισμὸν τῆς γνώσεως τῆς δόξης τοῦ θεοῦ ἐν προσώπῳ ['Ιησοῦ] Χριστοῦ (shined in our hearts to give us the light of the glorious knowledge of God in the face of Christ)* in 4:6. The genitive τῆς γνώσεως (of the knowledge) is probably an epexegetical genitive. Hence, φωτισμὸν (light) is τὴν γνώσεως τῆς δόξης τοῦ θεοῦ (the glorious knowledge of God). The two phrases, ἐν ταῖς καρδίαις ἡμῶν (in our hearts) and ἐν προσώπῳ ['Ιησοῦ] Χριστοῦ (in the face of [Jesus] Christ), is of interest.[107] Although καρδία and πρόσωπον (face) are not set in opposition, the existence of the two words may well be set up for their later reappearance in 5:12. The genitive possessive pronoun ἡμῶν (our) refers to the Christian community upon which Christ's light shines. The inwardness of καρδία is emphasised, as the light shines into the inner and invisible notion of humans, and importantly into the community of Christ under the ministry of Paul.[108]

---

[107] Moule (1959:184) argues that ἐν προσώπῳ (in face) is a translation of a Hebrew prepositional phrase, and in the case of 2 Cor. 4:6, the phrase means in the face (countenance) or person. Nguyen (2008:160) argues that πρόσωπον (face) can mean mask, portraying the social authority of Moses.

[108] Jewett (1971:329) argues for the polemical usage of καρδία, and suggests that the divine-man-missionaries are concerned only about the face, the external. Regardless of the legitimacy of Jewett's theory of the divine-man-missionaries, the polemical use of the contrast between πρόσωπον (face) and καρδία is evident in 2 Cor 4–5. Lambrecht (1999:66) regards the expression ἐν ταῖς καρδίαις ἡμῶν (in our hearts) is equivalent to ἐν ἡμῖν (in you) in Gal 1:16. Although Lambrecht's assertion appears to be sound (which may well be the case), we must not overlook the emphasis on the outward-inward juxtaposition. Contextually, the juxtaposition is so prominent that it could overshadow the suggested synonymy. Thrall (1994:405) ties 3:3 and 5:12 together, and argues that πρόσωπον (face), as attested with the old covenant, is set in contrast to καρδία, as related to the gospel in the new covenant. The association is strong and persuasive, given that Paul's entire defence centres on his apostolicity in 2:14–7:4.

In 4:18, Paul concludes his argument: μὴ σκοπούντων ἡμῶν τὰ βλεπόμενα ἀλλὰ τὰ μὴ βλεπόμενα (we are not seeing the things that can be seen but the things that cannot be seen). The contrast between 'seen' and 'unseen' is emphasised. Paul then accuses his opponents in 5:12: τοὺς ἐν προσώπῳ καυχωμένους καὶ μὴ ἐν καρδίᾳ (those who are boasting in face and not in heart). The juxtaposition between outward (seen) and inward (unseen) is fully manifested in Paul's usage of καρδία in 5:12 after developing this concept in the previous context. The concept of "seen" alludes to the old Mosaic covenant in which the external glory and credentials are accentuated; and the concept of "unseen" points to the new covenant in which the Spirit operates within humans. Most importantly, the antithesis of καρδία-πρόσωπον (heart-face) is clearly expressed, with the word καρδία appearing in its singular form. In other words, the antithesis of the outward and inward is exemplified by the occurrence of the singular καρδία in 5:12. Behm (1965:612) also notes this contrast. In his recent work, Nguyen (2008:1–2) argues that the interplay between πρόσωπον (face) and καρδία is of great significance in Paul's argument in the wider context of 2:14–7:4. As previously mentioned, he contends that the occurrences of καρδία in this segment (3:2, 3, 15; 4:6; 5:12) denote the inward spiritual dimension of a Christian identity as opposed to the outward identity marked by superficial values in the Corinthian society. This Christian identity, for Nguyen (2008:1–2), is the social identity of the church communities.[109] I concur with Nguyen; and further argue that this singular καρδία portrays this common communal identity: the Christian community in which the inward identity instead the outward appearance is of central importance (Nguyen 2008:153, 172). Furthermore, the recent work by Vegge (2008:363) indicates that 2:14–7:4 is a key part for Paul to present his argument for achieving full reconciliation between the Corinthians and himself. As such, the communal aspect is fully emphasised in this semantic unit, with the singular καρδία emphasising the corporate identity of the church community.

In Paul's final plea in this semantic unit, there is a common understanding regarding the link between 6:11 and 7:3. In both verses, καρδία is related to emotion (Barrett 1973:204; Furnish 1984:360; Martin 1986:219; Thrall 1994:484; Lambrecht 1999:119). As defending his apostolicity, Paul expresses in 6:11: Τὸ στόμα ἡμῶν ἀνέῳγεν πρὸς ὑμᾶς, Κορίνθιοι, ἡ καρδία ἡμῶν πεπλάτυνται (We have spoken freely to you, Corinthians; our heart has been opened wide to you)*. As previously discussed, there are only three out of 21 cases in Paul's

---

[109] Matera (2003:131) interprets καρδία in 5:12 as a reality instead of an appearance. Lambrecht (1999:93) contends that καρδία denotes honesty instead of insincerity. Notably, Thrall (1994:405) suggests that Paul is responding to the opponents who are criticising him for the lack of Mosaic glory, since they fail to recognise the credentials of the apostle in the form of the community he has founded. Although Thrall does not directly define καρδία as pointing to the church community, her explanation does carry this allusion.

letters in which καρδία occurs in an abnormal singular construct. One of the three cases is ἡ καρδία ἡμῶν (our heart) in 6:11. Paul expresses his affection towards the Corinthians through the clause ἡ καρδία ἡμῶν πεπλάτυνται (our heart has been opened wide). He later elaborates his assertion, and informs them that στενοχωρεῖσθε δὲ ἐν τοῖς σπλάγχνοις ὑμῶν (but you are restricted in your affections for us)* in 6:12. The word σπλάγχνον means affection and love (Bauer 1979:763). There is a close association between σπλάγχνον (affection) and καρδία. Thus, the affection demonstrated by the word σπλάγχνον reveals the emphasis on emotion underlined by καρδία.

Regarding ἡμῶν (our), the plural pronoun does not necessarily denote a plural reality because Paul may use the epistolary plural. Paul depicts his own heart rather than a group of people as signified by ἡμῶν (our).[110] 6:11 is located in 2:14–7:4, a segment in which Paul defends his apostolic ministry among the Corinthians. Paul appeals to the Corinthians by expressing his affection towards them.[111] Hence, ἡμῶν (our) logically refers to Paul—his heart is wide open to the Corinthians as he emphatically addresses them as Κορίνθιοι (Corinthians) in the same verse.[112] Thus, it is reasonable to conclude that καρδία in 6:11 is not a distributive singular. Rather, it refers to the heart of Paul alone. This view is also common held by various commentators,[113] with ἡμῶν (our) considered as an epistolary plural.[114]

Nonetheless, it is more important to note that καρδία portrays the communal relationship between Paul and the Corinthians in this context. The word does not simply denote emotion. Rather, it is used to describe the relationship

---

[110] Blass and Debrunner (1961:146–147) call it the literary plural, a widespread usage amongst contemporary Greek authors. However, Robertson (1934:677–678) argues that this kind of editorial plural is not common in the Pauline epistles, since Paul sometimes associates himself with others in addressing to an audience. Moule (1959:118) is cautious about the epistolary plural as he states that it is not as common as some claim, and each passage must be examined individually. Wallace (1996:394) distinguishes the two terms, epistolary plural and literary plural, and argues that latter is a better terminology.

[111] Although Paul includes Timothy at the beginning of the epistles, Παῦλος...καὶ Τιμόθεος (Paul...and Timothy), in 1:1, the ἡμῶν (our) in 6:11 does not automatically include Timothy who is not the key character in this segment.

[112] This is the only occasion in 2 Corinthians on which they are called.

[113] Scholars commonly consider the phrase ἡ καρδία ἡμῶν (our heart) as the portrayal of Paul alone, although they do not define the plural pronoun as an epistolary plural (Plummer 1925:203; Hughes 1967:239; Barrett 1973:191; Martin 1986:185–186; Thrall 1994:468–469; Witherington 1995:400; Barnett 1997:335; DeSilva 1998:32; Lambrecht 1999:120; McCant 1999:61; Matera 2003:161; Keener 2005:191; Harris 2005:488–489; Roetzel 2007:87). Apart from commentators, Kijne (1966:174) also considers that the first person plural pronoun in 2 Cor 6:10–12 depicts Paul himself.

[114] Without specifying 6:11, Verhoef (1996:423) argues that an epistolary plural can explain some of the occurrences of the plural pronoun in 2 Corinthians, but he contends that each occurrence must be judged individually based on the context.

between Paul and the community. The invitation to this relational reconciliation is accentuated by the use of the vocative Κορίνθιοι (Corinthians).

In 7:3, Paul continues his argument by disclosing to the Corinthians that they are ἐν ταῖς καρδίαις ἡμῶν ἐστε εἰς τὸ συναποθανεῖν καὶ συζῆν (you are in our hearts so that we die together and live together with you)*. The denotation of καρδία as inward affection is evident. Καρδία in both 6:11 and 7:3 is linked to emotion. Similar to 6:11, καρδία in this context highlights the communal relationship between the apostle and the Corinthian community.

In summary, the overall occurrences of καρδία in this semantic unit point to the community, instead of individual, under the new covenant. This coherent usage of καρδία is extended from its usage in Unit A, 1:22 in particular, in which the phrase τὸν ἀρραβῶνα τοῦ πνεύματος ἐν ταῖς καρδίαις ἡμῶν (the pledge, which is the Spirit, in our hearts) denotes the work of God in a new dispensation. The comparison between the old dispensation and the new dispensation illustrated by the occurrences of καρδία in 2 Cor 3–4, combined with the antithesis of καρδία-πρόσωπον (heart-face) in 5:12, dominates Unit B. Therefore, the thematic meaning of καρδία elucidates a community that operates under the new dispensation. As such, the cry of Paul in 6:11 should not be merely regarded as his emotional cry to the Corinthians, as if the apostle craves their acceptance. Rather, καρδία is employed to convey a subtle message: the Corinthian community, which is a corporate entity under the new dispensation, should accept Paul's apostolic ministry. This ministry of reconciliation is ordained by God and operated under the new covenant. Accordingly, the corporate identity is the thematic meaning carried by καρδία in Unit B.

Καρδία in Unit D

In Unit D, Paul commences a new discussion, focusing on the collection. In this semantic unit, καρδία only occurs twice: 8:16 and 9:7.

The phrase τῇ καρδίᾳ Τίτου (in the heart of Titus) (8:16) conveys the zeal (σπουδή) of Titus, the same σπουδή shared by Paul. Σπουδή (zeal) occurs five times in this epistle.[115] Three of them occur in 2 Cor 8, depicting the zeal of the Corinthians (8:7), the zeal of others (possibly the Macedonians in 8:8), and the zeal of Titus (8:16).[116] Σπουδή in this unit probably connotes the eagerness and the zeal, with reference to a relationship.[117] Thus, the

---

[115] From this point onwards, the English translation, zeal, is not provided in this chapter.

[116] Σπουδή also occurs in 7:11–12, in which Paul praises the Corinthians for their σπουδή in response to his confrontation. It may not be a coincidence for Paul to reiterate σπουδή in chapter 8 for rhetorical reasons, urging the Corinthians to contribute to the offering for those who are in need in Jerusalem.

[117] The word is used in contemporary Greek literature to denote a civil or a religious responsibility, as well as personal devotion to other's welfare (Bauer 1979:763).

word exemplifies an underlying notion of both emotion and volition.[118] The use of καρδία in this verse concerns the relationship between Titus and the Corinthians. More importantly, Paul uses the phrase τὴν αὐτὴν σπουδὴν (the same zeal) to suggest that he shares the same zeal.[119] This indirectly elucidates Paul's relational zeal for the Corinthians. A relational aspect is highlighted by the use of καρδία in this context.

In 9:7, Paul reminds the Corinthians that they should give what προῄρηται τῇ καρδίᾳ, μὴ ἐκ λύπης ἢ ἐξ ἀνάγκης (has decided in his heart, not out of grief or out of distress).[120] The dative of καρδία serves as an indirect object of the verb προαιρέω (to decide), a word carrying a sense of volition. Paul informs the Corinthians to make their own decision. He elaborates in 9:7b that the decision must be μὴ ἐκ λύπης ἢ ἐξ ἀνάγκης (not out of grief or out of distress). Syntactically, the sentence can be rendered as προῄρηται τῇ καρδίᾳ, μὴ (προῄρηται) ἐκ λύπης ἢ ἐξ ἀνάγκης (decided in the heart, not [decided] out of grief or out of distress). The emotional notion signified by λύπη (grief) and ἀνάγκη (distress) is in parallel with καρδία.[121] Καρδία is certainly connected with an infinitive that denotes volition, but it can also be regarded as in parallel with the two nouns that represent emotion. In either case, the association between καρδία and volition or emotion is obvious. Nonetheless, the use of the singular καρδία is intriguing. The

---

[118] However, Betz (1985:58) interprets σπουδή as speediness and efficiency. Betz argues that σπουδή is found in many administrative letters in the Greco-Roman era. Hence, σπουδή in 8:16 refers to Paul's authorisation and commendation and of Titus as an efficient administrator of the envoys for the church, overseeing the collection and delivery of the offering to the designated group (Betz 1985:70). However, the previous mentioning of σπουδή in chapter 7 probably negates his definition. Σπουδή in chapter 7 reflects the emotional state of both Paul and the Corinthians, and has nothing to do with administration. Thrall (2000:545) also argues against Betz's view for a similar reason—σπουδή has been used in 8:7, 8 where the word does not refer to Titus but the Corinthians and the Macedonians.

[119] The reference of τὴν αὐτὴν σπουδὴν (the same zeal) is not explicit in the sentence. According to Thrall (2000:544–545), it can refer to the Macedonians, Paul, or even the Corinthians themselves. However, the wider context suggests that it probably refers to Paul. Many commentators maintain that the phrase refers to Paul (Plummer 1925:247; Barrett 1973:227; Furnish 1984:421; Martin 1986:273; Barnett 1997:418; Harris 2005:595; Roetzel 2007:50). However, Matera (2003:196) asserts that it is a God-given zeal, without referring to Paul or the Macedonians. Lambrecht (1999:139) is indecisive in determining what the phrase refers to.

[120] This is a literal translation of the text; alternative translations include "not out of pain or out of [a sense of] necessity" and "not reluctantly or under compulsion"*.

[121] Harris (2005:635) notes the commonality of all three words: καρδία, λύπη (grief), and ἀνάγκη (distress). Thrall (2000:576) argues that the phrase οὐ λυπηθήσῃ τῇ καρδίᾳ "not be grieved in the heart" in Deut 15:10 (LXX) is in parallel with 2 Cor 9:7. Thrall's argument further confirms that καρδία in 9:7 is related to emotion. Bruce (1996:227) regards καρδία as referring to the mind, but he does not provide sufficient evidence to support his view.

singular καρδία is clearly employed to point to the heart of the Corinthians. The singular form points to the single heart, single mind or common emotion, of the Corinthian community. In other words, the corporate unity is noticeably carried by the καρδία in 9:7.

5.2.2.2 Sociolinguistic aspect

Paul calls himself ἀπόστολος Χριστοῦ Ἰησοῦ (apostle of Christ Jesus) at the beginning of the epistle, and he defends his apostolic ministry in 2 Cor 1–9.[122] However, his utterance in 6:13 is particularly intriguing. Paul affirms his parental love to the Corinthians: ὡς τέκνοις λέγω (I speak as to my children)*. In other words, he appeals to them like a loving parent to his children instead of affirming his apostolic authority among the Corinthians.[123] As such, relational reconciliation is the key theme in 2 Cor 1–9. As much as Paul attempts to defend his apostolicity, he desires to strengthen a relational bond with the Corinthians by using the language of a family.

5.2.3 Thematic meaning of καρδία

As indicated by my analysis of 2 Cor 1–9 thus far, the overall occurrences of καρδία in all the major semantic units show a strong corporate reference. In Unit A, καρδία is used to depict the corporate identity of the Corinthian community (1:22) and the relationship between Paul and the Corinthians (2:4). In Unit B, the occurrences of καρδία (in 2 Cor 3–7), including the καρδία-πρόσωπον (heart-face) antithesis, highlight the Christian identity of the Corinthian community under a new dispensation in which Paul is its minister. In Unit D, καρδία indirectly highlights the relationship between Paul and the community (8:16) and the corporate unity of the community (9:7). Additionally, through studying the discourse structure, the macro-structure of 2 Cor 1–9 centres on Paul's relationship with the Corinthians. In particular, the discourse concerns the defence of his apostolic ministry among the Corinthian community. This is further confirmed by a brief review of the sociolinguistic aspect, since the parent-children relationship is portrayed in the letter. In conclusion, the thematic meaning of καρδία in 2 Cor 1–9 carries a relational and corporate connotation.

5.2.3.1 The flow of discourse and peak

The discourse peak is usually located near the end of a discourse, showing a shift in the proportion of use of one or more particular grammatical devices (including an increase in parallelism or tautologies) to highlight the climax.

---

[122] For a discussion of the sociolinguistic aspect associated with the use of ἀπόστολος (apostle), see § 3.2.2.1.

[123] For a discussion of the sociolinguistic implication of the parent-child language, see § 3.2.2.3.

In Unit C, there is an influx of words that portray emotions, including the following nouns: φόβος (fear) in 7:5, 11, 15; ἐπιπόθησις (longing) in 7:7, 11; ὀδυρμός (mourning) in 7:7; ζῆλος (jealousy) in 7:7, 11; λύπη (grief) in 7:10; σπουδή (zeal) in 7:11, 12; χαρά (joy) in 7:4, 13; σπλάγχνον (affection) in 7:15; τρόμος (trembling) in 7:15; and the following verbs: χαίρω (to rejoice) in 7:7, 9, 16; λυπέω (to grieve) in 7:8 (twice), 9 (thrice), 11; μεταμέλομαι (to regret) in 7:8; θαρρέω (to be brave) in 7:16. As shown above, some of these words are repeated in this semantic unit. Although Unit C is related to the Corinthians' response to Paul's earlier letter, the influx of words, with some appearing in parallel, shows that this is the climax of 2 Cor 1–9. The unit begins with the portrayal of Paul's φόβος (fear) in 7:4, but ends with the depiction of his joy: χαίρω ὅτι ἐν παντὶ θαρρῶ ἐν ὑμῖν (I rejoice because in everything I am fully confident in you)* in 7:16. Paul affectionately calls for a relational reconciliation between him and the community in the peak episode. Figure 5.10 shows the flow of discourse of 2 Cor 1–9.

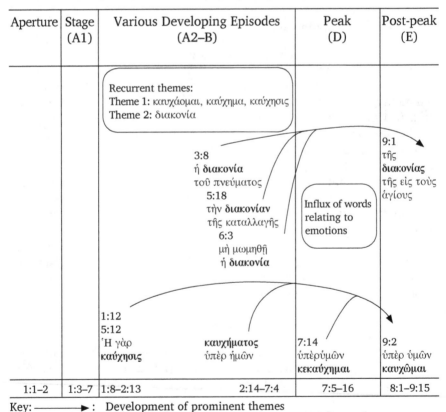

Key: ———▶ : Development of prominent themes

Figure 5.10. The flow of discourse of 2 Cor 1–9.

5.2.4 Summary

The sentence meaning of various occurrences of καρδία in 2 Cor 1–9 denotes mind, the seat of emotion and volition, or the inner person. Nonetheless, the thematic meaning of the term signifies the corporate entity of the Corinthians, and the relationship between Paul and the Corinthians. Of interest, Paul defends his apostleship, and uses καρδία in the καρδία-πρόσωπον (heart-face) antithesis to highlight the corporate identity of the Corinthians under a new dispensation in which Paul is its minister ordained by God.

5.3 Καρδία in other Pauline epistles

Although Romans and 2 Corinthians are my focus in this chapter, I also provide a brief analysis of καρδία in other Pauline epistles. The word occurs once in both 1 Thessalonians and Galatians, twice in Philippians, and four times in 1 Corinthians.[124] Given that καρδία in Philippians has already been discussed, I only examine its occurrences in the remaining epistles.

5.3.1 Καρδία in 1 Corinthians

Καρδία occurs in 1 Cor 4:5; 7:37 (twice); 14:25. As explained below, there is no evidence that the term carries any communal or corporate connotation.

The first occurrence is located in Unit A (1:10–4:21) that discusses church division.[125] In 4:5, Paul urges the Corinthians to refrain from being judgmental, by teaching them that the Lord φωτίσει τὰ κρυπτὰ τοῦ σκότους καὶ φανερώσει τὰς βουλὰς τῶν καρδιῶν (will bring to light the hidden things of darkness and reveal the motives of hearts)*. The word βουλή means intention or decision. Of interest, the metaphor of light shining into σκότος (darkness) is employed. It is logical to deduce that καρδία illustrates the "inner" notion of a human. In other words, although there is an association between καρδία and intention, the phrase τὰς βουλὰς τῶν καρδιῶν (the hidden things of the hearts) can simply be rendered as "inner thoughts" of humans.[126] There is no particular communal or corporate reference denoted by καρδία here.

In discussing marriage, in Unit C (7:1–40), Paul uses καρδία twice in 7:37, possibly alluding to mind and decision. Words like θέλημα (will) and κρίνω (to judge) show that the passage is related to decision and will. Καρδία is strongly associated with violation, if not directly denoting this, as

---

[124] The occurrences of καρδία are as follows: 1 Thess 2:4; Gal 4:6; Phil 1:7, 4:7; 1 Cor 4:5, 7:37 (twice); 14:25.

[125] Refer to chapter 3 for an explanation of discourse structure, including the major semantic units in 1 Corinthians.

[126] Fee (1987:164) interprets the phrase as the inner recesses of one's own thoughts. Barrett (1994:103) renders it as inward thought.

Paul informs the concerning party to make their own decision concerning marriage.[127] Nonetheless, καρδία does not have any communal or corporate connotation.

In Unit G (12:1–14:40), Paul discusses different spiritual gifts operating in a Christian community. Paul reiterates the same idea in 14:25 by saying that τὰ κρυπτὰ τῆς καρδίας αὐτοῦ φανερὰ γίνεται (the secrets of his heart are disclosed)*. Although καρδία is not overtly related to any words that depict emotion or volition, based on the striking parallel between 14:25 and 4:5, this study argues that καρδία points to the "inner" aspect of a human. It is reasonable to conjecture that κρυπτός (secret) may denote "thoughts and intention" as suggested in 4:5. In this context, καρδία depicts the heart of an unbeliever who visits the community. Hence, the term is used in describing an individual instead of a community.

In summary, none of the occurrences of καρδία in 1 Corinthians connote any corporate or relational reference. As shown in the discourse analysis of 1 Corinthians in chapter 3, corporate unity is the focus of the epistle and is vividly highlighted by the occurrences of σῶμα (body). The brief analysis of καρδία seems to indicate that Paul uses σῶμα (body) instead of καρδία to highlight the social and corporate reference in 1 Corinthians.

5.3.2 Καρδία in 1 Thessalonians

Καρδία occurs three times in 1 Thessalonians (2:4, 2:17, and 3:13). All of the three occurrences occur in Unit A (1:2–3:13).[128] In this unit, Paul encourages the Thessalonians to stand firm in their faith as they are waiting for the Lord's coming.

Καρδία first appears in 2:4.[129] In this context, Paul recollects his suffering during his time in Philippi (2:2). He denies that his ministry is out of an impure motive (2:3), since he has been approved by God. The word δοκιμάζω (to approve) appears twice in 2:4, as a perfect indicative verb in

---

[127] Both Barrett (1994:184) and Fee (1987:353) interpret καρδία in 7:37 as mind.

[128] The discourse structure of 1 Thessalonians is presented in chapter 6. For detailed account of various semantic units, see § 6.1.1.2.

[129] Marshall argues that the meaning of καρδία is derived from the Hebraic understanding, and thus the term should be understood as "the centre of the personality, the seat of thinking, feeling and willing," and he suggests that καρδία is the inner motive in 2:4 and inner character in 3:13 (Marshall 1983:65, 85, 101). Williams (1992:39, 55, 67) adopts the all-in-one definition, καρδία is the comprehensive self with emotion, volition and ration. Witherington (2006:79) adopts the same approach, and defines καρδία as the seat of thought, feeling, and will. These scholars seem to adopt a diachronic approach in their interpretation of καρδία. They draw on the so-called OT equivalent of καρδία, and then apply the definition universally for all the occurrences of καρδία without considering its context. This is a flawed approach as discussed in chapter 2. Other scholars seem to consider the meaning of καρδία as the same in all three occurrences (Richard 1995:80; Morris 1991:64). Again, their lack of examining the context is problematic.

the clause δεδοκιμάσμεθα ὑπὸ τοῦ θεοῦ (we have been approved by God)*, and as a present participle with an adjectival function to portray the character of God in the clause θεῷ τῷ δοκιμάζοντι τὰς καρδίας ἡμῶν (God, who examines our hearts)*.[130] Hence, καρδία probably points to Paul's mind (with a pure motive), which has been examined and approved by God. The word καρδία does not denote a communal aspect, and instead is used to indicate the heart of Paul.

In 2:17, καρδία is an antithesis of καρδία-πρόσωπον (heart-face). Despite his desire to visit the Thessalonians in person, Paul is unable to do so. Paul emphasises that he is not separated from them in καρδίᾳ. Based on the context, the term illustrates the relationship between Paul and the Thessalonians, pointing to a shared emotional bond.[131]

The last occurrence of καρδία occurs in 3:13. 3:11–13 is a benediction.[132] 3:13 depicts Paul's benediction for the Thessalonians: εἰς τὸ στηρίξαι ὑμῶν τὰς καρδίας ἀμέμπτους ἐν ἁγιωσύνῃ ἔμπροσθεν τοῦ θεοῦ (so that your hearts are strengthened in holiness to be blameless before our God)*. The phrase ὑμῶν τὰς καρδίας (your hearts) is synonymous with ὑμᾶς (you),[133] emphasizing the inwardness of the inner being strengthened by God. Καρδία occurs in its plural form, combined with the plural ὑμῶν (your). Unlike the case of a singular καρδία combined with ὑμῶν (your), which elucidates the connotation of corporate entity or corporate unity, the plural καρδία does not directly carry a corporate reference. However, based on the context of this benediction, Paul articulates 3:13 to a Christian community instead of an individual. Therefore, καρδία is used in the context of portraying the Thessalonian community.

---

[130] Fee (2009:62) observes the parallel between 1 Thess 2:4 and Jer 11:20 (LXX), in both cases the plural form of καρδία is linked with δοκιμάζω (to approve). Then, he argues that καρδία is the centre and source of the whole inner life. Frame (1912:97) also suggests a similar parallel, by indicating the parallel between 1 Thess 2:4 and Ps16:3.

[131] Ivor Jones (2005:35) defines καρδία in 2:17 as equivalent to the mind.

[132] A detailed analysis of 3:11–13, and explanation of its connection with 5:23, is presented in chapter 6.

[133] Morris (1991:110) argues that καρδία means the whole inner life. Bruce (1982a:72) renders it as the inner motives. Both of them repudiate any nuance of emotion in the word. Richard (1995:166) considers ὑμῶν τὰς καρδίας (your hearts) as a substitution for ὑμᾶς (you), with an emphasis on the inner being of a human. I concur with this view.

5.3.3 Καρδία in Galatians

Καρδία only occurs one time in Galatians, in Unit B (3:1–4:31).[134] In this semantic unit, Paul argues that both the Gentiles and the Jews are justified by faith of Christ and are one in Christ.

In 4:6, Paul portrays the Galatians as children. Various scholars consider the phrase εἰς τὰς καρδίας ἡμῶν (into our hearts) as either synonymous with ἡμῖν (in us) (Longenecker 1990:174; Matera 1992:151) or the depiction of the centre of will and emotion of a person (Dunn 1993:220; Fung 1988:184; Bruce 1982b:198; Tarazi 1994:211).[135] It is obvious that the καρδία is not associated with any words that are related to emotion, volition, and reason. However, the preposition εἰς (into) alludes to the "inner" essence of a human. Hence, it is likely that καρδία denotes "inwardness," whilst bearing the synonymous nuance of ἡμῖν. Καρδία occurs in its plural form, combined with ἡμῶν. Unlike the case of a singular καρδία combined with ἡμῶν, which elucidates the denotation of corporate entity or corporate identity, the plural of καρδία in 4:6 does not directly carry a corporate reference. However, the word occurs in the context that points to a corporate reference as explained below. The macrostructure of Galatians highlights a new corporate identity of the Galatians in a new dispensation, in which the Jews and the Gentiles are one in Christ.[136] In 4:6, τὰς καρδίας ἡμῶν (our hearts) is employed in the context in which believers are compared with their former state as non-believers (4:8–9). Therefore, the contrast of believers and non-believers is emphasised. As such, the usage of καρδία in 4:6 alludes to a new corporate identity, pointing to the believers who are blessed by God. This corporate identity is further illustrated by the following verse: εἶ...υἱός (you are...son) in 4:7. Of interest, Paul uses the clause ἐστε υἱοί (you are sons) in 4:6 to address the Galatians, and then he shifts to the second person singular verb εἶ (you are) and the singular noun υἱός (son) in 4:7 to address the Galatian Christians. Thus, based on this context the Galatians are depicted as having one corporate identity and the Holy Spirit dwells in the members (τὰς καρδίας ἡμῶν, our hearts) of this community.

5.3.4 Summary

A brief examination of the occurrences of καρδία in other Pauline epistles demonstrated that the communal and corporate connotation is attached to some of the occurrences, including 1 Thess 2:17, 3:13, and Gal 4:6.

---

[134] The discourse structure of Galatians is presented in chapter 6. For detailed account of various semantic units in Galatians, see § 6.2.1.1.

[135] The most problematic issue of their argument is that they directly derived καρδία from לֵב in the OT. This derivation is overly diachronic, and the approach becomes problematic when the consideration of the textual context is absent.

[136] For the discussion of the macrostructure of Galatians, see § 6.2.1.1.

5.4 Conclusion

This chapter has examined the occurrences of καρδία in Romans and 2 Corinthians by applying discourse analysis. The thematic meaning of καρδία in both epistles carries communal and corporate connotations. In Romans, καρδία appears in clustered patterns that are associated with different communities: Gentiles, Jews, and Christians. The term points to the corporate response of these communities to God and his salvation in Christ. In 2 Corinthians, καρδία depicts the corporate identity of the Corinthian community and the relationship between Paul and the Corinthians. In the καρδία-πρόσωπον (heart-face) antithesis, καρδία highlights the Christian identity of the community under the new dispensation in which Paul is the minister.

6

Anthropological terms in Pauline benedictions

6.0 Introduction

In this chapter we address Stage IV of this study—multiple anthropological terms within multiple discourses. We focus on the occurrences of πνεῦμα (spirit), σῶμα (body), and ψυχή (soul) in the Pauline benedictions. One or more of these key anthropological terms occur in two types of Pauline benedictions: καὶ ὁλόκληρον ὑμῶν τὸ πνεῦμα καὶ ἡ ψυχὴ καὶ τὸ σῶμα ἀμέμπτως...τηρηθείη (may your spirit and soul and body be kept entirely blameless)* in 1 Thess 5:23; and Ἡ χάρις τοῦ κυρίου ἡμῶν Ἰησοῦ Χριστοῦ μετὰ τοῦ πνεύματος ὑμῶν (The grace of our Lord Jesus Christ be with your spirit)* in Gal 6:18; Phlm 1:25; and Phil 4:23. In these benedictions, the terms occur in the abnormal singular construct. As argued in previous chapters, the abnormal construct must not be explained by automatically defining the singular term as a distributive singular. Instead, previous analyses have shown that a singular anthropological term can be a normal singular, which carries social and corporate and connotations that point to communal relationship or unity. As such, we aim to ascertain if these connotations are also present in the benedictions. In this chapter we initially consider 1 Thess 5:23 and then examine the identical benediction in Gal 6:18, Phlm 1:25, and Phil 4:23.

187

6.1 The tripartite formula in 1 Thess 5:23 in light of discourse analysis

In this section we discuss the benediction in 1 Thess 5:23, by initially identifying the discourse structure of 1 Thessalonians. Then we review previous explanations of the phrase, which is also known as the tripartite formula, ὑμῶν τὸ πνεῦμα καὶ ἡ ψυχὴ καὶ τὸ σῶμα (the spirit and the soul and the body of you), before analysing its grammatical and syntactical features. Our analysis, as a result, provides insights into the meaning of the anthropological terms.

6.1.1 Discourse structure of 1 Thessalonians

As with the previous chapters, an analysis of the discourse structure elucidates the major semantic units in 1 Thessalonians by investigating the discourse markers, examining the discourse coherence, and ascertaining the macrostructure.

6.1.1.1 Discourse markers

Three discourse markers demarcate the semantic units in 1 Thessalonians: change of verb mood, formulas, and use of the vocative.

Change of verb mood

The concentrated use of the imperative verbs usually signifies a hortatory section. There are 20 imperative verbs in 1 Thessalonians. Figure 6.1 shows that 19 of them occur in 5:11–26.[1] From the usage of the imperative, a major semantic unit, an exhortatory segment, may well be situated in the latter part of chapter 5.

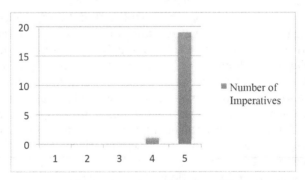

Figure 6.1. The imperative verbs in 1 Thessalonians.

---

[1] The imperatives occur in 4:18; 5:11 (twice), 13, 14 (four times), 15 (twice), 16, 17, 18, 19, 20, 21 (twice), 22, 25, 26.

Formulas

There are four types of formulas in 1 Thessalonians which function as discourse markers: benediction, formulaic praise, verb-conjunction-ὑμᾶς-ἀδελφοί,[2] and the conjunctive formula περὶ δὲ (now concerning).

Two optative clauses in 3:11–13, as indicated by two aorist optatives: κατευθύναι (he may keep) in 3:11 and πλεονάσαι (he may increase) in 3:12, and another in 5:23, as indicated by the optative τηρηθείη (may be kept), are two prayers of blessing,[3] which can also be considered as two benedictions.[4] The two benedictions carry a parenthetical function,[5] and delineate the boundary of 4:1–5:22, by highlighting the exhortatory segment within. 4:1–5:22 contains various exhortations.

The formulaic praise Εὐχαριστοῦμεν τῷ θεῷ πάντοτε (We thank God always)* occurs in 1:2 following the initial greeting. This formula marks Paul's first topic, discussing his relationship with the Thessalonians (1:2–3:13).

There are three occurrences of the verb-conjunction-ὑμᾶς-ἀδελφοί formula. First, Paul uses the formula ἀδελφοί, ἐρωτῶμεν ὑμᾶς καὶ παρακαλοῦμεν (brothers, we ask and urge you) in 4:1 after the benediction (3:11–13) to commence the parenthetical exhortation in 4:1–5:22.[6] Second, the formula οὐ θέλομεν δὲ ὑμᾶς ἀγνοεῖν, ἀδελφοί (but we do not want you to be ignorant, brothers)* in 4:13 begins the discussion of the death of loved ones (4:13–18). Since it occurs within the parenthetical segment, this formula marks the beginning of a minor segment. Third, the formula Ἐρωτῶμεν δὲ ὑμᾶς, ἀδελφοί (but we ask you, brothers) occurs in 5:12. As previously mentioned, there is an influx of the imperatives in the second half of chapter 5. Thus, the formula marks the general exhortations near the end of the epistle. Since it occurs in the parenthetical segment, it begins a minor semantic unit.

The conjunctive formula περὶ δὲ (now concerning) in 5:1 occurs within the parenthetical segment. Thus, it marks a minor semantic unit, in which Paul discusses the expectation of the Parousia (5:1–12).

---

[2] Translation: verb-conjunction-you-brothers.

[3] An optative can elucidate either a wish or a prayer; it is normally employed to denote a wish especially in the presence of ἄν. Since 3:11–13 and 5:23 are two independent clauses without ἄν, the optatives are best understood as volitive optatives denoting prayer. Wallace (1996:481) calls this kind of optative, voluntative optative or volitive optative; Moulton (1906:196) calls this optative of wish.

[4] For example, Jewett (1971:175) regards 5:23 as a benediction. Bruce (1982a:128) and Furnish (2007:122–123) call it a wish-prayer and a benedictory prayer, respectively. In this chapter, this kind of prayer of blessing is called benediction or benedictory prayer.

[5] Both Bruce (1982a:128) and Wanamaker (1990:205–206) favour this view. This is further discussed in the later section of this chapter.

[6] In this case, ἀδελφοί (brothers) is placed in front of verb-conjunction-you.

Vocative

There are 14 occurrences of ἀδελφοί (brothers).[7] The frequent occurrences of this vocative are striking when comparing with its occurrences in the other Pauline epistles. This will be further discussed in the section of prominence. Most of its occurrences do not function as discourse markers. Nonetheless, two occurrences are worth mentioning.

The vocative ἀδελφοί in 4:1 is combined with the adverb λοιπὸν (finally)[8] and the conjunction οὖν (therefore) to begin the parenthetical segment.[9] In other words, the beginning of the parenthetical segment is marked by three different discourse markers: the benediction in 3:11–13, the verb-conjunction-ὑμᾶς-ἀδελφοί formula in 4:1, and the vocative ἀδελφοί combined with λοιπὸν (finally) in 4:1.

Finally, the ἀδελφοί in 5:25 marks Paul's closing remark in the epistle.

6.1.1.2 Semantic units

Through the four identified discourse markers, 1 Thessalonians can be divided into: the letter-opening, two major semantic units, and the letter-closing. Table 6.1 outlines the semantics units in 1 Thessalonians, and table 6.2 outlines the perspectives of other scholars.[10]

---

[7] The occurrences of ἀδελφοί in 1 Thessalonians: 1:4; 2:1, 9, 14, 17; 3:7; 4:1, 10, 13; 5:1, 4, 12, 14, 25. From this point onwards, the English translation, brothers, is not provided in this chapter.

[8] The word λοιπὸν connotes remaining or the rest; and in this context, it means finally.

[9] The analysis of Philippians shows that the combination of λοιπὸν (finally) and ἀδελφοί (brothers) is a discourse marker. For a detailed discussion of this, see § 4.1.2.3.

[10] Table 6.2 does not present the full outline of each scholar. Rather, it presents the scholars that identify the same or similar unit as each of my units.

Table 6.1. Semantic units of 1 Thessalonians

Major Units		A 1:2–3:13	B 4:1–5:22			
Minor Units			B1 4:1–12	B2 4:13–5:11	B3 5:12–23	
Discourse Markers DM1: Change of Verb Mood					Imperative: 14/20	
DM2: Formulas	Letter-opening (1:1–2)	Εὐχαριστοῦμεν τῷ θεῷ πάντοτε (1:2) Benediction: κατευθύναι... πλεονάσαι (3:11–13)	ἐρωτῶμεν ὑμᾶς καὶ παρακαλοῦμεν (4:1)	Οὐ θέλομεν δὲ ὑμᾶς ἀγνοεῖν, ἀδελφοί (4:13)	Ἐρωτῶμεν δὲ ὑμᾶς, ἀδελφοί, (5:12)	Letter-closing (5:25–28)
DM3: Vocative			Λοιπὸν οὖν, ἀδελφοί (4:1)			
New Topic		Paul and the Thessalonians	Exhortations in light of the Parousia			

Table 6.2. Outline of 1 Thessalonians by scholars[a]

My Outline	Semantic Unit A 1:2–3:13[b]	Semantic Unit B 4:1–5:22[c]
Outline of Scholars	Fee Frame Furnish Malherbe Sterner Witherington	Best Bruce Frame Furnish Moore Malherbe Richard Sterner Wanamaker

[a] For detailed outlines, see Best 1972:153; Bruce 1982a:3; Frame 1912:17; Furnish 2007:7–8; I. Jones 2005:vi–vii; Malherbe 2000:viii; Marshall 1983:10–11; Moore 1969:v; Morris 1991:vi–vii; Richard 1995:v–vi; Sterner 1998:7; Wanamaker 1990:viii; Witherington 2006:vii–ix.

[b] Fee considers 1:1–3:13 a major segment. Both Frame and Witherington consider the prayer in 3:11–13 a separate segment (apart from 1:2–3:10).

[c] Best, Frame, Moore, and Wanamaker consider 4:1–5:22 a major segment, containing many sub-segments in it. For Bruce and Furnish, 4:1–5:24 is a major unit, containing many sub-segments. For Richard, 5:12–22 is one of the sub-segments under the major segment 4:3–5:28.

As shown in table 6.2, my outline of the semantic units is similar to those proposed by various scholars.

6.1.1.3 Discourse coherence

Thematic prominence and lexical cohesion are useful in ascertaining the coherent message of 1 Thessalonians. My examination below shows that relationship is a prominent theme in this epistle.

Thematic prominence

Relationship is a prominent theme. In the first semantic unit, Paul discusses his relationship with the Thessalonian community (1:3–6; 2:6–12, 17–19; 3:6–10). His language is full of affection and kinship, as illustrated by the following examples: μνημονεύοντες ὑμῶν τοῦ ἔργου (recall...your work)* in 1:3; ὡς ἐὰν τροφὸς θάλπῃ τὰ ἑαυτῆς τέκνα (like a nursing mother caring for her own children)* in 2:7; οὕτως ὁμειρόμενοι ὑμῶν (with such affection for you)* in 2:8; ἀπορφανισθέντες ἀφ' ὑμῶν (we were separated from you)* in 2:17;[11] πάσῃ τῇ χαρᾷ ᾗ χαίρομεν δι' ὑμᾶς (all the joy we feel because of you)* in 3:9.

---

[11] Ἀπορφανίζω means "make an orphan of someone" (Bauer 1979:98).

   In the second and last major semantic unit, Paul discusses the communal relationship among the Thessalonians (4:6–13, 5:13–15). In Unit B1 (4:1–12), Paul is concerned about sexual immorality and exploitation (4:3–8). The noun τὸν ἀδελφὸν (the brother) in 4:6 points out the occurrence of sexual immorality amongst the Thessalonians. As well argued by Wanamaker (1990:155), this kind of action "could threaten the very existence of the community."[12] In Unit B2 (4:13–5:11), Paul explains to the Thessalonians about the fate of those who died in Christ, οἱ νεκροὶ ἐν Χριστῷ (the dead in Christ)* in 4:16, and teaches them not to engage in excessive grief. Obviously, this discussion centres on the death of believers, alluding to those who belong to the community.[13] In Unit B3 (5:12–23), the apostle discusses life in a community, as illustrated by the following examples: εἰδέναι τοὺς κοπιῶντας ἐν ὑμῖν (to acknowledge those who labor among you)* in 5:12; ἀντέχεσθε τῶν ἀσθενῶν, μακροθυμεῖτε πρὸς πάντας (help the weak, be patient toward all)* in 5:14; τὸ ἀγαθὸν διώκετε [καὶ] εἰς ἀλλήλους (pursue what is good for one another)* in 5:15.

Lexical cohesion

There are several patterns of lexical cohesion (see Appendix 5). The first pattern is the repetition of παρουσία (coming). Παρουσία (coming) only occurs 11 times in the Pauline letters, four of which occur in 1 Thessalonians.[14] Its occurrences distribute throughout the epistle (2:19; 3:13; 4:15; 5:23). In all four cases, the noun portrays the coming (παρουσία) of Christ.[15] The second pattern is the repetition of ἐλπίς (hope), indicating the motif of hope. It occurs four times throughout the epistle (1:3; 2:19; 4:13; and 5:8).[16] These two motifs intertwine with each other, forming a key message: the coming of the Lord would bring hope to the Thessalonians who face various challenges, including tribulation (θλῖψις, in 1:6; 3:3, 7) and impurity (ἀκαθαρσία, in 2:3; 4:7).

---

[12] According to Wanamaker (1990:155–156), sexual immorality could destroy the community by breaking down the ethical boundary that separates believers from pagans and by destroying the kinship within the Thessalonian community.

[13] Fee (2009:166) also holds this view, arguing that the concern is not for people in general, but only for those who were a part of the believing community.

[14] The occurrences of παρουσία (coming) in Paul's letters: Romans: 0. 1 Corinthians: 2. 2 Corinthians: 3. Galatians: 0. Philippians: 2. 1 Thessalonians: 4. Philemon: 0.

[15] Παρουσία (coming) is modified by either τοῦ κυρίου (of the Lord) in 3:13, 4:15, 5:23, or αὐτοῦ (of him) in 2:19.

[16] Ἐλπίς (hope) occurs 25 times in all of the Pauline epistles. Its occurrence usually concentrates in a few chapters within a letter instead of displaying an even distribution. For example, in 1 Corinthians, ἐλπίς (hope) only occurs in chapters 9 (twice) and 13 (once). In Galatians and Philippians (the length of both epistles is similar to that of 1 Thessalonians), ἐλπίς (hope) only occurs once in each epistle.

However, the third pattern strongly indicates the relational reference in this epistle. The vocative ἀδελφοί (brothers) has an unusually high frequency in 1 Thessalonians.[17] The word is the third most frequent noun in the letter (see Appendix 5). Figure 6.2 shows that the occurrences of ἀδελφοί (brothers) are distributed throughout the whole epistle. The unusually frequent occurrences of ἀδελφοί (brothers) highlight the relationship between Paul and the Thessalonian community.

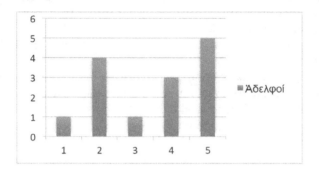

Figure 6.2. The vocative ἀδελφοί in 1 Thessalonians.

6.1.1.4 *Macrostructure and sociolinguistic aspect*

From the topic in each semantic unit and the findings of the discourse coherence, we propose that the macrostructure of 1 Thessalonians can be understood as follows: Paul reminds the Thessalonian community of the kinship and loving relationship shared between himself and the community, and encourages the community to live in love and hope whilst waiting for the coming of the Lord.

As previously discussed, Paul's expression in this epistle is full of affection. This affection is further illustrated by taking the sociolinguistic aspect into consideration. Paul does not call himself an apostle in the letter-opening. The phrase Χριστοῦ ἀπόστολοι (apostles of Christ) in 2:7 is the only instance that Paul mentions his apostleship. However, Paul immediately compares himself as νήπιοι (infant)[18] and τροφός (nursing

---

[17] The vocative ἀδελφοί occurs in 1:4; 2:1, 9, 14, 17; 3:7; 4:1, 10, 13; 5:1, 4, 12, 14, 25. When counting all the occurrences of ἀδελφοί (brothers) in all of the Pauline epistles, 23% of them occur in 1 Thessalonians. The epistle displays the highest ratio of occurrences if the length of each Pauline epistle is taken into consideration. The ratio of the occurrences of the vocative ἀδελφοί (brothers) in each epistle based on the total hits per 1000 words is as follows: Romans: 1.41; 1 Corinthians: 2.92; 2 Corinthians: 0.67; Galatians: 4.03; Philippians: 3.67; 1 Thessalonians: 9.43; Philemon: 0.

[18] There is a textual variant in 2:7. The manuscripts that support the reading of νήπιοι (infants) includes B, D*, 6, 33, 104, 81, 1739, and 1881. Nonetheless, νήπιοι is replaced by τύπους in the following manuscripts: ℵ, A, C, D2, F, G, and Ψ. Τύπους means example (Bauer 1979:830). It would be a smoother reading to describe Paul as an example amongst the Thessalonians than to depict him as a child. Thus,

mother)[19] in 2:7. The humility displayed by νήπιοι (infants) and the parental care depicted by τροφός (nursing mother) are further accentuated by the proceeding phrase ὡς πατὴρ τέκνα ἑαυτοῦ (as a father his children) in 2:11 and the extraordinary frequent occurrence of ἀδελφοί (brothers) in the whole epistle. Instead of asserting his authority, Paul compares his relationship with the community as a caring family.[20]

6.1.1.5 The flow of discourse and peak

The peak of 1 Thessalonians is located in Unit B2 (4:13–5:11), which is indicated by the following linguistic phenomena: the re-emergence of key prominent themes, τὴν παρουσίαν τοῦ κυρίου (the coming of the Lord) and ἐλπίς (hope); rare grammatical devices, οὐ μὴ (definitely not) and λόγῳ κυρίου (by word of Lord); multiple parallelisms, formed by words relating to καθεύσω (to sleep) and the repetition of παρακαλεῖτε ἀλλήλους (encourage one another); and B2 being the centre of a seemingly chiastic structure.

First, παρουσία (coming) and ἐλπίς (hope) are the two prominent themes that reappear in B2: τὴν παρουσίαν τοῦ κυρίου (the coming of the Lord), in 4:15; and ἐλπίς, in 4:13; 5:8. Notably, the concept of having hope in light of the παρουσία (coming), which is first mentioned in 2:19, re-emerges in 4:13–15.

Second, two grammatical devices that rarely occur in the Pauline epistles are found in B2. The first device is the emphatic negation οὐ μὴ (definitely not). The occurrence of οὐ μὴ (definitely not) is rare in Paul's work: it occurs only five times in all of the Pauline epistles.[21] However, οὐ μὴ (definitely not) occurs twice in 1 Thessalonians in close proximity, only five verses apart (4:15b and 5:3). Both of them are related to the coming of the Lord: οἱ ζῶντες οἱ περιλειπόμενοι εἰς τὴν παρουσίαν τοῦ κυρίου οὐ μὴ φθάσωμεν τοὺς κοιμηθέντας (that we who are alive, who are left until the coming of the Lord, will surely not go ahead of those who have fallen asleep)* in 4:15b; and ὅταν λέγωσιν εἰρήνη καὶ ἀσφάλεια, τότε αἰφνίδιος αὐτοῖς ἐφίσταται ὄλεθρος...καὶ οὐ μὴ ἐκφύγωσιν (now when they are

---

τύπους would likely be a correction intended by some scribers, whereas νήπιοι is more likely the original reading.

[19] The word τροφός connotes nurse. In this context, however, it depicts a nursing mother.

[20] See § 3.2.2.3 for the discussion of sociolinguistic implication concerning the parent-child language. Burke (2012:286) argues that Paul uses this parent-child relationship to emphasise his leadership role, an apostle who regards himself as being at the apex of the familial pyramid. Burke also suggests that the roles depicted by νήπιοι (infants) and τροφός (nursing mother) remain contentious; but he fails to explain the unusually frequent occurrences of ἀδελφοί (brothers), the vocative used by Paul to address the Thessalonians.

[21] The occurrences of οὐ μὴ (definitely not): once in Romans; once in 1 Corinthians; once in Galatians; and twice in 1 Thessalonians.

saying, "There is peace and security," then sudden destruction comes on them…and they will surely not escape)* in 5:3. The first usage is directed to the believers, and the second usage, non-believers. The second rare device is the occurrences of this peculiar clause: Τοῦτο γὰρ ὑμῖν λέγομεν ἐν λόγῳ κυρίου (For we tell you this by the word of the Lord)* in 4:15a. This clause is placed in front of the first emphatic negation. The anarthrous phrase λόγῳ κυρίου (by word of Lord) is a hapax legomenon in Paul's work.[22] A similar articulation is also found in 1:8: ὁ λόγος τοῦ κυρίου (the word of the Lord).[23]

Third, repeated words also appear in the form of parallelism, in three sets nonetheless. The first set, as previously mentioned, is the repetition of οὐ μὴ (definitely not). The emphatic negation is directed to two groups: believers and non-believers. The second is the repetition of the substantival participle of κοιμάω (to sleep). The word is recurrent in 4:13, 14, and 15, denoting those who died in Christ. Another verb with a similar meaning, καθεύδω (to sleep), is also recurrent in 5:6, 7, and 10; with its substantival participle denoting the non-believers, οἱ καθεύδοντες (those who sleep), in 5:7. The striking contrast between believers and non-believers is again highlighted by this parallel. Third, the imperative clause παρακαλεῖτε ἀλλήλους (encourage one another) is repeated in 4:18 and 5:11. The clause in 4:18 immediately follows the discussion of the resurrection of believers in Christ's παρουσία (coming); and the clause in 5:11 concludes the discussion of the παρουσία (coming) of the Lord. Most fascinatingly, παρακαλεῖτε (encourage) is the very first imperative verb that occurs in this epistle.

Finally, B2 is set in the centre of the parenthetical exhortation, appearing in the centre of a seemingly chiastic structure. The phrase θέλημα τοῦ θεοῦ (will of God) is found in both the previous unit (4:3, in Unit B1) and the following unit (5:18, in Unit B3). In both minor semantic units, the Thessalonians are urged to live a holy and godly life. However, the discussion of παρουσία (coming) in B2 is set in the middle of B1 and B3.

The occurrences of rare grammatical devices, multiple parallels, re-emergence of prominent themes, and being the centre of a chiasm indicate that B2 is the discourse peak. In this peak, the Thessalonians are treated as a group that is in contrast with the non-believers. The contrastive fate of the two groups during the παρουσία (coming) is emphasised. Thus, the corporate aspect is highlighted. As a faith community that would receive the ultimate blessing (including both the living and the dead members), the Thessalonian community is distinct from the non-believers.

The benediction, which is the centre of this analysis, occurs after the peak. Thus, it belongs to the post-peak episode. Figure 6.3 shows the discourse flow.

---

[22] Paul's disputed letters have also been considered.

[23] As well as 1 Thessalonians, this phrase only occurs in 2 Thess 3:1.

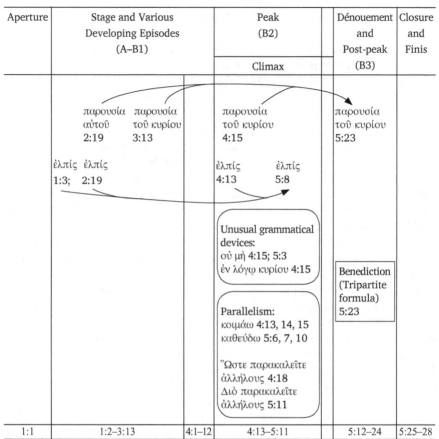

Aperture	Stage and Various Developing Episodes (A–B1)		Peak (B2)		Dénouement and Post-peak	Closure and Finis
			Climax		(B3)	

Key: ——► : Development of prominent themes

Figure 6.3. The flow of discourse of 1 Thessalonians.

6.1.2 Previous explanations of the tripartite formula

The phrase ὑμῶν τὸ πνεῦμα καὶ ἡ ψυχὴ καὶ τὸ σῶμα (the spirit and the soul and the body of you) is part of the benediction in 1 Thess 5:23. The benediction is located in close proximity with another benediction at the end of the epistle, Ἡ χάρις τοῦ κυρίου ἡμῶν Ἰησοῦ Χριστοῦ μεθ᾽ ὑμῶν (The grace of our Lord Jesus Christ be with you)* in 5:28. In the tripartite formula, the three articular anthropological terms are combined with the plural pronoun ὑμῶν (your), forming the abnormal singular construct. In previous scholarship, there are four main explanations of the meaning of these anthropological terms.

First, some suggest that Paul employs Hellenistic anthropology to depict the trichotomic nature of a human being, a human with three ontological parts: spirit, soul, and body. This view was once strongly upheld. For example, Heard (1882:98) asserts that 1 Thess 5:23 teaches us in the first place, that there are three parts in man. Schweizer (1968:435) is another proponent of this view, who argues that the three terms denote the constituent parts of a human person. However, a number of modern scholars repudiate this view, by arguing that Paul does not make a precise anthropological definition of different constituents of a human being (Bruce 1982a:130; Wanamaker 1990:207; Morris 1991:182; Malherbe 2000:339; Witherington 2006:173; Fee 2009:228). Of interest, the notion of a human person consisting of various constituent parts, for example, soul and body, is a Platonic view. As mentioned in chapter 2, modern scholarly works show that Paul adheres to Stoic philosophy instead of Platonic philosophy (Lee 2006:6; Martin 1995:6–7, 14; Engberg-Pedersen 2009:179–197).

The second explanation is a variation of the first one. Although the three terms do not denote three constituent parts of a human being, they denote different elements in human personality. For example, Marshall (1983:163) argues that the three terms should be understood as follows: πνεῦμα (spirit) depicts a believer's life in relationship with God, ψυχή (soul) denotes human personality, and through σῶμα (body) a believer expresses himself and acts.[24] Frame (1912:209) similarly argues that ψυχή (soul) and σῶμα (body) denote human elements, human personality in particular.[25] However, this explanation is not widely accepted in modern scholarship.[26]

The third explanation is proposed by Jewett (Jewett 1971:175–183, 250–251), who contends that Paul employs the terms for an anti-Gnostic polemical purpose. The summary of Jewett's argument is that the Thessalonians are confronted by the Gnostic polemic that emphasises the superiority of spirit over body. Hence, sexual immorality is considered to be unimportant, which leads to the indulgence of physical pleasure and abandonment of daily physical labour (as indicated in 1 Thess 4:6, 11).[27] Since the tripartite formula is originally a Gnostic usage,[28] Paul adapts his opponents' ideas, and employs the terms in a rhetorical manner to repudiate the superiority of spirit over body by emphasising the equal importance of body and spirit. Jewett's proposal is problematic on two grounds. First, there is little evidence in the epistle suggesting that Paul tackles the Gnostic teaching. For example, σῶμα (body) is never mentioned once in the whole

---

[24] Likewise, Jones (2005:77) argues that the Thessalonians might embrace a Hellenistic Jewish understanding that considers a human as a living being (ψυχή), having a physical body (σῶμα) and capacity to connect with God (πνεῦμα). His view assumes that the audience would understand a human being according to contemporary Hellenistic Judaism, for example, Philo's philosophy.

[25] For Frame, πνεῦμα (spirit) points to the divine element.

[26] For example, Witherington (2006:173) rejects Marshall's understanding, arguing that ψυχή (soul) does not depict the immaterial part of human in 1 Cor 15:44–46. Rather, it connotes the natural and physical aspect.

[27] Jewett (1971:250–251) argues that the "Libertinists" among the Thessalonians place the importance of human spirit over physical body.

[28] Jewett (1971:181) suggests that πνεῦμα-ψυχή-σῶμα (spirit-soul-body) triad itself was most popular in Gnostic circles.

epistle except in the tripartite formula, let alone mentioning its connection with πνεῦμα (spirit).[29] Second, if Gnostic polemic is in Paul's mind, then solely using a benediction to address such an important issue would be totally inadequate.[30] Jewett's explanation is rejected by a number of modern scholars (Marshal 1983:163; Wanamaker 1990:206; Richard 1995:285–286; Malherbe 2000:339; Furnish 2007:123). In addition, it is doubtful whether Gnostic influence was prominent in the first century, since 1 Thessalonians is possibly one of the earliest Pauline epistles.[31]

The fourth explanation argues that Paul does not provide a precise anthropological definition of a human being. Rather, the three terms exemplify different "parts" of a human person, and the phrase emphasises the wholeness of a human person. In other words, Paul arbitrarily chooses the three terms to illustrate that all of the different parts of a person are kept blameless (Fee 2009:227).[32] A number of modern scholars adopt this explanation.[33] Two detailed aspects of this view are worth mentioning.

First, Fee further argues that the tripartite formula, which is in the second part of 5:23, is in parallel with the first part of the verse. There is shift within the same verse, by focusing on the community in the first half, by using ὑμᾶς (you), and then focusing on each individual person in the second half. In other words, the phrase ὑμῶν τὸ πνεῦμα καὶ ἡ ψυχὴ καὶ τὸ

---

[29] Furnish (2007:123) repudiates Jewett's proposal by arguing that the issue of Gnostic influence is nowhere mentioned in the letter, including the absence of the word σῶμα (body) in the letter except its sole occurrence in the tripartite formula. Marshall (1983:163) also argues that there is no evidence in the epistle referring to any Gnostic type of anthropology.

[30] Wanamaker (1990:206) argues that it seems doubtful that a wish-prayer was either an appropriate or an adequate place for Paul to address the Gnostic teaching.

[31] Following the discovery of the Nag Hammadi, an international congress, which convened in Messina in 1966, defined Gnosticism as "a certain group of systems" which could be dated in the second century (King 2003:169). Thus, it is highly doubtful if Paul addressed the Gnostic polemic when he wrote 1 Thessalonians in the first century. If people assume the presence of any anti-Gnostic components in Paul's work, according to King (2003:174), they must be aware of the fact that the extant materials simply do not support a pre-Christian dating of Gnosticism, however it is defined.

[32] This arbitrary description of a human being is also adopted by Bruce (1982a:130) who argues that it is difficult to pinpoint the exact meaning of the terms. Rather, the clause basically means "May every part of you be kept entirely without fault." In addition, Bruce also notes the phrase ὑμῶν τὰς καρδίας (your hearts) in 3:13.

[33] They include Bruce (1982a:130), Witherington (2006:173), and the following commentators who provide further explanation, arguing that the emphasis of the tripartite formula is as follows: "in every particular, in their wholeness as human beings" (Moore 1969:86); "complete human beings" (Wanamaker 1990:207); "the entire person" (Morris 1991:182; Malherbe 2000:339); "whole" (Best 1972:244). Donfried (2002:48) similarly contends that the phrase highlights the totality of their existence.

σῶμα (the spirit and the soul and the body of you) in 23b denotes a single human person, but the pronoun ὑμᾶς (you) in 23a denotes a community (Fee 2009:227).[34] However, this study argues that this shift is contextually incoherent.

Second, some scholars further argue that there is an intertextual parallel between Deut 6:5 and 1 Thess 5:23. According to Richard (1995:285) and Malherbe (2000:339), Deut 6:5, which is quoted in Matt 22:37 and Mark 12:30, can be used to explain 1 Thess 5:23. Their argument is summarised as follows. The two benedictions (1 Thess 3:11–13 and 5:23) are considered parallel.[35] Together their anthropological terms ὑμῶν τὰς καρδίας (your hearts), in 3:13; and ὑμῶν τὸ πνεῦμα καὶ ἡ ψυχὴ καὶ τὸ σῶμα (the spirit and the soul and the body of you), in 5:23, resemble those in Deut 6:5 (with all your heart, and with all your soul, and with all your mind). Since the Jewish mindset regards a human person as a whole being, "heart," "soul," and "mind" are used metaphorically to emphasise the "whole" human person by combining different hypothetical "parts." Thus, 1 Thess 3:13 and 5:23 should be understood in the same way: καρδία (heart), πνεῦμα (spirit), ψυχή (soul), and σῶμα (body) are different hypothetical parts for portraying a whole human person. Despite this insightful suggestion, this argument does not explain a major difference between Deut 6:5 and the tripartite formula. In Deut 6:5, the pronoun is singular, in the form of the suffix ך (you).[36] Conversely, the pronoun in 1 Thess 5:23 is plural ὑμῶν (your).[37]

Out of these four explanations, the fourth one is the predominant view in modern scholarship. Nonetheless, the explanation fails to address the abnormal singular construct: the combination of three articular singular anthropological terms and a plural possessive pronoun. Regarding the two detailed aspects of the fourth explanation, the suggestion of a shift from community to individual is contextually inconsistent, and the explanation of an intertextual parallel between Deut 6:5 and 1 Thess 5:23 does not account for the difference in pronoun.

---

[34] Richard (1995:285–286) similarly argues that the tripartite formula in the second part of the prayer is synonymously parallel to the first part of the prayer, thus equating the three terms with "you," pointing to the unity of the person in all aspects.

[35] The wishes articulated in both benedictions are similar: the Thessalonians would be blameless at the coming of the Lord.

[36] In both Matthew and Mark, a second singular pronoun σου (your) is employed to reflect its Hebrew equivalent.

[37] This difference is discussed in the later section of this chapter.

6.1.3 Textual analysis of 1 Thess 5:23

6.1.3.1 Syntactical analysis of 1 Thess 5:23a

The clause αὐτὸς δὲ ὁ θεὸς τῆς εἰρήνης ἁγιάσαι ὑμᾶς ὁλοτελεῖς (Now may the God of peace himself make you completely holy)* in 5:23a forms the first half of the sentence. Δέ (now) is a transitional conjunction, introducing the concluding remark of the epistle. The optative ἁγιάσαι (make holy) is the main verb in this clause. As previously discussed, it denotes a prayer of blessing as Paul prays for the Thessalonians to be ὁλοτελεῖς (whole). The adjective is a hapax legomenon in the NT, derived from ὅλος (whole) by combining ὅλος (whole) and τέλος (completion) to create an intensive form, illustrating completion or end, pointing to the meaning of wholeness.

Since the two benedictory prayers, 3:11–13 and 5:23, are in parallel, together they carry a parenthetical function, highlighting the exhortation (4:1–5:22) between them. This parenthetic exhortation, as indicated by words relating to holiness—ἁγιασμὸς (holiness) in 4:3, 4, 7; and ἅγιος (holy) in 4:8—encourages the Thessalonians to live a holy life and not be defiled by sexual immorality in light of the coming of the Lord. As such, 5:23a can be interpreted as a benedictory prayer that concludes the parenthetical exhortation: "I pray that the God of peace would sanctify."

6.1.3.2 Syntactical analysis of 1 Thess 5:23b

The connective conjunction καί (and) begins the second half of the sentence: ὁλόκληρον ὑμῶν τὸ πνεῦμα καὶ ἡ ψυχὴ καὶ τὸ σῶμα ἀμέμπτως...τηρηθείη (may the spirit and the soul and the body of you be kept whole and blamelessly). This is another independent clause, in which the optative τηρηθείη (it may be kept) acts as the main verb. A predicate adjective ὁλόκληρον (whole) precedes the nouns in this clause, and it means complete or sound in an ethical or moral sense.[38] Its meaning is very close to that of ὁλοτελεῖς (whole) in the previous clause, suggesting a strong parallel between the two.[39] Ὁλόκληρον (whole) appears before the tripartite formula, though this is not grammatically required. The word order strongly suggests that the adjective is deliberately placed.

---

[38] Both Bauer and Foerster disagree on the semantic nature of ὁλόκληρος (whole). Bauer (1979:564) defines the adjective as a qualitative term, suggesting an ethical sense. Foerster (1965:767) classifies it as a quantitative term, denoting extent or compass. However, Foerster argues that the adjective in 1 Thess 5:23 expresses a specific idea that τὸ πνεῦμα καὶ ἡ ψυχὴ καὶ τὸ σῶμα (the spirit and the soul and the body) would not be affected by evil. Foerster's interpretation apparently alludes to a qualitative sense. Despite the two different views (quantitative vs. qualitative), the connotation behind the word carries an ethical sense according to both scholars.

[39] This parallel extends beyond the use of two similar adjectives. As previously mentioned, both Richard (1995:285–286) and Fee (2009:227) also argue that the first half and the second half of 5:23 form a parallel.

Thus, the emphasis on wholeness is reiterated, which points to ὑμᾶς (you) in 5:23a. However, in 5:23b, the subject of wholeness points to a more elaborated description, which is the tripartite formula: ὑμῶν τὸ πνεῦμα καὶ ἡ ψυχὴ καὶ τὸ σῶμα (the spirit and the soul and the body of you). The parallel between ὑμᾶς (you) and ὑμῶν τὸ πνεῦμα καὶ ἡ ψυχὴ καὶ τὸ σῶμα (the spirit and the soul and the body of you) in these two consecutive clauses becomes obvious. Of interest, the two clauses form a parallel with one another as shown in table 6.3.

Table 6.3. Comparison of 1 Thess 5:23a and 5:23b[a]

5:23a	5:23b
Αὐτὸς δὲ **ὁ θεὸς** τῆς εἰρήνης (1)	ἐν τῇ παρουσίᾳ τοῦ κυρίου ἡμῶν ᾽Ιησοῦ Χριστοῦ (8)
ἁγιάσαι (2)	*τηρηθείη* (9)
ὑμᾶς (3)	ὑμῶν τὸ πνεῦμα καὶ ἡ ψυχὴ καὶ τὸ σῶμα (6)
ὁλοτελεῖς (4)	ὁλόκληρον (5) ... ἀμέμπτως (7)

[a] Elements that are parallel are marked by the same highlight. The number in parenthesis represents the word order in the sentence.

Not only is the overall meaning of both clauses in parallel, the individual elements in both clauses are also in parallel. There are three elements clearly in parallel: the two adjectives ὁλοτελεῖς (whole) and ὁλόκληρον (whole), the two optatives ἁγιάσαι (he may sanctify) and τηρηθείη (it may be kept), and the nouns ὁ θεὸς (God) and ᾽Ιησοῦ Χριστοῦ (Jesus Christ). As such, it is logical to view ὑμᾶς (you) as parallel with ὑμῶν τὸ πνεῦμα καὶ ἡ ψυχὴ καὶ τὸ σῶμα (the spirit and the soul and the body of you),[40] which will be further discussed in the following section.

An adverbial phrase ἐν τῇ παρουσίᾳ τοῦ κυρίου ἡμῶν (in the coming of our Lord) concludes this benedictory prayer. Paul prays that the Thessalonians would be kept whole and blameless when Christ returns. This prayer echoes with the previous prayer in 3:11–13, in which Paul prays that the Thessalonians would be blameless and holy when the Lord returns.

6.1.3.3 Grammatical and syntactical features of the tripartite formula

One of the challenges in interpreting the tripartite formula is that it is not found elsewhere in the Pauline epistles.[41] Identifying the exact meanings

---

[40] Richard (1995:286) suggests a different view, arguing that ὑμῶν (your) is connected to ὁλόκληρον (whole), meaning your whole being. The anthropological terms are then appositional to your whole being.

[41] Witherington (2006:172–173) asserts that the tripartite phrase (in this exact form) is not found elsewhere, including in contemporary Greek literature. This phase is believed to be adopted in some early Church Fathers' work.

of πνεῦμα (spirit), ψυχή (soul), and σῶμα (body) proves to be difficult. As previously mentioned, modern scholars widely agree that Paul does not write this formula to provide a consistent and theological definition for each anthropological term.

To understand the meaning of the terms, it is essential to discuss their peculiar syntax. There are three problems concerning the formula's grammatical construction. First, the three articulated nouns, πνεῦμα (spirit), ψυχή (soul), and σῶμα (body), are combined with a personal plural pronoun ὑμῶν (you)— the abnormal singular construct. Of interest, none of the scholarly works reviewed in this chapter, though far from exhaustive, mentions this unusual construct. It is very likely that focus has always been on the identification and interpretation of the three terms. Second, the aorist passive optative verb τηρηθείη (it may be kept) is singular, although the subject of this verb consists of three definite nouns. Both observations thus far go against the normal rule of accordance. Third, the predicative adjective ὁλόκληρον (whole) agrees only with πνεῦμα (spirit) and σῶμα (body) in terms of gender, case and number; ψυχή (soul) does not agree with ὁλόκληρον (whole) in gender. These three problems will be dealt with as follows.

With the first problem, as repeatedly argued, the abnormal construct must not be explained by automatically defining the singular term as the distributive singular. In the tripartite formula, the use of a plural possessive pronoun, despite being at odds with the singular nouns, is possible if the construct alludes to the whole community. Paul does not teach about individual spirit, soul, or body. Rather, he focuses on the Christian community in Thessalonica.[42] The church in Thessalonica consists of different people, as illustrated by a plural ὑμῶν (your), and they belong to a single community in Christ, as illustrated by the singular πνεῦμα (spirit), ψυχή (soul), and σῶμα (body). The above-mentioned parallel, ὑμᾶς (you) in 5:23a and ὑμῶν τὸ πνεῦμα καὶ ἡ ψυχὴ καὶ τὸ σῶμα (the spirit and the soul and the body of you) in 5:23b, supports this view. In addition, this explanation can provide an account for the second and the third peculiar grammatical problems.

The second problem, the use of the singular aorist optative τηρηθείη (it may be kept), can be explained as follows. First, the tripartite formula denotes a single community. Thus, the singular optative τηρηθείη (it may be kept) refers to this community, highlighting the corporate entity as denoted by πνεῦμα (spirit), ψυχή (soul), and σῶμα (body). Second, the structure emphasises the "wholeness" depicted in the context. Although there are three articular nouns, the wholeness of a single community is emphasised by the use of a singular verb.

The third problem with the combination of the singular predicate adjective ὁλόκληρον (whole) and the subject phrase τὸ πνεῦμα καὶ ἡ ψυχὴ καὶ

---

[42] For example, Currie (2006:447) argues that the paraenetic passage in 1 Thess 5:12–24 is concerned about communal life, emphasising life together and the need of striving for peace within the whole community.

τὸ σῶμα (the spirit and the soul and the body) can be explained by a focus on a single community. Grammatically, the adjective ὁλόκληρον (whole) is supposedly to be in plural form, since there are three subjects to be modified. However, ὁλόκληρον (whole) is a singular predicate adjective. Thus, one could argue that the adjective modifies the noun that follows: πνεῦμα (spirit). According to this understanding, πνεῦμα (spirit) might represent the entire person, with ψυχή (soul) and σῶμα (body) elaborating what this person consists of. This view upholds a dichotomous view of the human person with an immaterial part (ψυχή) and a material part (σῶμα). In other words, the text should be understood as: "May your entire person, the soul and the body, be kept whole."[43] However, this understanding is problematic on three grounds. First, a singular adjective modifying a series of nouns is not uncommon in the NT.[44] Second, this understanding undermines the essence of "totality," illustrated by the repeated use of words relating to ὅλος (whole) in the context.[45] Third, it also undermines the significance of placing ὑμῶν (your) at the front of this clause, which possibly emphasises the single community as a whole. As such, the singular predicate adjective ὁλόκληρον (whole) is best understood as modifying a single entity: the community as illustrated by the tripartite formula.

Besides these three grammatical problems, it is important to discuss the intertextual echo between Deut 6:5 and 1 Thess 5:23. As previously mentioned, some scholars argue that the benediction in 5:23 carries an intertextual echo of Deut 6:5. In Deut 6:5 a second person singular pronoun, in the form of the

---

[43] Hendriksen (1955:148–150) holds a different view based on a similar grammatical understanding, arguing that the text should be interpreted as "May the whole person, the soul and the body, be kept blameless." His argument is problematic, since ὁλόκληρον (whole) is treated as attributive. However, ὁλόκληρον is clearly a predicate adjective, and thus should be interpreted as "May... be kept whole."

[44] Various examples can be found in the NT, including Acts 7:11; Rom 1:29; Eph 1:21; 4:31. There are cases in which a singular adjective modifies a series of nouns, and only the case and number of both groups agree. For example, in Eph 4:31, πᾶσα πικρία καὶ θυμὸς καὶ ὀργὴ καὶ κραυγή (every kind of bitterness, anger, wrath, quarreling)*, the feminine singular adjective πᾶσα (every) modifies several proceeding nouns, including the feminine singular πικρία (bitterness), the masculine singular θυμός (anger), the feminine singular ὀργή (wrath), the feminine singular κραυγή (quarreling). It is unimaginable (from the perspectives of syntax and context) to suggest that πᾶσα (every) only modifies πικρία (bitterness), and the rest of the group, θυμός (anger), ὀργή (wrath), and κραυγή (quarreling) simply elaborates πικρία (bitterness).

[45] Morris opposes the view of Hendriksen. Morris (1991:182) considers the possessive pronoun ὑμῶν (your) as non-emphatic, and therefore, the adjective ὁλόκληρον (whole) should also be considered as non-emphatic. In other words, ὁλόκληρον (whole) does not merely modify πνεῦμα (spirit), it refers to all three nouns. Thus, all three nouns indicate one whole person who is to be kept whole and blameless. I agree with Morris, since his grammatical analysis is sound, supported by the contextual evidence.

suffix ךָ, is used. The LXX also has the singular pronoun σου (your). The singular pronoun in Deuteronomy obviously depicts the nation of Israel as a singular entity according to the context. Conversely, the pronoun in 1 Thess 5:23 is in plural form, ὑμῶν (your). We propose that Paul uses the anthropological terms in their singular form to depict the singular entity of the Thessalonian community, whilst using the plural pronoun ὑμῶν (your) to indicate the multiplicity of the members in this community. In other words, although the singularity of the community is emphasised in both texts, Deut 6:5 and 1 Thess 5:23 use different grammatical devices to achieve this emphasis.

Thus, the key to understanding the tripartite formula is that Paul prays that the whole community would be sanctified by God in all its totality. This understanding of the tripartite formula and the meaning of the anthropological terms is further examined by considering the findings of the discourse structure.

6.1.4 The tripartite formula in light of discourse analysis

In light of the discourse structure and the discourse flow, the tripartite formula in the benediction should be understood as follows. The benediction in 5:23 is part of the prominent theme of communal relationship. The teaching of παρουσία (coming) does not solicit an individual response. Instead, the Thessalonians are exhorted to respond to the παρουσία as a corporate entity. Hence, the tripartite formula is used to highlight this "wholeness" and "singleness" of this faith community. In the παρουσία, the community will be made whole and blameless, including the members who have died and those who are alive. Paul does not aim to provide an account of the individual human person through the tripartite formula. Instead, the anthropological terms are used to heighten the essence of wholeness. The singularity elucidates one corporate entity of this faith community, a community that resembles a human being, having different "parts" as exemplified by τὸ πνεῦμα καὶ ἡ ψυχὴ καὶ τὸ σῶμα (the spirit and the soul and the body). In other words, the anthropological terms are used as a metaphor to portray the community as a corporate entity, a single communal being, which would receive the ultimate blessing during the παρουσία. This community is portrayed as in contrast to another group, the non-believers, which would face a doomed fate.

6.2 Πνεῦμα in the grace benediction

In the second section of this chapter we examine the meaning of πνεῦμα (spirit) in the Pauline benedictions in Gal 6:18, Phil 4:23, and Phlm 1:25. We initially identify the discourse structures of Galatians and Philemon,[46]

---

[46] This chapter refers to the findings of the discourse structure of Philippians presented in § 4.1.3.

before focusing on the benedictions. Since the three benedictions are identical in form, the textual analysis will treat them as a single benediction, by examining its form and function, reviewing the explanation of πνεῦμα in previous scholarship, and conducting syntactical analysis. The findings of both the discourse structure of each epistle and the textual analysis of the benediction will be referred to in order to ascertain the meaning of πνεῦμα in each of the three epistles.

6.2.1 Discourse structures of Galatians and Philemon

6.2.1.1 Discourse structure of Galatians

An analysis of the discourse structure elucidates the major semantic units in Galatians, by investigating the discourse markers, examining the discourse coherence, and ascertaining the macrostructure.

Discourse markers

Three discourse markers demarcate the semantic units in Galatians: formulas, use of the vocative, and lexical cohesion.

Formulas

There is only one occurrence of the verb-conjunction-ὑμᾶς[47] formula in Galatians. The formula Γνωρίζω γὰρ ὑμῖν, ἀδελφοί (I want you to know, brothers)* in 1:11 begins the first discussion of Paul who rebukes the Galatians for abandoning the gospel truth and following the teaching of οἱ ταράσσοντες (the ones who trouble) in 1:7, the Judaizers.[48]

Vocative

Two vocatives, Γαλάται (Galatians) and ἀδελφοί (brothers), are discourse markers in Galatians. Paul addresses the Galatians emphatically in 3:1: Ὦ ἀνόητοι Γαλάται (You foolish Galatians!)* Then he explains the concept of justification in 3:1–4:31. Thus, Γαλάται (Galatians) begins a new discussion.

---

[47] English translation: verb-conjunction-you.

[48] Fee (2007:6) explains that the term "Judaizers" is derived from Ιουδαϊκῶς ζῆς (you live like a Jew) in 2:14, pointing to those who force the Gentiles to follow the Jewish Law. Fee prefers to call them "agitators" due to the misleading overtones of being legalistic. However, this study uses the term Judaizers to denote those who force the Gentile Christian to observe the Jewish Law. The Judaizers are commonly believed to be Paul's opponents in Galatians (Dunn 1993:9; Fung 1988:7; Matera 1992:5–6).

The vocative ἀδελφοί (brothers) occurs nine times.[49] Most of the occurrences demarcate a major topic of discussion. The first occurrence of ἀδελφοί in 1:11 is combined with a formula as mentioned above. In 3:1–4:31, Paul explains the justification of both Jews and Gentiles. This discussion ends with two occurrences of ἀδελφοί (4:28 and 4:31). In 5:11, ἀδελφοί ends another discussion in which the Galatians are warned against practising circumcision for the purpose of justification (5:1–12). In 5:13, ἀδελφοί begins a new topic in which the Galatians are urged to live by the Spirit (5:13–26). In 6:1, ἀδελφοί begins the general exhortation (6:1–10). In 6:18, ἀδελφοί ends the benediction at the end of the epistle.

On the other hand, the occurrences of ἀδελφοί in 3:15 and 4:12 begin two minor semantic units. In his discussion of justification, Paul explains the relation between the Law and justification (3:15–4:11), which is marked by ἀδελφοί (3:15). In 4:12, Paul concludes his major discussion of justification (4:12–31) by appealing to the Galatians.

Lexical cohesion

There are five patterns of lexical cohesion: νόμος (law),[50] δικαιόω (to justify) and its cognate δικαιοσύνη (righteousness), περιτέμνω (to circumcise) and its cognate περιτομή (circumcision), σάρξ (flesh), and πνεῦμα (spirit), illustrating different discussion topics (see Appendix 6).

First, the occurrences of νόμος (law) are concentrated in Gal 2–4, 25 out of 32 occurrences of νόμος occur in this segment.[51] This indicates that the Law is the central point of discussion in these three chapters as shown in figure 6.4.

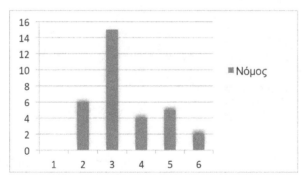

Figure 6.4. The occurrences of νόμος in Galatians.

---

[49] The occurrences of the vocative ἀδελφοί: 1:11; 3:15; 4:12, 28, 31; 5:11, 13; 6:1, 18.
[50] This is the second most frequent noun in the letter.
[51] The occurrences of νόμος (law) in Gal 3 are as follows: verses 2, 5, 10 (twice), 11, 12, 13, 17, 18, 19, 21 (thrice), 23, 24.

Second, the occurrences of δικαιόω (to justify) and δικαιοσύνη (righteousness) indicate the discussion of justification. The two words largely congregate in Gal 2–3, as shown in figure 6.5.[52]

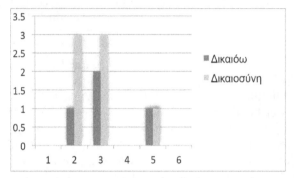

Figure 6.5. The occurrences of δικαιόω and δικαιοσύνη in Galatians.

Third, the occurrences of περιτομή (circumcision) and its corresponding verb περιτέμνω (to circumcise) indicate the discussion of circumcision. The two words, which illustrate the discussion of circumcision, congregate in Gal 2 and Gal 5 respectively (see figure 6.6).[53] In Gal 5, all four occurrences (two of περιτομή and two of περιτέμνω) occur in 5:1–12, with zero occurrences in 5:13–26. This suggests that the discussion of circumcision is confined to only 5:1–12 (see figure 6.7).

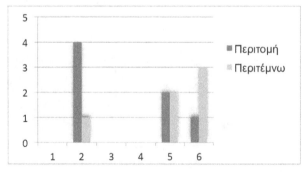

Figure 6.6. The occurrences of περιτομή and περιτέμνω in Galatians.

---

[52] The occurrences of δικαιοσύνη (righteousness) are as follows: 2:21; 3:6, 21; 5:5. The occurrences of δικαιόω (to justify) are as follows: 2:16 (thrice), 17; 3:8, 11, 24; 5:4.

[53] The occurrences of περιτομή (circumcision) are as follows: 2:7, 8, 9, 12; 5:6, 11; 6:15. The occurrences of περιτέμνω (to circumcise) are as follows: 2:3; 5:2, 3; 6:12, 13 (twice).

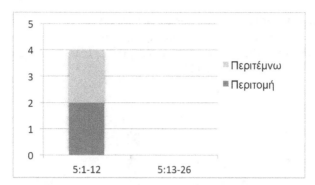

Figure 6.7. The occurrences of περιτομή and περιτέμνω in Gal 5.

Fourth, the occurrences of σάρξ (flesh) indicate the discussion of the flesh. Σάρξ occurs 18 times, mainly congregating in Gal 2–6 (see figure 6.8).[54] However, it does not occur in 5:1–12 (see figure 6.9). The following figures show these observations.

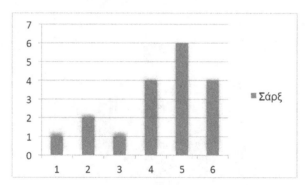

Figure 6.8. The occurrences of σάρξ in Galatians.

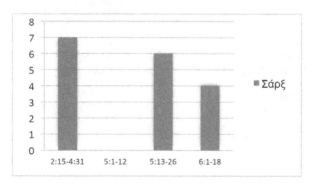

Figure 6.9. The occurrences of σάρξ in Gal 4–6.

[54] The occurrences of σάρξ (flesh) are as follows: 1:16; 2:16, 20; 3:3; 4:13, 14, 23, 29; 5:13, 16, 17 (twice), 19, 24; 6:8 (twice), 12, 13.

The last pattern is the occurrence of πνεῦμα (spirit). Πνεῦμα occurs 18 times in the letter, mainly congregating in Gal 5 in particular (see figure 6.10).[55] Resembling the occurrence of σάρξ (flesh), πνεῦμα (spirit) is nearly absent in 5:1–12 (see figure 6.11).

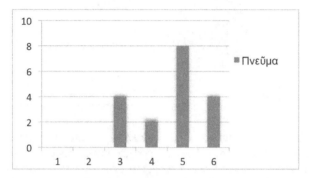

Figure 6.10. The occurrences of πνεῦμα in Galatians.

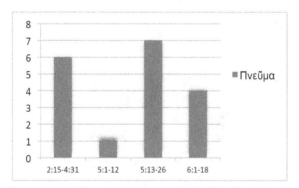

Figure 6.11. The occurrences of πνεῦμα in Gal 2–6.

Semantic units

Through the three identified discourse makers, Galatians can be divided into: the letter-opening, five major semantic units, and the letter-closing.

---

[55] The occurrences of πνεῦμα (spirit) are as follows: 3:2, 3, 5, 14; 4:6, 29; 5:5, 16, 17 (twice), 18, 22, 25 (twice); 6:1, 8 (twice), 18.

Table 6.4. Semantic units of Galatians

		A 1:11–2:21	B 3:1–4:31			C 5:1–12	D 5:13–26	E 6:1–10	
Minor Units			B1 3:1–14	B2 3:15–4:11	B3 4:12–31				
Discourse Markers DM 1: Formulas		Γνωρίζω γὰρ ὑμῖν, ἀδελφοί (1:11)							
DM 2: Vocatives			Γαλάται (3:1) ἀδελφοί (4:28, 31)			ἀδελφοί (5:11)	ἀδελφοί (5:13)	ἀδελφοί (6:1)	
DM 2: Lexical Cohesion		περιτομή and περιτέμνω	νόμος δικαιόω and δικαιοσύνη πνεῦμα			περιτομή and περιτέμνω Absence of σάρξ Near absence of πνεῦμα	Absence of περιτομή and περιτέμνω σάρξ πνεῦμα		
New Topic		Deviation of the Galatians	Justified by faith for Jews and Gentiles			Circumcision and Justification	Spirit-led Life	General Exhortations	

(Left vertical label: Letter-opening (1:1–10); Right vertical label: Letter-closing (6:11–18))

As shown in table 6.4, each major semantic unit contains a specific topic: Unit A: The deviation of the Galatians (1:11–2:21); Unit B: Justification by faith for Jews and Gentiles (3:1–4:31); Unit C: Circumcision and Justification (5:1–12); Unit D: Spirit-led Life (5:13–26); and Unit E: General Exhortations (6:1–10). Table 6.5 outlines the perspectives of other scholars, regarding the major semantic units in Galatians.[56]

---

[56] Table 6.5 does not present the full outline of each scholar. Rather, it presents the scholars that identify the same or similar unit as each of my units.

Table 6.5. Outline of Galatians by scholars[a]

My Outline	Unit A 1:11–2:21	Unit B 3:1–4:31	Unit C 5:1–12[b]	Unit D 5:13–26[c]	Unit E 6:1–10[d]
Outline of Scholars	Burton Dunn Fee Findlay Guthrie Martyn Matera Rogers	Betz Burton Ebeling Guthrie Lightfoot Morris	Betz Bligh Bruce Burton Ebeling Martyn Morris Lightfoot Longenecker	Bruce Burton Longenecker	Bruce Cousar Longenecker Morris
		Cousar Dunn Findlay Matera Rogers		Dunn Fee Fung Findlay Martyn Matera Rogers	

[a] For detailed outlines, see Betz 1979:vii-viii; Bruce 1982b:viii–ix; Dunn 1993:21–22; Fung 1988:v–viii; Matera 1992:v–vi; Bligh 1969:xiii–xiv; Guthrie 1981:v; Cousar 1982:ix; Morris 1996:30; Martyn 1997a:24–27; Burton 1921:lxxii–lxxiv; Findlay 1908:v–viii; Ebeling 1985:v–vi; Fee 2007:v–vi; Lightfoot 1902:65–7; Longenecker 1990:vii–viii; Rogers 1989:8–9.

[b] Betz, Morris, Burton, Ebeling, and Lightfoot consider 5:1–12 as a minor division of the major segment 5:1–6:10. For Bruce and Martyn, this segment begins in 5:2. For Bligh, this segment begins in 4:31. Longenecker considers 5:1–12 as the sub-division of 4:12–5:12.

[c] For Burton, 5:13–26 is a sub-division of a major segment 5:1–6:10.

[d] For Cousar, 6:1–10 is a sub-division of a major segment 5:13–6:18. Morris considers 6:1–10 as a sub-division of a major segment 5:1–6:10.

As shown in table 6.5, my outline is similar to those proposed by various scholars.

Discourse coherence

In terms of discourse coherence, there are two particular patterns of lexical cohesion worth noting. These patterns elucidate the relationship between Paul and the Galatians.

As previously mentioned, the key motifs in Galatians, including justification, the Law, circumcision, flesh, and the Spirit, are illustrated by the lexical cohesion of νόμος (law), δικαιόω (to justify) and its corresponding noun, περιτέμνω (to circumcise) and its corresponding noun, σάρξ (flesh) and πνεῦμα (spirit) respectively. However, two patterns of lexical cohesion, the occurrences of ἀδελφοί and πνεῦμα (spirit), signify a strong social reference in Galatians.[57]

As for ἀδελφοί, the vocative occurs nine times in Galatians. As previously shown, most of them are discourse markers. However, many of them are also employed to highlight the relationship between Paul and the Galatians.

First, a problem is mentioned in the letter-opening (1:6–7a): the relationship between Paul and the Galatians is at stake. Then, in Unit A, Paul uses ἀδελφοί (1:11) to remind them of the gospel that is preached by him: ὑπ᾽ ἐμοῦ (by me). The vocative portrays the relationship between Paul and the community.[58]

In Unit B, there are three occurrences of ἀδελφοί (4:12, 28, 31). The first occurrence of vocative occurs in 4:12. The vocative is then followed by Paul's emphatic call, δέομαι ὑμῶν (I beg you)* in 4:12,[59] and an emotional exclamation of his personal agony, ὥστε ἐχθρὸς ὑμῶν γέγονα ἀληθεύων ὑμῖν; (So then, have I become your enemy by telling you the truth?)* in 4:16. Then, two occurrences of vocative are found in 4:29 and 4:31, the ending of this unit. The use of vocative is to emphasise the relationship between Paul and the Galatians.[60]

In the two subsequent major semantic units, two vocatives appear in close proximity: 5:11 (Unit C), and 5:13 (Unit D). In the middle of them, there is an exceptionally passionate expression: Ὄφελον καὶ ἀποκόψονται οἱ ἀναστατοῦντες ὑμᾶς (I wish those agitators would go so far as to castrate themselves)* in 5:12. This illustrates Paul's passion for the Galatians who are disturbed by the Judaizers.[61] Thus, the two vocatives elucidate

---

[57] Of interest, Martyn (1997b:267–278) analyses Gal 5, and argues that the epistle illustrates a communal discord. This discord is caused by some people who attempt to teach the Galatian community the formula of combining Christ and the Sinaitic Law. This argument sheds light on the purpose of Galatians. Paul does not merely address a theological issue, he also addresses a communal problem.

[58] Dunn (1993:52) argues that the occurrence of ἀδελφοί strikes a conciliatory note given the departure from his usual etiquette in 1:6–10.

[59] Fee (2007:160–161) comments on the strong intensity of this personal appeal, and argues that it informs us much about the personal struggle Paul himself is going through, and this is a Paul we are simply not used to. For Martyn (1997b:419–420), this vocative reflects Paul's close and affectionate relationship with the Galatians, and the adverb ὡς (as) reflects a mutual friendship between them.

[60] As well argued by Matera (1992:162), these verses carry a strong personal and emotional appeal, as Paul unexpectedly appeals to the strong ties which once united him and the Galatians.

[61] For Longenecker (1990:234), this expression is the crudest and rudest of all Paul's extant statements.

this deep passion.[62] Furthermore, each vocative is accompanied with an emphatic personal pronoun: Ἐγὼ δέ, ἀδελφοί (Now I, brothers) in 5:11; and Ὑμεῖς γὰρ...ἀδελφοί (For you...brothers) in 5:13.[63]

In 6:18, ἀδελφοί occurs the last time in Galatians. Amongst all the Pauline epistles, this is the only occurrence in which ἀδελφοί appears adjacent to the benediction. Longenecker, joining a list of scholars, notes this unusual occurrence (Betz 1979:325; Dunn 1993:347–348; Fee 2007:254; Fung 1988:315; Guthrie 1981:153; Longenecker 1990:300; Martyn 1997a:569; Matera 1992:227; Morris 1996:191). He argues that the vocative is an expression of Paul's affection towards the converts despite his stern message. Whilst summarising his argument, οὔτε γὰρ περιτομή τί ἐστιν οὔτε ἀκροβυστία ἀλλὰ καινὴ κτίσις (For neither circumcision nor uncircumcision counts for anything; the only thing that matters is a new creation)* in 6:15, Paul reminds the Galatians of the shared kinship by using ἀδελφοί one last time. Paul and the Galatians are ἀδελφοί in this new creation.

Concerning πνεῦμα (spirit), the term occurs 18 times in Galatians.[64] Although it does not occur throughout the epistle,[65] it is a prominent term in Gal 3–6, Unit D in particular. Putting aside πνεῦμα in the benediction (6:18), all of them denote the Holy Spirit. In other words, the Holy Spirit is the sentential meaning in all of its occurrences. However, the thematic meaning of πνεῦμα in Galatians is different, which will be discussed below.

In Unit B, πνεῦμα (spirit) occurs six times. Paul argues that the Galatians are no longer under the Law. They have received the Holy Spirit (3:2, 3, 5, 14) and are God's children according to the Holy Spirit (4:6, 29). In other words, the context of πνεῦμα points to a new dispensation in which the Galatian community belong to, and they are different from those who are under the Law (4:29).

In Unit C, πνεῦμα (spirit) occurs once. Paul argues that the Galatians belong to Christ, instead of being justified by the Law (5:4). Through the Holy Spirit (5:5), the Galatians wait for the future hope. Again, a new dispensation is highlighted through the usage of πνεῦμα.

In Unit D, πνεῦμα (spirit) occurs seven times. Paul urges them to be led by the Holy Spirit instead of following the flesh (5:16, 17, 18) and to live by the Spirit (5:22, 25). The term is used in contrast to σάρξ (flesh), referring

---

[62] For Martyn (1997b:476), this ἀδελφοί in 5:11 shows the affectionate address made by Paul to the Galatians.

[63] Dunn (1993:278) suggests that Paul uses the emphatic personal pronoun in 5:11 for distancing himself from "the trouble maker." Fung (1988:244) argues that Paul uses the emphatic personal pronoun in 5:13 to forcefully distinguish his Galatian converts from the agitators.

[64] The occurrences of πνεῦμα (spirit) in Galatians: 3:2, 3, 5, 14; 4:6, 29; 5:5, 16, 17 (twice), 18, 22, 25 (twice); 6:1, 8 (twice), 18.

[65] The first occurrence of πνεῦμα (spirit) in Galatians appears in 3:2.

to a new dispensation in which the Galatians are in Christ and no longer under the Law.

In Unit E, Paul reminds the Galatians of their Christian identity that is marked by the Holy Spirit (6:1). Thus, they should follow the Spirit instead of the flesh (6:8).

Some scholars also note the significance of this usage. For example, Matera (1992:206) comments on the occurrence of πνεῦμα (spirit) in 5:16–18, and argues that the Spirit signifies those who have been incorporated into Christ. Longenecker (1990:246) considers the overall usage of πνεῦμα in Gal 5, and contends that the occurrences of πνεῦμα remind the Galatians of their new life (a life that is contrast to the teaching of the Judaizers). For Fung (1988:248), πνεῦμα signifies a new dispensation prophesised in Jer 31:31–34.[66] I agree with their arguments. Although the sentential meaning of πνεῦμα is the Holy Spirit, its thematic meaning in Galatians elucidates a key topic: the Galatian community belongs to Christ under a new dispensation, and is no longer under the Law in the old dispensation. The strong corporate reference of a Christian community with a new corporate identity (in this new dispensation) is highlighted by the overall occurrences of πνεῦμα.

Macrostructure and sociolinguistic aspect

From the identified semantic units and the analysis of discourse coherence, the macrostructure of Galatians can be understood as follows. Paul emphatically warns the Galatians against the necessity of circumcision. He expresses his affection to the Galatians, and reiterates that they are justified by God through faith of Christ, not by observing the Law, particularly practising circumcision. In Christ, Jews and Gentiles are one, a new creation in a new dispensation. Therefore, the community that has received the Spirit should live by the Spirit under this new dispensation.

In terms of sociolinguistic aspect, Paul invokes his apostleship to amplify the magnitude of his warning and teaching. In 1:1, he uses the self-designation, ἀπόστολος...διὰ Ἰησοῦ Χριστοῦ (apostle...through Jesus Christ). Agosto argues that this self-designation is employed to "re-establish his authority" (Agosto 2005:102). Although Paul also calls himself Χριστοῦ δοῦλος (a slave of Christ) in 1:10, it must not be mistaken as a mere expression of humility. As previously discussed, this self-designation carries a specific denotation, signifying Paul's leadership by alluding to the noble status of an imperial slave or the power possessed by a slave agent.[67]

---

[66] Fee (2007:208) similarly argues that walking by the Spirit is the primary new covenant imperative. Dunn suggests (1993:296) that the Spirit is employed in contrast to the living by the Law. For Bruce (1982b:245), Paul makes "led by the Spirit" antithetical to "under law."

[67] As previously mentioned, Martin (1990:75–76) further argues that this self-designation depicts Paul as a slave agent, leading and managing other Christians

The flow of discourse and peak

In the stage (1:1–10), Paul denounces the Galatians for their abandonment of the gospel truth (1:6) that he has preached. Various themes, including the Law, circumcision, and justification, are being developed in the following episodes (Units A and B) to form an argument: the Galatians are justified through the faith of Christ, instead of through observing the Law. In the pre-peak episode (Unit B3), the Galatians are portrayed as the children of promise, who are no longer under the Law. Meanwhile, Paul provides a strong summative argument in the peak episode (Unit C), in which the climax of the discourse is located.

Several features demonstrate that 5:1–12 is the peak of Galatians (and 5:1–6 is the climax within). Not only is the semantic unit located near the end of the letter, the unit is also a zone of grammatical turbulence that exhibits many intriguing grammatical phenomena.

First, the two imperative verbs in 5:1b are grammatically unique. Paul exhorts the Galatians: στήκετε οὖν καὶ μὴ πάλιν ζυγῷ δουλείας ἐνέχεσθε (Stand firm, then, and do not be subject again to the yoke of slavery)* in 5:1b. This is the only occasion in Galatians, where both a positive imperative verb and a negative one co-exist in the same clause: στήκετε…μὴ…ἐνέχεσθε (stand…do not be subject). The two imperatives are in parallel, elucidating the same concept. Most intriguingly, one imperative is placed at the beginning of the clause, whilst the other, the end of it. In other words, the parallel is also constructed in a unique word order, possibly capturing attention and providing emphasis.

Second, Paul employs an expression to draw the attention of the Galatians: Ἴδε ἐγὼ Παῦλος λέγω ὑμῖν (Listen! I, Paul, tell you)* in 5:2. This expression also occurs in 2 Cor 10:1, 1 Thess 2:18, and Phlm 1:19. In all three cases, Paul makes an emphatic expression.[68] The relationship between Paul and the Galatians is clearly highlighted.

Third, parallelism is a prominent device in 5:2–4, 5:2–3 in particular. Not only are 5:2 and 5:3 in parallel, they also contain the re-emergence of some key themes in Galatians. The message, Ἴδε ἐγὼ Παῦλος λέγω ὑμῖν ὅτι ἐὰν περιτέμνησθε, Χριστὸς ὑμᾶς οὐδὲν ὠφελήσει (Listen! I, Paul, tell you that if

---

who are the slaves of Christ. The use of slavery language seems to be a paradox, since Gal 5:1 teaches about freedom from slavery. However, Martin (1990:60) states that Paul, resembling a slave agent who is an authoritative representative of the power owner, uses this self-designation to imply his power and authority in his address to the Galatians.

[68] Paul defends his apostleship: δὲ ἐγὼ Παῦλος παρακαλῶ ὑμᾶς (Now I, Paul, appeal to you personally)* in 2 Cor 10:1. Paul expresses his genuine desire to visit the Thessalonians: διότι ἠθελήσαμεν ἐλθεῖν πρὸς ὑμᾶς, ἐγὼ μὲν Παῦλος καὶ ἅπαξ καὶ δίς, καὶ ἐνέκοψεν ἡμᾶς ὁ σατανᾶς (For we wanted to come to you (I, Paul, in fact tried again and again) but Satan thwarted us)* in 1 Thess 2:18. Paul makes a personal emphatic plea to Philemon: ἐγὼ Παῦλος ἔγραψα τῇ ἐμῇ χειρί, ἐγὼ ἀποτίσω (I, Paul, wrote this with my own hand: I will repay it)* in Phlm 1:19. As well as the clause in Galatians 5:2, all of these expressions follow the pattern of ἐγὼ Παῦλος.

you let yourselves be circumcised, Christ will be of no benefit to you at all)*
in 5:2, is immediately reiterated in the next verse, μαρτύρομαι δὲ πάλιν παντὶ
ἀνθρώπῳ περιτεμνομένῳ ὅτι ὀφειλέτης ἐστὶν ὅλον τὸν νόμον ποιῆσαι (And I
testify again to every man who lets himself be circumcised that he is obligated
to obey the whole law)* in 5:3. Four elements are in parallel between these
two verses. The clause Ἴδε ἐγὼ Παῦλος λέγω ὑμῖν (Listen! I, Paul, tell you)*
in 5:2a is synonymous with the clause μαρτύρομαι δὲ πάλιν (And I testify
again)* in 5:3a. The concept expressed in the clause Χριστὸς ὑμᾶς οὐδὲν
ὠφελήσει (Christ will be of no benefit to you)* in 5:2b is in parallel with
ὀφειλέτης ἐστὶν ὅλον τὸν νόμον ποιῆσαι (he is obligated to obey the whole
law)* in 5:3b, by employing the antithetical themes: Χριστός (Christ) and
νόμος (law). The word περιτέμνω (to circumcise) is repeated in both verses.
The two words, ὠφελήσει (he will benefit, 5:2b) and ὀφειλέτης (debtor, 5:3b),
share the same semantic root, since ὀφειλέτης (debtor) is the corresponding
noun of ὀφείλω (to benefit). In addition to the parallel, the two key themes
in Galatians, circumcision and the Law, join together in 5:3. Of interest, this
is the first occasion in this epistle that the concept of circumcision, denoted
by περιτέμνω (to circumcise), and the concept of the Law, denoted by νόμος
(law) appear in the same clause. Then, 5:2–3 is followed by a summative
statement that again mentions the two antithetical themes: κατηργήθητε ἀπὸ
Χριστοῦ, οἵτινες ἐν νόμῳ δικαιοῦσθε (you who are trying to be declared
righteous by the law have been alienated from Christ)* in 4a. As such, the use
of parallelism is extremely prominent in 5:2–4.

Finally, Paul introduces a resolution in 5:5: ἡμεῖς γὰρ πνεύματι ἐκ
πίστεως ἐλπίδα δικαιοσύνης ἀπεκδεχόμεθα "For through the Spirit, by faith,
we wait expectantly for the hope of righteousness."* Then he employs the
contrast of περιτομή (circumcision) and ἀκροβυστία (uncircumcision) in
5:6 to summarise his argument: ἐν γὰρ Χριστῷ Ἰησοῦ οὔτε περιτομή τι
ἰσχύει οὔτε ἀκροβυστία ἀλλὰ πίστις δι᾽ ἀγάπης ἐνεργουμένη (For in Christ
Jesus neither circumcision nor uncircumcision carries any weight—the
only thing that matters is faith working through love)*. A similar expression also occurs near the end of the letter: οὔτε γὰρ περιτομή τί ἐστιν οὔτε
ἀκροβυστία ἀλλὰ καινὴ κτίσις (For neither circumcision nor uncircumcision counts for anything; the only thing that matters is a new creation)* in
6:15. This reflects the significance of the argument in 5:6. In 5:1–6, all the
key words representing the key themes of this epistle occur: περιτομή (circumcision), νόμος (law), δικαιόω (to justify), Χριστός (Christ), and πνεῦμα
(spirit). They simultaneously appear within six verses, congruently forming
a core message of Galatians (as shown in the discussion of macrostructure).

In summary, the influx of many intriguing grammatical devices within
six verses, including both positive and negative imperative verbs in the same
clause, an emphatic expression, multiple parallels, and key thematic words
of the epistle, demonstrates that 5:1–12 is the discourse peak, in which
5:1–6 is the climax. Figure 6.12 shows the discourse flow of Galatians.

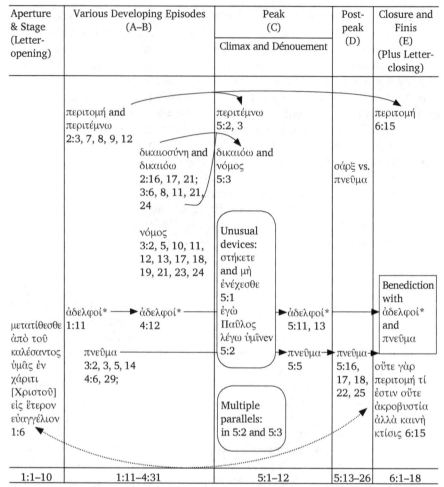

Aperture & Stage (Letter-opening)	Various Developing Episodes (A–B)	Peak (C) Climax and Dénouement	Post-peak (D)	Closure and Finis (E) (Plus Letter-closing)
μετατίθεσθε ἀπὸ τοῦ καλέσαντος ὑμᾶς ἐν χάριτι [Χριστοῦ] εἰς ἕτερον εὐαγγέλιον 1:6	περιτομή and περιτέμνω 2:3, 7, 8, 9, 12	περιτέμνω 5:2, 3		περιτομή 6:15
	δικαιοσύνη and δικαιόω 2:16, 17, 21; 3:6, 8, 11, 21, 24	δικαιόω and νόμος 5:3	σάρξ vs. πνεῦμα	
	νόμος 3:2, 5, 10, 11, 12, 13, 17, 18, 19, 21, 23, 24	Unusual devices: στήκετε and μὴ ἐνέχεσθε 5:1		Benediction with ἀδελφοί* and πνεῦμα
	ἀδελφοί* 1:11 → ἀδελφοί* 4:12	ἐγὼ Παῦλος λέγω ὑμῖν 5:2 → ἀδελφοί* 5:11, 13		
	πνεῦμα 3:2, 3, 5, 14 4:6, 29;	→ πνεῦμα 5:5	πνεῦμα 5:16, 17, 18, 22, 25	οὔτε γὰρ περιτομή τί ἐστιν οὔτε ἀκροβυστία ἀλλὰ καινὴ κτίσις 6:15
		Multiple parallels: in 5:2 and 5:3		
1:1–10	1:11–4:31	5:1–12	5:13–26	6:1–18

Key: ——▶ : Development of themes; ◀┈┈▶: Contrastive themes; *: Ἀδελφοί (emphasises relational bond)

Figure 6.12. The flow of discourse of Galatians.

6.2.1.2 Discourse structure of Philemon

Philemon is the shortest of all the Pauline epistles. Despite its shortness, the epistle can still be analysed by adopting the same method based on discourse analysis.

Discourse markers

Four discourse markers demarcate the semantic units in Philemon: use of the vocative, change of verb mood, formulas, and lexical cohesion.

Vocative

Paul addresses two target audiences in Philemon: Φιλήμων (Philemon) in 1:1; and several recipients including τῇ κατ᾽ οἶκόν σου ἐκκλησίᾳ (to the church that meets in your house)* in 1:2. However, Φιλήμων (Philemon) is the primary addressee.[69] Hence, the vocative ἀδελφέ (brother) is employed, and it occurs twice in Philemon (1:7 and 1:20). The first vocative ends the discussion in which Paul recalls his relationship and passion towards Philemon before the emergence of a new discussion in 1:8. The second vocative ends a major discussion of Onesimus. Thus, both vocatives demarcate two major semantic units: 1:4–7 and 1:8–20.

Change of verb mood

There are four imperative verbs (1:17, 18, 20, 22). All of them occur near the end of the epistle, signifying the boundary of 1:17–20. Although this segment is in the middle of the discussion of Onesimus, Paul shifts to articulate the actions that Philemon should take for Onesimus, as indicated by the influx of imperative verbs. Thus, 1:17–20 is a minor semantic unit within the major discussion of Onesimus (1:8–20).

Formulas

The only formula in Philemon is the formulaic praise Εὐχαριστῶ τῷ θεῷ μου πάντοτε (I always thank my God)* in 1:4. It begins the first topic of this epistle following the initial greeting (1:1–3).

Lexical cohesion

There are two patterns of lexical cohesion in Philemon: the recurrence of δέσμιος (prisoner) and its cognate δεσμός (imprisonment), and the repetition of παρακαλέω (I urge) (see Appendix 7). Both patterns occur in the major discussion of Onesimus. Thus, they both indicate a minor unit within 1:8–20. First, δέσμιος (prisoner) and δεσμός (imprisonment) occur four times (δέσμιος, in 1:1, 9; δεσμός, in 1:10, 13). They indicate that imprisonment is the topic in 1:8–16, discussing the imprisonment of both Paul and Onesimus: Παῦλος δέσμιος Χριστοῦ (a prisoner of Christ)* in 1:1; τοῦ ἐμοῦ τέκνου...ἐν τοῖς δεσμοῖς, Ὀνήσιμον (my child...during my imprisonment, that is, Onesimus)* in 1:10. Second, in the discussion of imprisonment,

---

[69] This is demonstrated by the frequent occurrences of the second person singular personal pronouns throughout the whole letter (20 in total). Although Ἀπφία (Apphia), Ἄρχιππος (Archippus), and τῇ κατ᾽ οἶκόν σου ἐκκλησίᾳ (the church at your house) are mentioned in 1:2, there are only four second person plural personal pronouns (1:3, 22 (twice), 25).

παρακαλέω (to urge) is repeated twice in close proximity (1:9, 10). Both occurrences depict Paul's plea to Philemon concerning Onesimus.

Semantic units

Through the four identified discourse markers, the epistle can be divided into: the letter-opening (1:1–3); two major semantic units; and the letter-closing (1:21–25). The two major units are Unit A (Paul's affection for Philemon, in 1:4–7) and Unit B (Paul's plea to Philemon for Onesimus, in 1:8–20). Table 6.6 shows the major semantic units of Philemon. Table 6.7 outlines the perspectives of other scholars, regarding the major semantic units in Philemon.[70] As shown in the table, my outline is similar to those proposed by various scholars.

---

[70] Table 6.7 does not present the full outline of each scholar. Rather, it presents the scholars that identify the same or similar unit as each of my units.

Table 6.6. Semantic units of Philemon

Major Units		A 1:4–7	B 1:8–20		
				B1 1:8–16	B2 1:17–20
Discourse Markers: DM1: Vocative		ἀδελφέ (1:7)			ἀδελφέ (1:20)
DM2: Change of Verb Mood					Imperatives: 3/4
DM3: Formulas	Letter-opening (1:1–3)	Εὐχαριστῶ τῷ θεῷ μου (1:4)			
DM4: Lexical Cohesion				δέσμιος and δεσμός παρακαλέω	
New Topic		Paul's affection for Philemon		Paul's plea to Philemon for Onesimus	

(The rightmost spanning column is labelled: Letter-closing (1:21–25))

Table 6.7. Outline of Philemon by scholars[a]

My Outline	Opening 1:1–3	Semantic Unit A 1:4–7	Semantic Unit B 1:8–20	Closing 1:21–25
Outline of Scholars	Barth Bruce Dunn Fitzmyer Lohse Martin Moo Nordling Thurston	Barth Bruce Dunn Fitzmyer Lohse Martin Moo Nordling Thurston	Dunn Fitzmyer Lohse Martin Moo Thurston	Barth Dunn Fitzmyer Lohse Martin Moo Thurston

[a] Barth and Blanke (2000:280) argue that the phrase πάντας τοὺς ἁγίους refers to both the believers assembled in Philemon's house and the believers visiting Colossae. Nordling (2004:202–203) suggests that the church and the saints are two interchangeable terms.

Discourse coherence

Although Paul primarily addresses Philemon in this letter, communal relationship is a coherent theme. Philemon is not a private letter per se. The
major issue in the epistle is also the concern of Christian community gathered in Philemon's house. As previously mentioned, the recipients of this
epistle include τῇ κατ' οἶκόν σου ἐκκλησίᾳ (to the church that meets in your
house)* in 1:2, as indicated by plural pronoun ὑμῖν (to you) in the initial
greeting, χάρις ὑμῖν (grace to you) in 1:3.

In Unit A, Paul praises Philemon for his love. Philemon shows his love
to πάντας τοὺς ἁγίους (all the saints)* in 1:5, and refreshes τῶν ἁγίων (the
saints)* in 1:7. The saints refer to believers, possibly including those who
gather in Philemon's house. Thus, instead of depicting Philemon's love in a
general sense, the repetition of οἱ ἅγιοι (the saints) could be a subtle reference to the worship community at Philemon's house.[71]

In Unit B, the topic is about Paul's plea to Philemon for Onesimus.
However, several observations show that this issue is also a concern of the
Christian community. First, Paul appeals to Philemon to receive Onesimus
διὰ τὴν ἀγάπην (because of love, 1:9). The word ἀγάπη (love) mentioned
in 1:5 and 1:7 is now reiterated in 1:9. This pattern of lexical cohesion
indicates that the appeal is not merely a private matter. Rather, it is related
to Philemon's love, his love for the Christian community in particular. Upon
his return to Philemon, Onesimus, a new Christian convert, would likely
be joining the community that is described by Paul as τῇ κατ' οἶκόν σου
ἐκκλησίᾳ (to the church that meets in your house)*. Not only would his
return affect Philemon, it would also impact the Christian community gathered in Philemon's house. As noted by Wilson (1992:112), Philemon has
now become a valuable member of the community.

In the letter-closing, the request and the final greeting involve two
communities (1:23–24): Philemon and his house church, and the prison
community, including Ἐπαφρᾶς (Epaphras), Μᾶρκος (Mark), Ἀρίσταρχος
(Aristarchus), Δημᾶς (Demas), and Λουκᾶς (Luke). Although Paul portrays
Μᾶρκος, Ἀρίσταρχος, Δημᾶς, and Λουκᾶς as his co-workers, mentioning
their names may allude to their regular visit to the prison where Paul and
Ἐπαφρᾶς are. Thus, the fate of Onesimus would be witnessed by both
communities.

Notably, when Paul makes a request for a guest room, instead of using
a second person personal singular pronoun (as in the case of 1:4–21), he
uses two plural pronouns to indicate his wish: διὰ τῶν προσευχῶν ὑμῶν
χαρισθήσομαι ὑμῖν (through your prayers I will be given back to you)* 1:22.

---

[71] Barth and Blanke (2000:280) argue that the phrase πάντας τοὺς ἁγίους (all the
saints) refers to both the believers assembled in Philemon's house and the believers
visiting Colossae. Nordling (2004:202–203) suggests that the church and the saints
are two interchangeable terms.

This indicates that Paul addresses both Philemon and the members of his house church.[72] This reinforces our theory that the issue of Onesimus is also the concern of the community.

Onesimus is a slave of Philemon (1:16) and a fellow prisoner of Paul (1:10). Although his name is not mentioned in both the initial greeting (1:1–3) and the letter-closing (1:21–25), he belongs to two communities. As such, his return would definitely not be a private matter between Paul and Philemon. Rather, it would be the concern of both the prison community and the Christian community that worshipped in Philemon's house. As well argued by Barth and Blake (2000:493–494), Paul makes this letter a matter of the church, so that Philemon must respond for his good or bad behaviour before the community. According to Fitzmyer (2000:81), Paul's concern is for the Christian community that would be involved in the way Onesimus is to be welcomed back by Philemon.

Macrostructure and sociolinguistic aspect

The macrostructure of Philemon can be understood as follows. Paul makes known his desire to Philemon that he would like to keep Onesimus (a slave of Philemon), but he also urges Philemon to welcome Onesimus back, as if welcoming Paul himself. This issue is the concern of two communities: the prison community and the Christian community gathered in Philemon's house. In terms of the sociolinguistic aspect, the relationship between Paul, Onesimus, and Philemon is intriguing. Philemon, as a master, has authority over his slave Onesimus. On the other hand, Paul, as an apostle, has authority over Philemon. Given the social hierarchy in the Graeco-Roman world, Paul's courteous plea to Philemon, requesting him to accept Onesimus, appears as a subversive gesture. It highlights the new paradigm that Paul encourages Christians to follow: fellow believers should be treated as brothers and sisters.

The flow of discourse and peak

Paul develops his argument in various developing episodes, focusing on his relationship with Philemon: χαρὰν γὰρ πολλὴν ἔσχον καὶ παράκλησιν ἐπὶ τῇ ἀγάπῃ σου (I have had great joy and encouragement because of your love)* in 1:7; διὰ τὴν ἀγάπην μᾶλλον παρακαλῶ (I would rather appeal to you on the basis of love)* in 1:9; and εἰ οὖν με ἔχεις κοινωνόν (Therefore if you regard me as a partner)* in 1:17. The peak of this epistle is located in Unit B2 (1:17–20). This is demonstrated by the influx of imperative verbs and the occurrences of several grammatical devices in B2.

---

[72] A number of commentators hold this view (Nordling 2004:285; Dunn 1996:346; Thurston and Ryan 2005:256; Lohse 1971:207; Fitzmyer 2000:123).

There are four imperative verbs in this epistle, and three of them occur in B2. Of interest, these three imperatives reflect the macrostructure of this epistle. The first imperative clause προσλαβοῦ αὐτὸν ὡς ἐμέ (accept him as you would me)* in 1:17 expresses Paul's desire: Onesimus could be welcomed by Philemon. The second imperative clause τοῦτο ἐμοὶ ἐλλόγα (charge what he owes to me)* in 1:18 is Paul's rhetorical strategy, emphasising the seriousness of Paul's desire. Although Paul instructs Philemon to charge his account for what Onesimus owes Philemon, Paul immediately reminds Philemon of what he owes Paul: σεαυτόν μοι προσοφείλεις (you owe me your very self)* in 1:19. The third imperative clause ἀνάπαυσόν μου τὰ σπλάγχνα (refresh my heart)* in 1:20 summarises Paul's desire stated in 1:17. According to the context, Philemon could refresh Paul if he follows Paul's command, προσλαβοῦ αὐτὸν ὡς ἐμέ (accept him as you would me)* in 1:17. The imperative ἀνάπαυσόν (accept) also echoes with its previous occurrence in 1:7 (ἀναπέπαυται), in which Philemon is praised for refreshing the saints. In summary, none of the three imperatives signify general exhortation. Rather, they are specific, personal, and related to the same issue.

Unit B2 also displays some captivating grammatical devices. First, two first class conditional sentences occur in adjacent verses: εἰ οὖν με ἔχεις κοινωνόν (Therefore if you regard me as a partner)* in 1:17a; and εἰ δέ τι ἠδίκησέν σε ἢ ὀφείλει (Now if he has defrauded you of anything or owes you anything)* in 1:18a. Of interest, they are the only conditional clauses in this epistle. Second, Paul uses an emphatic pronoun twice in the same verse: ἐγὼ Παῦλος (I, Paul)* in 1:19a; and ἐγὼ ἀποτίσω (I will repay)* in 19b. The pronoun ἐγώ (I) is not redundant. Rather, it illustrates emphasis. Third, there are 17 first person singular pronouns in this epistle. Approximately half of them occur in 1:17–20: με (me) and ἐμέ (me) in 17; ἐμοὶ (to me) in 18; ἐγώ (I), twice in 19, and μοι (to me) in 19; ἐγώ (I) and μου (of me) in 20.

In summary, B2 exhibits a zone of grammatical turbulence as indicated by the influx of imperative verbs (which focus on the same issue) and the occurrences of several grammatical devices (the adjacent conditional sentences, the emphatic expressions, and the concentrated occurrence of first person singular pronouns). As such, I propose that B2 is the peak of this epistle.

The clause in 1:21, Πεποιθὼς τῇ ὑπακοῇ σου ἔγραψά σοι (Since I was confident that you would obey, I wrote to you)*, has a summative purpose as Paul expresses his confidence in Philemon's favourable response. This can be considered as the dénouement in the post-peak episode. Figure 6.13 shows the discourse flow of Philemon.

Aperture & Stage	Various Developing Episodes (A–B1)			Peak (B2)	Post-peak Dénouement	Closure & Finis
	Relationship between Paul and Philemon: χαρὰν γὰρ πολλὴν ἔσχον καὶ παράκλησιν ἐπὶ τῇ ἀγάπῃ σου (1:7)	Relationship between Paul and Philemon: διὰ τὴν ἀγάπην μᾶλλον παρακαλῶ (1:9)		Relationship between Paul & Philemon + Paul's request to Philemon: εἰ οὖν με ἔχεις κοινωνόν, προσλαβοῦ αὐτὸν ὡς ἐμέ (1:17)	Paul's request to Philemon: Πεποιθὼς τῇ ὑπακοῇ σου ἔγραψά σοι (1:21)	
			Paul 's plea to Philemon: Ὀνήσιμον... ὃν ἀνέπεμψά σοι... ὃν ἐγὼ ἐβουλόμην πρὸς ἐμαυτὸν κατέχειν (1:10–13, excerpt)	Grammatical Devices: Influx of imperatives in 1:17–20 (3/4)# Two adjacent first class conditional sentences Influx of first person singular pronoun i n 1:17–20 (8/17)# Emphatic expressions: ἐγὼ Παῦλος (1:19a) ἐγὼ ἀποτίσω (1:19b)		Benediction: Ἡ χάρις... μετὰ τοῦ πνεύματος ὑμῶν(1:25)
χάρις ὑμῖν (1:3)	Communal reference: πάντας τοὺς ἁγίους (1:5) τῶν ἁγίων (1:7)					Communal reference: τῶν προσευχῶν ὑμῶν χαρισθήσομαι ὑμῖν (1:22)
1:1–3	1:4–7	1:8–14		1:15–20	1:21	1:22–25

Key: ——▶: Development of prominent theme; ◀·······▶ :Inclusio;
#: Occurrences/total occurrence in the letter

Figure 6.13. The flow of discourse of Philemon.

6.2.2 Textual analysis of the grace benediction

6.2.2.1 Form and function

Paul always ends his epistles with a "grace benediction,"[73] using the phrase ἡ χάρις τοῦ κυρίου (the grace of the Lord). This phrase is followed by different variants: μεθ' ὑμῶν (with you) in Rom 16:20; 1 Cor 16:23; 1 Thess 5:28; μετὰ πάντων ὑμῶν (with all of you) in 2 Cor 13:13; and μετὰ τοῦ πνεύματος ὑμῶν (with your spirit) in Gal 6:18; Phil 4:23; Phlm 1:25.[74] The form of this grace benediction has two different explanations of its origin. First, Jewett argues that all the benedictions in the NT are derived from a single formula, which is a free variation of the basic Hebraic form of the Aaronic Blessing (Num 6:24–26) (Jewett 1969:30–31). Since the form of the grace benediction is absent in contemporary Greek literature, Jewett contends that it must be derived from the OT. Mullins holds a similar view, and argues that the NT benedictions, including Paul's, follow a basic form that is derived from several texts in the LXX, including 2 Kgs 24:23; Ruth 2:4; and Num 6:24 (Mullins 1977:61–63). For Mullins (1977:61), these passages consist of three basic elements—wish, divine source, and recipient.

On the other hand, Stirewalt, White, and Weima adopt the second explanation. Stirewalt (2003:51) and White (1983:438) compare the Pauline epistles with ancient Greek official letters, and argue that the farewell section in those letters is replaced by a benediction in Pauline epistles.[75] Weima (1994:86–87) similarly contends that Paul uses the "health wishes" in the standard closing formula of contemporary Greco-Roman letters as a template to create a unique grace benediction that is absent in contemporary letters.

Neither explanation should be regarded as mutually exclusive, since they can be combined to explain the form of Paul's grace benediction. Whilst adopting the Greco-Roman letter-closings to address a community with a partial Gentile audience, Paul uses the basic elements in the Hebraic Blessing to compose his grace benediction with three variations: μεθ' ὑμῶν (with you); μετὰ πάντων ὑμῶν (with all of you); and μετὰ τοῦ πνεύματος ὑμῶν (with your spirit).[76]

---

[73] I adopt this term from Weima (1994:78).

[74] The benedictions in Paul's disputed letters follow a similar pattern: ἡ χάρις (the grace) is employed with μετὰ πάντων ὑμῶν (with all of you) in 2 Thessalonians and Titus; μεθ' ὑμῶν (with you) in 1 and 2 Timothy; or μετὰ πάντων τῶν ἀγαπώντων (with all the ones who love) in Ephesians. None of the disputed letters uses the phrase μετὰ τοῦ πνεύματος ὑμῶν (with your spirit). In other words, anthropological terms are absent in all the benedictions in the disputed letters.

[75] White details his analysis in another study (White 1972).

[76] Regardless of the possibility of this theory, Roetzel (2009:70) argues that the grace benediction is the most stable element in the Pauline letter-closings, with only minor variations.

As for the function, there are two contrastive views. First, the benediction is simply a formula that is alienated from the letter body, as Champion (1934:25) claims, it can easily be separated from its wider context, since it may not even have originated with Paul and could just be comprised of some well-known phrases circulated among Christians. Conversely, some scholars argue that there is a connection between a benediction and the letter content. Jewett (1969:24–25, 34) contends that the NT benedictions, including the Pauline benedictions, aim to summarise the arguments presented in the main body of a letter.[77] By examining the usage of εἰρήνη (peace) in the benedictions of 1 Thessalonians and Galatians, Weima (1995:177–197) explains how the concept of peace is central to the purpose of these two epistles.

According to Bahr (1968:27–41), an ancient author would usually employ a scribe to write the letter body, but the author would write the last closing remarks to signify his or her signature, which Bahr calls subscription. If Bahr is correct, then the closing remarks of all the Pauline epistles, including the benedictions, essentially reflect what Paul desires to convey. Based on the findings of Bahr and White, we can assume that the variant form, μετὰ τοῦ πνεύματος ὑμῶν (with your spirit), in the grace benedictions of Galatians, Philippians, and Philemon, is not random but rather is closely related to the letters' content as Paul deliberately chooses to depart from the usual formula: μεθ᾽ ὑμῶν (with you).

Given the close connection between the letter content and the benediction, discourse analysis is an effective method to ascertain the meaning of πνεῦμα (spirit) in the grace benediction. In the following sections, we initially review the explanations of πνεῦμα (spirit) in previous scholarship, then investigate its abnormal singular construct, and finally apply the previous findings of discourse structure to ascertain the meaning of πνεῦμα (spirit) in Gal 6:18, Phil 4:23, and Phlm 1:25. I would like to show that πνεῦμα (spirit) carries a social and corporate connotation by indicating the connection between the chosen variant form and the core message of each letter.

6.2.2.2 Explanations of πνεῦμα in previous scholarship

The most problematic element in the grace benediction is arguably the definite singular genitive noun τοῦ πνεύματος (the spirit). In previous scholarship, there are three major interpretations of the meaning of πνεῦμα (spirit): (1) it denotes the Holy Spirit; (2) it carries an ontological sense, describing a human spirit; (3) the phrase μετὰ τοῦ πνεύματος ὑμῶν (with your spirit) is considered as synonymous with μεθ᾽ ὑμῶν (with you).[78] Some scholars

---

[77] However, Jewett does not investigate this benedictory phrase and its variant in his study.

[78] From this point onwards, the English translations for the following phrases (partial or whole) are not provided in this chapter: πνεῦμα (spirit); μετὰ τοῦ

adopt one interpretation; others hold a combination of different interpretations. However, some scholars simply ignore or provide little analytical comment of the grace benediction.[79]

According to the first explanation, πνεῦμα is treated as a normal singular noun, denoting the Holy Spirit. Jewett is a proponent of this view.[80] In interpreting πνεῦμα in Gal 6:18 and Phil 4:23, he argues that the reference of πνεῦμα "is clearly being made to the single divine spirit" (Jewett 1971:184). For Jewett, there is no such distinction between the divine spirit and the human spirit in Paul's work, since πνεῦμα means "the apportionment of the divine spirit given to each Christian" (Jewett 1971:197).[81] This view does not receive wide support in scholarship. Fee argues that it is a futile attempt to link the πνεῦμα in Gal 6:18 to the Holy Spirit as Jewett's assumption is not as "clear" as he states.[82] I also repudiate this explanation. If the singular πνεῦμα is a normal singular noun, denoting the Holy Spirit, it would be theologically absurd to interpret that Paul wishes Christ's grace to be in company with the Holy Spirit.

The second explanation is a common view. Πνεῦμα connotes the human spirit,[83] denoting: the "anthropological πνεῦμα" (Schweizer 1968:435),[84] depicting the psychical functions of humans; "inner personality" (Hendriksen 1968:249), functioning as a contact point between

πνεύματος ὑμῶν (with your spirit); μετὰ πάντων ὑμῶν (with all of you); μεθ᾽ ὑμῶν (with you).

[79] For example, some commentators either ignore or mention little about the grace benediction in Phil 4:23 (Synge 1951:48; Johnstone 1977:477–478; Cousar 2009:90–91).

[80] Reumann also shares Jewett's view. In commenting the πνεῦμα in Phil 4:23, Reumann (2008:732) defines the term as God's Spirit that is apportioned to one and all.

[81] Bauer (1979:675) also argues that in some contemporary Greek literature, πνεῦμα connotes a divine spirit in the actual soul: τὸ πνεῦμα τῇ ψυχῇ (the spirit in the soul).

[82] Referring to the singular use of πνεῦμα, Fee (1994:469) argues the reference is clearly being made to the single divine spirit. Apparently, Fee responds to Jewett's word "clearly."

[83] A number of scholars hold this view (Betz 1979:325; Bockmuehl 1998:271; Collange 1979:155; Dunn 1996:349; Ellicott 1867:140; Fee 1995:461; Fung 1988:315; Hansen 2009:332; Hawthorne 1983:215–216; Matera 1992:227; Moo 2008:442; Muller 1955:211; Schweizer 1968:435). Some of these scholars hold a combination of several views. For example, Fung (1988:315) argues that the πνεῦμα in Gal 6:18 denotes the human spirit, referring to God conscious aspect of a human. However, Fung also supports the view in which μετὰ τοῦ πνεύματος ὑμῶν and μεθ᾽ ὑμῶν are synonymous.

[84] Schweizer considers that πνεῦμα carries the same meaning in Phil 4:23, Phlm 1:25, and Gal 6:18. Whilst suggesting an ontological connotation of πνεῦμα, Schweizer also emphasizes the synonymy between μετὰ τοῦ πνεύματος ὑμῶν and μεθ᾽ ὑμῶν.

humans and God; the individual human spirits of the readers (Dunn 1996:349); or the "whole personality" (Collange 1979:155), emphasising its mental and spiritual aspects. Amongst the scholars who advocate this explanation, some also argue that the singular πνεῦμα is a distributive singular noun, pointing to each spirit of the reader.[85] However, most of these interpreters provide very little evidence of how this kind of ontological connotation is derived from the text.[86] The most problematic issue of all, they, with only a few exceptions,[87] usually analyse the benediction by singling it out the context of an epistle, as if the benediction is a separate piece of work that is totally disconnected from the rest of the letter. As previously argued, a benediction is closely associated with the letter content. As such, I also repudiate this explanation. The problem of this explanation can be demonstrated by the following example. In Galatians, the concept of the human spirit is nowhere found in Galatians. The core message of the epistle is totally unrelated to the discussion of the human spirit. Thus, the emergence of πνεῦμα as the human spirit in Gal 6:18 is incoherent with the entire epistle.[88]

The third explanation is that the phrase μετὰ τοῦ πνεύματος ὑμῶν is synonymous with the phrase μεθ' ὑμῶν. This view can be traced back to an early Church Father in the fourth century AD, John Chrysostom,[89] who argues that Paul deliberately uses μετὰ τοῦ πνεύματος ὑμῶν instead of μεθ' ὑμῶν for the purpose of redirecting the Galatians away from "carnal things" that sprung from their "judaizing error."[90] The interpretation of Chrysostom indicates that the benediction is of two natures: both a benediction and an

---

[85] Bockmuehl (1998:271), Fee (1995:461), Hansen (2009:332), and Hawthorne (1983:215–216) define the πνεῦμα in Phil 4:23 as a distributive singular. For instance, Bockmuehl asserts that the benediction should be interpreted as follows: "God's grace to be with the people's individual human spirits as united in Christ's fellowship."

[86] For instance, Betz (1979:325) notes that πνεῦμα throughout Galatians denotes the Holy Spirit. Without providing further explanation, he then argues that only the πνεῦμα in 6:18 connotes the human spirit.

[87] In interpreting the πνεῦμα in Gal 6:18, Dunn (1993:347) argues that the term denotes the human spirit that is bonded with the Holy Spirit, a bonding that elucidates the new identity of the Christian community that should not be defined by ethnicity. His interpretation seems to take the context of the epistle into consideration.

[88] A detailed discussion of πνεῦμα in Gal 6:18 will later be presented in this chapter.

[89] I do not suggest that this view was originated by John Chrysostom. His argument only serves as an example to illustrate how early the discussion of μετὰ τοῦ πνεύματος ὑμῶν was. Chrysostom's view is mentioned by scholars in the last two centuries, including Schlier (1962:285) and Lightfoot (1902:226).

[90] Chrysostom (1889:13.47–48) subtly points out the synonymous nature of μετὰ τοῦ πνεύματος ὑμῶν and μεθ' ὑμῶν, although his focus is to highlight the connection between the word πνεῦμα and the issues faced by the Galatians. This subtle allusion has probably inspired many contemporary commentators.

exhortation. Centuries later, some scholars adopt this explanation, suggesting that μετὰ τοῦ πνεύματος ὑμῶν is simply an abbreviation of μεθ' ὑμῶν or μετὰ πάντων ὑμῶν.[91] I argue that the synonymy suggested by Chrysostom is sound. Since the phrase ἡ χάρις τοῦ κυρίου (the grace of the Lord) is followed by μεθ' ὑμῶν, μετὰ πάντων ὑμῶν, or μετὰ τοῦ πνεύματος ὑμῶν, it is logical to consider μετὰ τοῦ πνεύματος ὑμῶν as synonymous with μεθ' ὑμῶν. In addition, despite his problematic conclusion (the "judaizing error"), Chrysostom's attempt of connecting the benediction with the letter content is admirable. The meaning of the variant form, μετὰ πάντων ὑμῶν, should be ascertained by referring to the letter content, an approach that I adopt. However, this explanation does not account for the abnormal singular construct.

Although there is an attempt to define πνεῦμα in the grace benediction, most scholars fail to assert their view by providing a clear and persuasive argument. Furthermore, there is a common failure in explaining the singular πνεῦμα in the abnormal singular construct. Many scholars ignore this abnormal construction. For those who attempt to address it, the singular form is simply interpreted as the distributive singular.[92] As previously argued, it must not be assumed that the distributive singular always explains the abnormal singular construct in the Pauline epistles. Fee sharply points out that the attempt by scholarship to explain this abnormal singular construct in the grace benediction "has tended to draw blanks" (Fee 1994:469).[93] Weima (1995:180–182) provides a good reason for this failure

---

[91] Bruce (1982b:277), Burton (1921:362), and McDonald (1973:157) adopt this view in their comments of Gal 6:18. Burton further argues that the phrase denotes the spiritual fellowship among the Galatians. Likewise, Martin (1981:170), Lohse (1971:208), Bruce (1984:225), and Fee (1994:635) adopt this view in their comments on Phlm 1:25. However, most of them do not provide any detailed explanations. For example, Lohse does not explain why he holds this view. Martin simply quotes the work of Schweizer, arguing that τοῦ πνεύματος ὑμῶν is equivalent to ὑμεῖς (you).

[92] There is one notable observation. This peculiar grammatical construct is rarely mentioned in the commentaries of Gal 6:18 as very few scholars notice the singular form of πνεῦμα modified by the plural pronoun, ὑμῶν. Conversely, there is a sudden swarm of works interpreting the πνεῦμα in Phil 4:23 as the distributive singular. Regarding Phlm 1:25, the benediction does not interest some commentators, let alone the abnormal singular construct. For example, Muller (1955:193) does not include any analysis of the benediction in his work; and Vincent (1897:192–193) only briefly mentions the text. Lightfoot (1892:344) simply mentions that the benediction in Philemon is the same as in Galatians without any elaboration. Thompson (2005:227) regards ὑμῶν as referring to the church that congregates at Philemon's house. Nothing is mentioned regarding πνεῦμα. Williams (1907:191) simply argues that this benediction is a prayer.

[93] This is Fee's conclusion in commenting on the benediction in Gal 6:18.

by arguing that there is a common disinterest in the closing sections of the Pauline epistles.[94]

In summary, many scholars either ignore the connection between the grace benediction and the letter content, or overlook the peculiar abnormal singular construct. Some scholars do not provide a persuasive reason, and simply suggest that πνεῦμα denotes the Holy Spirit, the human spirit, or a hybrid formed by the combination of the Holy Spirit and the human spirit.

6.2.2.3 *The abnormal singular construct in the grace benediction*

To accurately ascertain the meaning of πνεῦμα in the grace benediction, it is crucial to explain the abnormal singular construct. In the grace benediction, the singular form of πνεῦμα is combined with the second person plural possessive pronoun ὑμῶν. This combination is not found in the NT except in the Pauline Epistles,[95] and only occurs four times in Paul's letters. Three out of the four occurrences appear as the identical benedictions in Gal 6:18, Phil 4:23, and Phlm 1:25.[96]

This study proposes that the variant form μετὰ τοῦ πνεύματος ὑμῶν is not a random insertion. It is a purposefully chosen alternative that is connected with the coherent message in the context of the relevant epistle. The singular πνεῦμα in the grace benediction denotes neither the human spirits (as the distributive singular) nor the Holy Spirit. Rather, the singular πνεῦμα is a normal singular noun, metaphorically employed to denote the corporate entity of a faith community. This explanation becomes evident when the discourse structure of each epistle is considered, whereas corporate entity or communal unity is a prominent theme in Galatians, Philippians, and Philemon. This explanation also accounts for the synonymous nature of μετὰ τοῦ πνεύματος ὑμῶν and μεθ᾽ ὑμῶν. Instead of using ὑμῶν, Paul uses the variant form with the singular πνεῦμα to highlight the corporate and communal unity.

Several scholars advocate this view, including Beare, Reed, Martin, Thurston and Ryan. Although Beare and Reed advocate this view, they do

---

[94] Some commentators do not provide any interpretation of μετὰ τοῦ πνεύματος ὑμῶν.

[95] In addition, the combination of the second person plural possessive pronoun and the plural form of πνεῦμα is entirely absent in the NT.

[96] The fourth occurrence is located near the end of 1 Cor 16:18, ἀνέπαυσαν γὰρ τὸ ἐμὸν πνεῦμα καὶ τὸ ὑμῶν (For they refreshed my spirit and yours)*. Πνεῦμα is connected to two possessive pronouns, ἐμὸν (mine), referring to Paul, and ὑμῶν, denoting the Corinthians. It is highly unlikely that the word denotes the Holy Spirit, since Paul portrays that his πνεῦμα and the πνεῦμα of the Corinthians are refreshed by Stephanas, Fortunatus and Achaicus (16:17). However, this clause is not the subject of this analysis, since it is not a benediction.

not explain the rationale behind it.[97] Thurston and Ryan support this view in their analysis of Phil 4:23. They first pinpoint the synonymous nature of μετὰ τοῦ πνεύματος ὑμῶν and μεθ' ὑμῶν, and then propose the communal connotation of πνεῦμα. They argue that the term denotes the community resembling an entire "person," echoing the emphasis of one-mindedness of the church in the epistle. Since they examine the wider textual context of the epistle and connect the benediction with another text in the letter body: ἑνὶ πνεύματι, μιᾷ ψυχῇ (in one spirit, in one soul), in 1:27, their argument is persuasive (Thurston and Ryan 2005:161). Martin (1989:171) similarly considers that πνεῦμα refers to the unity of the body of believers in which one spirit to be found, pointing to the entire person of the believers assembled as a congregation, as indicated by the singular use of the noun.[98]

6.2.3 The meaning of πνεῦμα in light of discourse analysis

As previously argued, defining πνεῦμα as the Holy Spirit (as a normal singular noun) or the human spirit (as a distributive singular noun) in the grace benediction is problematic. The meaning of πνεῦμα in Gal 6:18, Phil 4:23, and Phlm 1:25 must satisfy the following three criteria: to account for the abnormal singular construct, to be coherent with the discourse structure of the respective epistle; and to explain the reason behind adopting this particular variant form.

6.2.3.1 *Πνεῦμα in Gal 6:18 in light of discourse analysis*

Through our discourse analysis of Galatians, Ἡ χάρις τοῦ κυρίου ἡμῶν Ἰησοῦ Χριστοῦ μετὰ τοῦ πνεύματος ὑμῶν, ἀδελφοί ἀμήν (The grace of our Lord Jesus Christ be with your spirit, brothers. Amen) in 6:18 is connected with the entire epistle in the following ways.

First, ἀδελφοί indicates Paul's affection towards the Galatians, which is expressed through the lexical cohesion of ἀδελφοί throughout the epistle. The last occurrence of ἀδελφοί in 6:18 immediately follows the grace benediction. Hence, the benediction does not serve as a mere benediction. Paul employs the vocative to refer to the previous context, and reminds the Galatians of the relational bond between Paul and them, highlighting the Pauline gospel that they once received.

---

[97] For Beare (1959:158), the singular form of πνεῦμα in Phil 4:23 elucidates that the Philippians are all animated by the one spirit. However, he does not explain his argument. Reed (1997:306) defines πνεῦμα in 4:23 as the collective spirit of the Philippians. Likewise, he does not provide further elaboration. Of interest, although Moo (2008:442) interprets πνεῦμα in Phlm 1:25 as the human spirit, he does suggest that this grammatical construction reinforces the oneness in spirit of the congregation.

[98] However, this view is not popular in modern scholarship.

Second, as previously discussed, the thematic meaning of πνεῦμα points to the Galatian community under a new dispensation in which the community is incorporated in Christ. The singular πνεῦμα in the benediction highlights this corporate reference, since the term denotes the corporate entity of this community as a new single creation. This connotation is also expressed in the preceding context of the benediction. In 6:15, Paul reiterates the contrast between circumcision and new creation by providing a summative statement: οὔτε γὰρ περιτομή τί ἐστιν οὔτε ἀκροβυστία ἀλλὰ καινὴ κτίσις (For neither circumcision nor uncircumcision counts for anything; the only thing that matters is a new creation!)* Notably, the clause is almost identical to the summative statement in the climax: ἐν γὰρ Χριστῷ ᾿Ιησοῦ οὔτε περιτομή τι ἰσχύει οὔτε ἀκροβυστία ἀλλὰ πίστις δι᾿ ἀγάπης ἐνεργουμένη (For in Christ Jesus neither circumcision nor uncircumcision carries any weight—the only thing that matters is faith working through love)* in 5:6. The οὔτε...οὔτε (neither...nor) expression resembles a statement in 3:28: οὐκ ἔνι ᾿Ιουδαῖος οὐδὲ ῞Ελλην, οὐκ ἔνι δοῦλος οὐδὲ ἐλεύθερος, οὐκ ἔνι ἄρσεν καὶ θῆλυ· πάντες γὰρ ὑμεῖς εἷς ἐστε ἐν Χριστῷ ᾿Ιησοῦ (there is neither Jew nor Greek, there is neither slave nor free, there is neither male nor female–for all of you are one in Christ Jesus)*. In Christ, both the Jews and the Gentiles are one, a new creation. The Galatian community belongs to this new creation under a new dispensation. Following this important concept expressed in earlier passages (3:28; 5:6; 6:15), the grace benediction again highlights this concept using the singular πνεῦμα. Therefore, the plural ὑμῶν in the phrase μετὰ τοῦ πνεύματος ὑμῶν illustrates the members of the Galatian community, and the singular πνεῦμα represents the corporate entity, depicting the community in Christ as a single person, a new creation in a new dispensation. The term does not point to the Holy Spirit, nor does it denote the human spirit. In summary, not only is the variant form μετὰ τοῦ πνεύματος ὑμῶν synonymous with μεθ᾿ ὑμῶν, it also highlights the corporate entity of the Galatian community.[99]

6.2.3.2 *Πνεῦμα in Phlm 1:25 in light of discourse analysis*

Although the letter primarily addresses Philemon, the discourse coherence illustrates that the letter is of concern to two communities: the prison community and the Christian community gathered at Philemon's house. Onesimus is not a private matter between Paul and Philemon. Rather, Onesimus, who carries the letter with him, is about to shift from the prison community to Philemon's house church, and Onesimus now belongs to a part of the community that is ἐν Χριστῷ (in Christ, 1:20). Paul uses this

---

[99] Burton (1921:362) does not indicate that πνεῦμα in 6:18 carries a corporate dimension, but he does highlight the communal aspect of the term by interpreting it as spiritual fellowship.

subtle but logical emphasis of community to persuade Philemon who has the authority to treat Onesimus otherwise.

As such, the benediction χάρις...μετὰ τοῦ πνεύματος ὑμῶν (grace... with your spirit) is not a mere benediction. Rather, the singular πνεῦμα points to the corporate unity of a community in which both Philemon and Onesimus are tied together ἐν Χριστῷ (in Christ). Paul metaphorically employs the singular πνεῦμα to denote the Christian community of which Onesimus is now a part. The term also highlights the communal relationship shared by Philemon and Onesimus (a new convert) under the grace of Christ. Had Paul employed μεθ' ὑμῶν, the subtle message would not have been as effective as μετὰ τοῦ πνεύματος ὑμῶν.

6.2.3.3 *Πνεῦμα in Phil 4:23 in light of discourse analysis*

From the discourse analysis presented in chapter 4, the coherent theme displayed in Philippians focuses on the corporate unity and communal relationship (among the Philippians, and between Paul and the Philippians). The analysis of the anthropological terms shows that the corporate and social aspect is illustrated by the use of various anthropological terms: καρδία (heart); ψυχή (soul), including σύμψυχοι (fellow-souled) and ἰσόψυχον (same-souled); πνεῦμα (spirit); and σῶμα (body). Although each of the anthropological terms carries a specific meaning in its sentence, their overall occurrences share a common thematic meaning. This is indicated by the coherent pattern displayed by the following expression: διὰ τὸ ἔχειν με ἐν τῇ καρδίᾳ ὑμᾶς (because I have you in my heart), in 1:7b; στήκετε ἐν ἑνὶ πνεύματι (stand in one spirit), in 1:27; μιᾷ ψυχῇ συναθλοῦντες (striving together in one soul), in 1:27; κοινωνία πνεύματος (spiritual fellowship), in 2:1; ἰσόψυχον (like-minded, or literally, same-souled) in 2:20; ἤγγισεν παραβολευσάμενος τῇ ψυχῇ (risking in the soul), in 2:30; τὸ σῶμα τῆς ταπεινώσεως ἡμῶν (our humble body), in 3:21; σύμμορφον τῷ σώματι τῆς δόξης αὐτοῦ (likeness of his glorious body), in 3:21; and τὰς καρδίας ὑμῶν (your hearts), in 4:7. The common thematic meaning points to the corporate unity and communal relationship of the Philippians.

In terms of πνεῦμα in Philippians, there are three occurrences (1:27; 2:1; 4:23). The following summarises the key findings presented in chapter 4. In 1:27, the terms πνεῦμα and ψυχή (soul) denote the Christian community, and do not connote the human soul and the human spirit with an ontological reference. Rather, they carry a metaphorical sense, and are parallel in meaning. The adjacent clauses, στήκετε ἐν ἑνὶ πνεύματι, μιᾷ ψυχῇ συναθλοῦντες, mean "stand unitedly (as if one corporate being) by fighting unitedly (as if one corporate being)." Regarding 2:1, this book has demonstrated that the anarthrous genitive term πνεύματος in κοινωνία πνεύματος does not denote the Holy Spirit. Rather, the phrase means "spiritual fellowship."

From the findings of the discourse flow, the coherent theme is corporate unity. The Philippian community is metaphorically portrayed as a single corporate being, being depicted as having a πνεῦμα or a ψυχή (soul), and having a mind with the capacity τὸ αὐτὸ φρονεῖν (to think the same). Paul regards the members of this corporate being as Paul's συνεργοί (co-workers) and συγκοινωνοί (partakers). As being his σύμψυχοι (fellow-souled), Paul calls this community σύζυγε (fellow worker); and he urges its members with this exhortation: συγχαίρετέ (rejoice together). Furthermore, Paul considers himself part of this community as indicated by the usage of words with a συν- prefix, a prefix indicating "together with," highlighting the partnership between Paul and the community.

Since the benediction is part of the epistle, the departure from the variant form μεθ' ὑμῶν is not random. Based on the findings summarised above, the phrase μετὰ τοῦ πνεύματος ὑμῶν is closely connected to the entire epistle. Πνεῦμα in the grace benediction does not denote the Holy Spirit, nor does it point to the human spirit as a distributive singular. The term echoes ἐνὶ πνεύματι (in one spirit) in 1:27 and κοινωνία πνεύματος (spiritual fellowship) in 2:1, signifying a corporate entity. In other words the corporate unity is reiterated in μετὰ τοῦ πνεύματος ὑμῶν—the singular πνεῦμα signifies a united community, a corporate entity, and the plural ὑμῶν indicates different members it.

6.3 Conclusion

In this chapter I have shown the corporate and relational dimensions of the anthropological terms within the tripartite formula (1 Thess 5:23) and the grace benediction (Gal 6:18; Phlm 1:25; Phil 4:23) by examining the discourse structure, analysing the key terms in various semantic units, exploring the sociolinguistic aspect, and identifying the flow of discourse. In 1 Thess 5:23, the anthropological terms in the tripartite formula denote the corporate entity of the Thessalonian community, highlighting "wholeness" and "oneness." In Gal 6:18, Phlm 1:25, and Phil 4:23, πνεῦμα is used in a metaphorical sense to indicate a social and corporate reference.

Further research is required to explore the use of other variant forms, μεθ' ὑμῶν and μετὰ πάντων ὑμῶν, in other Pauline benedictions. As previously discussed, μεθ' ὑμῶν is used in Rom 16:20, 1 Cor 16:23, 1 Thess 5:28, and μετὰ πάντων ὑμῶν is used in 2 Cor 12:14. Based on a brief analysis of these Pauline texts, the argument of this study is as follows. Whilst Paul addresses various communities in Romans, particularly the Gentiles, communal unity is not his primary concern. Therefore, using μετὰ τοῦ πνεύματος ὑμῶν to illustrate unity would be unnecessary. Likewise, community schism is not a concern of 1 Thessalonians. Instead, the focus is the corporate entity, in contrast with the non-believers. The tripartite formula in the benediction illustrates this aspect, and Paul resorts to μεθ' ὑμῶν to conclude the epistle. Similarly, 2 Corinthians focuses on the relationship between Paul and the Corinthians. There is no need for Paul to emphasise unity among the Corinthians by employing μετὰ τοῦ πνεύματος ὑμῶν. However, in 1 Corinthians, corporate unity is the focus and is vividly highlighted throughout the whole epistle by the occurrences of σῶμα. Whilst it would seem more appropriate for Paul to use μετὰ τοῦ πνεύματος ὑμῶν, σῶμα instead of πνεῦμα is the key term used by Paul. It is possible that Paul avoids using πνεῦμα in the benediction. Nevertheless, I have not specifically addressed the above arguments, and they are only conjectures. Further research is needed to verify my speculative arguments.

7

Conclusion

7.1 The purpose of this book

A solid understanding of Paul's anthropology inevitably requires an investigation of the apostle's key anthropological terms. Such analysis provides an important resource for reflecting on and understanding Christian theological anthropology. In this book we have revisited and investigated Paul's anthropological terms with particular focus on their corporate, relational, and thus ecclesiological connotations. We have focused on four key terms, πνεῦμα (spirit),[1] ψυχή (soul), σῶμα (body), and καρδία (heart), as they occur in seven epistles that are commonly considered Paul's authentic work: Romans, 1 Corinthians, 2 Corinthians, Galatians, Philippians, 1 Thessalonians, and Philemon.

7.2 The findings of our analyses

As initially raised in chapter 1, we have explored the following questions. First, what are the social and corporate connotations of Paul's anthropological terms, and what are the implications of this for understanding of Paul's anthropology? Second, how are the key anthropological terms understood given Paul's wider thought about the person of Christ and the identity of the church? Based on the findings of our analyses, the responses are as

---

[1] To be more specific, it is πνεῦμα τοῦ ἀνθρώπου (spirit of a human person).

follows. First, Paul's anthropological terms are principally concerned with community, and person to person relationship in community. Relationship and unity, both between Paul and the community, and among the community, is highlighted. As such, Paul does not generally use anthropological terms to identify and denote the ontology of a human person. Second, the nature of communal identity is grounded on Christ and his work. Therefore, the corporate and social connotations of the key anthropological terms are intertwined with Paul's Christological and ecclesiological vision. The details of our findings are as follows.

In chapter 2, we have reviewed scholarship examining Paul's anthropological terms over the last 50 years. Our review has shown that previous work failed to fully attend to the key comments of James Barr, in *The Semantics of Biblical Language*, which prioritised the textual context of a word, including its place in the whole discourse. Thus, I have proposed a method that seriously attends to the synchronic dimension of semantic study. We have identified basic principles of discourse analysis, and then employed them to examine Paul's anthropological terms. We have devised four research stages: a single anthropological term within a single discourse, multiple anthropological terms within a single discourse, a single anthropological term within multiple discourses, and multiple anthropological terms within multiple discourses. Furthermore, to provide a synchronic linguistic context for this research, we have given an overview of the semantic range of the key terms in the first century Koine Greek literature.

In chapter 3, we have conducted Stage I—a single anthropological term within a single discourse: the corporate dimension of σῶμα in 1 Corinthians. We have examined the discourse structure, the overall occurrences of clustered σῶμα in various semantic units in 1 Corinthians, and the sociolinguistic aspect. Our analysis has concluded that a corporate and communal connotation is present in the meaning of σῶμα. In particular, the phrase ἓν σῶμα (one body) is used by Paul to remind the Corinthians of their ecclesiological identity, as a single community because of Christ. In the epistle, this community is called τὸ σῶμα τοῦ Χριστοῦ (the body of Christ). The use of the anthropological term σῶμα intertwines with the apostle's Christology and ecclesiology. However, Paul's anthropology cannot be delineated from his Christology and ecclesiology. This corporate and communal connotation, imbued in the phrases τὸ σῶμα τοῦ Χριστοῦ and ἓν σῶμα (one body), is widely accepted in Pauline scholarship. As such, this examination demonstrated the value of discourse analysis by verifying the connotation of σῶμα in 1 Corinthians.

In chapter 4, we have conducted Stage II—multiple anthropological terms within one discourse: the key anthropological terms in Philippians. We have analysed the terms ψυχή (soul), πνεῦμα (spirit), καρδία (heart), and σῶμα (body). We have investigated the discourse structure, the anthropological terms in various semantic units, the sociolinguistic aspect, and the flow of discourse. Our examination has concluded that a common thematic meaning is connoted by ψυχή (soul), πνεῦμα (spirit), καρδία (heart), and σῶμα (body). Many occurrences of the key terms, combined with εἷς (one, masculine gender), μία (one, feminine gender), and the prepositional prefix συν- prefix (a prefix indicating together with), highlight the communal relationship and corporate unity among the Philippians, and the friendship between Paul and the Philippians. In particular, Paul responds to the conflict among the Philippians, and the relational crisis between himself and the Philippians. He exhorts the Philippians by employing the anthropological terms in phrases, such as ἐνὶ πνεύματι, μιᾷ ψυχῇ (in one spirit, 1:27) and μετὰ τοῦ πνεύματος ὑμῶν (with your spirit, 4:23). The key terms are employed metaphorically to depict the ecclesial community. This community is grounded on the gospel of Christ, which is evident in the clauses preceding and following 1:27: ἀξίως τοῦ εὐαγγελίου τοῦ Χριστοῦ πολιτεύεσθε (conduct yourselves worthy of the gospel of Christ) and συναθλοῦντες τῇ πίστει τοῦ εὐαγγελίου (work together in the faith of the gospel). Our examination of the key anthropological terms in Philippians has revealed a profound correlation between three aspects of Paul's theology: his anthropology, his ecclesiology, and his Christology.

In chapter 5, we have conducted Stage III—a single anthropological term within multiple discourses: καρδία (heart) in Romans, 2 Corinthians, Philippians, and 1 Thessalonians. Given that 71% of occurrences of καρδία are found in Romans and 2 Cor 1–9, our analysis has focused on these discourses. Our examination has concluded that the thematic meaning of καρδία, in both epistles, carries communal and corporate connotations. In Romans, καρδία occurs in clustered patterns that are associated with different communities in Rome: Gentiles, Jews, and Christians. The term points to the corporate response of these communities to God and his salvation in Christ. In 2 Cor 1–9, καρδία depicts the identity of the Corinthian community, and also the relationship between Paul and the Corinthians. In particular, the term elucidates the community under, a new dispensation, a new covenant in which Paul is chosen as the minister of Christ. The καρδία-πρόσωπον (heart-face) antithesis, and the juxtaposition of καρδία and λίθος (stone) are employed to contrast the old covenant and the new covenant, the gospel. Therefore, as well as denoting the community under a new dispensation, καρδία also highlights that the community is under the ministry of Christ through the apostle. The interconnection of Paul's anthropology, Christology, and ecclesiology is prominent through the use of καρδία.

In chapter 6, we have conducted Stage IV—multiple anthropological terms within multiple discourses: a focus on Pauline benedictions. The terms analysed were πνεῦμα (spirit), σῶμα (body), and ψυχή (soul) in the benediction in 1 Thessalonians, and πνεῦμα in the benedictions in Galatians, Philippians, and Philemon. This investigation concluded that corporate and relational connotations are present in the anthropological terms in the tripartite formula (1 Thess 5:23) and the grace benediction (Gal 6:18; Phlm 1:25; Phil 4:23). The terms, πνεῦμα, σῶμα, and ψυχή are used metaphorically to portray the corporate entity of a faith community. In 1 Thess 5:23, the tripartite formula highlights the wholeness of the faith community. However, this wholeness hinges upon the truth in the following formula: ἐν τῇ παρουσίᾳ τοῦ κυρίου ἡμῶν Ἰησοῦ Χριστοῦ (in the coming of our Lord Jesus Christ). The interconnection of Paul's anthropology, Christology, and ecclesiology is clearly marked by these chosen anthropological terms. In the grace benediction (Gal 6:18; Phlm 1:25; Phil 4:23), the use of πνεῦμα highlights corporate unity, whereby the phrase μετὰ τοῦ πνεύματος ὑμῶν (with your spirit) conveys the oneness of the Christian community. This phrase is also attached to the preceding noun clause: χάρις τοῦ κυρίου (grace of the Lord). Thus, there is an undeniable correlation between Paul's anthropology, Christology, and ecclesiology.

7.3 The verification of the hypotheses

Our examination of Paul's anthropological terms in light of discourse analysis has verified that many occurrences of the terms have corporate and relational dimensions. Whilst not all occurrences have social and corporate connotations, many occurrences do, which indicates a coherent thematic meaning. In other words, not only do some occurrences have corporate and relational dimensions in their immediate context (sentential and paragraphic), some overall occurrences also have social and corporate connotations, which form a pattern within a discourse.

Therefore, through the use of key anthropological terms Paul encourages the Christian community to be united as a single entity because of Christ. This communal entity operates under the new dispensation of Christ's grace. Although facing various challenges, this communal entity should stand together for the sake of the gospel of Christ, wait for the eschaton in which God will educe the perfection and wholeness of the community through Christ, and share the same mind with Paul who is an apostle of Christ.

7.4 The implications of the findings

Based on our findings, a pragmatic implication is that Christian practice should not be understood as an individualistic endeavour. Rather, it must be accomplished in and through community. Most importantly, we conclude that the three aspects of Paul's theology, his anthropology, ecclesiology, and Christology, are inseparable.

Although we have focussed on Paul's anthropology, an ancient theology, our findings could provide some theological insights for the contemporary

Christian church as it considers and addresses some controversial issues. As such, how might a better understanding of Paul's anthropological terms assist Christian reflection on the nature of the human person? Our modern church is currently examining and debating the topic of bioethics, and needs to articulate a coherent theology regarding the nature of the human person.[2] For example, issues of human cloning and stem cell research involve a discussion about the human person.[3] Any theological account will inevitably draw on biblical resources, especially those examining Paul's anthropology, Paul's anthropological terms in particular. Our study has shown that Paul does not use the terms to provide a precise description of the ontology of a human person. Rather, Paul uses the anthropological terms to elucidate his ecclesiology, which is a theme that is inseparable from his Christology. Some theologians, in response to the issue of human cloning, debate whether a cloned human person has a "soul" based on an analysis of ψυχή (soul) in the Pauline epistles.[4] However, given the findings in our study, this kind of analysis may be in vain. The identity of a cloned human person, in light of our findings, must take into account the significance of relationship. Karen Lebacqz articulates the various questions raised regarding the identity of a cloned human person, stating that the "secular way of putting the questions is to ask whether clones will have sufficient personality or distinctiveness or individuality to qualify as fully human … [the] theological way… is to ask whether clones will have that elusive quality that we know as 'soul'" (Lebacqz 1997:1). Lebacqz (1997:4) argues that the notion of soul is not an individual possession but a statement about relationship. Soul has to do with our standing before God. She concludes by highlighting the communal

---

[2] Gene Green (2007:3–21) provides an overview of the relationship between human identity in biblical theology and contemporary challenges.

[3] Some of the work discussing these issues includes the following: Chan, Mark L. Y., and Roland Chia, eds. 2003. *Beyond Determinism and Reductionism: Genetic Science and the Person.* Hindmarsh, South Australia: ATF Press; Cole-Turner, Ronald. 1993. *The New Genesis: Theology and the Genetic Revolution.* Louisville, KY: John Knox; Waters, Brent, and Ronald Cole-Turner, eds. 2003. *God and the Embryo: Religious Voices on Stem Cells and Cloning.* Washington DC: Georgetown University Press; Maienschein, Jane. 2003. *Whose View of Life? Embryos Cloning and Stem Cells.* Cambridge, MA: Harvard University Press; Peters, Ted. 2003. *Science, Theology, and Ethics.* Aldershot, Hants: Ashgate; Peters, Ted, Karen Lebacqz, and Gaymon Bennett. 2008. *Sacred Cell? Why Christians Should Support Stem Cell Research.* Lanham, MD: Rowman & Littlefield; Carnley, Peter. 2004. *Reflections in Glass.* Sydney: HarperCollins; Ford, Norman M., and Michael Herbert. 2003. *Stem Cells: Science, Medicine, Law and Ethics.* Melbourne: St Paul's; Snow, Nancy E., ed. 2003. *Stem Cell Research: New Frontiers in Science and Ethics.* Notre Dame, IN: University of Notre Dame Press; Rae, Scott B., and Paul M. Cox. 1999. *Bioethics: A Christian Approach in Pluralistic Age.* Grand Rapids, MI: Eerdmans.

[4] The analysis of Peters (2003:165–168) aims to respond to the question "Can souls be Xeroxed?" Some theologians also wrestle with this question (Rae and Cox 1999:114).

aspect, stating that "the real question is not whether a clone will be unique, or whether it will have soul … [t]he question is why we would choose to do this in the human community" (ibid. 5).[5] Although Lebacqz's response does not draw on an analysis of Paul's anthropological terms, her attempt to articulate a theological anthropology and consider the question of human identity from the perspective of community and relationship with God is more appropriate than analysing whether Paul's anthropological term, ψυχή (soul), has any ontological connotation.

7.5 Areas for further research

Due to the limitations of this book, the following areas require further research. First, we have not examined every occurrence of σῶμα (body), ψυχή (soul), πνεῦμα (spirit), and καρδία (heart) in the Pauline epistles. Second, the following Pauline anthropological terms have not been investigated: σάρξ (flesh), νοῦς (mind), συνείδησις (conscience), and ἔσω ἄνθρωπος (inner person). Third, the disputed Pauline epistles have not been included: Ephesians, Colossians, 2 Thessalonians, 1 Timothy, 2 Timothy, and Titus. Fourth, a synchronic study should consider contemporary literature, including biblical and non-biblical literature. Although the usage of the key anthropological terms in non-biblical literature has been studied, further research on the usage of these terms in non-Pauline biblical literature should also be conducted. Fifth, the contemporary Jewish culture and Paul's cultural context, in particular Stoicism, are not adequately addressed in this book. Sixth, we have not paid much attention to the diachronic approach. Nonetheless, further study should focus on intertextuality, a diachronic method, by examining the allusion and echo of the Hebrew Scripture and the Septuagint in Paul's letters. Seventh, this book has not referred to other modern yet important theories, including semantic field theory, metaphor theory, cognitive linguistics, and postmodern hermeneutics. In conclusion, these areas should be addressed in future research in order to elaborate and provide a more holistic understanding of Paul's anthropological terms.

---

[5] Peters (2003:169) also highlights the communal aspect of human identity in his discussion of human of cloning. He argues that our identities come from God's continuing grace and from our desire or lack of desire to live in close communion with God. Souls do not come in any final form with our DNA. Likewise, in the bioethical debate about stem cell research some theologians describe the notion of soul as "centered selves [which] are formed by and developed in spiritual relationship," with this relationship realised "in relationship to community and to God" (Peters, Labacqz, and Bennett 2008:207).

Appendix A

Nouns in 1 Corinthians

There are 1368 nouns in the letter. The following lists the nouns that occur more than once in 1 Corinthians. Σῶμα is the fourth most frequent noun, ranking only behind θεός, κύριος, and Χριστός. This demonstrates a very strong pattern of lexical cohesion.

θεός 106
κύριος 66
Χριστός 64
σῶμα 46
γυνή 41
πνεῦμα 40
ἀδελφός 39
ἀνήρ 32
ἄνθρωπος 31
Ἰησοῦς 26
ἐκκλησία 22
γλῶσσα 21
κόσμος 21
λόγος 17
σοφία σοφός 17
μέλος 16
δύναμις 15
ἀγάπη 14
δόξα 12
σάρξ 11
ἀπόστολος 10
γνῶσις 10
ἐξουσία 10
κεφαλή 10
χάρις 10
νόμος 9
αἰών 8
ἔργον 8
εὐαγγέλιον 8
θάνατος 8
Παῦλος 8
ποτήριον 8
συνείδησις 8
Ἀπολλῶς 7
ἄρτος 7
ἡμέρα 7
μέρος 7
νοῦς 7
πίστις 7
χάρισμα 7

βρῶμα 6
μυστήριον 6
ὄνομα 6
παρθένος 6
πατήρ 6
προφήτης 6
βασιλεία 5
δοῦλος 5
καρδία 5
μωρία 5
οἰκοδομή 5
ὀφθαλμός 5
πορνεία 5
προφητεία 5
ἄγγελος 4
αἷμα 4
ἁμαρτία 4
ἀνάστασις 4
ἀφθαρσία 4
δαιμόνιον 4
εἰδωλολάτρης 4
εἴδωλον 4
εἰρήνη 4
Ἕλλην 4
ζύμη 4
Κηφᾶς 4
μισθός 4
ναός 4
οἶκος 4
πόρνος 4
πούς 4
τιμή 4
φωνή 4
χείρ 4
Ἀδάμ 3
ἀνάγκη 3
ἀπαρχή 3
ἀποκάλυψις 3
ἀστήρ 3
γένος 3

γῆ 3
γνώμη 3
διαίρεσις 3
ἔθνος 3
εἰκών 3
ἐλπίς 3
θέλημα 3
θεμέλιος 3
θυσιαστήριον 3
ἴαμα 3
ἰδιώτης 3
καιρός 3
καύχημα 3
κήρυγμα 3
κοινωνία 3
κρίμα 3
νῖκος 3
πλεονέκτης 3
πρόσωπον 3
πῦρ 3
Στεφανᾶς 3
σχίσμα 3
τέκνον 3
τέλος 3
χρεία 3
ἀδελφή 2
ἀήρ 2
ἀθανασία 2
ἀκοή 2
ἀκροβυστία 2
ἀλήθεια 2
ἀνάθεμα 2
ἀνάμνησις 2
ἄρχων 2
ἀσθένεια 2
ἀτιμία 2
βοῦς 2
γάλα 2
γραφή 2
δεῖπνον 2

διακονία 2
διδάσκαλος 2
διδαχή 2
ἐνέργημα 2
ἐντολή 2
ἐντροπή 2
ἐπιστολή 2
ἐπιταγή 2
ἔρις 2
ἑρμηνεία 2
Ἔφεσος 2
ζωή 2
θάλασσα 2
κακία 2
κέντρον 2
κλῆσις 2
κοιλία 2
κοινωνός 2
κόπος 2
κριτήριον 2
λαός 2
λογεία 2
λοίδορος 2
Μακεδονία 2
μέθυσος 2
μιμητής 2
Μωϋσῆς 2
νεφέλη 2
ὁδός 2
οἰκία 2
οἰκονόμος 2
οὐρανός 2
οὖς 2
παρουσία 2
πειρασμός 2
πέτρα 2
ποίμνη 2
πόρνη 2
σάλπιγξ 2
σατανᾶς 2

σημεῖον 2
σταυρός 2
συνήθεια 2
Τιμόθεος 2
τόπος 2
τράπεζα 2
υἱός 2
φθορά 2
φρήν 2
φύραμα 2
χρόνος 2
ὥρα 2

Appendix B

Verbs in Philippians

There are 256 verbs in the letter; 212 of them only occur once. The following lists the verbs that occur more than once in Philippians. Among all the verbs, φρονέω and χαίρω are the third and the fourth most frequent verbs respectively. Apart from the common verbs, εἰμί and ἔχω, the occurrence of φρονέω and χαίρω surpasses 252 verbs in Philippians, demonstrating a very strong pattern of lexical cohesion.

εἰμί 17
ἔχω 10
φρονέω 10
χαίρω 9
γίνομαι 6
ἡγέομαι 6
οἶδα 6
πείθω 6
γινώσκω 5
πέμπω 5
περισσεύω 5
ἀκούω 4
λέγω 4
ὁράω 4
πληρόω 4
ἀσπάζομαι 3
βλέπω 3
διώκω 3
ἔρχομαι 3
καταλαμβάνω 3
ποιέω 3
ὑπερέχω 3
ἀσθενέω 2
γνωρίζω 2
ἐλπίζω 2
ἐνεργέω 2
ἐπιζητέω 2
ἐπιποθέω 2
εὑρίσκω 2
ζάω 2
καταγγέλλω 2
λαμβάνω 2
λογίζομαι 2
μανθάνω 2
μεριμνάω 2
παρακαλέω 2
περιπατέω 2

σκοπέω 2
στήκω 2
συγχαίρω 2
συναθλέω 2
ταπεινόω 2
ὑπάρχω 2
χαρίζομαι 2

Appendix C

Nouns and verbs in Romans

There are 1680 nouns in the letter. The following list shows the nouns that occur more than thrice in Romans. Ἁμαρτία and πίστις are the fourth and the sixth most frequent noun respectively, demonstrating two very strong patterns of lexical cohesion. Although the occurrence of Ἰσραήλ does not seem to be frequent, the word also demonstrates a pattern of lexical cohesion in that among all the proper names in the letter, including Ἀβραάμ, Ἕλλην, Ἠσαΐας, Ἰερουσαλήμ, and Μωϋσῆς, Ἰσραήλ is the most frequent name apart from Χριστός.

θεός 153	ὀργή 12	τέκνον 7	σωτηρία 5
νόμος 74	υἱός 12	ὑπακοή 7	τέλος 5
Χριστός 65	ἀκροβυστία 11	φύσις 7	φόβος 5
ἁμαρτία 48	ἡμέρα 11	Ἕλλην 6	χρηστότης 5
κύριος 43	Ἰσραήλ 11	καιρός 6	ἀπιστία 4
πίστις 40	εἰρήνη 10	κρίμα 6	διακονία 4
Ἰησοῦς 36	μέλος 10	νοῦς 6	διάκονος 4
δικαιοσύνη 34	Ἀβραάμ 9	στόμα 6	ἐκλογή 4
πνεῦμα 34	ἀγάπη 9	τιμή 6	θέλημα 4
ἔθνος 29	ἀνήρ 9	ὑπομονή 6	Ἰερουσαλήμ 4
ἄνθρωπος 27	εὐαγγέλιον 9	χάρισμα 6	καρπός 4
σάρξ 26	κόσμος 9	αἰών 5	κληρονόμος 4
χάρις 24	παράπτωμα 9	δικαίωμα 5	Μωϋσῆς 4
θάνατος 22	σπέρμα 9	δοῦλος 5	ὁμοίωμα 4
ἀδελφός 19	ἀλήθεια 8	ἐκκλησία 5	πλήρωμα 4
δόξα 16	δύναμις 8	ἐξουσία 5	πρόσκομμα 4
ἔργον 15	ἐπαγγελία 8	ἐπιθυμία 5	ῥῆμα 4
καρδία 15	λαός 8	Ἠσαΐας 5	σκάνδαλον 4
περιτομή 15	ἀδικία 7	θλῖψις 5	φρόνημα 4
ζωή 14	γραφή 7	κλάδος 5	ψυχή 4
πατήρ 14	ἐντολή 7	ὄνομα 5	
ἐλπίς 13	κτίσις 7	πλοῦτος 5	
σῶμα 13	λόγος 7	ῥίζα 5	

There are 1169 verbs in Romans. The following list shows the 15 verbs that have the highest occurrences. Δικαιόω is on this list. The word displays a very strong pattern of lexical cohesion when taking its meaning into consideration. All the verbs that occur more frequently than δικαιόω carry a general and "non-technical" meaning. However, δικαιόω is arguably the only verb that carries a specific theological connotation in Romans on this list.

εἰμί 113	ἔχω 25	γράφω 21	οἶδα 16
λέγω 48	ζάω 23	πιστεύω 21	δικαιόω 15
γίνομαι 35	ποιέω 23	λογίζομαι 19	θέλω 15
ἀποθνῄσκω 23	ἀσπάζομαι 21	κρίνω 18	

Appendix D

Nouns in 2 Corinthians 1–9

There are 629 nouns in 2 Cor 1–9. The following list shows the nouns that occur more than once in 2 Cor 1–9. Τίτος is among the most frequent nouns on the list. Furthermore, among all the proper names, including Μακεδονία, Μωϋσῆς, Ἀχαΐα, Ἰσραήλ, Κόρινθος, Μακεδών, Τιμόθεος, it is the most frequent name apart from Χριστός. The unusually frequent occurrence of Τίτος suggests a strong pattern of lexical cohesion.

θεός 63
Χριστός 30
κύριος 20
δόξα 19
χάρις 16
'Ιησοῦς 15
πνεῦμα 14
διακονία 11
καρδία 11
παράκλησις 11
ἀδελφός 9
θλῖψις 9
πρόσωπον 9
θάνατος 8
ἀγάπη 7
Τίτος 7
δικαιοσύνη 6
ἐκκλησία 6
ζωή 6
ἡμέρα 6
λόγος 6
λύπη 6
σάρξ 6
ἄνθρωπος 5
δύναμις 5
ἐπιστολή 5
εὐαγγέλιον 5
Μακεδονία 5
πίστις 5
σπουδή 5
σῶμα 5
φόβος 5
χαρά 5
ἀλήθεια 4

ἁπλότης 4
γνῶσις 4
εὐλογία 4
κάλυμμα 4
καύχησις 4
μέρος 4
πατήρ 4
προθυμία 4
σωτηρία 4
υἱός 4
ὑπερβολή 4
ἄνεσις 3
γράμμα 3
δοκιμή 3
εὐχαριστία 3
ζῆλος 3
καιρός 3
καύχημα 3
κοινωνία 3
κόσμος 3
Μωϋσῆς 3
νόημα 3
ὀσμή 3
πάθημα 3
πεποίθησις 3
συνείδησις 3
ὑστέρημα 3
αἰών 2
ἁμαρτία 2
ἀνάγκη 2
ἀπόστολος 2
ἀρραβών 2
Ἀχαΐα 2
δέησις 2

διαθήκη 2
διάκονος 2
εἰκών 2
εἰλικρίνεια 2
ἐλπίς 2
ἐπαγγελία 2
ἐπιπόθησις 2
θέλημα 2
ἰσότης 2
'Ισραήλ 2
κατάκρισις 2
καταλλαγή 2
κοινωνός 2
Κόρινθος 2
Μακεδών 2
μετάνοια 2
ναός 2
οἰκία 2
οὐρανός 2
παρουσία 2
παρρησία 2
περίσσευμα 2
πλάξ 2
πτωχεία 2
σκῆνος 2
σκότος 2
σπλάγχνον 2
σπόρος 2
τέλος 2
Τιμόθεος 2
ὑπομονή 2
φῶς 2
φωτισμός 2

Appendix E

Nouns in 1 Thessalonians

There are 317 nouns in 1 Thessalonians. The following list shows the nouns in the letter. The occurrence of ἀδελφός is strikingly frequent in that it is the third most frequent noun on the list, demonstrating a very strong pattern of lexical cohesion. Both ἐλπίς and παρουσία are also among the most frequent nouns on the list, demonstrating two additional strong patterns of lexical cohesion.

θεός 36
κύριος 24
ἀδελφός 19
Ἰησοῦς 16
Χριστός 10
λόγος 9
πίστις 8
εὐαγγέλιον 6
ἡμέρα 6
νύξ 6
ἀγάπη 5
ἄνθρωπος 5
πατήρ 5
πνεῦμα 5
ἐλπίς 4
παρουσία 4
χαρά 4
χρεία 4
ἁγιασμός 3
δόξα 3
εἰρήνη 3
θλῖψις 3
καρδία 3
κόπος 3
Μακεδονία 3
ὀργή 3
πρόσωπον 3
Τιμόθεος 3
υἱός 3
ἀκαθαρσία 2
Ἀχαΐα 2
ἔθνος 2
εἴσοδος 2
ἐκκλησία 2
ἐπιθυμία 2
ἔργον 2
θέλημα 2

κλέπτης 2
καιρός 2
μάρτυς 2
μιμητής 2
μνεία 2
οὐρανός 2
Παῦλος 2
σκότος 2
σωτηρία 2
τέκνον 2
χάρις 2
ψυχή 2
ἁγιωσύνη 1
ἀγών 1
ἀήρ 1
Ἀθῆναι 1
ἀκοή 1
ἁμαρτία 1
ἀνάγκη 1
ἀπάντησις 1
ἀπόστολος 1
ἀρχάγγελος 1
ἀσφάλεια 1
βάρος 1
βασιλεία 1
γαστήρ 1
δόλος 1
δύναμις 1
εἶδος 1
εἴδωλον 1
ἐκλογή 1
ἐπιστολή 1
εὐχαριστία 1
Θεσσαλονικεύς 1
θώραξ 1
Ἰουδαία 1
καύχησις 1

κέλευσμα 1
νεφέλη 1
κολακεία 1
μόχθος 1
ὁδός 1
ὄλεθρος 1
πάθος 1
παραγγελία 1
παράκλησις 1
περικεφαλαία 1
περιποίησις 1
πλάνη 1
πλεονεξία 1
πληροφορία 1
πορνεία 1
πρᾶγμα 1
προσευχή 1
πρόφασις 1
προφητεία 1
προφήτης 1
σάλπιγξ 1
σατανᾶς 1
Σιλουανός 1
σκεῦος 1
στέφανος 1
συμφυλέτης 1
σῶμα 1
τέλος 1
τιμή 1
τόπος 1
τροφός 1
τύπος 1
ὑπομονή 1
ὑστέρημα 1
φιλαδελφία 1
φίλημα 1
Φίλιπποι 1

φωνή 1
φῶς 1
ὥρα 1
χείρ 1
χρόνος 1
ὠδίν 1

Appendix F

Nouns and verbs in Galatians

There are 527 nouns in Galatians. The list shows the nouns that occur more than once; νόμος is the second most frequent noun, showing a very strong lexical cohesion. Both πνεῦμα and σάρξ are the fifth most frequent words, also showing strong lexical cohesion.

Χριστός 38	διαθήκη 3	εἰρήνη 3	ἡμέρα 2
νόμος 32	παιδίσκη 5	ἐκκλησία 3	Ἰερουσαλήμ 2
θεός 31	πατήρ 5	ἔτος 3	Ἰουδαϊσμός 2
πίστις 22	σπέρμα 5	Ἰάκωβος 3	λόγος 2
πνεῦμα 18	τέκνον 5	Ἰεροσόλυμα 3	μεσίτης 2
σάρξ 18	δικαιοσύνη 4	καιρός 3	μήτηρ 2
Ἰησοῦς 17	δοῦλος 4	κατάρα 3	ὄρος 2
ἄνθρωπος 14	ἐλευθερία 4	κληρονόμος 3	ὀφθαλμός 2
υἱός 13	Κηφᾶς 4	κόσμος 3	παιδαγωγός 2
ἀδελφός 11	ἀγάπη 3	πρόσωπον 3	Παῦλος 2
ἔθνος 10	ἄγγελος 3	σταυρός 3	Πέτρος 2
ἐπαγγελία 10	αἰών 3	Ἁγάρ 2	πραΰτης 2
Ἀβραάμ 9	ἀκροβυστία 3	ἀκοή 2	Σινά 2
ἔργον 8	ἀλήθεια 3	ἀνάθεμα 2	στοιχεῖον 2
εὐαγγέλιον 7	ἁμαρτία 3	ἀποκάλυψις 2	Τίτος 2
περιτομή 7	ἀπόστολος 3	Ἀραβία 2	φύσις 2
χάρις 7	Βαρναβᾶς 3	δουλεία 2	χείρ 2
κύριος 6	γραφή 3	Ἕλλην 2	χρόνος 2
γραφή 3	διαθήκη 3	ἐπιθυμία 2	

There are 416 verbs in Galatians. The following list shows the verbs that occur more than once in the letter. The high occurrence rates of both δικαιόω and περιτέμνω are evident. These two strong patterns of lexical cohesion become more prominent when considering their respective cognates, the nouns δικαιοσύνη and περιτομή.

εἰμί 53	βαστάζω 4	πείθω 3	ἐξαποστέλλω 2
γίνομαι 12	γινώσκω 4	προλέγω 3	καυχάομαι 2
λέγω 11	δουλεύω 4	σπείρω 3	κηρύσσω 2
ζάω 9	ἐνεργέω 4	σταυρόω 3	κληρονομέω 2
θέλω 9	θερίζω 4	τρέχω 3	παραλαμβάνω 2
δικαιόω 8	καλέω 4	ἀγαπάω 2	πάρειμι 2
ἔρχομαι 8	ὁράω 4	ἀθετέω 2	πορθέω 2
γράφω 7	πιστεύω 4	ἀναβαίνω 2	προσανατίθημι 2
εὐαγγελίζω 7	ἀκούω 3	ἀνέρχομαι 2	στοιχέω 2
δίδωμι 6	ἀναγκάζω 3	ἀποθνήσκω 2	συγκλείω 2
περιτέμνω 6	γεννάω 3	ἀποκαλύπτω 2	ταράσσω 2
ποιέω 6	ἔνειμι 3	ἀρέσκω 2	ὑπάρχω 2
διώκω 5	ζηλόω 3	ἀφορίζω 2	φοβέω 2
δοκέω 5	λαμβάνω 3	διαφέρω 2	ὠδίνω 2
ἔχω 5	οἶδα 3	ἐξαγοράζω 2	

Appendix G

Nouns and verbs in Philemon

There are 81 nouns in Philemon as shown on the following list. The recurrence of δέσμιος, together with its cognate, δεσμός, is evident. The total occurrence of the word group is equal to that of ἀδελφός, placing it just behind three other nouns on the list. This indicates a strong pattern of lexical cohesion displayed by the word group.

Χριστός 8   Ἀρίσταρχος 1   παράκλησις 1
Ἰησοῦς 6   Ἄρχιππος 1   παρρησία 1
Κύριος 5   γνώμη 1   πατήρ 1
ἀδελφός 4   Δημᾶς 1   πνεῦμα 1
ἀγάπη 3   εἰρήνη 1   πρεσβύτης 1
Παῦλος 3   ἐκκλησία 1   σάρξ 1
σπλάγχνον 3   Ἐπαφρᾶς 1   συναιχμάλωτος 1
δέσμιος 2   ἐπίγνωσις 1   συστρατιώτης 1
δεσμός 2   εὐαγγέλιον 1   τέκνον 1
δοῦλος 2   κοινωνία 1   Τιμόθεος 1
θεός 2   κοινωνός 1   ὑπακοή 1
πίστις 2   Λουκᾶς 1   Φιλήμων 1
προσευχή 2   Μᾶρκος 1   χαρά 1
χάρις 2   μνεία 1   χείρ 1
ἀδελφή 1   ξενία 1   ὥρα 1
ἀνάγκη 1   οἶκος 1
Ἀπφία 1   Ὀνήσιμος 1

There are 44 verbs in Philemon as shown below. The repetition of παρακαλέω places the word only behind ἔχω, εἰμί, and ποιέω in terms of the rate of occurrence. This repetition indicates a pattern of lexical cohesion.

ἔχω 4   ἀσπάζομαι 1   ὀνίνημι 1
εἰμί 3   βούλομαι 1   ὀφείλω 1
ποιέω 3   γεννάω 1   πείθω 1
ἀναπαύω 2   γίνομαι 1   προσλαμβάνω 1
γράφω 2   διακονέω 1   προσοφείλω 1
λέγω 2   ἐλλογέω 1   χαρίζομαι 1
παρακαλέω 2   ἐλπίζω 1   χωρίζω
ἀδικέω 1   ἐπιτάσσω 1
ἀκούω 1   ἑτοιμάζω 1
ἀναπέμπω 1   εὐχαριστέω 1
ἀνήκω 1   θέλω 1
ἀπέχω 1   κατέχω 1
ἀποτίνω 1   οἶδα 1

References

Abasciano, Brian J. 2006. Corporate election in Romans 9: A reply to Thomas Schreiner. *Journal of the Evangelical Theological Society* 49:351–371.

Agosto, Efrain. 2005. *Servant leadership: Jesus & Paul.* St. Louis, MO: Chalice.

Alexander, Loveday. 1989. Hellenistic letter-forms and the structure of Philippians. *Journal for the Study of the New Testament* 37:87–101.

Amador, J. D. H. 2000. Revisiting 2 Corinthians: Rhetoric and the case for unity. *New Testament Studies* 46:92–111.

Bahr, Gordon J. 1968. Subscriptions in Pauline letters. *Journal of Biblical Literature* 87:27–41.

Bailey, Kenneth E. 1983. The structure of I Corinthians and Paul's theological method with special reference to 4:17. *Novum Testamentum* 25:152–181.

Bailey, Kenneth E. 2011. *Paul through Mediterranean eyes: Cultural studies in 1 Corinthians.* Downer Grove, IL: IVP Academic.

Balentine, Samuel E., and John Barton, eds. 1994. *Language theology and the Bible: Essays in honour of James Barr.* Oxford: Clarendon.

Banker, John. 1987. *A semantic and structural analysis of Titus.* Semantic and Structural Analysis Series. Dallas, TX: Summer Institute of Linguistics.

Banker, John. 1996. *A semantic and structural analysis of Philippians.* Semantic and Structural Analysis Series. Dallas, TX: Summer Institute of Linguistics.

Banker, John. 1999. *A semantic and structural analysis of Philemon.* Semantic and Structural Analysis Series. Dallas, TX: Summer Institute of Linguistics.

Barclay, John M. G. 1987. Mirror-reading a polemic letter: Galatians as a test case. *Journal for the Study of the New Testament* 10:73–93.

Barclay, John M. G. 2008. Is it good news that God is impartial? A response to Robert Jewett, Romans: A commentary. *Journal for the Study of the New Testament* 31:89–111.

Barnett, Paul. 1997. *The second epistle to the Corinthians*. The New International Commentary on the New Testament. Grand Rapids, MI: Eerdmans.

Barr, James. 1961. *The semantics of biblical language*. London: Oxford University Press. Reprinted in 1983, London: SCM.

Barrett, C. K. 1973. *A commentary on the second epistle to the Corinthians*. Black's New Testament Commentaries. London: A & C Black.

Barrett, C. K. 1991. *The epistle to the Romans*. Black's New Testament Commentaries. London: A & C Black.

Barrett, C. K. 1994. *A commentary on the first epistle to the Corinthians*. Black's New Testament Commentaries. London: A & C Black.

Barth, Markus, and Helmut Blanke. 2000. *The letter to Philemon: A new translation with notes and commentary*. Eerdmans Critical Commentary. Grand Rapids, MI: Eerdmans.

Bauer, Walter. 1979. *A Greek-English lexicon of the New Testament and other early Christian literature*. William F. Arndt and F. Wilbur Gingrich, trans. Chicago, IL: University of Chicago Press.

Beare, F. W. 1959. *A commentary on the epistle to the Philippians*. Black's New Testament Commentaries. London: A & C Black.

Beasley-Murray, George R. 1987. *John*. Word Biblical Commentary 36. Dallas, TX: Word Books.

Beaugrande, Robert-Alain de, and Wolfgang Ulrich Dressler. 1983. *Introduction to text linguistics*. London: Longman.

Beekman John, John Callow, and Michael Kopesec. 1981. *The semantic structure of written communication*. Dallas, TX: Summer Institute of Linguistics.

Behm, Johannes. 1965. Καρδία. In vol. 3 of *Theological dictionary of the New Testament*, 608–614. Gerhard Kittel and Gerhard Friedrich, eds. Geoffrey W. Bromiley, trans. 10 vols. Grand Rapids, MI: Eerdmans, 1964–1976.

Berding, Kenneth. 2000. Confusing word and concept in 'spiritual gifts': Have we forgotten James Barr's exhortation. *Journal of the Evangelical Theological Society* 43:37–51.

Berry, Ken L. 1996. The function of friendship language in Philippians 4:10–20. In John T. Fitzgerald (ed.), *Friendship, flattery, and frankness of speech: Studies on friendship in the New Testament world*, 107–124. Novum Testamentum Supplementary Series 82. Leiden, Netherlands: Brill.

Bertram, Georg. 1974. Φρήν. In vol. 9 of *Theological dictionary of the New Testament*, 220–235. Gerhard Kittel and Gerhard Friedrich, eds. Geoffrey W. Bromiley, trans. 10 vols. Grand Rapids, MI: Eerdmans, 1964–1976.

Best, Ernest. 1955. *One body in Christ: A study in the relationship of the church to Christ in the epistles of the Apostle Paul*. London: SPCK.

Best, Ernest. 1972. *A commentary on the first and second epistles to the Thessalonians*. Black's New Testament Commentaries. London: A & C Black.

Betz, Hans Dieter. 1979. *Galatians: A commentary on Paul's letter to the churches in Galatia*. Hermeneia: A Critical and Historical Commentary on the Bible. Philadelphia, PA: Fortress.

Betz, Hans Dieter. 1985. *2 Corinthians 8 and 9: A commentary on two administrative letters of the Apostle Paul*. Hermeneia: A Critical and Historical Commentary on the Bible. Philadelphia, PA: Fortress.

Betz, Hans Dieter. 2000a. The concept of the 'inner human being' (ὁ ἔσω ἄνθρωπος) in the anthropology of Paul. *New Testament Studies* 46:315–341.

Betz, Hans Dieter. 2000b. The human being in the antagonisms of life according to the Apostle Paul. *Journal of Religion* 80:557–575.

Black, David Alan. 1995. The discourse structure of Philippians: A study in textlinguistics. *Novum Testamentum* 37:16–49.

Blakemore, Diane. 2002. *Relevance and linguistic meaning: The semantics and pragmatics of discourse markers*. Cambridge Studies in Linguistics 99. Cambridge: Cambridge University Press.

Blakemore, Diane. 2003. Discourse and relevance theory. In Deborah Schiffrin, Deborah Tanner, and Heidi E. Hamilton (eds.), *The handbook of discourse analysis*. Blackwell Handbooks in Linguistics. Malden, MA: Blackwell.

Blanton, Thomas. 2010. Spirit and covenant renewal: A theologoumenon of Paul's opponents in 2 Corinthians. *Journal of Biblical Literature* 129:129–151.

Blass F., and A. Debrunner. 1961. *A Greek grammar of the New Testament and other early Christian literature*. Translated and revised by Robert W. Funk. Chicago, IL: University of Chicago Press.

Bligh, John. 1969. *Galatians: A discussion of St Paul's epistle*. Householder Commentaries 1. London: St. Paul Publications.

Bockmuehl, Markus. 1998. *The epistle to the Philippians*. Black's New Testament Commentary. Peabody, MA: Hendrickson.

Bodine, Walter R. ed. 1995. *Discourse analysis of biblical literature: What it is and what it offers*. The Society of Biblical Literature Semeia Studies. Atlanta, GA: Scholars Press.

Brakke, David. 2000. The body in early eastern Christian sources. *Bulletin of the American Society of Papyrologists* 37:119–134.

Brodie, T. L. 2009. Countering Romans. In Udo Schnelle (ed.), *The letter to the Romans*, 519–542. Bibliotheca Ephemeridum Theologicarum Lovaniensium 226. Leuven: Uitgeverij Peeters.

Brown, Gillian, and George Yule. 1983. *Discourse analysis*. Cambridge: Cambridge University Press.

Brown, Michael Joseph. 2001. Paul's use of ΔΟΥΛΟΣ ΧΡΙΣΤΟΥ ΙΗΣΟΥ in Romans 1:1. *Journal of Biblical Literature* 120:723–737.

Brown, Roger, and Albert Gilman. 2003. The pronouns of power and solidarity. In Christina Bratt Paulston and G. Richard Tucker (eds.), *Sociolinguistics: The essential reading*, 156–176. Malden, MA: Blackwell.

Bruce, F. F. 1965. *An expanded paraphrase of the epistles of Paul: Printed in parallel with the Revised Version, with fuller references by Drs. Scrivener, Moulton, and Greenup.* Exeter, Devon: Paternoster.

Bruce, F. F. 1982a. *1 and 2 Thessalonians.* Word Biblical Commentary 45. Waco: Word Books.

Bruce, F. F. 1982b. *The epistle to the Galatians: A commentary on the Greek text.* The New International Greek Testament Commentary. Grand Rapids, MI: Eerdmans.

Bruce, F. F. 1984. *The epistles to the Colossians, to Philemon, and to the Ephesians.* The New International Commentary on the New Testament. Grand Rapids, MI: Eerdmans.

Bruce, F. F. 1996. *1 and 2 Corinthians.* New Century Bible. Grand Rapids, MI: Eerdmans.

Burk, Denny. 2008. Discerning Corinthian slogans through Paul's use of the diatribe in 16:12–20. *Bulletin for Biblical Research* 18:99–121.

Burke, Trevor J. 2012. Paul's new family in Thessalonica. *Novum Testamentum* 54:269–287.

Burton, Ernest De Witt. 1898. *Syntax of the moods and tenses in New Testament Greek.* Edinburgh, UK: T. & T. Clark.

Burton, Ernest De Witt. 1921. *A critical and exegetical commentary on the epistle to the Galatians.* International Critical Commentary on the Holy Scriptures of the Old and New Testaments. Edinburgh, UK: T. & T. Clark.

Byrne, Brendan. 1996. *Romans.* Sacra Pagina 6. Collegeville, MN: Liturgical Press.

Calloud, Jean. 1976. *Structural analysis of narrative.* The Society of Biblical Literature Semeia Supplements. William A. Beardslee, ed. Daniel Patte, trans. Philadelphia, PA: Fortress.

Callow, John. 2000. *A semantic and structural analysis of 2 Thessalonians.* Semantic and Structural Analysis Series. Dallas, TX: Summer Institute of Linguistics.

Callow, John. 2002. *A semantic and structural analysis of Colossians.* Semantic and Structural Analysis Series. Dallas, TX: Summer Institute of Linguistics.

Carnley, Peter. 2004. *Reflections in glass.* Sydney: HarperCollins.

Carson, D. A. 1998. *Exegetical fallacies.* Second edition. Grand Rapids, MI: Baker.

Carter, Timothy L. 2008. Looking at the metaphor of Christ's body in 1 Corinthians 12. In Stanley E. Porter (ed.), *Paul: Jew, Greek, and Roman*, 93–115. Pauline Studies 5. Leiden, Netherlands/Boston, MA: Brill.

Champion, L. G. 1934. *Benedictions and doxologies in the epistles of Paul.* Oxford: Kemp Hall.

Chan, Mark L. Y., and Roland Chia, eds. 2003. *Beyond determinism and reductionism: Genetic science and the person.* Hindmarsh, South Australia: ATF Press.

Chen, Sunny. 2015. The distributive singular in Paul: The adequacy of a grammatical category. *Journal of Greco-Roman Christianity and Judaism* 11:104–130.

Childs, Brevard S. 1970. *Biblical theology in crisis.* Philadelphia, PA: Westminster.

Christensen, Duane L. 2001. *Deuteronomy 1:1–21:9 Revised.* Word Biblical Commentary 6A. Nashville, TN: Thomas Nelson.

Chrysostom, John. 1889. Commentary of St. John Chrysostom Archbishop of Constantinople on the epistle of St. Paul the Apostle to the Galatians. In vol. 13 of *The Nicene and post-Nicene fathers.* Philip Schaff, ed. Buffalo, NY: Christian Literature Company.

Ciampa, Roy E., and Brian S. Rosner. 2010. *The first letter to the Corinthians.* The Pillar New Testament Commentary. Grand Rapids, MI: Eerdmans.

Clendenen, Ewell Ray. 1987. The structure of Malachi: A textlinguistic study. *Criswell Theological Review* 2:3–17.

Cole-Turner, Ronald. 1993. *The new Genesis: Theology and the genetic revolution.* Louisville, KY: John Knox.

Collange, Jean-François. 1979. *The epistle of Saint Paul to the Philippians.* A. W. Heathcote, trans. London: Epworth.

Collin, Finn, and Finn Guldmann. 2005. *Meaning, use and truth: Introducing the philosophy of language.* Hampshire, UK: Ashgate.

Collins, Raymond F. 1999. *First Corinthians.* Sacra Pagina 7. Collegeville, PA: Liturgical Press.

Combes, I. A. H. 1998. *The metaphor of slavery in the writings of the early Church: From the New Testament to the beginning of the fifth century.* Journal for the Study of the New Testament Supplement Series 156. Sheffield, UK: Sheffield Academic.

Conzelmann, Hans. 1975. *1 Corinthians: A commentary on the first epistle to the Corinthians.* George W. MacRae, ed. James W. Leitch, trans. Hermeneia: A Critical and Historical Commentary on the Bible. Philadelphia, PA: Fortress.

Cousar, Charles B. 1982. *Galatians.* Interpretation: A Bible Commentary for Teaching and Preaching. Atlanta, GA: John Knox.

Cousar, Charles B. 2009. *Philippians and Philemon: A commentary.* Louisville, KY: Westminster John Knox.

Craddock, Fred B. 1985. *Philippians: Interpretation: A Bible commentary for teaching and preaching.* Atlanta, GA: John Knox.

Cranfield C. E. B. 1975. *Romans 1–8.* Vol. 1 of A critical and exegetical commentary on the epistle to the Romans. 2 vols. The International Critical Commentary. Edinburgh, UK: T. & T. Clark, 1975–1979.

Cranfield C. E. B. 1979. *Romans 9–16.* Vol. 2 of A critical and exegetical commentary on the epistle to the Romans. 2 vols. The International Critical Commentary. Edinburgh, UK: T. & T. Clark, 1975–1979.

Currie, Thomas W. 2006. Between text & sermon: 1 Thessalonians 5:12–24. *Interpretation: A Bible commentary for teaching and preaching* 60:446–449.

Dahl, Nils A. 2004. Paul and the church at Corinth. In Edward Adams and David G. Horrell (eds.), *Christianity at Corinth: The quest for the Pauline church,* 85–95. Louisville, KY: Westminster John Knox.

Dana, H. E., and Julius R. Mantey. 1928. *A manual grammar of the Greek New Testament.* London: Society for Promoting Christian Knowledge.

Deibler, Ellis W. 1998. *A semantic and structural analysis of Romans.* Semantic and Structural Analysis Series. Dallas, TX: Summer Institute of Linguistics.

Deming, Will. 1996. The unity of 1 Corinthians 5–6. *Journal of Biblical Literature* 115:289–312.

DeSilva, David A. 1993. Measuring penultimate against ultimate reality: An investigation of the integrity and argumentation of 2 Corinthians. *Journal for the Study of the New Testament* 52:41–70.

DeSilva, David A. 1998. *The credential of an Apostle: Paul's gospel in 2 Corinthians 1–7.* Bibal Monograph Series 4. N. Richland Hills, TX: Bibal.

Destro, Adriana, and Mauro Pesce. 1998. Self, identity, and body in Paul and John. In A. I. Baumgarten, J. Assmann, and G. G. Stroumsa (eds.), *Self, soul and body in religious experience,* 184–197. Studies in the History of Religions 78. Leiden, Netherlands: Brill.

Dihle, Albert. 1974. Ψυχή. In vol. 9 of *Theological dictionary of the New Testament,* 608–617. Gerhard Kittel and Gerhard Friedrich, eds. Geoffrey W. Bromiley, trans. 10 vols. Grand Rapids, MI: Eerdmans, 1964–1976.

Dijk, Teun A. van. 1977. *Text and context: Explorations in the semantics and pragmatics of discourse.* Longman Linguistics Library 21. New York: Longman.

Doble, Peter. 2002. 'Vile bodies' or transformed persons? Philippians 3.21 in context. *Journal for the Study of the New Testament* 86:3–27.

Donfried, Karl Paul. 2002. *Paul, Thessalonica, and early Christianity.* Grand Rapids, MI: Eerdmans.

Dooley, Robert A., and Stephen H. Levinsohn. 2001. *Analyzing discourse: A manual of basic concepts.* Dallas, TX: SIL International.

Driver, S. R. 1896. *A critical and exegetical commentary on Deuteronomy.* The International Critical Commentary. Edinburgh, UK: T. & T. Clark.

Dunn, James D. G. 1988a. *Romans 1–8.* Word Biblical Commentary 38A. Dallas, TX: Word Books.

Dunn, James D. G. 1988b. *Romans 9–16.* Word Biblical Commentary 38B. Dallas, TX: Word Books.

Dunn, James D. G. 1993. *A commentary on the epistle to the Galatians.* Black's New Testament Commentaries. London: A & C Black.

Dunn, James D. G. 1996. *The epistles to the Colossians and to Philemon: A commentary on the Greek text.* The New International Greek Testament Commentary. Grand Rapids, MI: Eerdmans.

Dunn, James D. G. 2002. How are the dead raised? With what body do they come? Reflections on 1 Corinthians 15. *Southwestern Journal of Theology* 45:4–18.

Dunn, James D. G. 2006. *The theology of Paul the Apostle.* Grand Rapids, MI: Eerdmans.

Dunn, James D. G. 2008. *The new perspective on Paul.* Grand Rapids, MI: Eerdmans.

Dunson, Ben C. 2011. Faith in Romans: The salvation of the individual or life in community? *Journal for the Study of the New Testament* 34:19–46.

Dunson, Ben C. 2012. *Individual and community in Paul's letter to the Romans.* Wissenschaftliche Untersuchungen zum Neuen Testament II 332. Tübingen: Mohr Siebeck.

Ebeling, Gerhard. 1985. *The truth of the Gospel: An exposition of Galatians.* David Green, trans. Philadelphia, PA: Fortress.

Edgar, Brian G. 2000. Paul and the person. *Science and Christian Belief* 12:151–164.

Ellicott, Charles J. 1867. *St. Paul's epistle to the Galatians: With a critical and grammatical commentary.* London: Longmans, Green, Reader, & Dyer.

Elliger, K., and W. Rudolph., eds. 1990. *Biblica Hebraica Stuggartensia.* Stuttgart: Deutsche Bibelgesellschaft.

Elliott, John H. 1991. Temple versus household in Luke-Acts: A contrast in social institutions. In Jerome H. Neyrey (ed.), *The social world of Luke-Acts: Model for interpretation*, 211–240. Peabody, MA: Hendrickson.

Ellis, E. Earle. 1990. Sōma in first Corinthians. *Interpretation* 44:132–144.

Endsjø, Dag Øistein. 2008. Immortal bodies, before Christ: Bodily continuity in ancient Greece and 1 Corinthians. *Journal for the Study of the New Testament* 30:417–436.

Engberg-Pedersen, Troels. 2009. The material spirit: Cosmology and ethics in Paul. *New Testament Studies* 55:179–197.

Fantin, Joseph D. 2010. *The Greek imperative mood in the New Testament: A cognitive and communicative approach.* Studies in Biblical Greek 12. New York: Peter Lang.

Fee, Gordon D. 1987. *The first epistle to the Corinthians.* The New International Commentary on the New Testament. Grand Rapids, MI: Eerdmans.

Fee, Gordon D. 1994. *God's empowering presence: The Holy Spirit in the letters of Paul.* Peabody, MA: Hendrickson.

Fee, Gordon D. 1995. *Paul's letter to the Philippians.* The New International Commentary on the New Testament. Grand Rapids, MI: Eerdmans.

Fee, Gordon D. 2007. *Galatians.* Pentecostal Commentary. Blandford Forum, Dorset: Deo.

Fee, Gordon D. 2009. *The first and second letters to the Thessalonians*. The New International Commentary on the New Testament. Grand Rapids, MI: Eerdmans.

Findlay, George G. 1908. *The epistle to the Galatians*. The Expositors Bible. London: Hodder and Stoughton.

Fiore, Benjamin. 2003. Paul, exemplification, and imitation. In J. Paul Sampley (ed.), *Paul in the Greco-Roman world: A handbook*, 228–257. Harrisburg, PA: Trinity Press International.

Fitzgerald, John T. 1996. Philippians in the light of some ancient discussions of friendship. In John T. Fitzgerald (ed.), *Friendship, flattery, and frankness of speech: Studies on friendship in the New Testament world*, 141–160. Novum Testamentum Supplementary Series 82. Leiden, Netherlands: Brill.

Fitzgerald, John T., ed. 1996. *Friendship, flattery, and frankness of speech: Studies on friendship in the New Testament world*. Supplements to Novum Testamentum 82. Leide, Netherlands: Brill.

Fitzgerald, John T. 2007. Christian friendship: John, Paul, and the Philippians. *Interpretation* 61:284–296.

Fitzmyer, Joseph A. 1993. *Romans: A new translation with introduction and commentary*. The Anchor Bible 33. New York: Doubleday.

Fitzmyer, Joseph A. 2000. *The letter to Philemon: A new translation with introduction and commentary*. The Anchor Bible 34C. New York: Doubleday.

Fitzmyer, Joseph A. 2008. *First Corinthians*. The Anchor Yale Bible 32. New Haven, CT: Yale University Press.

Foerster, Werner. 1965. Ὁλόκληρία. In vol. 3 of *Theological dictionary of the New Testament*, 767–769. Gerhard Kittel and Gerhard Friedrich, eds. Geoffrey W. Bromiley, trans. 10 vols. Grand Rapids, MI: Eerdmans, 1964–1976.

Ford, Norman M., and Michael Herbert. 2003. *Stem cells: Science, medicine, law and ethics*. Melbourne, Australia: St. Paul's.

Fowl, Stephen E. 2005. *Philippians*. The Two Horizons New Testament Commentary. Grand Rapids, MI: Eerdmans.

Frame, James Everett. 1912. *A critical and exegetical commentary on the epistles of St. Paul to the Thessalonians*. International Critical Commentary on the Holy Scriptures of the Old and New Testaments. Edinburgh, UK: T. & T. Clark.

Fung, Ronald Y. K. 1988. *The epistle to the Galatians*. The New International Commentary on the New Testament. Grand Rapids, MI: Eerdmans.

Furnish, Victor Paul. 1984. *II Corinthians: A new translation with introduction and commentary*. The Anchor Yale Bible 32A. New York: Doubleday.

Furnish, Victor Paul. 2007. *1 Thessalonians, 2 Thessalonians*. Abingdon New Testament Commentaries. Nashville, TN: Abingdon.

Garland, David E. 1985. The composition and unity of Philippians. *Novum Testamentum* 27:141–173.

Georgakopoulou, Alexandra, and Dionysis Goutsos. 2004. *Discourse analysis: An introduction.* Second edition. Edinburgh, UK: Edinburgh University Press.

Gosnell, Peter W. 2009. Law in Romans: Regulation and instruction. *Novum Testamentum* 51:252–271.

Green, Gene L. 2007. Lexical pragmatics and biblical interpretation. *Journal of the Evangelical Theological Society* 50:799–812.

Green, Joel B. 2008. *Body, soul, and human life: The nature of humanity in the Bible.* Studies in Theological Interpretation. Grand Rapids, MI: Baker Academic.

Green, Joel B. 2010. Discourse analysis and New Testament interpretation. In Joel B. Green (ed.), *Hearing the New Testament strategies for interpretation,* 218–239. Grand Rapids, MI: Eerdmans.

Grice, H. P. 1991. Utterer's meaning, sentence-meaning, and word-meaning. In Steven Davis (ed.), *Pragmatics: A reader,* 65–76. New York: Oxford University Press.

Gundry, Robert H. 1976. *Sōma in biblical theology: With emphasis on Pauline anthropology.* Society for New Testament Studies Monograph Series 29. Cambridge: Cambridge University Press.

Gupta, Nijay K. 2010. Which "body" is a temple (1 Corinthians 6:19)? Paul beyond the individual/communal divide. *Catholic Biblical Quarterly* 72:518–536.

Guthrie, Donald. 1981. *Galatians.* The New Century Bible Commentary. Grand Rapids, MI: Eerdmans.

Guthrie, Donald. 1990. *New Testament introduction.* Fourth edition. Downers Grove, IL: Intervarsity Press.

Guthrie, George H. 1994. *The structure of Hebrews: A text-linguistic analysis.* Supplements to Novum Testamentum 73. Leiden, Netherlands: Brill.

Halliday, M. A. K. 2002. *Linguistic studies of text and discourse.* Jonathan Webster, ed. London: Continuum.

Halliday, M. A. K., and Ruqaiya Hasan. 1986. *Language, context, and text: Aspects of language in a social-semiotic perspective.* Burwood, Australia: Deakin University Press.

Hansen, Walter. 2009. *The letter to the Philippians.* The Pillar New Testament Commentary. Grand Rapids, MI: Eerdmans.

Harris, Murray J. 2005. *The second epistle to the Corinthians: A commentary on the Greek Text.* The New International Greek Testament Commentary. Grand Rapids, MI: Eerdmans.

Harrison, P. N. 1936. *Polycarp's two epistles to the Philippians.* Cambridge: Cambridge University Press.

Hart, George, and Helen Hart. 2001. *A semantic and structural analysis of James.* Semantic and Structural Analysis Series. Dallas, TX: Summer Institute of Linguistics.

Hawthorne, Gerald F. 1983. *Philippians*. Word Biblical Commentary 43. Waco, TX: Word Books.

Hays, Richard B. 1989. *Echoes of scripture in the letters of Paul*. New Haven, CT: Yale University Press.

Hays, Richard B. 1997. *First Corinthians*. Interpretation: A Bible Commentary for Teaching and Preaching. Louisville, KY: John Knox.

Heard, J. B. 1882. *The tripartite nature of man: Spirit, soul, and body*. Edinburgh, UK: T. & T. Clark.

Heil, John Paul. 2010. *Philippians: Let us rejoice in being conformed to Christ*. Early Christianity and its Literature 3. Atlanta, GA: Society of Biblical Literature.

Hendriksen, William. 1955. *Exposition of I and II Thessalonians*. New Testament Commentary. Grand Rapids, MI: Baker.

Hendriksen, William. 1968. *Exposition of Galatians*. New Testament Commentary. Grand Rapids, MI: Baker.

Héring, Jean. 1967. *The second epistle of Saint Paul to the Corinthians*. A. W. Heathcote and P. J. Allcock, trans. London: Epworth.

Hill, David. 1967. *Greek words and Hebrew meanings: Studies in the semantics of soteriological terms*. Society for New Testament Studies Monograph Series 5. Cambridge: Cambridge University Press.

Holmås, Geir Otto. 2005. 'My house shall be a house of prayer': Regarding the temple as a place of prayer in Acts within the context of Luke's apologetical objective. *Journal for the Study of the New Testament* 27:393–416.

Holmberg, Bengt. 1980. *Paul and power: The structure of authority in the primitive church as reflected in the Pauline epistles*. Philadelphia, PA: Fortress.

Horn, L. 1997. Presupposition and implicature. In Shalom Lappin (ed.), *The handbook of contemporary semantic theory*. Oxford: Blackwell.

Horsley, Richard A. 1998. *1 Corinthians*. Abingdon New Testament Commentaries. Nashville, TN: Abington.

Hughes, Philip Edgcumbe. 1967. *Paul's second epistle to the Corinthians*. The New International Commentary on the New Testament. Grand Rapids, MI: Eerdmans.

Hultgren, Arland J. 2011. *Paul's letter to the Romans: A commentary*. Grand Rapids, MI: Eerdmans.

Hurd, John Coolidge. 1983. *The origin of I Corinthians*. Macon, GA: Mercer University Press.

Huttunen, Niko. 2009. *Paul and Epictetus on law*. Library of New Testament Studies 405. London: T. & T. Clark.

Jewett, Robert. 1969. The form and function of the homiletic benediction. *Anglican Theological Review* 51:18–34.

Jewett, Robert. 1970. The epistolary thanksgiving and the integrity of Philippians. *Novum Testamentum* 12:40–53.

Jewett, Robert. 1971. *Paul's anthropological terms: A study of their use in conflict settings*. Leiden, Netherlands: Brill.

Jewett, Robert. 2007. *Romans: A commentary*. Hermeneia: A Critical and Historical Commentary on the Bible. Minneapolis, MN: Fortress.

Johanson, Bruce C. 1987. *To all the brethren: A text-linguistic and rhetorical approach to 1 Thessalonians*. Coniectanea Biblica: New Testament Series 16. Stockholm: Almqvist & Wiksell.

Johnson, Edna. 1988. *A semantic and structural analysis of 2 Peter*. Semantic and Structural Analysis Series. Dallas, TX: Summer Institute of Linguistics.

Johnson, Edna. 2008. *A semantic and structural analysis of Ephesians*. Semantic and Structural Analysis Series. Dallas, TX: Summer Institute of Linguistics.

Johnson, Luke Timothy. 2010. *The writings of the New Testament*. Minneapolis, MN: Fortress.

Johnstone, Robert. 1977. *Lectures on the epistle to the Philippians*. Minneapolis, MN: Klock & Klock.

Jones, Ivor H. 2005. *The epistles to the Thessalonians*. Epworth Commentaries. Suffolk, UK: Epworth.

Jones, Maurice. 1918. *The epistle to the Philippians*. London: Methuen.

Käsemann, Ernst. 1971. *Perspectives on Paul*. Margaret Kohl, trans. London: SCM.

Käsemann, Ernst. 1980. *Commentary on Romans*. Translated and edited by Geoffrey W. Bromiley. Grand Rapids, MI: Eerdmans.

Keener, Craig S. 2005. *1–2 Corinthians*. New Cambridge Bible Commentary. New York: Cambridge University Press.

Kempson, Ruth M. 1997. Semantic, pragmatics, and natural-language interpretation. In Shalom Lappin (ed.), *The handbook of contemporary semantic theory*. Oxford: Blackwell.

Kempthorne, R. 1968. Incest and the body of Christ: A study of I Corinthians vi. 12–20. *New Testament Studies* 14:568–574.

Ker, Donald P. 2000. Paul and Apollos—Colleagues or rivals? *Journal for the Study of the New Testament* 77:75–97.

Kibrik, Andrej A. 2011. *Reference in discourse*. Oxford Studies in Typology and Linguistic Theory. Oxford: Oxford University Press.

Kijne, J. J. 1966. We, us and our in I and II Corinthians. *Novum Testamentum* 8:171–179.

Kim, Dongsu. 2010. Reading Paul's καὶ οὕτως πᾶς Ἰσραὴλ σωθήσεται (Rom. 11:26a) in the context of Romans. *Calvin Theological Journal* 45:317–334.

Kim, Yung Suk. 2008. *Christ's body in Corinth: The politics of a metaphor*. Minneapolis, MN: Fortress.

King, Karen L. 2003. *What is gnosticism?* Cambridge, MA: Belknap Press of Harvard University Press.

Kinneavy, James L. 1971. *A theory of discourse: The aim of discourse.* Englewood Cliffs, NY: Prentice-Hall.

Kleinknecht, Hermann. 1968. Πνεῦμα. In vol. 6 of *Theological dictionary of the New Testament,* 332–359. Gerhard Kittel and Gerhard Friedrich, eds. Geoffrey W. Bromiley, trans. 10 vols. Grand Rapids, MI: Eerdmans, 1964–1976.

Krentz, Edgar. 2008. Civic culture and the Philippians. *Currents in Theology and Mission* 35:258–263.

Kümmel, Werner Georg. 1963. *Man in the New Testament.* John J. Vincent, trans. London: Epworth.

Kwon, Yon-Gyong. 2008. Ἀρραβών as pledge in second Corinthians. *New Testament Studies* 54:525–541.

Laato, Timo. 1995. *Paul and Judaism: An anthropological approach.* South Florida Studies in the History of Judaism 115. Atlanta, GA: Scholars Press.

Laato, Timo. 2004. Paul's anthropological considerations: Two problems. In D. A. Carson, Peter T. O'Brien, and Mark A. Seifrid (eds.), *Justification and variegated nomism II: The paradoxes of Paul.* Wissenschaftliche Untersuchungen zum Neuen Testament 181. Tübingen: Mohr Siebeck.

Lambrecht, Jan. 1999. *Second Corinthians.* Sacra Pagina 8. Collegeville, PA: Liturgical Press.

Lebacqz, Karen. 1997. *Ethics & Policy; Newsletter of the Center for Ethics & Social Policy of the Graduate Theological Union 4.* Theological Union.

Lee, Jae Hyun. 2010. *Paul's gospel in Romans: A discourse analysis of Romans 1:16–8:39.* Linguistic Biblical Studies 3. Leiden, Netherlands: Brill.

Lee, Michelle V. 2006. *Paul, the Stoics, and the body of Christ.* Society for New Testament Studies Monograph Series 137. New York: Cambridge University Press.

Lemke, Jay L. 1995. Intertextuality and text semantics. In Peter H. Fries and Michael Gregory (eds.), *Discourse in society: Systemic functional perspectives, meaning and choice in language: Studies for Michael Halliday,* 85–114. Advances in Discourse Processes 50. Norwood, NJ: Ablex.

Levinsohn, Stephen H. 2000. *Discourse features of New Testament Greek: A coursebook on the information structure of New Testament Greek.* Second edition. Dallas, TX: Summer Institute of Linguistics.

Levinson, Stephen C. 1989. *Pragmatics.* Cambridge Textbooks in Linguistics. Cambridge: Cambridge University Press.

Lightfoot, J. B. 1892. *Saint Paul's epistles to the Colossians and to Philemon.* London: Macmillan.

Lightfoot, J. B. 1902. *Saint Paul's epistle to the Galatians.* London: Macmillan.

Lightfoot, J. B. 1913. *Saint Paul's epistle to the Philippians.* London: Macmillan.

Lohse, Eduard. 1971. *A commentary on the epistles to the Colossians and to Philemon.* Hermeneia: A Critical Commentary on the Bible. Philadelphia, PA: Fortress.

Long, A. A. 2004. *Epictetus: A Stoic and Socratic guide to life.* Oxford: Clarendon Press/New York: Oxford University Press.

Longacre, Robert E. 1983. *The grammar of discourse.* Second edition. Topics in Language and Linguistics. New York: Plenum.

Longenecker, Richard N. 1990. *Galatians.* Word Biblical Commentary 41. Waco, TX: Word Books.

Longinus.1995. *On the sublime.* W. H. Fyfe. Revised by Donald Russell, trans. Loeb Classical Library 199. Cambridge, MA: Harvard University Press.

Louw, J. P. 1973. Discourse analysis and the Greek New Testament. *The Bible Translator* 24:101–118.

Louw, J. P. 1982. *Semantics of New Testament Greek.* Atlanta, GA: Scholars Press.

Louw, J. P. 1987. *A semantic discourse analysis of Romans.* 2 vols. Pretoria, South Africa: University of Pretoria.

Lyall, Francis. 1984. *Slaves, citizens, sons.* Grand Rapids, MI: Zondervan.

Lyons, George, and Williams H. Malas. 2007. Paul and his friends within the Greco-Roman context. *Wesleyan Theological Journal* 42:50–69.

Maienschein, Jane. 2003. *Whose view of life? Embryos, cloning, and stem cells.* Cambridge, MA: Harvard University Press.

Malherbe, Abraham J. 1996. Paul's self-sufficiency (Philippians 4:11). In John T. Fitzgerald (ed.), *Friendship, flattery, and frankness of speech: Studies on friendship in the New Testament world,* 125–139. Novum Testamentum Supplementary Series 82. Leiden, Netherlands: Brill.

Malherbe, Abraham J. 2000. *The letters to the Thessalonians: A new translation with introduction and commentary.* The Anchor Bible 32B. New York: Doubleday.

Marchal, Joseph A. 2006. *Hierarchy, unity, and imitation: A feminist rhetorical analysis of power dynamics in Paul's letter to the Philippians.* Sharon H. Ringe, ed. Atlanta, GA: Society of Biblical Literature.

Marshall, I. Howard. 1983. *1 and 2 Thessalonians.* New Century Bible Commentary. Grand Rapids, MI: Eerdmans.

Marshall, I. Howard. 1992. *The epistle to the Philippians.* Epworth Commentaries. London: Epworth.

Martin, Dale B. 1990. *Slavery as salvation: The metaphor of slavery in Pauline Christianity.* New Haven, CT: Yale University Press.

Martin, Dale B. 1995. *The Corinthian body.* New Haven, CT: Yale University Press.

Martin, Ralph P. 1981. *Colossians and Philemon.* New Century Bible. Grand Rapids, MI: Eerdmans.

Martin, Ralph P. 1986. *2 Corinthians.* Word Biblical Commentary 40. Waco, TX: Word Books.

Martin, Ralph P. 1989. *Philippians.* New Century Bible. Grand Rapids, MI: Eerdmans.

Martin, Ralph P. 1997. *A hymn of Christ: Philippians 2:5–11 in recent interpretation & in the setting of early Christian worship*. Downers Grove, IL: InterVarsity.

Martin, Troy W. 2006. Paul's pneumatological statements and ancient medical texts. In John Fotopoulos (ed.), *New Testament and early Christian literature in the Greco-Roman context: Studies in honor of David E. Aune*, 105–126. Leiden, Netherlands: Brill.

Martyn, J. Louis. 1997a. *Galatians: A new translation with introduction and commentary*. The Anchor Bible 33A. New York: Doubleday.

Martyn, J. Louis. 1997b. *Theological issues in the letters of Paul*. London: T. & T. Clark.

Matera, Frank J. 1992. *Galatians*. Sacra Pagina 9. Collegeville, PA: Liturgical Press.

Matera, Frank J. 2003. *II Corinthians*. The New Testament Library. Louisville, KY: Westminster John Knox.

May, Alistair Scott. 2004. *The body for the Lord: Sex and identity in 1 Corinthians 5–7*. Journal for the Study of the New Testament Supplement Series 278. London: T. & T. Clark.

McCant, Jerry W. 1999. *2 Corinthians*. Readings: A New Biblical Commentary. Sheffield, UK: Sheffield Academic.

McDonald, H. D. 1973. *Freedom in faith: A commentary on Paul's epistle to the Galatians*. London: Pickering & Inglis.

Meeks, Wayne A. 2004. A Nazi New Testament professor reads his Bible: The strange case of Gerhard Kittel. In Hindy Najman and Judith H. Newman (eds.), *The idea of biblical interpretation: Essays in honor of James L. Kugel*, 513–44. Boston, MA: Brill.

Mey, Jacob L. 1993. *Pragmatics: An introduction*. Oxford: Blackwell.

Michaels, J. Ramsey. 2010. *The gospel of John*. The New International Commentary on the New Testament. Grand Rapids, MI: Eerdmans.

Mihaila, Corin. 2009. *The Paul-Apollos relationship and Paul's stance towards Greco-Roman rhetoric: An exegetical and socio-historical study of 1 Corinthians 1–4*. Library of New Testament Studies 402. London: T. & T. Clark.

Mitchell, Margaret M. 1989. Concerning ΠΕΡΙ ΔΕ in 1 Corinthians. *Novum Testamentum* 31:229–256.

Mitchell, Margaret M. 1993. *Paul and the rhetoric of reconciliation: An exegetical investigation of the language and composition of 1 Corinthians*. Louisville, KY: Westminster John Knox.

Moo, Douglas. 1996. *The epistle to the Romans*. The New International Commentary on the New Testament. Grand Rapids, MI: Eerdmans.

Moo, Douglas. 2008. *The letters to the Colossians and to Philemon*. Grand Rapids, MI: Eerdmans.

Moore, A. L. 1969. *1 and 2 Thessalonians*. The Century Bible. London: Nelson.

Morris, Leon. 1988. *The epistle to the Romans*. Grand Rapids, MI: Eerdmans.

Morris, Leon. 1991. *The first and second epistles to the Thessalonians*. The New International Commentary on the New Testament. Grand Rapids, MI: Eerdmans.

Morris, Leon. 1996. *Galatians: Paul's charter of Christian freedom*. Leicester, UK: Intervarsity.

Moule, C. F. D. 1959. *An idiom book of New Testament Greek*. Second edition. Cambridge: Cambridge University Press.

Moulton, James Hope. 1906. *Prolegomena*, vol. 1 of *A grammar of New Testament Greek*. James Hope Moulton, ed. 4 vols. Edinburgh, UK: T. & T. Clark, 1906–1976.

Moulton, James Hope, and George Milligan. 1930. *The vocabulary of the Greek Testament: Illustrated from the papyri and other non-literary sources*. London: Hodder and Stoughton. Reprinted Peabody, MA: Hendrickson, 1997.

Moxnes, Halvor. 1994. The quest for honor and unity of the community in Romans 12 and in the orations of Dio Chrysostom. In Troels Engberg-Pedersen (ed.), *Paul in his Hellenistic context*. Studies of the New Testament and its World, 203–230. Edinburgh, UK: T. & T. Clark.

Müller, Jac J. 1955. *The epistles of Paul to the Philippians and to Philemon*. New International Commentary on the New Testament. Grand Rapids, MI: Eerdmans.

Mullins, Terence Y. 1964. Disclosure: A literary form in the New Testament. *Novum Testamentum* 7:44–50.

Mullins, Terence Y. 1977. Benediction as a New Testament form. *Andrews University Seminary Studies* 15:59–64.

Murphy-O'Connor, Jerome. 1979. *1 Corinthians*. New Testament Message: A Biblical-Theological Commentary 10. Wilmington, DE: Michael Glazier.

Murphy-O'Connor, Jerome. 1996. *Paul: A critical life*. Oxford: Clarendon.

Murphy-O'Connor, Jerome. 2009. *Becoming human together: The pastoral anthropology of St. Paul*. Atlanta, GA: Society of Biblical Literature.

Murphy-O'Connor, Jerome. 2010. *Keys to First Corinthians: Revisiting the major issues*. Oxford: Oxford University Press.

Nelson, Richard D. 2002. *Deuteronomy: A commentary*. The Old Testament Library. Louisville, KY: Westminster John Knox.

Newton, Michael. 1985. *The concept of purity at Qumran and in the letters of Paul*. Society for New Testament Studies Monograph Series 53. Cambridge: Cambridge University Press.

Neyrey, Jerome H. 1986. Body language in 1 Corinthians: The use of anthropological models for understanding Paul and his opponents. *Semeia* 35:129–170.

Nguyen, V. Henry T. 2008. Christian identity in Corinth: *A comparative study of 2 Corinthians, Epictetus and Valerius Maximus*. Wissenchaftliche Untersuchungen zum Neuen Testament 2. Reihe 243. Jörg Freg, ed. Tübingen: Mohr Siebeck.

Nongbri, Brent. 2009. Two neglected textual variants in Philippians 1. *Journal of Biblical Literature* 128:803–808.

Nordling, John G. 2004. *Philemon.* Concordia Commentary. Saint Louis, MO: Concordia.

Norrick, Neal R. 2003. Discourse and semantics. In Deborah Schiffrin, Deborah Tanner, and Heidi E. Hamilton (eds.), *The handbook of discourse analysis.* Blackwell Handbooks in Linguistics. Malden, MA: Blackwell.

Novum Testamentum Graece. 2012. Nestle-Aland 28th edition. Stuttgart: Deutche Bibelgesellschaft.

Olsson, Birger. 1974. *Structure and meaning in the fourth gospel: A text-linguistic analysis of John 2:1–11 and 4:1–42.* Coniectanea Biblica: New Testament Series 6. Jean Gray, trans. Lund, Sweden: Gleerup.

Orr, William F., and James Arthur Walther. 1976. *1 Corinthians: A new translation.* The Anchor Bible 32. New York: Doubleday & Company.

Osborne, Grant R. 2006. *The hermeneutical spiral.* Downers Grove, IL: IVP Academic.

Osiek, Carolyn. 2000. *Philippians Philemon.* Abingdon New Testament Commentaries. Nashville, TN: Abingdon.

Pascuzzi, Maria. 2009. Baptism-based allegiance and the divisions in Corinth: A reexamination of 1 Corinthians 1:13–17. *Catholic Biblical Quarterly* 71:813–829.

Patte, Daniel. 2010. Three types of identity formation for Paul as servant of Christ Jesus in Romans. In Kathy Ehrensperger and J. Brian Tucker (eds.), *Reading Paul in context: Explorations in identity formation: Essays in honour of William S. Campbell,* 209–228. Library of New Testament Studies 428. London: T. & T. Clark.

Peterlin, Davorin. 1995. *Paul's letter to the Philippians in the light of disunity in the Church.* Novum Testamentum Supplementary Series 79. Leiden, Netherlands: Brill.

Peterman, G. W. 1997. *Paul's gift from Philippi: Conventions of gift-exchange and Christian giving.* Society for New Testament Studies Monograph Series 92. Cambridge: Cambridge University Press.

Peters, Ted. 2003. *Science, theology, and ethics.* Aldershot, UK: Ashgate.

Peters, Ted, Karen Lebacqz, and Gaymon Bennett. 2008. *Sacred cell? Why Christians should support stem cell research.* Lanham, MD: Rowman & Littlefield.

Pickering, Wilbur. 1980. *A framework for discourse analysis.* Publications in Linguistics 64. Dallas, TX: Summer Institute of Linguistics.

Pike, Kenneth L. 1967. *Language in relation to a unified theory of the structure of human behavior.* Second edition. Janue Linguarum Series Maior 24. Paris: Mouton.

Plummer, Alfred. 1925. *A critical and exegetical commentary on the second epistle to the Corinthians.* The International Critical Commentary. Edinburgh, UK: T. & T. Clark.

Polaski, Sandra Hack. 1999. *Paul and the discourse of power*. Gender, culture, theory 8. The Biblical Seminar 62. Sheffield, UK: Sheffield Academic.

Porter, Stanley E. 1994. *Idioms of the Greek New Testament*. Second edition. Biblical Languages: Greek 2. Sheffield, UK: Sheffield Academic.

Porter, Stanley E. 2012. *Why hasn't discourse analysis caught on in New Testament studies?* April 24, 2012. Accessed 15 June 2012. http://stanleyeporter.wordpress.com/2012/04/24/why-hasnt-discourse-analysis-caught-on-in-new-testament-studies.

Porter, Stanley E., ed. 1995. Discourse analysis and New Testament studies: An introductory survey. In Stanley E. Porter and D. A. Carson (eds.), *Discourse analysis and other topics in biblical Greek*, 14–35. Journal for the Study of the New Testament Supplement Series 113. Sheffield, UK: Sheffield Academic.

Porter, Stanley E., and Mark J. Boda, eds. 2009. *Translating the New Testament: Text, translation, theology*. Grand Rapids, MI: Eerdmans.

Rae, Scott B., and Paul M. Cox. 1999. *Bioethics: A Christian approach in a pluralistic age*. Grand Rapids, MI: Eerdmans.

Rahlfs, Alfred, and R. Hanhart, eds. 2006. *Septuaginta*. Second edition. Stuttgart: Deutche Bibelgesellschaft.

Reale, Giovanni. 1990. *The schools of the imperial age*. In vol. 6 of A history of ancient philosophy. John R. Catan, ed., trans. Albany: State University of New York Press.

Reed, Jeffrey T. 1991. The infinitive with two substantival accusatives: An ambiguous construction. *Novum Testamentum* 33:1–27.

Reed, Jeffrey T. 1995. Identifying theme in New Testament: Insight from discourse analysis. In Stanley E. Porter and D. A. Carson (eds.), *Discourse analysis and other topics in biblical Greek*, 75–101. Journal for the Study of the New Testament: Supplementary Series 113. Sheffield, UK: Sheffield Academic.

Reed, Jeffrey T. 1996. Philippians 3:1 and the epistolary hesitation formulas: The literary integrity of Philippians, again. *Journal of Biblical Literature* 115:63–90.

Reed, Jeffrey T. 1997. *A discourse analysis of Philippians: Method and rhetoric in the debate over literary integrity*. Journal for the Study of the New Testament: Supplementary Series 136. Sheffield, UK: Sheffield Academic.

Reed, Jeffrey T. 2002. Discourse analysis. In Stanley E. Porter (ed.), *A handbook to the exegesis of the New Testament*, 189–217. Boston, MA: Brill.

Renkema, Jan. 1993. *Discourse studies: An introductory textbook*. Amsterdam: John Benjamin.

Reumann, John. 1996. Philippians, especially chapter 4, as a "letter of friendship": Observation on a checkered history of scholarship. In John T. Fitzgerald (ed.), *Friendship, flattery, and frankness of speech: Studies on friendship in the New Testament world*, 83–106. Novum Testamentum Supplementary Series 82. Leiden, Netherlands: Brill.

Reumann, John. 2008. *Philippians: A new translation with introduction and commentary*. The Anchor Yale Bible 33B. New Haven, CT: Yale University Press.

Richard, Earl J. 1995. *First and Second Thessalonians*. Sacra Pagina 11. Collegeville, PA: Liturgical Press.

Ricoeur, Paul. 1974. *The conflict of interpretations: Essays in hermeneutics*. Don Ihde, ed. Evanston, IL: Northwestern University Press.

Robertson, Archibald, and Alfred Plummer. 1929. *A critical and exegetical commentary on the first epistle of St. Paul to the Corinthians*. The International Critical Commentary. Edinburgh, UK: T. &T. Clark.

Robertson, A. T. 1934. *A grammar of the Greek New Testament in the light of historical research*. Nashville, TN: Broadman.

Robinson, John A. T. 1952. *The body: A study in Pauline theology*. London: SCM.

Robinson, John A. T. 1979. *Wrestling with Romans*. London: SCM.

Roetzel, Calvin J. 2007. *2 Corinthians*. Abingdon New Testament Commentary. Nashville, TN: Abingdon.

Roetzel, Calvin J. 2009. *The letters of Paul: Conversations in context*. Fifth edition. Louisville, KY: Westminster John Knox.

Rogers, Elinor MacDonald. 1989. *A semantic and structural analysis of Galatians*. Semantic and Structural Analysis Series. Dallas, TX: Summer Institute of Linguistics.

Romaine, Suzanne. 1994. *Language in society: An introduction to sociolinguistics*. New York: Oxford University Press.

Runge, Steven E. 2010. *Discourse grammar of the Greek New Testament: A practical teaching and exegesis*. Peabody, MA: Hendrickson.

Russell, D. A. 1972. *Plutarch*. Classical Life and Letters. London: Duckworth.

Sanday, William, and Arthur C. Headlam. 1902. *A critical and exegetical commentary on the epistle to the Romans*. International Critical Commentary on the Holy Scriptures of the Old and New Testaments. Edinburgh, UK: T. & T. Clark.

Sanders, Jack T. 1962. The transition from opening epistolary thanksgiving to body in the letters of the Pauline corpus. *Journal of Biblical Literature* 81:348–362.

Saussure, Ferdinard de. 2006. *Writings in general linguistics*. Carol Sanders and Matthew Pires, trans. New York: Oxford University Press.

Schenk, Wolfgang. 1977. Textlinguistische Aspekte der Strukturanalyse, dargestellt am Beispiel von I Kor XV. 1–11. *New Testament Studies* 23:469–477.

Schiffrin, Deborah. 1987. *Discourse marker*. Studies in Interactional Sociolinguistics 5. Cambridge: Cambridge University Press.

Schiffrin, Deborah, Deborah Tanner, and Heidi E. Hamilton, eds. 2003. *The handbook of discourse analysis*. Blackwell Handbooks in Linguistics. Malden, MA: Blackwell.

Schlatter, Adolf. 1995. *Romans: The righteousness of God.* Siegfried S. Schatzmann, trans. Peabody, MA: Hendrickson.

Schlier, Heinrich. 1962. *Der Brief an die Galater.* Kritisch-exegetisches Kommentar über das Neue Testament 7. Göttingen: Vandenhoeck & Ruprecht.

Scholer, David M. 1993. Foreward: An introduction to Philo Judaeus of Alexandria. In *The works of Philo: Complete and unabridged.* C. D. Yonge, trans. Peabody, MA: Hendrickson.

Schreiner, Thomas R. 1998. *Romans.* Baker Exegetical Commentary on the New Testament. Grand Rapids, MI: Baker Academic.

Schreiner, Thomas R. 2006. Corporate and individual election in Romans 9: A response to Brian Abasciano. *Journal of the Evangelical Theological Society* 49:373–386.

Schweizer, Edward. 1968. Πνεῦμα. In vol. 6 of *Theological dictionary of the New Testament,* 389–455. Gerhard Kittel and Gerhard Friedrich, eds. Geoffrey W. Bromiley, trans. 10 vols. Grand Rapids, MI: Eerdmans, 1964–1976.

Schweizer, Edward. 1971a. Σάρξ. In vol. 7 of *Theological dictionary of the New Testament,* 98–105. Gerhard Kittel and Gerhard Friedrich, eds. Geoffrey W. Bromiley, trans. 10 vols. Grand Rapids, MI: Eerdmans, 1964–1976.

Schweizer, Edward. 1971b. Σῶμα. In vol. 7 of *Theological dictionary of the New Testament,* 1024–1094. Gerhard Kittel and Gerhard Friedrich, eds. Geoffrey W. Bromiley, trans. 10 vols. Grand Rapids, MI: Eerdmans, 1964–1976.

Schweizer, Edward. 1974. Ψυχή. In vol. 9 of *Theological dictionary of the New Testament,* 637–656. Gerhard Kittel and Gerhard Friedrich, eds. Geoffrey W. Bromiley, trans. 10 vols. Grand Rapids, MI: Eerdmans, 1964–1976.

Scornaienchi, Lorenzo. 2008. *Sarx und Soma bei Paulus: Der Mensch zwischen Destruktivität und Konstruktivität.* Novum Testamentum et Orbis Antiquus Studien zur Umwelt des Neuen Testaments 67. Göttingen: Vandenhoeck & Ruprecht.

Scroggs, Robin. 1972. Paul and the eschatological woman. *Journal of the American Academy of Religion* 40:283–303.

Sherman, Grace E., and John C. Tuggy. 1994. *A semantic and structural analysis of the Johannine Epistles.* Semantic and Structural Analysis Series. Dallas, TX: Summer Institute of Linguistics.

Silva, Moisés. 1983. *Biblical words and their meanings: An introduction to lexical semantics.* Grand Rapids, MI: Zondervan.

Silva, Moisés. 1992. *Philippians.* Baker Exegetical Commentary on the New Testament. Grand Rapids, MI: Baker.

Silva, Moisés. 1995. Discourse analysis and Philippians. In Stanley E. Porter and D. A. Carson (eds.), *Discourse analysis and other topics in biblical*

Greek, 102–106. Journal for the Study of the New Testament Supplement Series 113. Sheffield, UK: Sheffield Academic.

Smiga, George. 1991. Romans 12:1–2 and 15:30–32 and the occasion of the letter to the Romans. *Catholic Biblical Quarterly* 53:257–273.

Snow, Nancy E., ed. 2003. *Stem cell research: New frontiers in science and ethics.* Notre Dame, IN: University of Notre Dame Press.

Son, Sang-Won (Aaron). 2001a. *Corporate elements in Pauline anthropology: A selected study of terms, idioms, and concepts in the light of Paul's usage and background.* Analecta Biblica 148. Roma: Editrice Pontificio Istituto Biblico.

Son, Sang-Won (Aaron). 2001b. Implications of Paul's 'one flesh' concept for his understanding of the nature of man. *Bulletin for Biblical Research* 11:107–122.

Sperber, Dan, and Deidre Wilson. 1995. *Relevance: Communication & cognition.* Second edition. Oxford: Blackwell.

Stacey, W. David. 1956. *The Pauline view of man in relation to its Judaic and Hellenistic background.* London: Macmillan.

Stanley, Arthur Penrhyn. 1876. *The epistles of St. Paul to the Corinthians.* London: John Murray.

Staples, Jason A. 2011. What do the Gentiles have to do with "all Israel"? A fresh look at Romans 11:25–27. *Journal of Biblical Literature* 130:371–390.

Sterner, Robert H. 1998. *A semantic and structural analysis of 1 Thessalonians.* Semantic and Structural Analysis Series. Dallas, TX: Summer Institute of Linguistics.

Steven, E. 2010. *Discourse grammar of the Greek New Testament: A practical introduction for teaching and exegesis.* Lexham Bible Reference Series. Peabody, MA: Hendrickson.

Stirewalt, M. Luther. 2003. *Paul, the letter writer.* Grand Rapids, MI: Eerdmans.

Stowers, Stanley K. 1986. *Letter writing in Greco-Roman antiquity.* Library of Early Christianity. Wayne A. Meeks, ed. Philadelphia, PA: Westminster.

Stowers, Stanley K. 1991. Friends and enemies in the politics of heaven: Reading theology in Philippians. In Jouette M. Bassler (ed.), *Pauline theology volume 1: Thessalonians, Philippians, Galatians, Philemon,* 105–121. Minneapolis, MN: Fortress.

Stuhlmacher, Peter. 1994. *Paul's letter to the Romans: A commentary.* Edinburgh, UK: T. & T. Clark.

Sumney, Jerry L. 1990. *Identifying Paul's opponent. The question of method in 2 Corinthians.* Journal for the Study of the New Testament Supplementary Series 40. Sheffield, UK: Sheffield Academic.

Surburg, Mark P. 2000. Structural and lexical feature in 1 Corinthians 11:27–32. *Concordia Journal* 26:200–217.

Synge, F. C. 1951. *Philippians and Colossians: Introduction and commentary.* London: SCM.

Tarazi, Paul Nadim. 1994. *Galatians: A commentary.* Orthodox Biblical Studies. Crestwood, NY: St. Vladimir's Seminary Press.

Taylor, Richard A., and E. Ray Clendenen. 2004. *Haggai, Malachi.* The New American Commentary 21a. Nashville, TN: Broadman & Holman.

Terry, Ralph Bruce. 1992. Some aspects of the discourse structure of the book of James. *Journal of Translation and Textlinguistics* 5:106–125.

Terry, Ralph Bruce. 1995. *A discourse analysis of First Corinthians.* Dallas, TX: Summer Institute of Linguistics and the University of Texas at Arlington.

Terry, Ralph Bruce. *Peak in discourse.* Accessed 26 March 2019 http://bible.ovu.edu/terry/discourse/peak.htm.

Thiselton, Anthony C. 2000. *The first epistle to the Corinthians.* The New International Greek Testament Commentary. Grand Rapids, MI: Eerdmans.

Thompson, Marianne Meye. 2005. *Colossians and Philemon.* The Two Horizons New Testament Commentary. Grand Rapids, MI: Eerdmans.

Thrall, Margaret E. 1962. *Greek particles in the New Testament: Linguistic and exegetical studies.* New Testament Tools and Studies 3. Bruce M. Metzger, ed. Leiden, Netherlands: Brill.

Thrall, Margaret E. 1994. *2 Corinthians 1–7.* Vol. 1 of *A critical and exegetical commentary on the second epistle to the Corinthians.* International Critical Commentary. 2 vols. Edinburgh, UK: T. & T. Clark.

Thrall, Margaret E. 2000. *2 Corinthians 8–13.* Vol. 2 of *A critical and exegetical commentary on the second epistle to the Corinthians.* International Critical Commentary. 2 vols. Edinburgh, UK: T. & T. Clark.

Thurston, Bonnie B., and Judith M. Ryan. 2005. *Philippians and Philemon.* Sacra Pagina 10. Collegeville, PA: Liturgical Press.

Turner, Nigel. 1963. *Syntax.* Vol. 3 of *A grammar of New Testament Greek.* James Hope Moulton, ed. 4 vols. Edinburgh, UK: T. & T. Clark, 1906–1976.

Vegge, Ivar. 2008. *2 Corinthians: A letter about reconciliation: A psychagogical, epistolographical and rhetorical analysis.* Wissenschaftliche Untersuchungen zum Neuen Testament 2. Reihe 239. Tübingen: Mohr Siebeck.

Verhoef, Eduard. 1996. The senders of the letters to the Corinthians and the use of "I" and "we". In R. Bieringer (ed.), *The Corinthian correspondence,* 417–425. Bibliotheca Ephemeridum Theologicarum Lovaniensium 125. Leuven, Belguim: Leuven University Press.

Vincent, Martin R. 1897. *A critical and exegetical commentary on the epistles to the Philippians and to Philemon.* International Critical Commentary on the Holy Scriptures of the Old and New Testaments. Edinburgh, UK: T. & T. Clark.

Voelz, James W. 2005. Word order: Part 1. *Concordia Journal* 31:425–427.

Wallace, Daniel B. 1996. *Greek grammar beyond the basics: An exegetical syntax of the New Testament.* Grand Rapids, MI: Zondervan.

Wanamaker, Charles A. 1990. *The epistles to the Thessalonians: A commentary on the Greek text*. The New International Greek Testament Commentary. Grand Rapids, MI: Eerdmans.

Wasserman, Emma. 2007. The death of the soul in Romans 7: Revisiting Paul's anthropology in light of Hellenistic moral psychology. *Journal of Biblical Literature* 126:793–816.

Waters, Brent, and Ronald Cole-Turner, eds. 2003. *God and the embryo: Religious voices on stem cells and cloning*. Washington DC: Georgetown University Press.

Watson, Nigel. 1993. *The second epistle to the Corinthians*. Epworth Commentaries. London: Epworth.

Wegener, Mark I. 2004. The rhetorical strategy of 1 Corinthians 15. *Theology and Mission* 31:438–455.

Weima, Jeffrey A. D. 1994. *Neglected endings: The significance of the Pauline letter closings*. Journal for the Study of the New Testament Supplementary Series 101. Sheffield, UK: JSOT Press.

Weima, Jeffrey A. D. 1995. The Pauline letter closings: Analysis and hermeneutical significance. *Bulletin for Biblical Research* 5:177–197.

Welborn, L. L. 1987. On the discord in Corinth: 1 Corinthians 1–4 and ancient politics. *Journal of Biblical Literature* 106:85–111.

Westfall, Cynthia Long. 2005. *A discourse analysis of the letter to the Hebrews*. Library of New Testament Studies 297. London: T. & T. Clark.

White, John Lee. 1972. *The form and function of the body of the Greek letter: A study of the letter-body in the non-literary papyri and in Paul the Apostle*. Society of Biblical Literature Dissertation Series 2. Missoula, MT: Scholars Press.

White, John Lee. 1983. Saint Paul and the apostolic letter tradition. *Catholic Biblical Quarterly* 45:433–444.

White, L. Michael. 1990. Morality between two worlds: A paradigm of friendship in Philippians. In David L. Balch, Everett Ferguson, and Wayne A. Meeks (eds.), *Greeks, Romans, and Christians: Essays in honor of Abraham J. Malherbe*, 201–215. Minneapolis, MN: Fortress.

Williams, A. Lukyn, ed. 1907. *The epistles of Paul the Apostle to the Colossians and to Philemon*. Cambridge Greek Testament Commentaries. Cambridge: Cambridge University Press.

Williams, David John. 1992. *1 and 2 Thessalonians*. New International Biblical Commentary. Peabody, MA: Hendrickson.

Willis, Wendell Lee. 1985. *Idol meat in Corinth: The Pauline argument in 1 Corinthians 8 and 10*. Society of Biblical Literature Dissertation Series 68. Chico, CA: Scholars Press.

Wilson, Andrew. 1992. The pragmatics of politeness and Pauline epistolography: A case study of the letter to Philemon. *Journal for the Study of the New Testament* 48:107–119.

Wimbush, Vincent L. 1987. *Paul, the worldly ascetic: Response to the world and self-understanding according to 1 Corinthians 7.* Macon, GA: Mercer University Press.

Winer, G. B. 1877. *A treatise on the grammar of New Testament Greek: Regarded as a sure basis for New Testament exegesis.* W. F. Moulton, trans. Edinburgh, UK: T. & T. Clark.

Winter, Bruce W. 1997. *Philo and Paul among the Sophists.* Society for New Testament Studies Monograph Series 96. Cambridge: Cambridge University Press.

Winter, Bruce W. 2001. *After Paul left Corinth: The influence of secular ethics and social change.* Grand Rapids, MI: Eerdmans.

Winter, Sean F. 1997. 'Worthy of the gospel of Christ': A study in the situation and strategy of Paul's epistle to the Philippians. PhD dissertation. University of Oxford.

Witherington, Ben, III. 1994. *Friendship and finances in Philippi: The letter of Paul to the Philippians.* The New Testament in Context. Valley Forge, PA: Trinity Press.

Witherington, Ben, III. 1995. *Conflict and community in Corinth: A socio-rhetorical commentary on 1 and 2 Corinthians.* Grand Rapids, MI: Eerdmans.

Witherington, Ben, III. 2006. *1 and 2 Thessalonians: A socio-rhetorical commentary.* Grand Rapids, MI: Eerdmans.

Wojciechowski, Michael. 2006. Paul and Plutarch on boasting. *Journal of Greco-Roman Christianity and Judaism* 3:99–109.

Wuest, Kenneth S. 1947. *Romans in the Greek New Testament for the English reader.* London: Pickering & Inglis.

Yinger, Kent. 1998. Romans 12:14–21 and nonretaliation in second temple Judaism: Addressing persecution within the community. *Catholic Biblical Quarterly* 60:74–96.

Zerbe, Gordon. 2008. Paul on the human being as 'psychic body': Neither dualist nor monist. *Direction Journal,* Fall 2008, 37:168–184. Accessed 26 March 2019. http://www.directionjournal.org/issues/gen/art_1527_.html.

Zerbe, Gordon. 2009. Citizenship and politics according to Philippians. *Direction* 38:193–208.

Index

SIL International®
Publications in Translation and Textlinguistics Series
ISSN 1550-588X

8. **Studies in the Psalms: Literary-structural analysis with application to translation,** by Ernst R. Wendland, 2017, 538 pp., ISBN 978-1-55671-401-6.
7. **Prophetic rhetoric: Case studies in text analysis and translation.** Second edition, by Ernst R. Wendland, 2014, 719 pp., ISBN 978-1-55671-345-3.
6. **Orality and the Scriptures: Composition, translation, and transmission,** by Ernst R. Wendland, 2013, 405 pp., ISBN 978-1-55671-298-2.
5. **Lovely, lively lyrics: Selected studies in biblical Hebrew verse,** by Ernst R. Wendland, 2013, 461 pp., ISBN 978-1-55671-327-9.
4. **LiFE-style translating: A workbook for Bible translators.** Second edition, by Ernst R. Wendland, 2011, 509 pp., ISBN 978-155671-243-2.
3. **The development of textlinguistics in the writings of Robert Longacre,** by Shin Ja Hwang, 2010, 423 pp., ISBN 978-1-55671-246-3.
2. **Artistic and rhetorical patterns in Quechua legendary texts,** by Ågot Bergli, 2010, 304 pp., ISBN 978-1-55671-244-9.
1. **Translating the literature of Scripture: A literary-rhetorical approach to Bible translation,** by Ernst R. Wendland, 2004, 509 pp., ISBN 978-1-55671-152-7.

SIL International® Publications
7500 W. Camp Wisdom Road
Dallas, TX 75236-5629 USA

General inquiry: publications_intl@sil.org
Pending order inquiry: sales@sil.org
publications.sil.org

Rev. Dr Sunny Chen currently teaches New Testament Greek at Pilgrim Theological College, Melbourne, Australia. He is the Chaplaincy Coordinator at The University of Melbourne, and an Honorary Researcher at the University of Divinity, Melbourne. Before earning his Master of Theology with high honors at Dallas Theological Seminary and doctorate at the University of Divinity, he was a secondary school teacher in Hong Kong. The areas of his research interests include Pauline epistles, New Testament Greek, the Gospel of John, and intertextuality.

Passionate about education, Dr Chen is currently a member of Queen's College Council, The University of Melbourne, the Vice President of Wesley College Council, and he chairs the governance body of Pilgrim Theological College.

Recent publications

2019. Semantics of Suffering: Thematic Meaning of the Language of Suffering in Romans and 2 Corinthians. In Siu Fung Wu (ed.), *Suffering in Paul*. Eugene, OR: Wipf & Stock.

2016. The Wedding Imagery of Jesus and Adam: The Intertextual Connection of John 19:23–37 and Genesis 2:18–25. Paper presented at the annual meeting of the Society of Biblical Literature. San Antonio, TX, 20 November, 2016.

2015. The Distributive Singular in Paul: The Adequacy of a Grammatical Category. *Journal of Greco-Roman Christianity and Judaism* 11:104–130.

2015. Evangelism & Communicating the Good News (Acts 17:16–34). In *A New Season: Six Bible Studies Exploring 'Who is God Calling in this New Season of the Uniting Church.'* Uniting Church in Australia Synod of Victoria and Tasmania.